T0321852

Secure E-Government Web Services

Andreas Mitrakas
European Network and
Information Security Agency (ENISA), Greece

Pim Hengeveld
T-Systems, Belgium

Despina Polemi
University of Piraeus, Greece

Johann Gamper
Free University of Bozen-Bolzano, Italy

IDEA GROUP PUBLISHING

Hershey • London • Melbourne • Singapore

Acquisition Editor:	Kristin Klinger
Senior Managing Editor:	Jennifer Neidig
Managing Editor:	Sara Reed
Assistant Managing Editor:	Sharon Berger
Development Editor:	Kristin Roth
Copy Editor:	Larissa Vinci
Typesetter:	Jamie Snavely
Cover Design:	Lisa Tosheff
Printed at:	Integrated Book Technology

Published in the United States of America by
  Idea Group Publishing (an imprint of Idea Group Inc.)
  701 E. Chocolate Avenue
  Hershey PA 17033
  Tel: 717-533-8845
  Fax: 717-533-8661
  E-mail: cust@idea-group.com
  Web site: http://www.idea-group.com

and in the United Kingdom by
  Idea Group Publishing (an imprint of Idea Group Inc.)
  3 Henrietta Street
  Covent Garden
  London WC2E 8LU
  Tel: 44 20 7240 0856
  Fax: 44 20 7379 3313
  Web site: http://www.eurospan.co.uk

Copyright © 2007 by Idea Group Inc. All rights reserved. No part of this book may be reproduced in any form or by any means, electronic or mechanical, including photocopying, without written permission from the publisher.

Product or company names used in this book are for identification purposes only. Inclusion of the names of the products or companies does not indicate a claim of ownership by IGI of the trademark or registered trademark.

Library of Congress Cataloging-in-Publication Data

Secure E-government web services / Andreas Mitrakas ... [et al.], editors.
     p. cm.
   Summary: "This book addresses various aspects of building secure E-Government architectures and services; it presents views of experts from academia, policy and the industry to conclude that secure E-Government web services can be deployed in an application-centric, interoperable way. It addresses the narrow yet promising area of web services and sheds new light on this innovative area of applications"--Provided by publisher.
   Includes bibliographical references and index.
   ISBN 1-59904-138-3 (hardcover) -- ISBN 1-59904-139-1 (softcover) -- ISBN 1-59904-140-5 (ebook)
   1. Electronic government information--Security measures--United States. 2. Internet in public administration--United States. 3. Electronic government information--United States. I. Mitrakas, Andreas.
   JK468.A8S43 2007
   352.3'8028567--dc22
                              2006027726

British Cataloguing in Publication Data
A Cataloguing in Publication record for this book is available from the British Library.

All work contributed to this book is new, previously-unpublished material. The views expressed in this book are those of the authors, but not necessarily of the publisher.

Secure E-Government Web Services

Table of Contents

Preface

INTRODUCTION

This book is about security in e-government applications with emphasis on Web services. As e-government applications are coming of age, security has been gradually becoming more demanding a requirement for users, administrators, and service providers. The increasingly more widespread use of Web services facilitates the exchange of data among various e-government applications, and, therefore, paving the way for enhanced service delivery. This volume addresses various aspects of building secure e-government architectures and services and presents the views of experts from academia, policy, and the industry to conclude that secure e-government Web services can be deployed in an application-centric and interoperable way. The chapters of this book have been based on conference papers presented in the context of the eMayor project that aimed at secure interoperable e-government services. This book addresses the narrow yet promising area of Web services aiming at shedding new light to this innovative area of applications. Responding to the challenges previously presented, this book gathers contributions from scholars across Europe, the U.S., and China who present their views on secure e-government Web services. The intended readership for this book includes parties with an ongoing interest in e-government with emphasis on security of e-government applications.

BACKGROUND

The first chapter of this book is an introduction to secure e-government as an area of interdisciplinary interest that sets the stage for what will follow in this volume. The chapters of this volume have been presented in two discreet conferences regarding e-government Security. The first event was a conference entitled Trust and Confidence in a Fast Moving Environment that was presented as part of the activities of the eBusiness Forum Working Group ST-3 (www.ebusinessforum. gr). The objective of this working group has been to address security challenges of eBusiness services, applications, and underlying technologies in a broadband environment. An obvious extension to e-government was deemed necessary in view of the public conference organised on July 2, 2004 in Athens and it was hosted by the Athens Chamber of Commerce and Industry. Chapters II-X were presented at this conference.

The second event in which Chapters X-XVII were presented was entitled e-government: Towards Electronic Democracy. This international conference was organised on March 2-4, 2005, in Bozen-Bolzano, Italy. In the background of this conference, the European Science Foundation (ESF) has established the program, Towards Electronic Democracy (TED), with the overall objectives:

- To discuss and evaluate how advances of interactive decision-analytic tools might help develop e-democracy.
- To develop e-government systems which involve their citizens more fully in the public decision making process.

This conference on interdisciplinary methods and techniques addressed a large spectrum of issues that are relevant and have to be investigated for a successful transition from the traditional form of government to e-government. The conference had a strong interdisciplinary character and brought together people from different sectors, including researchers, technology providers, administrative staff, and politicians. This conference was initiated by the TED working group of the ESF and jointly organized with the Free University of Bozen-Bolzano, the City of Bozen-Bolzano, and the IFIP WG 8.5-Information Systems in Public Administration.

Both conferences belong to a broader initiative that aims at presenting a holistic approach on the design and use of secure and interoperable cross border e-government services in such areas as digital certificates, electronic invoicing, electronic procurement, etc. Experiences, case studies, lessons learned, and best practices are presented by various real life stakeholders that include municipalities, Chambers of Commerce, and Industry, as well as service providers. These views underline the services that have been adopted, reveal barriers, and propose potential solutions and measures that could assist adopting e-government services and increasing the level of privacy and trust in transactions with the European public sector.

BOOK LAYOUT

The following chapters were presented at the first conference in the Athens workshop.

Chapter I is a brief introduction to the area of secure e-government. Secure e-government has emerged as a critical goal for public administrations worldwide. While e-government services bring the promise of efficient online services closer to its intended beneficiaries, being citizens, organizations, and other public administration units, new challenges pose potential threats. Emphasis is placed on the evolution of Web services and security technologies as a plausible technology upon which e-government services can be based.

Chapter II focuses on the interoperability aspects of e-government. Research into initiatives worldwide show that some of the legal and organizational barriers for the adoption of new technologies in e-government have largely been addressed. Some additional prevailing requirements for e-government, however, challenge e-government architects. The authors consider Web services and PKI prominent ways to resolve these remaining issues. This chapter presents three innovative e-government services based on these technologies with emphasis on security and interoperability.

Chapter III introduces the notion of trust as a means to establish security in ubiquitous mobile applications. Burmester argues that while trust is an essential enabler of security in open networks, its role is exacerbated in ad hoc wireless environments where there is no network topology. In these networks, communication can be effected through trusted routes. It is therefore important to understand the limitations of such environments and to seek ways to support explicit or implicit trust. Burmester concludes by presenting several models that enable trust based on economic, insurance, information flow, and evolutionary paradigms.

Chapter IV argues that information society is increasingly dependent on distributed systems and infrastructures for critical functions. The increasing complexity of these systems is rapidly growing along with the pervasive use of open information infrastructures for applications and communications. For Servida, this trend exposes society to cyber vulnerabilities and threats that require control. This chapter outlines the main research directions that have are priority in EU research programmes.

Chapter V examines broadband communication networks and the repercussions of their excess capacity. In specific location-based services over wireless broadband networks are gradually becoming more widespread in an emerging ambient intelligence society. Location-based services over broadband and peer-to-peer networks user authentication ensures trust. Biometric authentication is an approach to providing irrefutable identity verification of a user, thus providing the highest level of security. This chapter addresses some of the issues associated with the use of biometric identity for user and device authentication over broadband wireless networks

Chapter VI presents an application centric overview of a topical case study. The liberalization of the energy market requires frequent online access to metering devices that is necessary for exchanging meter data. Integrating security is an essential requirement for online meter device access. Ruland presents the SELMA project (Secure Electronic Exchange of Metering Data) and emphasises on the security aspects and claims that the security concept includes the security mechanisms and cryptographic techniques applied to the metering data as well as the security management.

Chapter VII addresses reliable enforcement of security policies for e-government. While e-government organizations interact frequently with citizens and/or businesses to deliver paper-based and electronic services, they also interact also with each other in various contexts. The authors identify a clear need for a secure, interoperable, and cost-effective e-government platform that addresses the requirements of small e-government organizations.

Chapter VIII claims that the use of electronic technologies in e-government adds up to end user convenience in spite of the security threats that steel hamper its widespread use. Denial of service attacks are becoming an increasingly alarming a factor in e-government that highlights the seriousness of the situation. To limit the impact of denial of service attacks, the authors claim that the use of best practices along with a classification of attacks and defence mechanisms can lead to a resolution of the problem.

Chapter IX claims that secure e-government aims at supporting public administration in delivering enhanced public services. In e-government, electronic signatures and certification services are used to invoke trust and security in services and applications. The author sees a risk in certification services that if being on offer in an apparent geographical or contextual isolation threaten to create fault lines across e-government services. Limitations in interoperability of certification services might hamper trust and security in the whole value chain of e-government applications. Drawing from the case of small public administrations the author proposes a certification service architecture and approach to support interoperability in secure e-government services.

The following chapters were presented at Towards Electronic Democracy Conference, Bolzano, March 2005.

Chapter X addresses the widespread diffusion of online services provided by public and private organizations driven by e-government applications highlights the need for user authentication and authorisation. Single sign on technology combined with strong authentication meets the requirement of protecting against replay attacks. Additionally, PKI and digital identity concepts are presented in the framework of the PRIME project to conclude that multiple dependable identities that are needed in modern day transactions as a general solution for identity management has yet to come.

Chapter XI addresses ePolling systems that are a critical component in e-democracy services. In e-polling systems, security requirements remain a high level in spite of their acceptance error that does not affect the final result. This chapter proposes a protocol for accurate and anonymous ePolling in which trust is presented in a measurable way by permitting voters to verify that their casted votes have been counted.

Chapter XII presents a methodology for proving in zero knowledge, the validity of selecting a subset of a set belonging to a predefined family of sets. Applying the proposed methodology to electronic voting the authors can provide for extended ballot options. This chapter claims that complexity is linear with respect to the total number of participants in an election.

Chapter XIII addresses the issue of orchestrating secure and dependable e-government services by linking them at request. The chapter investigates the applicability of two existing reference models, the workflow reference model and the extended SOA reference model. This chapter makes recommendations toward ensuring correct and in-time service-delivery processes, secure information sharing, and transparent and accountable processes.

Chapter XIV presents model driven architecture, an approach to increase the quality of complex software systems by creating high-level system models and automatically generating system architectures and components. This chapter shows how this paradigm can be applied to model driven security for inter-organizational workflows in e-government. While the focus is on the realization of security critical inter-organizational workflows in the context of Web services, security requirements are specified at an abstract level using UML diagrams to produce security relevant artifacts for the target reference architecture based on Web service security standards.

Chapter XV seeks to sustain the quality of e-government services and solve the problem of efficient and secure electronic exchange and processing of governmental documents and data. The authors consider that a major difficulty in a distributed deployment is the heterogeneity of interconnected systems that are required operating in multiple organizational domains. This chapter presents how the ISO/RM-ODP standard offers a general framework to design and develop an open distributed system attuned to e-government, including a high-level case study of how this standard can be applied in system design in e-government.

Chapter XVI introduces the goal of ShanghaiGrid and its sub-project, e-government on the grid. This chapter asserts that the main existing problem of e-government is how to integrate each government agency's resources to form cross-agency services. A grid technique provides an ideal way to solve this problem while workflow middleware and a real-name citizen mailbox are also presented.

Chapter XVII proposes a new concept of e-government service marketplace (e-govSM). This chapter presents an overview of the architecture and implementation of e-govSM easing the automation of administrative processes involving several administrations and allowing the reuse of data. This architecture facilitates citizens' interaction with various public administrations by providing them a single and personalized access point to services. The e-govSM is formalized using a set of XML schema models to support an interoperable and open system. The architecture is based on four main functional modules for the creation and management of citizen unique identifiers, for the management of citizen interactions with the marketplace, for the management of administrative process execution, and for the management of all public administrations interactions with e-govSM.

NOTE

Nothing in this Preface or book may be interpreted or construed as representing the views and opinion of any other party except the authors of the chapters herein in any way whatsoever. The editors acknowledge that this volume represents their personal efforts; the opinions expressed herein do not represent the views of any third party including the editors' employers past or present in any way whatsoever.

Acknowledgments

This book was conceived in late 2004 between the two conferences organised in the context of the eMayor project. During eMayor, the editors realised the general lack of sufficient research material in the area of secure Web services for e-government. Additionally it was felt that the good papers presented in those two conferences merit additional attention in this emerging field of interest especially with regard to potential implications for both research and deployments by industry. This book aims at presenting applicable concepts in eGovernment that make use of Web services.

Several parties have contributed to this book directly or indirectly. The editors would like to express their gratitude to Dr. Paul Timmers, Mrs. Tiziana Arcarese, Dr. Aniyan Varghese, and Mr. Giuseppe Zilioli who have at different points in time managed the eMayor project on behalf of the European Commission. Additionally, the editors would like to thank Professor Christos Douligeris, Professor Reinhard Riedl, Professor Christoph Ruland, Professor Giancarlo Succi, Mr. Alexandros Kaliontzoglou, as well as all participants in the eMayor project who have contributed to this book. Special thanks also go to Dr. Mehdi Khosrow-Pour, Ms. Jan Travers, and Ms. Kristin Roth for their prompt support in the preparation of this volume.

For supporting their efforts to publish this book, the editors would also like to thank the following organisations: European Commission, European Network, and Information Security Agency (ENISA), Deloitte, Ubizen (a Cybertrust Company), Free University of Bozen-Bolzano, University of Piraeus, and Idea Group Publishing.

The Editors
August 2006

Chapter I

Towards Secure E-Government

Andreas Mitrakas, European Network and
Information Security Agency (ENISA), Greece

Pim Hengeveld, T-Systems, Belgium

Despina Polemi, University of Piraeus, Greece

Johann Gamper, Free University of Bozen-Bolzano, Italy

ABSTRACT

Secure e-government has emerged as a critical goal for public administrations across the world. While e-government services bring the promise of efficient online services, closer to its intended beneficiaries, being citizens, organisations, and other public administration units, new challenges pose potential threats. This book presents the views of academics and non-professionals from EU, USA, and China on pertinent e-government issues. The emphasis is on the evolution of Web services and security technologies as a plausible technology upon which e-government services can be based. The chapters of this book represent concepts that have been presented in the framework of the e-mayor project. This chapter addresses some of the basic concepts and objectives of this book and introduces the reader in the secure e-government Web services.

Copyright © 2007, Idea Group Inc. Copying or distributing in print or electronic forms without written permission of Idea Group Inc. is prohibited.

INTRODUCTION

Building trust and confidence in e-government is a main priority of modern day governments. The deployment of secure e-government services requires developing a secure electronic environment for such applications in view of exchanging government e-mail and accessing repositories of government information for authorized public servants and citizens. This environment can further be leveraged upon to develop shared applications, business processes, and workflow systems that enhance the performance of public administration. The establishing of interoperable public key infrastructures (PKI) offering secure and interoperable e-government services is a critical intermediary step toward such a secure environment. In addition, vulnerability assessments and the specific use of security tools can further enhance the level of trust in the offered services. The remainder of this chapter addresses the application framework for e-government and associated policy and organisational issues; it touches upon technical issues related to Web services and closes with some recommendations for future research and possible action.

APPLICATIONS FOR E-GOVERNMENT

While e-government is a means to modernize public administrations and strengthen support for public policies, it strives toward enhanced cooperation among public administrations and the private sector. In principle, e-government relies on personalised services for end users that are citizens, businesses, and other public administration units and aims at improved service toward those parties. Furthermore, e-government also broadens the potential of democratic participation and enhancing the way that public policy making is carried out. Ideally, transformation should occur jointly at federal, national, regional, and local levels. Specifically in Europe, the federal level can be seen as an EU wide area of development of e-government services. The impact of e-government depends on technology features as well as organisational resources available. It is necessary at all times to maintain a sense of strategic vision into perspective and keep the legal framework as an instrument to achieve the desired results in terms of transforming public sector processes to sensible e-government operations. In e-government, it is necessary to strive for meaningful applications that bring about improvements in the interactions of the stakeholders with public administrations.

Envisaged transactions for e-government require that the expectations of citizens and businesses alike be taken well into account when interacting with each other (UNCTAD, 2001). Early day doctrine suggests that typical e-government applications for citizens include examples such as proof of identity, taxation, social security services, health care services, issuance of permits, registration services, family status certificates, etc.

Furthermore, typical e-government applications for organisations include social security contributions, employment services, health and safety regulation, corporate

Copyright © 2007, Idea Group Inc. Copying or distributing in print or electronic forms without written permission of Idea Group Inc. is prohibited.

tax, VAT submissions, company registries, public procurement, electronic invoicing, customs declarations, etc. In certain areas new additional services emerge with regard to facilitating the way that markets operate, like for example in the liberalisation of energy markets. An area of particular interest for e-government is electronic direct democracy or e-democracy whereby information communication media are leveraged with regard to referenda and polling in a way that improves the deliberation process. A major challenge facing e-democracy regards voter identification in a way that ensures the secrecy of voting and the integrity of the process. Therefore, the link between security requirements in e-government applications becomes critical.

Some of the previously mentioned application areas already benefit from the significant interest of governments worldwide and in many cases, technology infrastructures are already in place and successfully used in e-government transactions. In addition, a comprehensive legal framework supports and facilitates technological deployments and business measures in a way that political goals are served. Such is the case of customs cooperation in the EU that has improved customs declarations by the evolution of electronic data interchange (EDI) and subsequent cooperation programmes that meet the goals of the EU Internal Market. While security has been critical in the evolution of public administration services, it has gained new momentum with the advent of Web services that can be leveraged for e-government. This volume addresses the area between applications, security, and Web services, as shown in Figure 1.

In e-government, the technological emphasis is placed on information technologies that are leveraged to deliver online services and back office functionalities. However, non Internet-based technologies can also be leveraged in terms of convergence and also to levels controlled by information technologies. Examples of reliance on services that are not specific to information technology include:

Figure 1. Secure e-government Web services

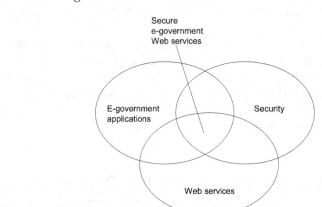

Copyright © 2007, Idea Group Inc. Copying or distributing in print or electronic forms without written permission of Idea Group Inc. is prohibited.

telecommunications issues in a government context (e.g., call/fax centres), mobile phone and personal digital assistant based services, services based on legacy systems, monitoring systems (e.g., CCTV), road traffic management, TV and radio based services (e.g., digital audio broadcasting), digital TV, and high definition TV.

Moreover, identifying the various stakeholders in an e-government environment helps identify risks undertaken in the relationships among these parties. Within e-government, typical roles include:

- **Application owner:** This is the e-government agency that owns and controls the e-government implementation that supports a smart card. The application owner may assume additional roles in line with the operational model at hand.
- **Application service provider:** Typically, an outsourced agent that carries out specific functions associated with an application at the request of the application owner.
- **E-government supervisor:** In some cases, the applications on offer might be supervised or even licensed through a registration scheme. Alternatively, in some cases, an accreditation mechanism might be in place to ensure the integrity of the procedures in place and the features of systems' in case several providers are used.
- **Security services provider:** This is an outsourced provider of security services that might additionally include certificate management services and so forth.
- **Token vendor:** This is a role reserved for an outsourced provider of tokens.
- **End user:** End users typically include citizens while other categories of users might also be included, such as agents of public administrations, business organisations, professionals, etc.
- **Other:** This category includes the various brokers that might be implicated in an e-government smart card based implementation such as an identity broker, a privacy broker to invoke privacy enhancing technologies, and so forth.

A clear definition of roles is a prerogative for e-government implementations to allow for a separation of duties and areas of responsibilities. In addressing requirements for e-government it must be noted that e-government is an area of interdisciplinary interest. As a consequence, this chapter addresses technological, organisational, and legal aspects involved in the life cycle and deployment of e-government applications and services (Lei & Mitrakas, 1996).

TRUST AND SECURITY IN E-GOVERNMENT

To Luhman, trust is the decision to enter into a relationship with others under conditions of risk perceived. Trust is characterized by the choice of an action against

Copyright © 2007, Idea Group Inc. Copying or distributing in print or electronic forms without written permission of Idea Group Inc. is prohibited.

other alternatives, such as confidence for example. For Williams, trust is related to cooperation that requires a joint action carried out by multiple agents. The objective of trust is to reach the purpose of cooperation even when the cooperating actors are not under the immediate control of other participants of the same process or context. In e-government trust is invoked by the interaction among actors that control, deliver, or benefit from the service. Adherence to the rule of law is a necessary condition to the success of e-government and is related to the public interest that is served through public administration. This principle of adherence to law for e-government services is typical as opposed to other forms of electronic transactions such as e-commerce for example.

The decision to trust a party requires a set of incentives that limit the non-dependent party to meet the requirements of trust. A system of incentives provides assurances to the dependent parties with regard to the expectations of each party toward one another. While a system of incentives could comprise moral obligations, self interest, reputation, and so forth, in e-government, it is based on law and contract and operates within a context of public interest. However, in e-government, the technical capability that mandates to public administration the lowering of transaction costs by implementing technical means implies a reductive vision of trust in electronic transactions. Fukuyama suggests, "Trust does not reside in integrated circuits or fibre optic cables. Although it involves an exchange of information, trust is not reducible to information." A virtual e-government organisation requires assurances when procuring supplier services, much like the beneficiaries of the e-government system need with regard to the identity of that organisation and associated services. Reciprocity and transparency are needed along with legal requirements in order to bring e-government services closer to beneficiaries. In the absence of trust, there can be a reverse trend that restores past procedures and relies on old hierarchies.

According to the Communication from the Commission COM (2001) 298 final, June 6, 2001, Network and Information Security: Proposal for A European Policy Approach "Network and Information Security can be understood as the ability of a network or an information system to resist, at a given level of confidence, accidental events, or malicious actions. Such events or actions could compromise the availability, authenticity, integrity, and confidentiality of stored or transmitted data as well as related services offered via these networks and systems." Information security typically addresses such areas as the protection of systems and data from unauthorized use. The goal of information security, however, stretches beyond the information technology security level to address all infrastructures that facilitate its use and include processes, technologies, and services. A major feature of information security is risk management that seeks to adapt the security requirements to a level commensurate with the service delivered or risk perceived. Contrary to a formalistic model that requires a static approach for information security, risk management takes into account the dynamic features of the environment and adapts the security objectives through a dedicated methodology (Ford & Baum, 2001).

Copyright © 2007, Idea Group Inc. Copying or distributing in print or electronic forms without written permission of Idea Group Inc. is prohibited.

Information security is an enabler in mitigating risk in e-government transactions. Information security rules allow assessing threats and set out the conditions to mitigate it. While a threat is the possibility of hindering the operation of an information system, risk is the probability that a threat might materialize. The principles of proportionality and reasonableness have been enshrined for example in the EU Directive 95/46/EC on the protection of personal data and they are used to assess a risk based model on information security. Data protection regulation requires for example setting up discreet environments to treat personal data in a way that leaking it to another environment is prevented or detected. If social security numbers are used as business identifiers, the resulting identification profiles that are merged into comprehensive databases must become known to the data subjects (i.e., citizens) much like all the parties that have access to them. A supervising authority may further audit and control such processes.

Information security objectives are used to detect the implementation of the following principles with evidence in hand:

- Confidentiality to ensure that information is accessible only to authorized parties.
- Integrity that prevents data from being changed, modified, altered, or destroyed at any operation, in line with an expectation of data quality.
- Availability that concerns the degree to which a system is able to operate and at a committable state at the start of an assignment.
- Accountability for acts performed which especially in white collar crime is often associated with governance, that is if particular significance in e-government and relates strongly with public interest.

These principles are fully observed within highly organized environments that operate based on audited security policies and practices. To determine information security benchmarks, it is typically required to carry out risk assessment by measuring two quantities of risk, the magnitude of the potential loss, and the probability that loss might occur. A vulnerability assessment complements a risk assessment in identifying and quantifying vulnerabilities in a system that seeks network and information security measures (Dunn & Wigert, 2004).

Information security provides the measurable assurance that end use of e-government systems require prior to trusting them. Information security methodologies that have been developed provide the approach to benchmarks risk and take mitigation measures. Trusting a system may happen under conditions that the risks are identified and mitigation measures are taken. In e-government a risk management approach is of paramount importance due to the interest in deploying services among large populations, as well as the requirement for transparency in public administration operations.

Copyright © 2007, Idea Group Inc. Copying or distributing in print or electronic forms without written permission of Idea Group Inc. is prohibited.

POLICY-MAKING CONSIDERATIONS

Policy making has two possible effects, redistribution and efficiency. To reduce the adverse effect of policy making on citizens efficiency should be sought to avoid the possibility of benefiting one part of the society at the expense of another. Producing results that are in the interest of everyone in the society, lies in the heart of modern day regulatory policy making. Typical modern day mechanisms to hedge the adverse effect of policy making or market inefficiencies include (Hix, 1999):

- Technical standards that enable consumers and business obtain information that would otherwise be unavailable.
- Safety standards that reduce the effect on the citizens that do not participate in those transactions.
- Competition policies to reduce the effect of state subsidies and monopolistic practices.

In e-government, the effect of policy making must take into account potential adversities cause to parts of the society that have limited or no access to electronic services. Consideration also merits the moderating of powers of e-government organisations through appropriate supervision and control mechanisms.

To the extent that regulatory policy is a politician's response to the pressure of private interests, e-government poses specific challenges due to limitations in interoperability and the role of technical standards. By using standards for harmonisation, Europe produces efficient policy outcomes in line with public interest (Stigler, 1971). As harmonisation may happen at a level that is higher than the one it succeeds, e-government is a response to present day inefficiencies and hurdles by utilizing more rather than less regulation. In this perspective, appropriate instruments for regulation might also include soft policies and codes of practice beyond law and contract.

A typical approach in EU policy making has been to level a stage of control over the Member States' action areas, without necessarily creating a new state or qualifying for statehood as such (Magnette, 2000). While the EU manages power delegated by its Member States, it sometimes empowers Member States or on other occasions it constrains them through a rational self-limitation process. In e-government the EU can determine applications that serve European policy goals (i.e., Internal Market) and strive toward removing technical, organisational, and legal hurdles associated with it. Examples of such applications include electronic procurement and electronic invoicing that have been subjected to comprehensive EU legislation.

A question emerges with regard to whether the EU level is the most appropriate to address e-government applications, reach consensus on services, and debate on the need to interoperate with each other. In addressing policy requirements in e-government, it is critical to adhere to the principles of proportionality and subsidiarity (Mousis, 2002). In e-government, applications and services cross-border

Copyright © 2007, Idea Group Inc. Copying or distributing in print or electronic forms without written permission of Idea Group Inc. is prohibited.

cooperation observes the principle of regulation at a national level within a Member State is coupled with action at EU level where necessary only.

In the e-mayor project that has been the driving force behind this book, e-government applications that have been developed within municipalities in the Member States have sought an interoperability layer that permits them to interoperate in line with EU policies in pertinent areas. These areas include the mobility of citizens within the internal market—an EU policy priority area. The EU layer that the e-mayor project has attained to, therefore, consists of a platform that allows for the transfer of data at the application level, which is controlled by a policy enforcer and supported by a certificate management mechanism. In e-mayor, certificate management also meets the requirement of interoperability by applying a root interoperability model (Mitrakas, 2006).

The conception of EU policy must proportionally select the instruments used with regard to the objectives pursued prior to launching an EU policy initiative it is essential to ensure the appropriateness of the EU level to facilitate communications (Hix, 1999).

In e-government, an application-centric approach is desirable to address the issues pertaining to applications such as identity management, e-procurement, and the way they interact in an e-government context. Identity management for example can play an important role in electronic public procurement in order to designate authentication requirements for end users. It is essential to take for example private law, privacy, and data protection rules into account by introducing appropriate policy levels that implement binding forms of identification and authentication.

TECHNICAL CONSIDERATIONS

Interoperability in general is the ability of products, systems, or business processes to work together to accomplish a common task. While interoperability is a technical consideration, it typically takes into account organisational interests. At a technical level, interoperability regards the ability of software to exchange data via a common set of procedures, to read and write the same file formats, use the same protocols, and ensure the translation of data from one format to another. With regard to e-government processes, interoperability covers how data is used or exchanged in the various public administration agencies, which parties have access to certain types of data, how that data is presented to different types of end users that might reside in different countries, etc. Factors contributing to determining the interoperability of a system include the way a system is built, trade secrets, and potential shortcomings in coordination. As a measure against these shortcomings, user communities and government agencies set up their shared interoperability structures (e.g., e-GIF in the UK, SAGA in Germany, etc.).

Further on the critical issue of interoperability, which makes the secure interconnection and cooperation between various secure e-government systems possible,

Copyright © 2007, Idea Group Inc. Copying or distributing in print or electronic forms without written permission of Idea Group Inc. is prohibited.

enhancing the feasibility and applicability at regional, national, and international levels of the application emerges as an additional requirement. At this level, the interconnection with the EU is highly desirable due to the increased demand for mobility of citizens and the criticality of the governmental data, which deem the secure and interoperable information exchange as an essential element in e-government services.

At the certificate management level like in PKI services, interoperability is typically addressed through cross-certification, which can be described as the way to establish chains of trust between various CAs. However, cross-certification is often a cumbersome process because it relies on non-automated and often time-consuming paper-based processes, which reduce the flexibility and usability of the approach (Nash, Duane, Brink, & Joseph, 2001).

The absence of automated cross-certification services is to a great extent due to the inadequate standardisation of the way Certificate Policies (CPs) and Certificate Practice Statements (CPSs) is applied in real life implementations. PKI certificate profiles often follow diverging approaches and therefore limit the ability of the relying party to positively compare them and establish trust and equivalence levels. More specifically, although the CP structure is defined in existing standards such as ETSI TS 101 456, there is still a significant gap in the standardisation of the way that the CP requirements are implemented in the CA domain like for example with regard to roles of the involved subjects, certification, and registration requirements, etc.

The previously mentioned limitations pose restrictions, especially in the light of the absence of an appropriate regulatory certificate management framework that does not allow for the automated comparison of CPs and CPSs in a meaningful way. As a consequence, automated cross-certification services are obstructed and there are obstacles to the secure electronic cooperation, information exchange, and knowledge sharing. Additionally the general absence of interoperability architectures for e-government exacerbates concerns related to policy management. In general, there are several interoperability models each with its own individual features that can be leveraged to facilitate interoperability in e-government certification services. The general distrust, however, among e-government actors in this area have resulted in very limited results thereto.

Although examples of certificate management services interoperability can be found in several Member States as well as in the U.S. and beyond, cross-certification at a pan European or global level can be evidenced only among commercial providers of such interoperability services. The ad hoc commercial application providers list the trusted roots of certificate service providers in their applications in a way that applications recognise them and hence, trust them by default, for example, the roots listed in browsers. Unfortunately the criteria to select the certification service providers to be listed are not always meaningful and at the same level among all providers. Sometimes, adhering to demanding accreditation schemes such as the WebTrust for CAs scheme is required. Others however, just apply a yearly fee in

Copyright © 2007, Idea Group Inc. Copying or distributing in print or electronic forms without written permission of Idea Group Inc. is prohibited.

return for the service. Even at this commercial level of application defined trust the decision on whether to trust an application or not is only made by the third party application itself and not necessarily by the relying party. The relying party would have to modify the settings of its applications as well as understand the implications of making such as decision prior to acting at the application level.

Although this is a general certificate management problem affecting all business sectors, there is also a need for a sector-specific analysis, especially in the CP standardisation part, where dedicated requirements of the underlying users' communities have to be considered taking into account the special CP-related needs of the latter.

The strategic objective is to introduce a flexible, extensible, and standards based CP comparison model that could serve as the base for the automated online cross-certification service, enabling public authorities offering interconnected security services. Possible implementations at the European level (i.e., IDABC of the EU Commission) like the European Bridge Certification Authority need to be considered to address the open issues of cross-recognition of e-government PKIs.

Automation and transparency in the PKI functionality needs to be provided in order to provide "pre-packaged" user-friendly secure e-government services to the citizens embedding human processes integrated into the business model that it serves. Figure 2 addresses the direction that present day e-government services are heading toward.

Integrated business models for e-government that leverage upon smart cards and PKI address complex problems such as liability and insurance. The public administrators should be able to make e-government services available via their trusted service providers based on service level agreements. This is a proposed solution to avoid huge start up costs, risk of the service, non-effective usage, use of not up to date technologies, and cost of recruitment and training of skilled people.

Figure 2. Trends in e-government

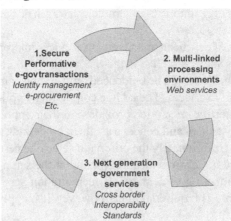

Copyright © 2007, Idea Group Inc. Copying or distributing in print or electronic forms without written permission of Idea Group Inc. is prohibited.

Interoperability among e-government services and applications is well acknowledged as a serious barrier in the evolution thereof. The creation of an XML strategy for e-government will contribute to the solution of interoperability at the application level. Close cooperation with the XML working group needs to be achieved in order to build a registry of government-specific XML tags and schemas that will be compiled into software components that government and industry can use to interface with one another.

Web services connect computers and devices with each other using widely accepted standards such as HTTP and XML to exchange and combine data in new ways. Web services are software objects that can be assembled over the Internet using standard protocols to perform functions or execute business processes. The critical feature of making Web services available is their ability to create on-the-fly services through the use of loosely-coupled, reusable software components (Hartman, Flinn, Beszosov, & Kawamoto, 2003). The use of Web services has fundamental implications in both technical and business terms:

- Software can be delivered and paid for as fluid streams of services as opposed to packaged products
- Interoperability between systems is achieved in an ad hoc automated manner to accomplish business tasks
- Organisational services can be completely decentralised and distributed over the Internet while they are accessed by a broad variety of communications devices
- Organisations can be freed from the burden of complex, slow, and expensive software integration while they focus instead on their core business and their mission critical tasks

Web services provide significant enhancements if compared with previous paradigms because they use a stable technical foundation based on a universally-agreed upon base specification (XML) for structured data representation and almost universally-agreed base specification simple object access protocol (SOAP) for structured message exchange. Web services combine multiple technical development strands into a single powerful vision for offering services online. Additionally Web services encompass the full spectrum of eCommerce in the broadest sense, through an architectural viewpoint that seeks to address all the requirements and functions of online transactions (within a domain, across domains, intra-organisation, inter-organisation, as well within and between parties involved in the transactions in their different roles and in different contents). Major IT vendors agree on the importance and primacy of Web services and the overall vision if not the individual details (Armstrong et al., 2002).

Available commercial middleware technologies and application server platforms are the software foundation of modern enterprise computing systems,

Copyright © 2007, Idea Group Inc. Copying or distributing in print or electronic forms without written permission of Idea Group Inc. is prohibited.

which process the requests coming through Web services gateways. An additional strength of Web services is the enhanced interoperability capabilities the feature. By definition, Web services depend only on passing standard XML messages. Web services applications do not need to make any assumptions about what lies on the other end of the information pipeline, except of assuming that the recipient of data can equally understand SOAP and WSDL as the originator does. As Web services clients and servers are implemented in many languages and on many platforms it is easy to use them to communicate between the various platforms even in distributed application environments.

Web services are a set of protocols based on Extensible Markup Language (XML). The following base protocols form the initial specification for Web services:

- **Simple Object Access Protocol (SOAP):** Defines the runtime message that contains the service request and response. SOAP is independent of any particular transport and implementation technology.
- **Web Services Description Language (WSDL):** Describes a Web service and the SOAP messages it understands. It provides a structured way to describe what a service does, paving the way for automation.
- **Universal Discovery, Description, Integration (UDDI):** UDDI is a cross-industry initiative to create a standard for service discovery together with a registry facility that facilitates the publishing and discovery processes.

Web services are founded on the universal acceptance of XML as the syntax for data communications and the increasing integration of SOAP as the mechanism for messaging. In addition to these two protocols, the Web Services Description Language (WSDL) is beginning to gain acceptance for enabling a common description of Web services (their interfaces and functions) and the universal description, discovery, and integration (UDDI) is gaining value for the aggregation and identification of WSDL documents by providing registry capabilities.

COMPETITION ASPECTS IN E-GOVERNMENT

While interoperability has emerged as a necessary condition for e-government, a question related to power and market dominance has been looming for a long time. Government agencies that rely on information technology to deliver their services rely much like any other user of information systems on market-based solutions for information technology. To the extent that these technologies originate from ad hoc monopolies raises issues regarding legitimacy and control of these market actors.

A fault line can therefore be noted between the legitimate market interests of service and application providers on one hand, and the interest of governments on the other, to reduce their reliance on monopolies to procure public services. The five-year investigations that the European Commission had launched demonstrate

Copyright © 2007, Idea Group Inc. Copying or distributing in print or electronic forms without written permission of Idea Group Inc. is prohibited.

the importance of power relationships in the area of information technology and systems interoperability (Commission IP/04/382 of March 24, 2004). While the European Commission deemed that in some cases market abuse could be proven and that restriction in interoperability between computers that use its own operating system and third party servers had occurred the company under investigation was able to acquire a dominant market position in the area of work group server operating systems. To reverse these adverse effects, the Commission deemed that disclosing documentation to rival vendors is beneficial in order to create a level playing field in this market.

Relying on software products that originate from a vendor with significant market power to provide e-government services to large populations may raise a question of legitimacy for the government agencies involved. The recent experience demonstrates that restrictions placed in an operating system at the network level, control the way that applications interact with this system and the further interoperate with each other. Open and transparent e-government may be at risk if it relies on a technical layer that limits its choices to a handful of options. Transparent e-government may also have the meaning of allowing the end user to know at all times which software runs on his computer and exactly which functions it carries out. Software that has been developed as a result of non-transparent software development can be a reason for end user concern and a risk for citizens, businesses, and third party public administrations.

Interoperability also associates with software patents that might be used in e-government. Typically, patented software allows for interoperability as long as the conditions of reasonable and non-discriminatory licensing are observed. If an e-government programme uses previously patented software to deliver a service, the end user might be asked to pay a higher price for the e-government service and a second time for the patent protected programme that the e-government programme is using. Although the information technology market is a typical example of an ad hoc monopoly of certain software vendors, the applications that e-government brings about could be projected by taking this assumption into account and project alternative scenarios that allows them to spread the risk instead of concentrating all their interest in a single arrangement. While open source might provide a way to improve market inefficiencies, the way that open source software is managed might not necessarily provide adequate assurances thereto and perpetuate the end user concerns on e-government.

STANDARDISATION PROCESS

Standardisation has emerged as a significant area of EU policy that sometimes might also complement the legislative process. With regard to products, technical standards have long been considered a critical area of EU activity. Since 1979 in the Cassis de Dijon case (ECJ 120/78 of 20/02/79) in which the European Court of

Copyright © 2007, Idea Group Inc. Copying or distributing in print or electronic forms without written permission of Idea Group Inc. is prohibited.

Justice ruled that a product meeting the requirements of one member state should be legally made available in another, mutual recognition of technical standards has emerged as a matter of significant interest for the evolution of the EU Internal Market. The EU approach to technical harmonisation has resulted in limiting standards to technical specifications and safety requirements while reserving a prominent place to EU standards organisations, European Committee for Standardisation (CEN), and the European Telecommunications Standards Institute (ETSI).

To avoid the emergence of obstacles based on technical standards, Member States have agreed to inform the Commission with regard to technical standards. Since the promulgation of Directive 1998/34/EC of the European Parliament and of the Council of June 22, 1998 laying down a procedure for the provision of information in the field of technical standards and regulations (OJ L 204, 21.7.1998) standardisation has gained new impetus in Europe. Standardisation might help e-government organisations to set out a level playing field with regard to the provision of services in a measurable way in the member states. Standardisation can also be sued a forum for the discussion and possible resolution of critical matters such as interoperability for example. It remains to be seen what level of applicability these requirements might have in the area of services with emphasis on public administration services such as e-government. While some measures toward harmonisation can be expected, full-scale harmonisation might still be out of reach.

In the case of Directive 1999/93/EC on a Community framework on electronic signatures, standards published in the Official Journal of the European Communities establish a presumption of conformity, meaning that the electronic signature products that meet their requirements also comply with the legal requirements. This approach has been underlined by the Commission Decision of July 14, 2003 on the publication of reference numbers of generally recognized standards for electronic signature products in accordance with Directive 1999/93/EC of the European Parliament and of the Council. This decision has endorsed and given legal effect to certain standards promulgated by the European Electronic Signatures Standardisation Initiative. Standards assume legal significance in cases where the law mandates them in order to give specific effect to a particular regulation within the EU. The regulation of electronic signatures in the EU has often been based on a co-regulation approach that encourages the cooperation between the legislator and industry in order to ensure an optimal level of technical standards, while allowing for space in order to take into account the requirements of the market actors when setting out a regulatory framework.

Hence, from a regulatory viewpoint, a standardisation layer addresses the input of industry and public interest standardisation organisations to the evolution of the internal market. Standards promulgated in Europe typically originate from the EU standardisation organisations, ETSI and CEN, while the International Standards Organisation operates at an international level that often provides input in EU standards. Such is the case of the security standard ISO 17799 that provides

Copyright © 2007, Idea Group Inc. Copying or distributing in print or electronic forms without written permission of Idea Group Inc. is prohibited.

recommendations on information security management for use by those who are responsible for initiating, implementing, or maintaining security in an organisation. This standard provides a common basis to pursue security management practices and indirectly to provide confidence in transactions. Obviously, other ad hoc standardisation initiatives are equally valid and often quite accepted, such as Identrus in the past and OASIS more recently, for example.

REGULATORY INSTRUMENTS FOR E-GOVERNMENT BEYOND LEGISLATION

While e-government is essentially based on law and contract policies aim at communicating operational conditions in a way that allows e-government organisations reaching out to their suppliers and recipients of services. Policies aim at underpinning transactions by spreading risk among the transacting parties. In this sense, policies reduce information asymmetry with regard to the internal workings of an e-government system that is prevalent in the relationship between the e-government organisation and the beneficiaries. Policies are unilateral declarations of will that complement transaction frameworks. Policies can be seen as guidelines that relate to the technical organisational and legal aspects of a transaction and they are rendered enforceable by means of an agreement that binds the transacting parties or on other cases directly by law.

A security policy is a critical element of security programmes because it identifies the rules and procedures that parties with access to information resources must adhere to in order to ensure the confidentiality, integrity, and availability of data and resources. Voluntary security frameworks are binding to the extent that this is the intent of the parties involved. From a regulatory viewpoint, it is interesting to examine the instruments through which security policies are enacted within a public interest, e-government organisation. This, however, is a broader consideration for other types of policies that are typically used to provide notice and knowledge of the prevailing legal terms and conditions of using systems that strive toward interoperability in e-government transactions.

As a security feature for e-government applications, PKI requires that CAs use legal stipulations through a certification practice statement that conveys legally binding limitations to certificate users, being subscribers and relying parties. A CPS is a statement of the practices that a CA employs in issuing certificates. In e-government electronic signatures play a multi-facet role in identifying a natural person or an organisation, as well as providing the means for the non-repudiation of transactions. As a security feature, electronic signatures often epitomize security requirements in specific environments that address certificate management. Therefore, electronic signature policies convey information necessary to the relying party to make an informed decision on whether to trust that e-government application from a technical and organisational point of view.

Copyright © 2007, Idea Group Inc. Copying or distributing in print or electronic forms without written permission of Idea Group Inc. is prohibited.

Assessing the validity of electronic signatures is yet another requirement of the end user most importantly, the relying parties (e.g., ETSI TR 102 041). A signature policy determines the validation conditions of an electronic signature within a given context. Potentially signature policies are adapted in large automated e-government environments in which they can offer added functionality with regard to the way to manage signature validations. When a role based system that uses attributes is in place transaction constraints designate roles or other attributes that are leveraged upon in the e-government transaction. Attribute certificates are used to convey such role constraints and are used to indicate a role, a function, or a transaction type constraint. In return attribute policies are used to convey limitations associated with the use and life cycle of such attributes (e.g., ETSI TS 101 058). As attributes can be seen roles under which e-government actors are acting for example.

An example of using policies can be seen in the context of processing signed electronic procurement transactions. A public authority that is the recipient of a tender might mandate by means of a signature policy a specific signature format and validation rules for that tender to be validly submitted. The sender of the tender might mandate that signing an invoice might only be carried out under a certain role, which is the e-government agent in charge of opening tenders; therefore, an attribute certificate issued under a specific attribute policy should in this case be mandated.

HORIZONTAL ISSUES

Beyond the already addressed vertical issues of interest for e-government, there are a number of horizontal areas of interest that need further attention from a systematic point of view. The cross-recognition and status information for electronic signatures can pave the way for an enhanced degree of interoperability among e-government services at the federal, national, regional, or local levels. While the primary scope of Directive 1999/93/EC has been the regulation of the non-repudiation function of electronic signatures. It has also addressed aspects of authentication based on electronic signatures. With regard to applications that are subject to legislation, the role of electronic signatures has yet to be addressed. Qualified electronic signatures meet the requirements for non-repudiation in electronic e-government processes. However, electronic signatures may only be recognised across multiple environments if a prior operational and legal relationship is established due to open issues related to the cross-recognition of top root hierarchies across multiple domains.

The standard ETSI TS 102 231 Harmonized TSP status information provides some preliminary means to create and distribute status information concerning trust service providers like a CA to relying parties. To interpret status information harmonized and widely accessible evaluations and approval criteria regarding the trust service providers must be put in place. In e-government applications, it is beneficial to consider harmonised approval criteria for the participating CAs. In the federative trust model of a Bridge-CA, for example, participating domains agree

Copyright © 2007, Idea Group Inc. Copying or distributing in print or electronic forms without written permission of Idea Group Inc. is prohibited.

on evaluation criteria (e.g., a standardised certification policy) and further arrange the managing and publishing of status information. While a top root arrangement for all domains requires the same type of harmonisation, it may be difficult to have it accepted across the board. For the information to become accessible online by the client software of the relying party, a standardised selection and profiling of access protocol(s) might be required. Addressing the requirements for CAs, issuing certificates is a matter that requires further attention. While the trust position of CAs issuing qualified certificates to individuals poses no problem to relying parties, trust in the certification path is a matter of concern. In e-government, further work is needed in trusting each CA along the certification path with particular emphasis on the requirements for top root CAs.

The mutual recognition, equivalence levels, and certificate validation across e-government organisations must be addressed beyond the boundaries of the requirements regarding the provision of harmonized trust service provider status information. Accessing validation data on certificates issued by a certificate services provider requires the implementation of real life models that address the concerns of relying parties and CSPs in a way that stretches beyond the obvious bilateral boundaries. Addressing the issue of interoperability in providing status information is a key issue to address in the interest of e-government applications.

In e-government electronic signatures provide for the authentication of parties and data exchanged by those parties involved in a transaction. Authentication has assumed legal content pursuant to the directive on electronic signatures. Authentication relates to another key area in e-government, namely identity management and especially public identity. Confirming that authentication standards meet the requirements of e-government is an additional requirement.

A signature policy is a set of rules to create and validate electronic signatures, under which an electronic signature can be determined to be valid in a particular transactions context. A signature policy describes the scope and the usage of such an electronic signature with a view to address the conditions of a given transaction context. In e-government there is a frequent requirement to have documents signed by several parties in parallel. Verifying that a transaction bears the right number of electronic signatures in the right order to represent a chain of authorisation and setting out the conditions to validate those signatures is a matter that requires further attention. Signature policies must additionally be used to include rules on the use and validation of timestamps together with electronic signatures.

When using XML documents in e-government to allow for a "what you see is what you sign" effect, it is necessary to work toward XML-based signatures in line with prevailing standards (e.g., ETSI TS 101 903 standard XML Advanced Electronic Signatures—XAdES). Relying on XML based solutions enhances interoperability and allows the use of advanced electronic signatures that remain valid over long periods while meeting legal requirements

Developments in information security and application tokens, such as smart cards, must remain closely monitored by standardisation actors in the area of e-

Copyright © 2007, Idea Group Inc. Copying or distributing in print or electronic forms without written permission of Idea Group Inc. is prohibited.

government since network security is a background requirement to ensure data integrity, confidentiality, and availability. It is necessary that lodging electronic files with e-government organisations is supported by sound security measures. A security policy sets out the permissions, restrictions, and applications under which systems are allowed to operate while the requirements in this area must comply with the ISO 17799 standard on security management.

Confidentiality in e-government is a general requirement that applies in all procedures and is a mandated requirement emanating from the general legal framework. Beyond the obvious protection against malicious attacks, additional application specific measures should be taken such as locking of submitted documents, for example, until such time when designated agents are allowed to access them.

Data integrity is necessary to ensure the interests of the communicating parties and it relates to the hash function that is used in an electronic signature process as well as specific network security features implemented in a communication. As data integrity is often a formal security requirement in e-government it is useful to examine its specific repercussions.

At the transaction level, it is necessary to address risk management issues with regard to the e-government application at hand. While a regulatory framework sometimes addresses certain aspects related to legal risk, it is desirable that further efforts focus on setting up an approach toward addressing risk management and mitigating risk in e-government. It is suggested that action be taken in the area of risk management for e-procurement by developing risk and risk mitigation models.

Quality assurance standards are also useful to build up confidence in e-government and assure users and relying parties that they meet the requirements stipulated in the legal framework. Additionally respect for the principles of transparency, competition and equal treatment must also be ensured. Trust labels, accreditation and rating schemes can support quality assurance in public procurement. Technical standards must aim at introducing a common methodology in setting up and auditing electronic public procurement systems Action in the form of technical standards must meet the requirement for formal recognition of quality labels.

VULNERABILITY ASSESSMENT ANALYSIS

As infrastructures in the public sector become more complex including various types of networks (e.g., mobile or ad hoc) offering a variety of electronic or mobile government services evaluating their vulnerabilities and detecting their security incidents becomes a difficult problem. A major challenge when performing a vulnerability analysis of a security-critical large-scale infrastructure today is the fact that the IT infrastructure surrounding it undergoes continuous changes involving a variety of fixed, mobile, and ad hoc networks. A new server, a new node, or network device and even the upgrade to a new version of software, introduces new vulnerabilities that, if exploited, may lead to unpredictable security breaches. Moreover,

Copyright © 2007, Idea Group Inc. Copying or distributing in print or electronic forms without written permission of Idea Group Inc. is prohibited.

even if a system remains the same for a period of time, new, previously unknown, vulnerabilities are discovered.

It is difficult for the security personnel to keep track of all these developments. Vulnerability assessment tools are a valuable aid in this area, as they contain assessment engines that are regularly updated with recently identified vulnerabilities. Moreover, vulnerability assessment tools test systems for vulnerability to large numbers of known attacks. Reports generated during a vulnerability assessment generate a brief overview of the security state of a system at a particular time, reveal the known weaknesses of the system, and allow the selection of appropriate countermeasures in a proactive manner.

Existing vulnerability assessment and intrusion detection tools are based on common methodologies originally designed to evaluate threats and respond against small-scale attacks. New methods for better assessing and more effectively detecting and responding to large-scale attacks will become an emerging need as infrastructures become large scale, more complex and security-critical (Valvis, Sklavos, Papadaki, & Polemi, 2002).

Various vendors of vulnerability assessment tools use different terminology to explain the same issue and there is a lack of machine-readable information. Thus, although the data provided by vulnerability assessment reports are detailed, are presented in an ambiguous textual form or in a proprietary data format. The effect is that a vulnerability report has become tightly coupled to specific tool and cannot easily be shared across different tools. This lack of common ground has hampered the ability to integrate diverse sources of available security data more effectively. The result is twofold: the security personnel is overloaded with redundant data and it is not feasible to fully utilize all possibly available data in making the most accurate diagnosis.

On the other hand the development of commonly agreed upon or standardized and extensible exchange formats will enable interoperability between commercial, open source, and research systems, allowing users to deploy their preferred systems according to their advantages in order to obtain an optimal implementation with improved response time.

The open problems that outline the above mentioned challenges can be categorized in theoretical, harmonisation and testing. In particular, the methods implemented in existing commercial vulnerability assessment and intrusion detection systems to date are based on limited decision-making techniques not capable of analyzing large amount of vulnerability assessment and intrusion detection data from various sources.

New promising research activities include the use of graph and game theory in the design of new methods of detecting and analyzing large-scale attacks. These methods have been implemented in prototypes (e.g., the GrIDS, Archipelago, RIDAN, CORE).

Vendors of vulnerability assessment and intrusion detection systems use different terminology to explain the same issue and there is a lack of machine-readable

Copyright © 2007, Idea Group Inc. Copying or distributing in print or electronic forms without written permission of Idea Group Inc. is prohibited.

information. Thus, although the data provided by vulnerability assessment and intrusion detection reports are detailed, they are presented in an ambiguous textual form or in a proprietary data format. The effect is that a vulnerability report has become tightly coupled to specific tool and cannot easily be shared across different tools. This lack of common ground has hampered the ability to integrate diverse sources of available security data more effectively.

To date vulnerability assessment tools and intrusion detection systems have been tested in small- to medium-scale facilities, which are not representatives of large operational networks or the portion of the Internet that could be involved in an attack. Testing and benchmarking vulnerability assessment and intrusion detection tools in these small size test beds are limited and not very useful when the test beds become large scale, which is often the case when evaluating these tools in critical infrastructures is needed. To make rapid advances in evaluating vulnerability assessment and intrusion detection tools in critical infrastructures it is necessary to first develop new frameworks for testing and benchmarking such tools in large-scale test beds.

The following directions and actions can further be considered in order to address open questions in vulnerability assessment.

- Identify barriers and gaps in existing analysis methods for the security assessment and detection of governmental critical infrastructures
- Provide new enhanced methods (in order to be implemented in next generation vulnerability assessment and intrusion detection systems and tools) capable to identify future threats
- Design and specify configurable, interoperable intrusion detection tools embedding these new methods
- Develop new frameworks and standards for testing and benchmarking intrusion detection in large-scale critical infrastructures
- Collaborate with all relevant standardisation bodies (e.g., IDMEF, IETF, and IODEF) for providing recommendations and receiving feedback.
- Experimental promising techniques based on various mathematical theories (game theory, graph theory, algebraic geometry) that lead to better decision-making models need to be explored

CHALLENGES IN THE SECURITY OF WEB SERVICES

The need for interoperable e-government services is addressed through the use of XML and Web services. XML is considered a proven method for enterprise application integration that improves extensibility and scalability and facilitates easy adoption of changes to the schemas and business processes to suit growing needs. Web services based on the widely accepted standard XML use the simple object

Copyright © 2007, Idea Group Inc. Copying or distributing in print or electronic forms without written permission of Idea Group Inc. is prohibited.

access protocol (SOAP) messages providing a communication channel among applications, which are able to run on different operating systems, with different technologies and programming languages that go beyond simple content delivery. XML distributed services are implemented preferably with open source tools, software implementations of the Web Services Description Language (WSDL 1.1) for the services' description, and the universal description discovery and integration protocol (UDDI 2.0) for directory publishing. The use of a UDDI creates standard interoperable platforms that enable service providers, mobile users, and the appropriate applications to quickly, easily, and dynamically find and use several Web services over the Internet.

Extensions (whether mobile or not) usually are being developed for leading Web services technology platforms provided by reputable software vendors. Both architectures can mitigate some of the limits of mobile computing but they are unlikely to provide many of the features usually associated with the Web services technology. However, in cases of different Web services, interoperability can be achieved between reputable software platforms following the release of the Basic Profile 1, by Web Services Interoperability (WS-I).

Popular and powerful protocols for transferring sensitive information over a secure connection are the SSL and the transport layer security (TLS). However, these protocols are designed and best suited for the old wired Internet topography. A number of serious problems arise when trying to apply SSL/TLS to new generation dynamic applications (whether wireless or not) such as:

- SSL/TLS is a point-to-point protocol that secures direct connections between hosts. Due to fact that the emerging Internet topography is based on Web services, it will require multiple intermediaries to help process and deliver XML-based services. Therefore, this topography requires end-to-end security
- Peer groups and subscription-based multicast applications will be a major model for the smart wireless applications of the future. Being a one-to-one protocol, SSL/TLS does not adequately support multicast applications
- SSL/TLS indiscriminately encrypts all data with the same key strength, which can be unnecessary or even undesirable for some mobile services applications

Measures for end-to-end security better suit the next generation. High-speed wireless governmental environments utilizing cryptographic operations on the data with technologies offering digital signatures and encryption. More advanced value added services such as time stamping, can additionally be implemented as well. Technologies used in e-government platforms (e.g., e-mayor), enabling digital signatures and encryption for XML content, are the W3C XML Signature Recommendation (XML-DSIG) and W3C XML Encryption draft standard. XML-DSIG defines a means of rendering a digital signature in XML and brings several benefits

Copyright © 2007, Idea Group Inc. Copying or distributing in print or electronic forms without written permission of Idea Group Inc. is prohibited.

of XML to digital signatures, making them human-readable, easily parsed, platform independent, and generally more advantageous for workflow environments that preceding standards like PKCS#7. Seamless integration into workflow processes is achieved in the mobile platform presented, using XML encryption, which allows the selective encryption of arbitrary portions of XML documents. In order to add encryption, digital signatures, and authorisation token support to SOAP messages for Web services an implementation of the OASIS WS-S (WS-security) has been used.

PKI technologies play an important role in implementing interoperable secure mobile services. Web services integration with a PKI is achieved by the W3C XML key management specification (XKMS) which is a building block for secure Web services (mobile or not) and a means of using Web services to simplify a number of PKI protocols. The use of XKMS enables the management of keys and certificates as part of the integrated mobile services applications and achieves Web services based registration, revocation and updates using SOAP over wireless network communication. Using PKI ensures the legal validity of digitally signed documents.

However, there are still various challenges facing the security of Web services including:

- XKMS defines a Web services interface to a public key infrastructure. This makes it easy for applications to interface with key-related services, like registration, revocation, location, and validation. Most developers will only ever need to worry about implementing XKMS clients. XKMS server components are mostly implemented by providers of public key infrastructure (PKI) providers, such as Entrust, Cybertrust and VeriSign.
- SOAP security extensions: Digital Signature (SOAP-DSIG) defines the syntax and processing rules for digitally signing SOAP messages and validating signatures. It is needed to further investigate the corresponding extensions in kSOAP messages in order to provide digital signatures through mobile devices.
- Existing standards on sets of SOAP extensions can be used when building secure Web services to implement message content integrity and confidentiality. These refer to a set of extensions and modules, as the "WSS: SOAP Message Security."
- XKMS integrated with kSOAP will simplify the deployment of enterprise-strength PKI services by transferring complex key verification processing tasks from the mobile device to a Trust Service thus dealing with the problem of large packages and limited memory as well as the low processing capacity of mobile devices.
- The implementation of appropriate user interfaces running on 3G mobile terminals, relying on the W3C XForms standard in order for the mobile browser

Copyright © 2007, Idea Group Inc. Copying or distributing in print or electronic forms without written permission of Idea Group Inc. is prohibited.

to enable the user to directly interact with the various mobile Web services, is a very interesting research area.

There has been enormous progress in the area of interoperability between various implementations of the SOAP protocol for different platforms. However, a similar effort concerning the kSOAP technology and the interoperability issues between kSOAP and Web services from various platforms has not been noticed yet and would be very interesting. For example:

- XML-based browsers for mobile devices, mobile Web services messaging, and security and cryptography on mobile Web services
- Design and development of XML based mobile browser
- Design and development of libraries for mobile Web services messaging
- Design and development of mobile Web Services Security and Cryptography libraries and toolkits

THE E-MAYOR PROJECT

The e-mayor project aims at providing a secure, interoperable, and affordable platform for Web services in e-government organisations. A novel feature of e-mayor is the emphasis it gives on the needs and requirements of small- and medium-sized government organisations (SMGOs) across Europe. The development of e-government Web services in smaller municipalities is often hindered by lack of financial, political, or legal support. Security and technical problems cannot be solved because the required expertise or infrastructure is not available. The e-mayor project looks into the issues which are the main barriers to progress. By creating an e-government platform e-mayor intends to help SMGOs overcome these barriers. The e-mayor project started on January 1, 2004 and was finalized in early 2006 and involved a number of highly specialized European Companies in information security technologies and management, a number of leading European universities in this field and five municipalities that were involved in the trials.

The main questions that the e-mayor project addressed are the following:

- How can one develop a secure, interoperable, affordable e-government platform that serves the needs of small- and medium-sized government organisations (i.e., municipalities) around Europe and enables them to make a next step in e-government?
- Is it possible to develop, maintain, and operate secure e-government Web services that would be able to support cross-border one-stop e-government services for citizens and regional G2G-cooperation activities?
- What are the main political and legal issues that affect the introduction of a secure Web service platform, and can recommendations be made regarding the

Copyright © 2007, Idea Group Inc. Copying or distributing in print or electronic forms without written permission of Idea Group Inc. is prohibited.

way the European Union further enhance secure Web services for e-government?

- How can small- and medium-sized municipalities face current problems (e.g., communication with other municipalities in order to issue documents for citizens)?
- How can they offer electronic and mobile services despite their own barriers (e.g., lack of infrastructure, limited expertise, etc.) for large groups of citizens (e.g., elder, youngsters, handicapped) and deal with cross-border communication?

Additionally, e-mayor was confronted with the following issues related to the proper methodological approach to trans-disciplinary engineering of e-government solutions both for IT solution providers and for SMGOs making use of prefabricated platforms. Thus, e-mayor developed a detailed, technologically, and organisationally validated IT architecture that holistically fulfils practical requirements and makes use of multi-disciplinary knowledge. Ulterior questions relate to the business case in delivering secure e-government services at various scales. Actually, e-government within municipalities is proceeding at a steady pace, with budgets roughly remaining constant over the years. From this, one may conclude that the business case for delivering value in terms of efficiency and effectiveness is there. However, the benefits can be reaped only at a modest pace in a controlled manner. This is typical for medium-sized organisations in general.

The e-mayor project aims at contributing toward the provision of secure and interoperable e-government services, by developing an affordable, ease of use electronic platform hosting secure municipal Web services. In order for an e-mayor platform to be successfully deployed across Europe, on one hand, a simple open solution based on widely accepted standards with good market support must be put in place. On the other hand, the platform must be Internet based to enable communication with legacy as well as newly developed systems residing on heterogeneous platforms. Web services and XML address both sets of requirements and therefore these technologies will form the core for the research and development effort and implementation. Security is centrepiece in the e-mayor architecture in order to ensure the trust of the users and the applicability of the platform in real life terms. e-mayor highly considers the barriers imposed on small- and medium-sized public organisations because of their small size and limited resources and it strives to meet their needs. The project puts an effort in promoting the e-mayor platform as de facto standard for such organisations.

The challenge for e-mayor is to develop and implement an open, secure, and affordable e-government platform for small and medium European public organisations in order to support the secure communication of municipalities amongst themselves, businesses, and citizens. Furthermore, the secure remote access and storage to repositories of municipal information for authorized civil servants and

Copyright © 2007, Idea Group Inc. Copying or distributing in print or electronic forms without written permission of Idea Group Inc. is prohibited.

citizens needs to be included. Finally, the platform should allow the support of pan European services enhancing their role, visibility, and mission.

The e-mayor platform must provide a sustainable basis for future, secure e-government and support the re-organisation of public administration which is foreseen by leading e-government experts. The platform should be deployable all over Europe and support cross-border processes and services. Thus it has to jointly fulfil highly demanding functional requirements, security requirements, highly heterogeneous legal and political requirements, usability and accessibility requirements, economic requirements, and requirements related to need for easy deployment and maintenance.

After describing the main requirements and drafting the e-mayor platform design in 2004, the consortium continued in 2005 with the implementation of the e-mayor platform. A multilingual static and dynamic Web page content that represents the graphical interface to the services using standard W3C guidelines with respect to accessibility for special groups was developed. e-mayor is fully equipped to handle digital identity cards, securing access to the online government services, signing digital forms, and for providing authentication services. Citizens, civil servants, or both may use the digital identity cards. The platform may connect to any PKI infrastructure and, depending on how this is offered, may support any type of digital certificate based on the X.509 standard or a secure token such as a smartcard. The e-mayor platform is based upon open source tools and software, and runs on well-known software environments. It is based upon modern XML and Web services standards.

The validation and verification activities were also on the agenda. The prototypical implementation of the e-mayor platform by itself had as a main aim to validate the architecture in two ways. Firstly, it should demonstrate the technological feasibility (if the prototype works). Secondly, it should form the basis for a number of pan-European trials, which help to validate the organisational feasibility and potential for real life implementation.

The main field trials formed the basis for an overall evaluation from a technical, user, legal, and financial perspective which in turn led to a refinement of the e-mayor platform architecture and implementation. Several cities across Europe have tried out the secure e-mayor Web services platform at a large scale and over 200 citizens and civil servants used the e-government services.

In Aachen, Germany, which is located close to the borders of Belgium and the Netherlands, the Municipality will try out a number of trans-border e-government services, with the aim of further developing online services in the region. Two cities in Italy, Bolzano, and Siena assess the usability of the e-mayor platform as a basis for providing services to the citizens with the help of digital ID-cards for identification. In Spain, the city of Seville worked out an ambitious set of ideas to further develop e-government. The applicability of e-mayor is being investigated for a number of important online services, including tax services.

Copyright © 2007, Idea Group Inc. Copying or distributing in print or electronic forms without written permission of Idea Group Inc. is prohibited.

The trials also included a number of cross-border e-government applications, where municipalities exchanged information on citizens, residence certificates, in a controlled and secure way, allowing for translation, security enforcement management, and multi-lingual e-forms access. The results of the trials showed the technical and organisational feasibility of cross-border e-government and integration, but left open a number of legal issues and questions regarding large-scale market validation.

The e-mayor project focuses on issues that are considered to be at the core of European e-government policies by addressing the main barriers against effective e-government. That is, apart from improving knowledge management, the interoperability between government organisations in general and between Member States in particular. The e-mayor project addresses all three aspects of interoperability of the European interoperability framework for Pan-European e-government services, namely organisational interoperability (i.e., the cross-border process itself), semantic interoperability (i.e., the transformation of the documents is an important step toward the desired direction, as well as the analysis of the different European national digital XML-standards), and technical interoperability (BPEL, E2M/M2E). The European interoperability framework provides guidelines for innovation toward interoperability and e-mayor achieved a successful realisation of those guidelines.

The e-mayor project also contributes to innovation in this respect, as it is the first really large-scale set of trials achieving interoperability among European municipalities. The technologies developed and reworked for these purposes, address a new way of handling the digital forms, the implementation of security enforcement module, the handling of language issues in cross-border e-government and the integration into one adaptable and easy to implement e-government platform. The e-mayor approach represents a lightweight implementation of a fully-fledged e-government platform that meets forthcoming requirements of exchanging documents between stakeholders. It appears that e-mayor is also successful due to the absence of a centralized architecture to address an e-government problem and as such it may form the basis of a number of applications that serve mobility in Europe.

Apart from the local advantages of e-mayor, for municipalities and other smaller government organisations, this solution for dealing with cross-border e-government is considered by the consortium as a possibility to work on politically important priority actions, like the Bolkestein directive, e-procurement for the public sector and secure exchange of information related to cross-border policing and homeland security. Although e-mayor does not aim at a market study, through the exploitation plans of the individual partners of e-mayor the viability of the business case for secure e-government services is also examined. The results of e-mayor also aim at providing input into the EU standardisation process with regard to specific areas within the realm of interest of e-mayor (e.g., electronic signatures, security, Web services, e-government).

Copyright © 2007, Idea Group Inc. Copying or distributing in print or electronic forms without written permission of Idea Group Inc. is prohibited.

CONCLUSION

While various security technologies have enhanced the security level of electronic services in e-government, there are still major challenges in order to reach a desired level of secure and interoperable architectures upon which user friendly, automated, interoperable, and secure e-government services can be leveraged. Interoperability requirement and the way they are implemented in real life applications are a critical consideration for e-government due to challenges posed by disparate requirements in applications at the various e-government levels or across borders. Intrusion detection systems and vulnerability assessment tools providing perimeter security face harmonisation, testing, and methodology challenges. The security promised by Web services in combination with PKI has emerged as a very appropriate combination for creating secure services, however, there are still open issues ahead. In brief, essential security features of e-government rollouts additionally include: trust status lists, confidentiality, integrity, the interconnection of registries and databases, and quality assurance and accreditation of services. In e-government, an application-centric approach is required to explore and resolve issues pertaining to applications such as identity management that is a lynchpin for applications in terms of setting out authentication requirements for end users and third party applications. While requirements for identity management might vary, EU Member States have a standing need to take the legal framework into account especially with regard to cross-border applications. Additional challenges related to the regulatory instruments to regulate e-government through law, contract, and policies merit further discussion. Finally, business aspects and especially competition challenges require close monitoring in an area of public interest such as e-government. The impact of e-government is likely to affect best practices in order for stakeholders to assess the approach they adopt toward e-government and other lateral applications that interact with private sector needs (e.g., e-invoicing). Best practices could also be considered to determine the rate of interaction between e-government and a broader framework of electronic applications and transactions.

NOTE

This chapter represents the authors' personal opinion and not the views of any third party including their employers past or present in any way whatsoever. The authors would like to thank Mrs. Isabella Santa for proofreading this chapter.

REFERENCES

Armstrong, E., Bodoff, S., Carson, D., Fisher, M., Green, D., & Haase, K. (2002). *The Java Web services tutorial*. Boston: Addison-Wesley.

Copyright © 2007, Idea Group Inc. Copying or distributing in print or electronic forms without written permission of Idea Group Inc. is prohibited.

Communication from the Commission COM. (2001). *298 final, June 6, 2001, Network and information security: Proposal for a European policy approach.*

Dunn, M., & Wigert, I. (2004). *Critical information infrastructure protection.* Zurich, Switzerland: Swiss Federal Institute of Technology.

Ford, W., & Baum, M. (2001). *Secure electronic commerce.* Upper Saddle River, NJ: Prentice Hall.

Fukuyama, F. (1995). *Trust: The social virtues and the creation of prosperity.* New York: Free Press.

Hix, S. (1999). *The political system of the European Union.* London: Palgrave.

Hartman, B., Flinn, D., Beszosov, K., & Kawamoto, S. (2003). *Mastering Web services security.* Hoboken, NJ: Wiley Publishing.

Lei, L., & Mitrakas, A. (1996, June 10-12). A multi disciplinary perspective for electronic commerce. In P. Swatman, J. Gricar, & J. Novak (Eds.), *Electronic commerce for trade efficiency and effectiveness. The 9th International Conference on EDI-IOS*, Moderna Organizacija, Kranj.

Luhmann, N. (1988). Familiarity, confidence, trust: Problems and alternatives. In D. Gambetta (Ed.), *Trust: Making and breaking cooperative relations* (pp. 94-107). New York: Basil Blackwell.

Magnette, P. (2000). *L'Europe, l'Etat et la démocratie.* Brussels: Complexe.

Mitrakas, A. (2006). Certificate management interoperability for e-government applications. In A. Mitrakas, P. Hengeveld, D. Polemi, & J. Gamper (Eds.), *Secure e-government Web services.* Hershey, PA: Idea Group Publishing.

Mousis, N. (2002). *Guide to European policies, European Study Service.* Rixensart, Belgium.

Nash, A., Duane, B., Brink, D., & Joseph, C. (2001). *PKI: Implementing and managing eSecurity.* Emeryville, CA: McGraw-Hill Osborn Media.

Stigler, G. J. (1971). The theory of economic regulation. *Bell Journal of Economics and Management Science, 6*(2), 3-21.

UNCTAD. (2001). *E-Commerce and development report 2001.* New York, United Nations.

Valvis, G., Sklavos, P., Papadaki. K., & Polemi, D. (2002, March) Overview of a network-based IDS solution. In *Proceedings of Applied Test Suites Conference,* Athens, Greece.

Williams, B. (1988). Formal structure and social reality. In D. Gambetta, (Ed.), *Trust making and breaking co-operative relation.* Oxford: Blackwell.

Copyright © 2007, Idea Group Inc. Copying or distributing in print or electronic forms without written permission of Idea Group Inc. is prohibited.

Chapter II

Building Innovative, Secure, and Interoperable E-Government Services

A. Kaliontzoglou, National Technical University of Athens, Greece

T. Karantjias, National Technical University of Athens, Greece

D. Polemi, University of Piraeus, Greece

ABSTRACT

Research into initiatives worldwide shows that although some of the legal and orga-nizational barriers for the adoption of new technologies in e-government have been lifted, there are still not many implementations of actual e-government services that have been designed based on a common and systematic approach. The prevailing requirements for e-government services, interoperability and security, pose major challenges to e-government architects and it is now being slowly understood that Web services in combination with public key infrastructures may provide the neces-sary solutions. In this context, this chapter presents three innovative e-government services based on these technologies, focusing on their security and interoperability aspects. The goal of the chapter is to demonstrate the services' specifications and use cases so that they may act as examples for further research and development.

Copyright © 2007, Idea Group Inc. Copying or distributing in print or electronic forms without written permission of Idea Group Inc. is prohibited.

INTRODUCTION

Nowadays it has become evident from the existing e-government initiatives and best practices that although most of the legal and organizational barriers for the wide adoption of e-government services have been lifted, there is still a lack for actual e-government services implementations. Services that make appropriate use of new and already established technologies, such as Web services and PKI, are considered promising in the sense that they satisfy the important e-government requirements of interoperability and security, respecting at the same time the business goals of public organizations and the expectations of citizens that interact with them.

Designing, building, and delivering e-government services that share a set of common requirements demands at first the introduction of a generic e-government architecture that fulfils those requirements, and then the change of focus to the specific requirements posed by each service to be deployed. Those special requirements might stem from the policies of the specific organizations wishing to deploy the service, or even by the legal framework set up by the state or country where the service is to be offered.

This chapter initially presents the major requirements of e-government services and references an existing e-government architecture that satisfies them. It then goes further into analyzing three distinct service implementations that rely on the architecture and leverage its common functionalities. These services include the issuance and distribution of public certification documents, such as birth certificates, electronic invoicing, and electronic ticketing. Their selection has been based on desk study and worldwide research results that demonstrate they are among the top services demanded by governmental organizations and citizens. Their implementation is based on Web services and PKI filling the gap of successful deployments of those technologies and demonstrating use cases that can be further consulted in the future for similar endeavours.

The chapter is structured as follows: "Generic E-Government Requirements and Architecture" focuses on the most important requirements that need to be satisfied by an e-government service and references a generic e-government architecture that has been already designed and has already been built in the European e-mayor project. "Three Innovative Secure and Interoperable E-Government Services" investigates in detail one by one the use cases of the three aforementioned innovative e-government services: issuance of public certification documents, e-invoicing, and e-ticketing. Finally, "Conclusion" draws conclusions.

GENERIC E-GOVERNMENT REQUIREMENTS AND ARCHITECTURE

This section describes firstly the basic requirements that need to be taken into account when building an e-government service and then goes on to give an

Copyright © 2007, Idea Group Inc. Copying or distributing in print or electronic forms without written permission of Idea Group Inc. is prohibited.

overview of an e-government architecture that may host e-government services that satisfy the requirements.

It should be noted that in the rest of the chapter when we refer to an e-government service, we specifically mean an enterprise service operated by a public organization that performs one instance of a business function, as for example the issuance of a certification document etc. The terms "enterprise service" and "e-government service" are therefore interchangeable in this context.

E-Government Requirements

Interoperability is a primary goal of an e-government service. Lack of interoperability amongst services is mainly due to the unhomogeneity of technical solutions deployed in the infrastructures that support the service itself, as well as the lack of well-defined service business functions.

The interconnection of governmental organizations that use various platforms and systems is a difficult task requiring easily identifiable and publishable e-services, as well as clear interfaces for the establishment of secure and reliable connection points.

Interoperability is satisfied by using widely deployed standards and technologies during the services' design and implementation phases.

Current practices indicate that in order for an e-government service to succeed in its business goals, it should be secure in all aspects so that the entities involved trust it. An e-government service should make use of security services and mechanisms supported by the environment or architecture where it is deployed.

There are five critical security requirements that need to be satisfied (Hartman, Flinn, Beszosov, & Kawamoto, 2003):

- **Authentication:** The method with which an entity is uniquely identified and its identity verified.
- **Integrity:** The method that ensures that every system, resource, file, and information in general can be modified only by authorized entities.
- **Privacy and confidentiality:** The method by which access to the content of information is available only to authorized recipients.
- **Non-repudiation:** The method that produces cryptographic data that ensure that an entity cannot repudiate its actions.
- **Availability:** The method that ensures that a system can fulfil its purpose with a given degree of success.

An e-government service can satisfy the security requirements by making use of a set of *security mechanisms* and a set of *security services*. Security mechanisms are stand-alone instances of components that are directly embedded within an e-government enterprise service and that address a security requirement based on a policy. Security services on the other hand, are independent services within

Copyright © 2007, Idea Group Inc. Copying or distributing in print or electronic forms without written permission of Idea Group Inc. is prohibited.

an e-government architecture that are available to any enterprise service wishing to perform a security goal as part of a policy. Security services integrate security mechanisms, and may interact with other security services as part of their operation. Security mechanisms may also interact with security services to send and receive information.

Yet another important requirement that an e-government service has to take into account is the friendliness towards users and respect to the way a user perceives the service itself.

This requirement is usually satisfied in two ways:

- With the support of applications with which most users are already accustomed and do not pose additional training requirements.
- With the provision of a high level of transparency for complex processes that the service entails, so that a user does not perceive the lower level technical details, without nevertheless losing the meaning of what process they are involved in and why.

Therefore, an e-government service should be supporting standard browsing facilities common in most computers nowadays and a high level of abstraction with respect to technical details.

Finally, a major requirement of e-government services is the compliance with the underlying legal and policy framework as dictated by the laws and directives of the states where the service is to be deployed and operated. The legal specificities are tightly coupled on one hand with the business functions of the service itself, and on the other with the security functions that it has to support, such as the restrictions posed by law regarding digital signatures and their equation with hand written ones under specific constraints. Furthermore, an e-government service has to abide by the organizational policies of the organization hosting it.

A Generic Secure E-Government Architecture

The study of previous e-government requirements has lead to the design of a new e-government architecture that on one hand is generic enough to accommodate them and on the other hand offers an adequate framework for the implementation and deployment of e-government services that achieve specific governmental business goals. This architecture is part of the work that has occurred in the E.C. funded "e-mayor project" (e-mayor, 2004) which has the purpose of building and evaluating a platform that is an instance of the architecture.

The architecture is depicted in Figure 1.

As can be seen in Figure 1, the architecture is divided into specific areas of services that perform core functions of an e-government architecture. These are the basic services, administration and orchestration services, security services, enterprise services, and existing infrastructure support services. A short description of these

Copyright © 2007, Idea Group Inc. Copying or distributing in print or electronic forms without written permission of Idea Group Inc. is prohibited.

Figure 1. A generic secure e-government architecture

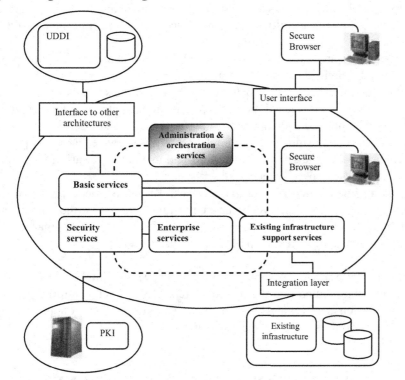

groups follows. The main concepts behind the systematic design approach of the architecture are based on the RM-ODP standard (e-mayor Consortium D3.1, 2004; Kaliontzoglou, Sklavos, Karantjias, & Polemi, 2004; Meneklis, Kaliontzoglou, Polemi, & Douligeris, 2005) for a more detailed analysis).

- **Administration and orchestration services:** These services perform two very important functions within the architectural framework: they manage all other services and orchestrate the enterprise services so that they successfully achieve the business goals. They are divided into access services, process coordination services, and user management services.
- **Basic services:** These provide the basic functions that are used by the archi-tecture as a whole to perform primitive tasks. Basic services are user interface services, message transformation services, message forwarding services, publication and query services, notification services, and printing services.
- **Security mechanisms and services:** These address the security requirements of Section 2. Security mechanisms that are supported are the following: digital signatures, advanced electronic signatures, and encryption. Security mecha-nisms are encapsulated into distinct components that are in turn, embedded into

Copyright © 2007, Idea Group Inc. Copying or distributing in print or electronic forms without written permission of Idea Group Inc. is prohibited.

any other component that needs them, based on the policies that govern the services. The security services that the e-government architecture comprises are the following: identity management, access control, time stamping and keys, and certificates management.

- **Enterprise services:** These are the actual e-government services. Enterprise services are divided into a set of atomic sub-processes and each one is mapped into a service. This achieves better coordination of the services and more efficient reuse where needed. For example, an atomic enterprise service might accept a completed and signed form by the user. This sub-service might be used in the composition of any complete enterprise service that encompasses such a process. The services that follow and that are the focus of this paper are examples of specific enterprise services.
- **Existing infrastructure support services:** These, in essence, manage the intermediate integration layer of the architecture that connects the architecture with services that operates on top of existing infrastructure of an organization (e.g., wrapper software on top of legacy databases etc.)

The enterprise services described in Section 3 have been implemented as Web services and incorporated into the previous architecture. Each enterprise service utilizes the previous services and resources of the e-mayor architecture appropriately in order to carry out its intended business purpose.

THREE INNOVATIVE SECURE AND INTEROPERABLE E-GOVERNMENT SERVICES

This section presents the three new services that are the focus of this chapter:

- **Issuance and distribution of public certification documents:** Involving the generation of digital certificates requested by citizens, bearing the proper credentials of public authorities
- **E-invoicing:** Involving the secure issuance and distribution of digital invoices among commercial partners
- **E/m-ticketing:** Involving the setup of an infrastructure for the creation and validation of digital tickets related to public transportation or events

Issuance and distribution of public certification documents is rated as a top candidate service for future deployment by municipalities worldwide. Something also shown by the research results of the e-mayor project (e-mayor Consortium D2.1, 2004), as well as the results of major e-government initiatives such as e-Gif

Copyright © 2007, Idea Group Inc. Copying or distributing in print or electronic forms without written permission of Idea Group Inc. is prohibited.

operated by the UK Office of the eEnvoy (UK Office of the eEnvoy, 2004) and SAGA (German Federal Ministry of Interior, 2003) in Germany. Furthermore, the value of invoices exchange has been emphasized by the European Union Directive on VAT legislation on electronic invoicing and electronic storage of invoices (The European Parliament, 2001), which has to be adapted in all European Union (EU) countries legislation by 2008. The report of the CEN/ISSS e-invoicing Focus Group on standards and developments on electronic invoicing (CEN/ISSS e-invoicing Focus Group, 2003) demonstrates the needs for electronic invoice implementations. Electronic ticketing has been receiving attention the last years mainly because buying and collecting tickets produces crunch times. Being competitive means changing business models from paper passed tickets to keep up with customers' changing habits and needs, adopting mobile for one. Electronic tickets enabled by mobile phones comprise an important class of everyday consumer transactions, fulfilling the requirement of governmental organizations to easily provide tickets to events, public museums, public transportation, and so forth.

In the sections that follow, each service is described in terms of what its business goals are in the context of e-government, what are the more specific requirements it poses in addition to the common e-government requirements described in the section "E-Government Requirements," which are its main actors and components, and which are its functional and operational phases and characteristics.

Figure 2. Certification document issuance

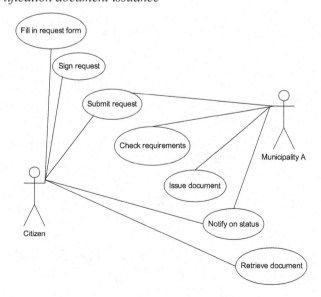

Copyright © 2007, Idea Group Inc. Copying or distributing in print or electronic forms without written permission of Idea Group Inc. is prohibited.

Issuance and Distribution of E-Certification Documents

Description and Purpose

This service deals with the secure issuance and distribution of certification documents. Example certification documents that can be reported are birth, death, or marriage certificates (we use the term certification document in this section in order to avoid any confusion with security certificates such as those complying with the X509 standard). In this section, we present a particular enterprise service that can be deployed in the reference architecture of section "A Generic Secure E-Government Architecture," in which municipalities (a representative governmental organization) are able to generate, issue. and deliver securely (to citizens or other municipalities) digitally signed birth certificates. The functionality and initial implementation aspects of the service are provided here where as a full implementation occurred as part of the e-mayor project.

The purpose of this service is to enable a citizen to interact with the intended municipality, regardless of the citizen's location, in order for him to make a secure request for a specific certification document that the municipality can provide.

As shown in the use case diagram of Figure 2, the citizen has to fill in certain forms, sign them, and then submit the request to the municipality. The municipality checks on whether it can issue the desired document. If yes, a civil servant issues the certification document, signs it, and notifies the citizen that he or she may retrieve it.

Figure 3. Certification document issuance with propagation

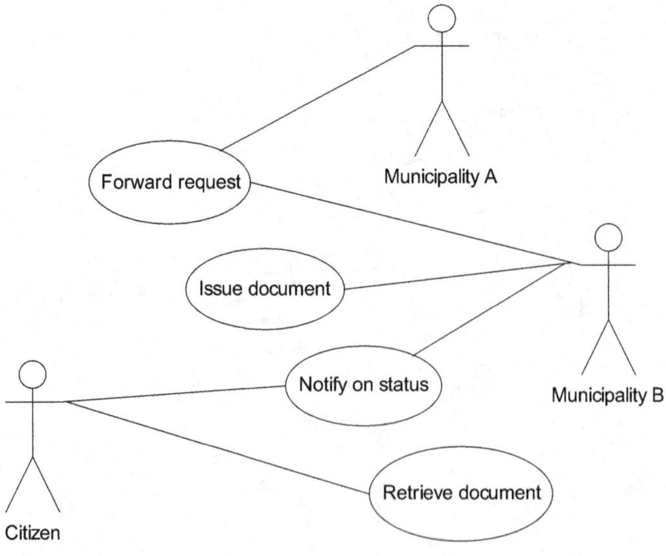

Copyright © 2007, Idea Group Inc. Copying or distributing in print or electronic forms without written permission of Idea Group Inc. is prohibited.

If not, as shown in the diagram of Figure 3, the request is propagated to the municipality that is indeed responsible for issuing the document, which may reside even on a different country, therefore requiring cross-border electronic communication.

Additional/Specific Service Requirements

There are two requirements posed by the "issuance and distribution of e-certification documents" e-government service in addition to the common ones of section "E-Government Requirements" and they are attributed to the fact that municipalities are small sized governmental organizations and that may have to interact with each other over country borders in order to deliver the requested services to their citizens.

- **Limited trained personnel:** Smaller sized governmental organizations suffer from a lack of personnel that is adequately trained to cope with the technologies introduced by IT. Furthermore, training the personnel has a greater impact on smaller governmental organizations because of the limited funds it usually has available
- **Cross border communication:** An ever increasing number of citizens change their location to work and live in other countries. This means that there is a definite demand to support them in everyday administrative procedures that include cross-border communication. In cross-border services, there is exchange of information, data, or documents between citizens and public administrations in an international context and across administrative boundaries

The enterprise service described in the following paragraphs has to take into account these additional requirements.

Main Service Components

The certification document issuance service operates as an enterprise service within the architecture. The WSDL description of the endpoint of the service can be published in a UDDI directory through the publication and query service. This allows searching for the specific enterprise service and comprehension of the messages this service understands so that messages can be sent to and received from it.

The enterprise service is running as a Web service in the architecture and it is managed by the orchestration service. It communicates with the following architecture services:

- With secure browsers through the access service
- With any required databases through an existing infrastructure support service

Copyright © 2007, Idea Group Inc. Copying or distributing in print or electronic forms without written permission of Idea Group Inc. is prohibited.

- The forwarding service of the architecture, in order to securely dispatch the certification document to its final destination
- The key and certificate management service for validation of key and certificates

An important part of the service is the format of the data that is being exchanged. It is evident from the fundamental e-government requirements of section "E-Government Requirements" that this format has to be XML to ensure interoperability. Further interoperability nevertheless has to be ensured with respect to the exact structure supported specifically for data related for example to address information or birth details, etc. Therefore, the messages have to be based on widely adopted e-government standards that define such XML data such as the following:

- The schemas produced under the UK eGif initiative (Hunter, 2004; Kent, 2003)
- The OASIS Universal Business Language (UBL) Schemas (Meadows & Seaburg, 2004)
- Schemas derived from the e-gov project–GovML (Kavvadias, Spanos, & Tambouris, 2002)
- The IDA e-procurement XML schemas initiative (IDA BC, 2004)

Transformations between formats and languages respecting semantic differences may be performed by using the message transformation services of the architecture.

Figure 4. Certification document issuance and delivery transaction scheme

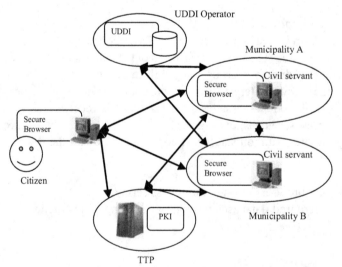

Copyright © 2007, Idea Group Inc. Copying or distributing in print or electronic forms without written permission of Idea Group Inc. is prohibited.

Entities and Actors

This section presents the entities involved in a typical certification document issuance and delivery and their roles. All entities and their relationships are depicted in Figure 4.

The actors that take part are:

- **The citizen:** The citizen is the consumer of any e-government service supported by the architecture. It has to communicate with the TTP to get the proper security credentials
- **Municipalities and personnel:** The municipalities are the governmental organizations that are part of the e-government architecture and host the services. Their personnel (civil servants, administrators etc.) are the internal users of the e-government services. They too have to communicate with the TTP to receive credentials. The service does not pose a limit to the number of municipalities that may participate in a transaction. This means that a citizen may request a certification document for which a number of municipalities shall have to cooperate to complete the service
- **The trusted third party (TTP):** Before any secure messaging can take place, all participants need to have established an adequate security framework. Such a framework may be an infrastructure based on TTP technologies (Nash, Duane, Brink, & Joseph, 2001). In our case, the required TTPs are at a minimum a certification authority (CA) and a registration authority (RA) offering the PKI services of registration, certification, and revocation status information with OCSP, as well as a time stamping authority (TSA) offering standard based time stamping services
- **Universal description, discovery, and integration (UDDI) directory operator:** This operator hosts a public UDDI directory where Web services can be published and thus become publicly available

Figure 5. Birth certificate service operation on municipality A

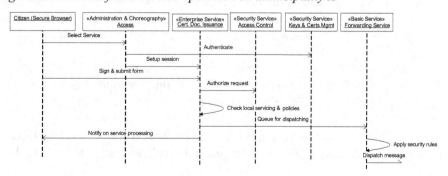

Copyright © 2007, Idea Group Inc. Copying or distributing in print or electronic forms without written permission of Idea Group Inc. is prohibited.

Functional and Operational Description

This section presents the functional description of a typical transaction that is supported by the enterprise service. More specifically, the section describes the sequences of operations that are carried out in order for a citizen in city A to receive a birth certificate from a municipality that is located in city B. In the paper world, a citizen would have to sign a formal request form in the premises of the municipality B and wait for a few days for the civil servant there to fill in and sign the birth certificate.

Supposing that an implementation of the e-government architecture of the section "A Generic Secure E-Government Architecture" has been deployed at both the municipalities A and B along with the enterprise service described here, the citizen may acquire the certificate in a more efficient manner.

The service execution has two main phases. The first one involves the actions that take place at the premises of municipality A and the second the actions that take place at municipality B. The first phase is depicted in the sequence diagram of Figure 5.

A description of the process is the following:

- **Selection of service, authentication, and submission of request:** The citizen logs on directly to the site of municipality A where he or she currently resides and selects the certification document issuance enterprise service. This is performed through a secure browser. The access service of the architecture authenticates the user utilizing proper calls to the keys and certificates management service. If authentication is successful, the citizen goes on to complete the specific form, declaring whether he would like to receive a signed paper document in municipality A, or a purely digital birth certificate in case this was acceptable. The citizen has the option to sign the form he completes. A user signature may be optional at this point, according to the active municipality policy.

- **Authorization:** The access service propagates the request to the actual enterprise service that runs as a Web service in the architecture. This enterprise service consults the access control service to take the necessary actions to authorize the citizen's request and provide him or her with a success or failure result. In case of success, the citizen is also provided with an estimation of time within which his or her request will be completed and served. More specifically, the enterprise service retrieves the form, checks its destination, and checks whether it adheres to a policy permitting it to exchange securely documents with the municipality B and whether it knows where to find corresponding services of the architecture at municipality B (based on new or previous queries on known UDDI registries).

- **Confirmation whether request can be served locally and request propagation:** According to this information and local database information, the

Copyright © 2007, Idea Group Inc. Copying or distributing in print or electronic forms without written permission of Idea Group Inc. is prohibited.

Figure 6. Birth certificate service operation at platform B

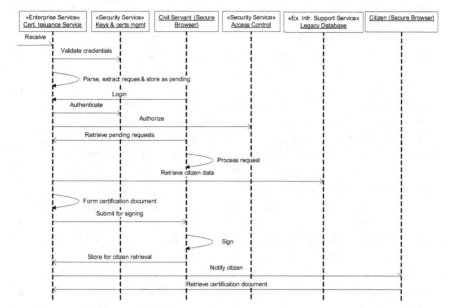

enterprise service checks whether it can serve the request locally, or the request has to be propagated to another municipality. Since the citizen requested a birth certificate from municipality B, the request needs to be propagated. The enterprise service takes the appropriate steps to wrap the request into a SOAP message, and send over to the forwarding service. The forwarding service checks what security rules must be applied to the message (e.g., apply WS-Security extensions), applies those rules and forwards the message to platform B.

The next part of the process takes place at platform B, as depicted in Figure 6. The steps of the second phase are the following:

a.   **Request retrieval, credentials validation, and request storage:** A corresponding enterprise service at platform B receives and parses the message and validates any security credentials applied to it by the service of platform A. This is performed with information acquired by the keys and certificates service in the architecture of municipality B. This security service will perform credentials validation, as is for example the validation of an X509 certificate through an OCSP or XKMS interface. If this process is successful, the citizens' request is extracted from the message and stored as pending.

b.   **Civil servant authentication and access to pending requests:** The procedure continues from the point where a civil servant at the municipality responsible

Copyright © 2007, Idea Group Inc. Copying or distributing in print or electronic forms without written permission of Idea Group Inc. is prohibited.

for processing requests and serving them, accesses through a secure browser the citizens pending request. The civil servant first has to strongly authenticate himself to the platform, based on deployed policies and credentials.

c.   **Service processing and issuance of XML birth certificate:** As part of normal processing, the civil servant checks whether the local database contains an entry verifying that the citizen is a person indeed born in municipality B. The database consulted may be a new one which is part of the platform or a legacy system which is contacted via an existing infrastructures support service. The next step is to transparently formulate a proper XML document with all the required information and present it to a proper official at municipality B to be signed, which may be the same civil servant or another person.

d.   **Signing of birth certificate with XAdES and storage of signed birth certificate:** The official uses the proper cryptographic token (smart card) to sign the document using the secure browser with the proper advanced electronic signature mechanism embedded on it. The electronic signature will be based on the XAdES standard (ETSI, 2002) and will have to abide by a signature policy used in the municipality which enables cross-border exchange of such electronic information with other public organizations. Finally, the signed document is stored for further retrieval by the citizen.

e.   **Retrieval of signed birth certificate:** Depending on the citizen's choice on the form in which he wants the document (paper or digital) the platform will employ different notification mechanisms:

   •   **Paper form:** The XML document is forwarded by the corresponding services from platform B back to platform A, which utilizes the printing service of the architecture to be printed under the supervision of a responsible civil servant. Platform A automatically contacts the citizen by e-mail and/or a message to his mobile phone to retrieve the paper document at the municipality A premises.

   •   **Digital form:** The platform B notification service notifies the citizen directly by e-mail and/or message to a mobile device that his digital birth certificate is ready to be collected. The citizen uses his secure browser to authenticate at platform B and retrieve his birth certificate.

The operation can alternatively be realized by having the citizen log on directly to the services at municipality B first to request the same data. The services at platform B would take the appropriate steps to contact platform A and automatically again receive the birth certificate.

The same architecture implementation could be operated on several other municipalities forming a network. The fact that it is based on XML and Web services enables other municipalities deploying their own solutions to find the platform's interfaces and use them. This would also ideally suit more complex cases where

Copyright © 2007, Idea Group Inc. Copying or distributing in print or electronic forms without written permission of Idea Group Inc. is prohibited.

people are married to foreigners and are living and working abroad, where getting a valid birth or marriage certificate from their hometown may be an extremely cumbersome process. Furthermore, businesses building proprietary Web services software to also access specific services provided by municipalities (for example services related to taxes).

Electronic Invoicing

Description and Purpose

A commercial invoice is the most important document exchanged between trading partners. In addition to its commercial value, an invoice is an accounting document that has legal implications to both transacting parties and constitutes the basis for value added tax (VAT) declaration, VAT reclamation, statistics declaration for intra community trade, and export and import declaration for extra community trade. Nevertheless, in order for e-invoicing implementations to be successful, they need to be in compliance with the EU Directive requirements (i.e., acceptable, interoperable, secure, and affordable by the majority of businesses and organizations operating in EU Member states).

As shown in CEN/ISSS E-Invoicing Focus Group (2003) and The European Parliament (2001), most contemporary e-invoicing implementations are based on EDI, which is an option covered by the Directive. The usage of advanced eSignatures is the other option suggested in the Directive, but their adoption in e-invoicing systems is

Figure 7. A typical e-invoice transaction

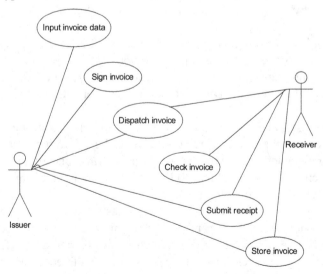

Copyright © 2007, Idea Group Inc. Copying or distributing in print or electronic forms without written permission of Idea Group Inc. is prohibited.

not widespread at the moment. The following sections present an alternative to EDI enterprise service of electronic invoicing that is an open, practical, cost-effective, and secure solution in accordance to EU legislation. This e-invoicing service has been presented so far as a reference implementation of a stand-alone e-invoicing service (CEN/ISSS e-invoicing Focus Group, 2003; Kaliontzoglou, Boutsi, Mavroudis, & Polemi, 2003; Kaliontzoglou, Boutsi, & Polemi, 2005), while in this chapter we present how it is embedded and deployed as an enterprise service in the architecture of section "A Generic Secure E-Government Architecture," further leveraging its interoperability and security features.

At an abstract business level, e-invoicing is about the exchange and storage of e-invoices.

As shown in the use case diagram of Figure 7, electronic invoicing starts with the completion of the invoice data by an employee of the organization that issues the invoice and the signing of the invoice based on a specific signature policy. The signed electronic invoice is then forwarded to the recipient organization that checks its content and cryptographic validity. The transaction is finalized by the submission of a confirmation receipt back to the issuing organization and storage of the invoice.

Additional/Specific Service Requirements

Council Directive 2001/115/EC of December 20, 2001 amends Directive 77/388/EEC with a view of simplifying, modernizing, and harmonising the conditions laid down for invoicing in respect of value added tax. This Directive clarifies the implementation of e-invoicing through the Member States and aims to introduce harmonized procedures for invoicing (paper or electronic invoicing) across Member State borders in a homogeneous home market. The Directive additionally promotes the use of PKI by obligating EU countries to accept digitally signed electronic documents.

As shown in Kaliontzoglou, Boutsi, and Polemi. (2005), this directive poses certain requirements to e-invoicing implementations. In addition to the common e-government requirements presented in the section "E-Government Requirements" that are indeed enforced by the Directive, further requirements are the following:

- **Electronic storage of e-invoices:** The conditions for electronic storage of e-invoices and the technical requirements of the electronic storage system are integral components of the security requirements concerning e-invoicing. Authenticity, integrity, and readability should be guaranteed throughout the storage period, according to the e-invoicing Directive.
- Integrity of the *sequence of the invoices* assists in avoiding any gaps occurring in the outgoing invoices and in strengthening company and tax authority control. This requirement is implementation specific and can be fulfilled by enforcing a tight sequence issuance scheme for the reference number embedded in each invoice.

Copyright © 2007, Idea Group Inc. Copying or distributing in print or electronic forms without written permission of Idea Group Inc. is prohibited.

These additional requirements are met by the enterprise service presented in the following paragraphs.

Main Service Components

The e-invoicing service operates as an enterprise service within the architecture. The WSDL description of the endpoint of the service can be published in a UDDI directory through the Publication and query service. This allows searching for the specific enterprise service and comprehension of the messages this service understands so that messages can be sent and received from it.

The enterprise service is running as a Web service in the architecture and it is managed by the orchestration service. It communicates with the following entities:

- With secure browsers through the access service
- The repository for e-invoices and receipts. This communication may be direct (i.e., the repository is a database directly controlled by the enterprise service) or indirect through an existing infrastructure support service of the architecture
- The forwarding service of the architecture, in order to securely dispatch the invoice to its final destination
- The key and certificate management service for validation of key and certificates

The repository for invoices and receipts may take many forms. In case it is part of the enterprise service itself, it may be any database. Due to the requirement imposed by the Directive that the invoices should retain their form while stored, a

Figure 8. e-invoicing transaction scheme

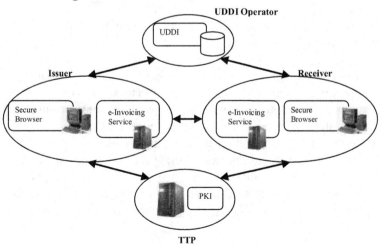

Copyright © 2007, Idea Group Inc. Copying or distributing in print or electronic forms without written permission of Idea Group Inc. is prohibited.

Native XML database implementation of such a repository is considered ideal. This is in contrast to a relational database that "breaks down" invoice elements to store them in distinct tables. Another option would be to use an existing system that is visible in the architecture through an existing infrastructure support service.

In order to promote interoperability with respect to the exact structure supported specifically for e-invoices, various business XML schemas that represent invoices have to be supported. The most widely adopted standards that define forms for e-invoices are the following:

- XML Common Business Library version 4.0 (xCBL 4.0) (xCBL.org, 2003)
- Business Application Software Developers Association (BASDA) electronic Business Interchange standard using XML (eBis-XML suite) (Business Application Software Developers Association, 2005)
- The Universal Business Language (UBL) (Meadows & Seaburg, 2004).
- The Open Applications Group Integration Specification (OAGIS) (Rowell, 2002)

Transformations between e-invoicing formats may be performed by using the message transformation services of the architecture. The more of this type of standards are supported by the enterprise service, the more increases the level of interoperability it offers.

Entities and Actors

This section presents the entities involved in an e-invoicing transaction with the e-invoicing enterprise service and their roles. As in common invoicing practice, an e-invoicing transaction occurs between the issuer for the invoice who charges for a set of services or products and the receiver who is called to pay for them. Both parties have to be able to view and process e-invoices and be able to understand the security policy applied in a user-friendly manner.

All entities and their relationships are depicted in Figure 8.

The actors that take part are:

a. **The Issuer:** This organization hosts the e-government architecture that operates the enterprise service. It takes the appropriate steps to deploy the service and publish it in the Registry, so that other organizations may find it. It also communicates with the TTP to get the proper security credentials.

b. **The Receiver:** The Receiver organization may be part of the same or similar e-government architecture, or may operate a completely independent e-invoicing service. In the latter case, the two services have to support at least one common e-invoicing schema. The Receiver organization will also have to communicate with the TTP to get its proper security credentials.

Copyright © 2007, Idea Group Inc. Copying or distributing in print or electronic forms without written permission of Idea Group Inc. is prohibited.

Figure 9. E-invoice issuance phase

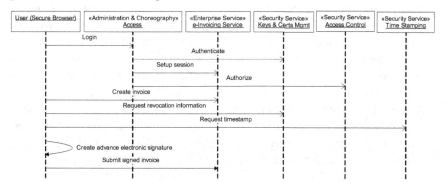

c.   **The TTP:** Before any secure messaging can take place, all participants need to have established an adequate security framework with Trusted Third Parties (TTPs) as described in the section "Entities and Actors" of the previous service.

d.   **UDDI directory operator:** This operator hosts a public UDDI directory where Web services can be published as described in the section "Entities and Actors" of the previous service.

Functional and Operational Description

The e-invoicing process can be divided into three phases: issuing, dispatch/reception, and storage. Credentials and security policy setup, as well as search and discovery in UDDI are considered already in carried out before these phases begin.

Figure 10. E-invoice dispatching and receipt phase

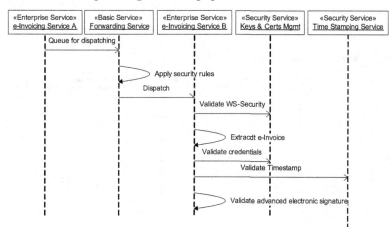

Copyright © 2007, Idea Group Inc. Copying or distributing in print or electronic forms without written permission of Idea Group Inc. is prohibited.

A. E-Invoice Issuance Phase

As depicted in the sequence diagram of Figure 9, an employee of the issuer organization (represented by the class user on the figure) initiates the e-invoicing process. He first authenticates himself by means of his smart card and PIN through the user interface. Based on the authentication credentials, the system performs an authorization check. The initial authentication and access control process through the access and access control services of the architecture are performed transparently.

The user interface transparently communicates with the enterprise service to enable the user to create a new invoice and supply the necessary data to complete the invoice or manage existing invoices (e.g., received, drafts etc.). This data input is automatically checked for prevention of errors. According to the user's privileges, the option for signing and dispatching the e-invoice is enabled or disabled. If the user has the right of signing and presses the "Sign and Send" button, the user interface transparently completes a series of steps:

- The form data are gathered and are used to structure an e-invoice
- The time stamps and revocation status information data are gathered from the corresponding time stamping service and keys and certificates management service of the architecture, and
- The XAdES signature is formulated based on the cryptographic primitives in the smart card, the user's certificate, and the invoice data

The distinction between types of users provides flexibility for both the employee that feeds in the data and the person who is responsible for signing the invoices, if they are not the same person.

The singing and authentication certificates might be different or they might be the same, something which is governed by the organizations policies. In case they are different, the user is prompted to use one or the other to according to what he is trying to accomplish at that particular time.

Figure 11. E-invoice storage phase

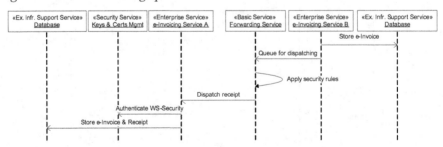

Copyright © 2007, Idea Group Inc. Copying or distributing in print or electronic forms without written permission of Idea Group Inc. is prohibited.

B. E-Invoice Dispatching and Receipt Phase

After the successful creation of the XAdES signature, the invoice is embedded in a SOAP message and sent to the forwarding service of the architecture, as shown on Figure 10. The forwarding service is responsible to extract the invoice, and pack it in a new message adding this time the specific security extensions mandated by the WS-Security standard, utilizing the xml digital signatures and encryption security mechanisms. The secure SOAP message is then dispatched to a corresponding e-invoicing/forwarding service on the receiver organization.

The receipt of the invoice is a fully automated process which does not require any human intervention. The SOAP message that contains the invoice is decrypted and the WS-Security based signature verified.

The next step is to extract the invoice itself and verify the credentials information that were used to create the advanced electronic signature along with any timestamps it contains. Finally, the XAdES signature itself is validated. These last steps all utilize the security services of the architecture.

C. E-Invoice Storage Phase

During the last phase, initially the e-invoice is stored in the database of the Receiver, as shown on Figure 11. That makes it available for parsing and further processing by the Receiver's users. The process is finalized by the dispatch of a SOAP reply (receipt), referencing the newly received invoice, and containing the status of the whole process. This reply is signed in a similar way using WS Security extensions by the Receiver's server in order to be valid as a receipt. When the Issuer service receives this signed SOAP reply, it is stored in the Issuer repository along with the sent invoice.

The full automation of the whole process for batch dispatching of the invoices is generally an open area of research, since it is a requirement usually posed by the organizations exchanging electronic invoices due to performance reasons, but it contradicts the related Directive and the application of advance electronic signatures.

Electronic Ticketing

Description and Purpose

Nowadays, the development and adoption of mobile technologies have enabled the introduction of new advanced services. The tremendous development of the Internet and related technologies, the understanding and exploitation of the business potentials that rest behind this trend, the boost of e-government frameworks and technologies, and the impressive growth of wireless mobile networks, are some of the main factors that contributed to this.

One of the core visions of IT is that the mobile phone has the potential to become the user's Personal Trusted Device, an accessory that is familiar and trusted from a security standpoint that will be used for much else than voice communications.

Copyright © 2007, Idea Group Inc. Copying or distributing in print or electronic forms without written permission of Idea Group Inc. is prohibited.

However, mobile payments alone are not sufficient to fully leverage the potential of the mobile phone as an essential and trusted personal accessory. Electronic tickets enabled by mobile phones comprise an important class of everyday consumer transactions, fulfilling the requirement of governmental organizations to easily provide tickets to events, public museums, public transportation, etc.

A ticket is considered as a proof of access or usage rights to a particular service. Electronic ticketing enabled by mobile devices:

- Eliminates paper tickets with digital codes displayed on mobile terminals
- Provides instant delivery
- Allows the usage of direct mobile marketing to offer discounts and promotions
- Offers lower costs such as paper, ink, printers, and manpower
- Adds convenience
- Protects the purchase due to the fact that there is no paper ticket to lose and a virtual record is tried to the user's mobile terminal number
- Provides versatile real-time database to compile reports and track attendance and solutions can be applied to all aspects of theatre or venue, including for example parking, vending machines, and concessions

Figure 12. E-ticketing business process

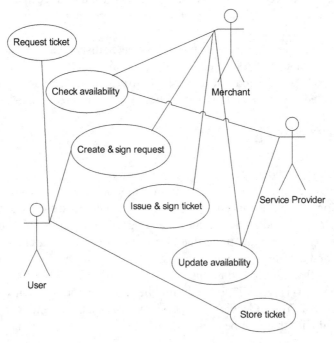

Copyright © 2007, Idea Group Inc. Copying or distributing in print or electronic forms without written permission of Idea Group Inc. is prohibited.

These tickets exist in two different types (Mobile Electronic Transactions, 2003), regarding the place that each ticket resides:

- **Virtual tickets:** Where the proof resides in a ticket issuer's server in which case the redemption of the ticket consists of online connection and user authentication to the server, at the usage point
- **PTD tickets:** Where the proof is an electronic data object carried in a mobile device in which an online connection to the ticket issuer's server is not required at the usage point.
- Actually, the possession of the particular data object is sufficient proof of access rights.

In this chapter, the electronic tickets that are generated are equivalent of physical tickets, as used in our everyday life. In particular, these tickets belong to the second type of tickets, as previously described. The ticketing system accommodates both single and multiple usages. However, the payment aspect of ticketing is not addressed in this chapter as it is considered largely independent of the ticketing aspect. The independence of this mobile ticketing architecture from the particularities of the various payment methods, which are out of the scope or can be themselves electronic services that can be offered from this platform, allows the adoption of multiple alternatives (credit cards, pre-paid cards, Web/mobile banking, or even charge of the user's bill)

As shown in the previous use case diagram, the user-citizen accesses the ticketing service and requests availability through the presented information from the merchant. The merchant checks for availability through the service provider, which is actually the governmental organization, and answers to the citizen.

The user in turn, fills in the request form, signs the form, and requests the specific ticket. The merchant issues the ticket and sends it to the citizen, informing the governmental organization for the previous issuance in order to update availability. The citizen stores the ticket in his or her mobile device and keeps it for further usage.

Additional Requirements

Nowadays, despite that 3G handheld devices provide additional functionality, mobile users have limited capability in changing contexts. Traditional techniques, which sometimes rely on powerful processors and extensive amounts of memory, are not suitable for wireless platforms, creating the need for new, wireless-specific technologies.

Furthermore, in the e/m-ticketing service there is the need to provide strong security mechanisms in the generated content and not only on the transferred messages (Josang & Sanderud, 2003). Indeed, the received ticket has to preserve the security credentials that strongly authenticate the merchant that issued the ticket.

Copyright © 2007, Idea Group Inc. Copying or distributing in print or electronic forms without written permission of Idea Group Inc. is prohibited.

Table 1. kSOAP Performance (Source: Nokia 9210)

	MIDlet Size	Request Setup	Request	Request Size	Reply Size
SOAP	~ 48 kb	~ 12.0 sec	~ 3 sec	529 bytes	594 bytes
Non-SOAP	~ 5 kb	~ 4.7 sec	~ 2.1 sec	18 bytes	34 bytes
%Overhead of SOAP	960 %	255 %	181 %	2939 %	1747 %

Similarly, the request of the citizen may need to preserve its confidentiality and integrity in specific parts that contain sensitive information regarding the payment procedure, which probably should be kept secret from the merchant or other intermediary entities. The enterprise service described in the following paragraphs has to take into account these additional requirements.

Main Service Components

The e/m-ticketing service operates as an enterprise service within the architecture. The WSDL description of the endpoint of the service can be published in a UDDI directory through the publication and query service. This allows searching for the specific enterprise service and comprehension of the messages this service understands so that messages can be sent and received from it.

The enterprise service is running as a Web service in the architecture and it is managed by the orchestration service. It communicates with the following entities:

- Secure mobile browsers through the access service
- The actual service provider hosting the repository for e/m-tickets and receipts. This communication may be direct (i.e., the repository is a database directly controlled by the enterprise service or indirect through an existing infrastructure support service of the architecture)
- The forwarding service of the architecture, in order to securely dispatch the ticket to its final destination
- The key and certificate management service for validation of keys and certificates

In order to promote interoperability with respect to the multiple mobile devices existing today and their different operation platforms, several third-party, lightweight XML parsers are used.

In the presented Web services platform, kXML by Enhydra (Enhydra, 2005) offers both Simple API for XML (SAX) (Megginson, 2005), and limited document object model (DOM) (Le Hégaret, 2004) capabilities. The implementation of the

Copyright © 2007, Idea Group Inc. Copying or distributing in print or electronic forms without written permission of Idea Group Inc. is prohibited.

various Web services uses the special utility of kXML, called kSOAP (Enhydra, 2005), for parsing SOAP messages (Table 1). The integration of mobile Web services, using kXML technology, allows business logic and data to reside and be executed at the most appropriate point on the network, as demanded by each service type. As a result, business processes are directly exposed to mobile services in a highly standardised and extensible manner.

However, the proposed platform offers the opportunity, to use other lightweight available technologies for the integration of the required Web services and secondly to interoperate with such implementations. Such a technology is the gSOAP Web services toolkit for C and C++, which is an open source development environment for Web services (Van Engelen, Gupta, & Pant, 2003). gSOAP supports pure C, which makes it essential for many embedded systems kernels and systems-oriented applications developed in C, providing performance that can surpass in some cases the corresponding performance of Java RMI and IIOP. Finally, the RPC compiler (Srinivasan, 1995) generates compact code and the runtime environment of the SOAP/XML engine has a small memory footprint, which is very important for the case of the mobile environment (Van Engelen, 2003).

Additionally, transformations in various e/m-ticketing formats may be performed by using the message transformation services of the architecture. The more ticket formats supported, the higher the level of interoperability.

Furthermore, as mentioned in the previous paragraph regarding the requirements of e/m-ticketing service, the need of an additional security level for the content itself

Figure 13. E-ticketing actors

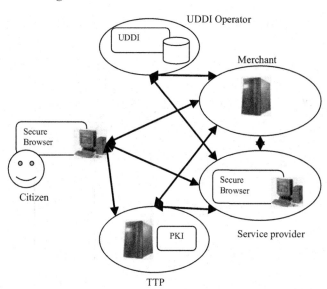

Copyright © 2007, Idea Group Inc. Copying or distributing in print or electronic forms without written permission of Idea Group Inc. is prohibited.

in order for the last to preserve the credentials of the involved entities, is fulfilled
with the integration of a mobile module, which provides the following:

- Generation and validation of XML digital signatures for mobile XML content
- Encryption/Decryption mechanisms for the previous content

This validation procedure is introduced in two different ways. The first involves
the downloading of the certification revocation lists (CRLs) from the PKI of the
presented platform and the execution of complex cryptographic operations in the
mobile device (Karantjias, Kaliontzoglou, Sklavos, & Polemi, 2004). However,
in most cases this is not feasible in many mobile devices that are used today. The
second solution is the integration and existence of a suitable interface that is used
in the mobile device in order to communicate with an XKMS server of the PKI.
This second solution suits more in the mobile environment because many complex
and heavy functionalities are lifted from the mobile terminal (Kasera, Mizikovsky,
& Sundaram, 2003).

Entities and Actors

This section presents the entities that may be involved in a typical ticketing
issuance and delivery and their roles. These entities, as well as their relationships
are depicted in Figure 13.

The actors that take part are:

a.   **The citizen:** The citizen is the consumer of any government service supported
     by the architecture. It has to communicate with the TTP in order to get the
     proper security credentials.

Figure 14. Availability request submission and checking

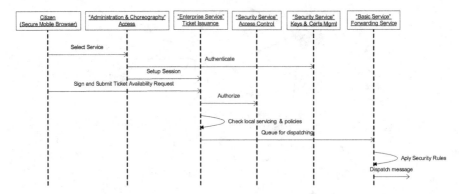

Copyright © 2007, Idea Group Inc. Copying or distributing in print or electronic forms without written permission of Idea Group Inc. is prohibited.

b.   **The merchant:** The merchant is the entity that hosts the main service platform and offers the required e/m-ticketing service, as well as other services, to mobile citizens. It has to communicate just like the citizen with the TTP to get the proper security credentials, as well as with the actual service provider described next in order to the required info regarding the ticket availability.

c.   **The service provider:** The service provider is the governmental organization that provides the e/m actual service, which in our case is the ticket provider. This entity could represent a public museum, stadium, or any governmental organization wishing to provide tickets to its citizens. The service provider communicates with the TTP to get the security credentials with the merchant in order to provide ticket availability and with the client at the time of ticket usage from the last mentioned. The platform could be hosted by the service provider (and therefore the roles of merchant and provider would be one and the same), but this is not a strong requirement. Some mobile and electronic service modules are needed to complement and communicate with the main components of the Web services platform.

d.   **The TTP:** Before any secure messaging can take place, all participants, need to have established an adequate security framework with trusted third parties (TTPs). The required TTPs are at a minimum a CA and a RA offering the PKI services of registration, certification, and revocation status information with OCSP, as well as TSA, offering standard based time stamping services.

e.   **UDDI directory operator:** This operator hosts a public UDDI directory where the various Web services are published and thus become publicly available to any user-citizen.

Figure 15. Request validation and availability response

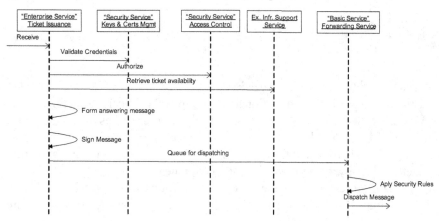

Copyright © 2007, Idea Group Inc. Copying or distributing in print or electronic forms without written permission of Idea Group Inc. is prohibited.

Figure 16. Service access and ticket formulation

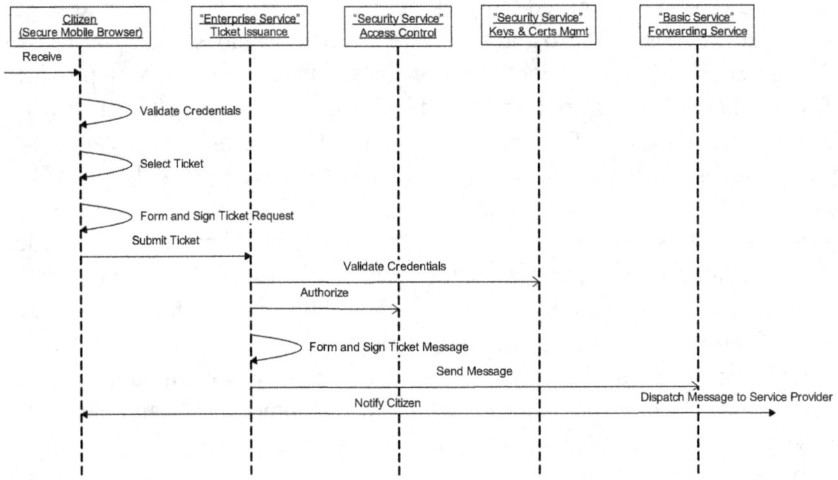

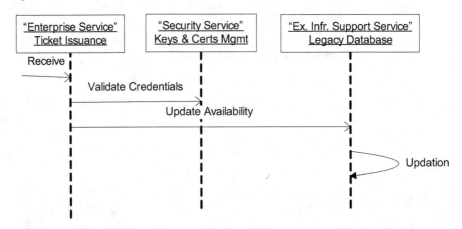

Figure 17. Availability update

Functional and Operational Description

This section presents the functional description of a typical transaction, which is supported by the enterprise service and describes the sequences of the operations that are carried out in order for a citizen to receive an electronic ticket using his mobile device. This functional description includes three different phases: request for ticket availability, ticket issuance, and ticket redemption.

The main prerequisite for the successful operation of the service is that an implementation of the e-government architecture of section "A Generic Secure

Copyright © 2007, Idea Group Inc. Copying or distributing in print or electronic forms without written permission of Idea Group Inc. is prohibited.

Figure 18. Ticket redemption

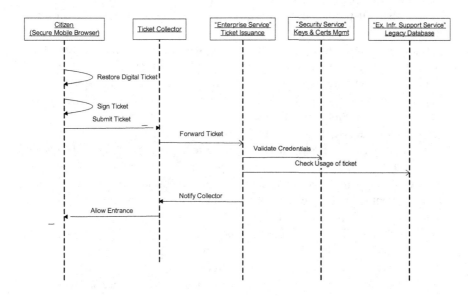

E-Government Architecture" has been deployed at both the merchant side and the governmental organization, which is the actual service provider. Additionally, we suppose that the citizen, who wishes to get an electronic ticket using his mobile device, has installed the required applications in order to structure the appropriate Web services for communicating with the e-government architecture, as well as the application module that is required for providing cryptographic mechanisms in the content.

The initial process that takes place is the request for ticket availability as follows:

a. **Selection of service, authentication, and submission of request for availability:** The citizen uses his mobile terminal to log on directly to the e-government architecture of the merchant and submits a signed request for ticket availability. This is performed through a secure browser. The access service of the architecture authenticates the user using utilizing proper calls to the keys and certificates management service. If the authentication procedure ends successfully, the connection remains open and the citizen waits for receiving the requested ticket availability. In every other case, the connection is closed and the citizen receives a failure message.

b. **Authorization:** The access service propagates the received request to the actual enterprise service that runs as a Web service in the architecture. This

Copyright © 2007, Idea Group Inc. Copying or distributing in print or electronic forms without written permission of Idea Group Inc. is prohibited.

enterprise service consults the access control service to take the necessary actions to authorize the citizen's request and provide him with a success of failure result. In particular, the enterprise service retrieves the request form and checks whether it adheres to a policy permitting it to access such a service.

c.   **Communication with the actual service provider:** The merchant digitally signs the submitted request for ticket availability and forwards it to the actual service provider. The last entity validates any security credentials applied to the received message, using the information acquired by the keys and certificates service in the architecture. This security service performs credential validation through an XKMS interface. If this process is successful, the forwarded citizens' request is extracted from the message and the service provider checks for ticket availability in its database through the "Existing infrastructure support services" of the architecture, as described in the section "A Generic Secure E-Government Architecture." It then structures an answered message providing the required information, digitally signs it, and sends it to the merchant.

d.s **Answer retrieval:** The merchant validates any security credentials applied to the received message following the previously described procedure (through an XKMS interface), digitally signs the received message, and forwards it to the citizen. The citizen following the same validating procedure on the security credentials of the message is now capable of choosing the desirable ticket.

Some of the steps described so far may be optional, especially in cases where the citizen does not have to choose a specific ticket. The ticketing process continues with the second phase, the issuance of the ticket, as follows:

a.   **Selection of desirable ticket and submission of the ticket request:** The citizen, using his mobile device and the advanced browser of it, is able to choose the desirable ticket and automatically structure the appropriate request of the selected ticket. It performs cryptographic mechanisms on the message; digitally signing the message and encrypting the sensitive parts of it, especially in cases where payment info is included (e.g., credit cards info, bank accounts, etc.). The citizen sends the ticket request to the merchant, waiting to receive the final ticket.

b.   **Issuance of the ticket and update of ticket availability:** The merchant receives the final ticket request from the citizen and performs cryptographic mechanisms on it, validating the signature of the sender, and decrypting the parts of the message that correspond to his private key. He then initializes the payment procedure, which as previously mentioned is out of the scope of the described service, but it could be another service integrated in the architecture. The successful finish of this   procedure is continued from the desirable ticket issuance. The merchant using the additional mobile module that provides security mechanisms on the content, as described in the previous paragraph, adds

Copyright © 2007, Idea Group Inc. Copying or distributing in print or electronic forms without written permission of Idea Group Inc. is prohibited.

his secure credentials (his digital signature) on the XML ticket as well as on the message that includes the first, and sends it to the citizen. Simultaneously communicates with actual ticket provider, which in the described case is a governmental organization, informing it for the citizens' ticket final selection, in order for message receiver to update the availability.

c.   **Receipt and storage of ticket**: The citizen receives the desirable ticket and validates the security credentials on message as well as the ticket itself. If the received message is valid, he then stores the XML ticket, which continues to carry the merchant's digital signature, on the mobile device, using the appropriate functions of the installed mobile application.

d.   **Ticket redemption**: The e/m-ticketing service continues with the last phase, the ticket redemption, which involves interaction between the mobile citizen and a ticket issuer terminal, which resides at the actual service provider. The citizen uses his mobile device to restore the digital ticket, to digitally sign and transmit it to the ticket collector's terminal via device independent, short-range communication technologies like the Infared or Bluetooth.

In particular, the service provider operates on the ticket issuer's terminal the module that provides security mechanisms on pure content. This module is able to receive the digitally signed XML document and to provide cryptographic mechanisms on it (e.g., in this case verifies the merchant's digital signature on the received message). Any related revocation material (e.g., CRLs) is already preinstalled on the device and is updated periodically in case XKMS has not been adopted for the communication with the corresponding PKI. If the device is connected with the main architecture, the XKMS interface is used instead.

If the signature is valid, the ticket issuer checks whether the ticket has been used again in order to prevent the use of copied tickets, receives clearance from the local server, updates its usage information and makes the mobile citizen able of using the ticket (e.g., entering an event, traveling, etc.).

In the case of disputes where the ticket appears invalid and the mobile citizen claims otherwise, the last has to vindicate that the XML ticket stored in his mobile device is signed with the following two valid signatures:

•   The mobile citizens' signature
•   The merchants' signature

If the verification process succeeds, the dispute resolution module in the ticket issuer checks the tickets' usage and its data. Thus, the citizen can prove ownership of his valid ticket and claim compensation. If the ticket is invalid (for example, if it has expired without being used) then the issuer is able to prove that the citizen's claim for compensation is false.

Copyright © 2007, Idea Group Inc. Copying or distributing in print or electronic forms without written permission of Idea Group Inc. is prohibited.

CONCLUSION

In this chapter, we have presented three new e-government services that are based on the Web services technology and leverage the functionality of an existing e-government architecture, with the purpose of filling in a gap of the lack of "killer applications" for e-government and presenting useful case study material to similar endeavours of public organizations in the future. Each service respects a set of common e-government requirements as well as some additional requirements imposed by its specific business goals and legal restrictions.

ACKNOWLEDGMENTS

The authors would like to thank the E.C. for its support in funding the e-mayor project (IST-2004-507217) and all the members of the project consortium for valuable discussions.

REFERENCES

Business Application Software Developers Association (BASDA). (2005). *eBIS-XML Specifications ver. (3.05)*. Retrieved from basda.net/twiki/pub/Core/DownloadTheSuite/eBIS-XML-3.05.zip

CEN/ISSS e-invoicing Focus Group. (2003). *Report and recommendations of CEN/ISSS e-invoicing focus group on standards and developments on electronic invoicing*. Retrieved from www.cenorm.be/isss/Projects/e-invoicing

e-mayor consortium D2.1. (2004). Deliverable D2.1: Municipal services–Analysis, requirements, and usage scenarios. *e-mayor project* (IST-2004-507217).

e-mayor consortium D3.1. (2004). Deliverable D3.1: e-mayor–System design. *e-mayor project* (IST-2004-507217).

e-mayor. (2004). Electronic and secure municipal administration for European citizens. E.C 6th Framework Programme, IST-2004-507217. Retrieved from www.emayor.org

Enhydra. (2005). *Open source for eBusiness*. Retrieved from http://www.enhydra.org

ETSI. (2002). ETSI TS 101 903 V1.1.1 - XML Advanced Electronic Signatures (XAdES). (Technical Specification.)

German Federal Ministry of Interior. (2003). *SAGA—Standards and Architectures for e-government Applications,* (version 2.0.)

Hartman, B., Flinn, D., Beszosov, K., & Kawamoto, S. (2003). *Mastering Web services security*. Indianapolis, IN: Wiley Publishing.

Hunter, R. (2004). E-government schema guidelines for XML. *Office of the eEnvoy,* (v3.1.) Retrieved from http://www.govtalk.gov.uk/documents/schema-guidelines-3_1.pdf

Copyright © 2007, Idea Group Inc. Copying or distributing in print or electronic forms without written permission of Idea Group Inc. is prohibited.

IDA BC. (2004). *IDA eProcurement XML schemas initiative—eOrdering and e-invoicing phases,* (v 2.0.) Retrieved from http://europa.eu.int/idabc/en/document/4721/5874

Josang, A., & Sanderud, G. (2003). Security in mobile communications: Challenges and opportunities. In *Proceedings of the Australasian Information Security Workshop* (AISW2003) Conference on ACSW Frontiers (Vol. 21, pp.43-48).

Kaliontzoglou, A., Boutsi, P., Mavroudis, I., & Polemi, D. (2003). Secure e-invoicing service based on Web services. In *Proceedings of the 1ˢᵗ Hellenic Conference on Electronic Democracy*, Athens, Greece.

Kaliontzoglou, A., Sklavos, P., Karantjias, T., & Polemi, D. (2004). A secure e-government platform architecture for small to medium sized public organizations. *Electronic Commerce Research & Applications, 4*(2), 174-186.

Kaliontzoglou, A., Boutsi, P., & Polemi, D. (2005). E-invoke: Secure e-invoicing based on Web services. Electronic Commerce Research, Kluwer (accepted for publication).

Karantjias, A., Kaliontzoglou, A., Sklavos, P., & Polemi, D. (2004). Secure applications for the Chambers of Commerce: Functionality and technical assessment. In *Proceedings of EUROSEC 2004 15ᵗʰ Forum on Information Systems and Security,* Paris.

Kasera, S., Mizikovsky, S., Sundaram, G. (2003). On securely enabling intermediary-based services and performance enhancements for wireless mobile users. In *Proceedings of the 2003 ACM workshop on Wireless security* (pp. 61-68).

Kavvadias, G., Spanos, E., & Tambouris, E. (Eds.). (2002). Deliverable D2.3.1 GovML syntax and filters implementation. *E-gov project* (IST-2000-28471). Retrieved from http://www.e-gov-project.org/e-govsite/e-gov_D231.zip

Kent, A. (2003). Address and personal details schema. *Office of the eEnvoy,* (v1.3) Retrieved from http://www.govtalk.gov.uk/documents/APD-v1-3.zip

Le Hégaret, P. (2004). *W3C document object model–DOM.* Retrieved from http://www.w3.org/DOM/

Meadows, B., & Seaburg, L. (2004). *Universal Business Language UBL 1.0. Official OASIS Standard.* Retrieved from http://docs.oasis-open.org/ubl/cd-UBL-1.0.zip

Megginson, D. (2005). *Simple API for XML–SAX.* Retrieved from http://www.saxproject.org/

Meneklis, B., Kaliotzoglou, A., Polemi, D., & Douligeris, C. (2005). Applying the ISO RM-ODP standard in e-government. In *Proceedings of E-government: Towards Electronic Democracy: International Conference,* Bolzano, Italy (LNCS 3416, pp. 213). Springer-Verlag GmbH.

Mobile Electronic Transactions. (2003). *MeT white paper on mobile ticketing.* Retrieved from http://www.mobiletransaction.org/

Nash, A., Duane, B., Brink, D., & Joseph, C. (2001). *PKI: Implementing & managing eSecurity.* Emeryville, CA: McGraw-Hill Osborn Media Publishing.

Copyright © 2007, Idea Group Inc. Copying or distributing in print or electronic forms without written permission of Idea Group Inc. is prohibited.

Rowell, M. (2002). OAGIS—A "Canonical" business language. *Open Applications Group, white paper,* (version 1.0.) Retrieved from www.openapplications. org/downloads/whitepapers/whitepaperdocs/20020429_OAGIS_A_Canonical_Business_Langugage-PDF.zip

Srinivasan, R. (1995). *Remote procedure call protocol specification version 2 (RPC) (RFC1831).* Retrieved from http://asg.web.cmu.edu/rfc/rfc1831.html

The European Parliament. (2001, December 20). *Council Directive 2001/115/EC, amending Directive 77/388/EEC with view to simplifying, modernizing, and harmonizing the conditions laid down for invoicing in respect of value added tax.*

UK Office of the eEnvoy. (2004). *UK GovTalk portal.* Retrieved from www.govtalk. gov.uk

Van Engelen, R. (2003). Pushing the SOAP envelope with Web services for scientific computing. In *Proceedings of the International Conference on Web services (ICWS)* (pp. 346-352).

Van Engelen, R., Gupta, G., & Pant, S. (2003). Developing Web services for C and C++. *In IEEE Internet Computing* (pp. 53-61).

xCBL.org. (2003). *XML common business library version 4.00* (xCBL v4.00). Retrieved from www.xcbl.org/xcbl40/xcbl40.html

Copyright © 2007, Idea Group Inc. Copying or distributing in print or electronic forms without written permission of Idea Group Inc. is prohibited.

Chapter III

Trust Models for Ubiquitous Mobile Systems

Mike Burmester, Florida State University, USA

ABSTRACT

This chapter introduces the notion of trust as a means to establish security in ubiquitous mobile network systems. It argues that trust is an essential requirement to enable security in any open network environments, and in particular, in wireless ad hoc environments where there is no network topology. In such environments, communication can only be achieved via routes that have to be trusted. In general it may be hard, or even impossible, to establish, recall, and maintain trust relationships. It is therefore important to understand the limitations of such environments and to find mechanisms that may support trust either explicitly or implicitly. We consider several models that can be used to enable trust in such environments, based on economic, insurance, information flow, and evolutionary paradigms.

Copyright © 2007, Idea Group Inc. Copying or distributing in print or electronic forms without written permission of Idea Group Inc. is prohibited.

INTRODUCTION

Wireless mobile networks are a paradigm for mobile communication in which wireless nodes do not rely on any underlying static network infrastructure for services such as packet routing, name resolution, node authentication, or distribution of computational resources. The communication medium is broadcast. Nodes in range communicate in a direct peer-to-peer manner, while nodes out of range establish routing paths dynamically through other nodes where possible. The recent rise in popularity of mobile wireless devices and technological developments have made possible the deployment of wireless mobile networks for several applications. Examples include emergency deployments, disaster recovery, search-and-rescue missions, sensor networks, military (battlefield) operations, and more recently e-commerce. Since the network nodes are mobile, the network topology frequently changes: Communication links are established or broken as nodes move in and out of range, and the network may get partitioned with the connectivity restricted to the partitions. As a result it may be much harder (or even impossible) to establish trust associations.

The trend in trust management is to view trust implicitly through delegation of privilege via certificates. Certificates can be chain-linked (linking à priori trust relationships) and used to propagate and distribute trust over insecure media, without the danger of being manipulated.

In this chapter, we give an overview of several models that can be used to support trust in mobile networks, based on economic, insurance, information flow, and evolutionary paradigms.

TRUST IN WIRELESS MOBILE NETWORKS

We consider environments in which there may be no fixed underlying network infrastructure, such as static base stations, for services such as packet routing, name resolution, node authentication, or the distribution of computational resources. In such environments, recalling and maintaining trust relationships is particularly challenging. Mobile systems share many of the complexities of fixed infrastructure systems. For example, nodes may have (Burmester & Yasinsac, 2004):

1.   No prior relationship or common peers
2.   No shared proprietary software
3.   Different transmission, memory and processing capabilities
4.   Different mobility characteristics
5.   Different lifetime properties

Copyright © 2007, Idea Group Inc. Copying or distributing in print or electronic forms without written permission of Idea Group Inc. is prohibited.

Defining Trust

Trust is a highly abstract concept and it is unlikely that any simple definition can comprehensively capture all the subtleties of its essence. Informally we may define trust as a behavioral expectation of one party toward another. There are two perspectives in this definition, one in which a party *awards* trust to another (Alice trusts that Bob's public key is PK(Bob)), the other in which a party *gains* trust from another (Alice has convinced Bob that her public key is PK(Alice)).

Representing Trust: Certificates vs. Tokens

In any stateful trust model, trust must be represented by some type of persistent structure. Certificates are the de facto standard for representing trust relationships that are protected by cryptography. Certificates are portable and bind a cryptographic key (a digital string) to an entity, thus guaranteeing the authenticity of actions performed by that entity. Trust tokens are another structure that can be used to represent trust in a more direct way, analogous to the relation between checks and cash. Checks guarantee payment by tying the purchaser to some identifying information (like a certificate), while the value of cash is self-contained.

Trusted Third Parties

A trusted third party (TTP) can facilitate significantly the establishment of trust in mobile environments. For example, if two parties A and B who do not know each other have a trust relationship with a third party T, then T can be an effective intermediary for transactions between A and B. However in general, wireless mobile networks may not have any infrastructure components that are typically used as TTPs. In such cases, TTPs have to be elected or assigned by using an appropriate election or assignment protocol.

MODELS FOR TRUST IN WIRELESS MOBILE ENVIRONMENTS

Trust is *context* driven (e.g., A may trust B for event x, but not for event y). Trust may also be qualitative rather than Boolean (e.g., A may trust B more than C). Finally, trust relationships may be fixed or dynamic. Dynamic trust relationships are most appropriate for the requirements of mobile environments.

Models for dynamic trust must support establishing, changing, and permanently revoking trust between parties, and must also consider network environment issues. In the following sections we shall consider several models that can be used to support trust in wireless mobile networks (Burmester & Yasinsac, 2004).

Copyright © 2007, Idea Group Inc. Copying or distributing in print or electronic forms without written permission of Idea Group Inc. is prohibited.

A Mathematical Model for Trust: The Trust Graph

We may represent the trust in a network by a directed graph, the *trust graph*, whose links (A, B) correspond to the explicit trust that node A has in node B. Such links are indicated by A $\Rightarrow$ B. The implicit trust that a node X has in another node Y is then represented by a trust path from X to Y:

$$X = X_0 \Rightarrow X_1 \Rightarrow X_2 \ldots \Rightarrow X_{n-1} \Rightarrow X_n = Y,$$

in which node X awards trust to node Y via a chain of intermediary nodes X_i, where X_i awards trust explicitly to the next node X_{i+1} in the chain. Such trust may be supported by certificates. For example, node X_i may certify (digitally sign) that key $PK(X_{i+1})$ is the public key of node X_{i+1}. A chain of certificates can then be used for implicit certification. This is essentially the trust model for the X509 PKI authentication infrastructure (ISO/IEC 9594-8, 1995). This particular trust infrastructure is hierarchical, with trust centrally managed (by a Root Certifying Authority, which is also a single-point-of-failure). PGP (Zimmermann, 1995) uses a web of trust in which trust is distributed "horizontally." See Burmester and Desmedt (2004) for a discussion on security issues of hierarchical vs. horizontal infrastructures.

In the basic trust graph model, trust is transitive but not necessarily reflexive. That is, even though A may award trust to B, B may not award trust to A. However, trust is binary: A $\Rightarrow$ B is either true or false. Therefore, there is a natural trust metric which is one unit for explicit trust. This is also the trust of a trust path that links A to B. In this model the trust that A awards to B is represented by the trust flow of A, B, which is also the connectivity of A, B. This model is appropriate for Byzantine faults environments in which the adversary can corrupt a bounded number of nodes, and trust has to be based on à priori beliefs, and not statistical profiles.

A Model Based on a Weighted Trust Graph

There are several other ways to define trust. For a stochastic model based on statistical profiling, we can define the explicit trust that A awards to (or has in) B as the probability with which A trusts B, based on, say, a history of good behavior by B. See the next section for a discussion on trust based on observed behavior. In this model we have a weighted trust graph in which each link A $\Rightarrow$ B is assigned a weight $t \in [0,1]$, which corresponds to the (explicit) trust that A has in B. If $\pi 1, \pi 2, \ldots, \pi n$ are (all) the trust paths that link X to Y, then the implicit trust that X has in Y can be computed as follows (Burmester, Douligeris, & Kotzanikolaou, 2006):

$$\sum_{\pi_i} \prod_{t \in \pi_i} t - \sum_{\pi_i \neq \pi_j} \prod_{t \in \pi_i \cup \pi_j} t + \ldots + (-1)^{n+1} \prod_{t \in \pi_1 \cup \ldots \cup \pi_n} t .$$

For example, if there are three disjoint paths from X to Y with trust weights (t_1, t_2), (t_3, t_4), (t_5, t_6) respectively, then the implicit trust that X has in Y is:

Copyright © 2007, Idea Group Inc. Copying or distributing in print or electronic forms without written permission of Idea Group Inc. is prohibited.

$$t_1t_2 + t_3t_4 + t_5t_6 - t_1t_2t_3t_4 - t_3t_4t_5t_6 + t_1t_2t_3t_4t_5t_6 \ .$$

One can extend this model to allow for a dynamic model in which trust is regularly updated, by using a trust-ranking algorithm similar to that used by Web search engines (e.g., PageRank of Google [PageRank, 1997]).

A Model Based on Observed Behavior

A natural way to acquire trust is through direct observation. At its most fundamental level, trust is a decision, subject to emotions and intuition. In this scenario, personal observation is preferred to second-hand methods because of hints, nuances, and feelings that can be garnered. Though feelings are not considered in computer trust systems, there are advantages in doing so. Not all actions give insight into trustworthiness. The challenge is to translate such observations into trust decisions.

A challenge to trust management systems is that trust relationships need to be constructed *before* they are exercised. There are four basic categories of activity that affect trust (Burmester & Yasinsac, 2004):

1. Trust earning actions over time
2. Trust earning actions by count
3. Trust earning actions by magnitude
4. Trust defeating actions

Combinations of the first three allow cautious parties to grant trust frugally. Untrustworthy parties will be challenged to conduct a sufficient quality and quantity of trustworthy actions to gain trust. On the other hand, observation of malicious, reckless, or otherwise unpredictable actions allows reduction or revocation of awarded trust.

A Model Based on the Internet Paradigm

The economic opportunity provided by the Internet has driven rapid establishment of many new trust models. Companies like eBay, Amazon, and Priceline conduct all of their business with customers with whom they have no personal relationship or interaction with. Early work on supporting trust models was from a business perspective (Pardue, 2000). Some work has been done more recently to identify models that support cryptographic protection of trust relationships. In Zhong, Chen, and Yang (2003), a token-based trust model is proposed in which parties accumulate trust, transaction-by-transaction. For trust-earning actions, parties are awarded tokens that can be retained and later presented to reflect the earned trust. If no additional trust information is gathered, tokens may be revoked or restricted. This novel approach to trust acquisition has many properties that are

Copyright © 2007, Idea Group Inc. Copying or distributing in print or electronic forms without written permission of Idea Group Inc. is prohibited.

well-suited to mobile networks. Tokens can be created, awarded, and verified via distributed algorithms, allowing a global aspect to trust decisions. Conversely, if the trust algorithm is well understood, parties that desire to perform malicious acts can become sleepers, behaving perfectly until they acquire sufficient trust to allow successful mischief.

Transitive Trust

Transitivity is in many respects a natural attribute of trust and is encountered in some of the most used security systems (Steiner, Neuman, & Schiller, 1988; Zhong et al., 2003). With transitive trust models, trust must be explicit (i.e., parties must know that if they place their trust in one party, then they are automatically placing their trust in other potentially unknown parties as well). For example, if Alice trusts Bob and Bob trusts Carol, then Alice must trust Carol. Such models make strong trust requirements on intermediaries or third parties. Unfortunately, there are inherent dangers in models with transitive trust (Christianson & Harbison, 1997).

A Model Based on Trust Classes

Trust may be considered as a two party relationship or there may be environments where nodes take on *class* trust properties, as in the Bell-LaPadula model (Bell & LaPadula, 1973). One way to form trust management functionality is to establish a trust promotion system. For example, consider a simple trust environment in which nodes can be categorized into the following five trust classes (from most to least trusted): *Highly trusted, Trusted, Unknown, Untrusted, Highly untrusted.* We can then establish a set of rules for promoting and demoting members between groups. These rules will be identified by the desired promotion rule. If promotion is not allowed for highly untrusted parties, then no rule is established for this class. The model may be further extended by designating a subset of the class of most trusted nodes as *promoters*. Promoters are responsible for determining if requestors meet the promotion requirements as designated in the promotion rules and in taking action to effect the justified group movement. While promotion is requested directly, demotion must be requested second hand.

A Financial Model

Trust can also be *contractually* secured. In this case, a Trusted Third Party guarantees the trust. As with secured loans, if the guaranteed trust is violated, the guarantor will deliver the promised security to the offended party. Secured trust is a pure form of transitive trust. It is unique in that its trust graph tree has height one and trust is secured by a contractually agreed value. As with secured financial interactions, the secured value may take many forms, including the following: a *co-signed trust certificate, a trust insurance policy, a trust bond and a trust collateral.*

Copyright © 2007, Idea Group Inc. Copying or distributing in print or electronic forms without written permission of Idea Group Inc. is prohibited.

These correspond to security mechanisms of the financial world. For a co-signed certificate, the co-signing party would have credentials that exceed those of the target and would assume liability for any adverse events that occur as a result of a trust breech. The insurance policy model is similar, except that the security is provided by a well recognized organization that promises benefits to the executor of the policy. The last two models are similar in that the trust target provides the value that secures the trust. The value can be monetary, property, or other items or issues of suitable value to the source.

CONCLUSION

We have considered several models that can be used to manage the trust in mobile wireless environments. These models are highly distributed and address many of the trust management properties that are needed to secure mobile environments.

ACKNOWLEDGMENTS

This material is based on work supported in part by the National Science Foundation under grant number NSF 0209092 and in part by the U.S. Army Research Laboratory and the Army Research Office under grant DAAD19-02-1-0235.

REFERENCES

Bell, D. E., & LaPadula, L. (1973). Secure computer systems: Mathematical foundations and model, *MITRE Corp.* M74-244, Bedford, MA.

Burmester, M., & Desmedt, Y. (2004). Is hierarchical public-key certification the next target for hackers? *Communications of the ACM, 47*(8), 68-74.

Burmester, M., & Yasinsac, A. (2004). Trust infrastructures for wireless mobile networks. *WSAES Transactions on Telecommunications* (pp. 377-381).

Burmester, M., Douligeris, C., & Kotzanikolaou, P. (2006). Security in mobile ad hoc networks. In C. Douligeris & D. Serpanos (Eds.), *Network security: Current status and future directions*. Piscataway, NJ: IEEE Press.

Christianson, B., & Harbison, W. S. (1997). Why isn't trust transitive? In *Proceedings of the 4th International Workshop on Security Protocols* (LNCS 1189, pp. 171-176).

ISO/IEC 9594-8. (1995). Information technology, Open Systems Interconnection. *The Directory: Overview of concepts, models, and services. International Organization for Standardization*. Geneva, Switzerland.

PageRank. (1997). Google. Retrieved from http://www.google.com/technology/

Copyright © 2007, Idea Group Inc. Copying or distributing in print or electronic forms without written permission of Idea Group Inc. is prohibited.

Pardue, H. (2000). A trust-based model of consumer-to-consumer online auctions. *The Arrowhead Journal of Business, 1*(1), 69-77.

Steiner, J., Neuman, C., & Schiller, J. I. (1988). Kerberos and authentication service for open network systems. In *Proceedings of USENIX*, Dallas, TX.

Zhong, S., Chen, J., & Yang, R. (2003). Sprite: A simple, cheat-proof, credit-based system for mobile ad hoc networks. In *Proceedings of INFOCOM 2003*.

Zimmermann, P. (1995). *The official PGP user's guide*. Cambridge, MA: MIT Press.

Copyright © 2007, Idea Group Inc. Copying or distributing in print or electronic forms without written permission of Idea Group Inc. is prohibited.

Chapter IV

Trust and Security in Ambient Intelligence:
A Research Agenda for Europe

Andrea Servida, Deputy Head of Unit, European Commission, Belgium

ABSTRACT

The information society is increasingly dependent on largely distributed systems and infrastructures for life-critical and business-critical functions. The complexity of systems in information society is rapidly growing because of a number of factors like their size, their unboundness, and interdependency, the multiplicity of involved actors, the need to pursue more decentralised control and, last but not least, the growing sophistication in functionality. This trend together with the pervasive use of open information infrastructures for communications as well as of freeware software and common application platforms expose our society to new cyber vulnerabilities and threats that deserve better understanding, assessment, and control. Building trust is essential for the development of the information society, and the electronic commerce in particular. This chapter outlines the main research directions that have been defined as the priority ones in which to engage the European research community in the thematic priority Information Society Technologies (IST) of the 6th Framework Programme. To this purpose, the chapter consolidates the results and recommendations of a number of consultation workshops that were organised by the Commission in the years 2000-2002.

Copyright © 2007, Idea Group Inc. Copying or distributing in print or electronic forms without written permission of Idea Group Inc. is prohibited.

INTRODUCTION

Our society is increasingly dependent on communication networks and information systems. Systems are more and more open, interconnected, and interoperable. "Plug and play" and "wireless in everything" technologies allow a large variety of devices to be connected and work in the background. The legacy of enterprises and administrations will soon become essentially a digital one and, therefore, "traceability of the bits" will have to be ensured. But while, formerly, data were just data and executable codes were just executable codes, "data" are now both "data and executable codes" and have become living and active objects. They can be downloadable software to give access to services on mobile devices, or agents acting on your behalf on the net, or multimedia content carrying with them their usage policy, and so forth. Their "semantics" can be "good," or "bad." At the same time, systems are becoming increasingly complex. They have short and diverse live cycles and require frequent updates. As a consequence, their management becomes vital. Terminals themselves become distributed and communicate: how can one verify/authenticate the various components? The boundaries of enterprises are blurring; enterprises are involved in multiple dynamic networks where information and functions are shared with others. The cosy closed enterprise is in the past: the mobile worker needs to access corporate data (B2E), suppliers get access to your design data, and you to share with them various business processes. In that context, who is an insider who is an outsider? All this brings complex security requirements at the application level.

The complexity is going to further develop in the Ambient Intelligence (Ducatel et al, 2001) vision (called in short AmI) that was developed by the Advisory Group (FP5 ISTAG, 2002) of the Information Society Technologies programme (IST Web site, 2005) in the course of the 5th Framework Programme. AmI drives and envisages the development of surrounding computing and wireless communication environments where "resources" would be available and shared. Users would be empowered through a digital environment that is aware of their presence and context, and is sensitive, adaptive, and responsive to their needs, habits, gestures, and emotions. AmI would be characterised by ubiquity, awareness, intelligence, and natural interaction. However, all developments in the AmI scenario would only be possible if they would be underpinned by novel security paradigms, concepts, models, architectures, and technologies.

As we move from the information and communication paradigm to the AmI one, we need to change our perspective to security and security technologies and look at them as key enablers to share, exploit, and manage our resources, knowledge, and values. Associated to this change, the human component would also play a key role for which we need to develop a culture of security that would make everybody understand that, in tightly interconnected and open environment of AmI, his or her security and his or her misbehaviour may be critical to the entire society. And,

Copyright © 2007, Idea Group Inc. Copying or distributing in print or electronic forms without written permission of Idea Group Inc. is prohibited.

we would also need to better understand both the nature of vulnerabilities of the information infrastructure and the scale of its interdependencies with other societal and economic systems and infrastructures that may be part of a broader reflection on how we would like or may need to depend on advanced and volatile technology and technological platforms.

In the AmI scenario, security can be seen at different levels:

- **Securing the individual and his or her personal info sphere:** Privacy of the individual has to be guaranteed also in the virtual world. It entails confidentiality, integrity, availability of personal data, anonymity in e-vote, pseudo-anonymity when buying on the Internet, and so forth. Preserving the balance between transparency and opacity of every individual has still to be found in the virtual world: one should not get the impression that he or she is permanently tracked. At the same time, non-repudiation (who has done what) has to be guaranteed in e-business transactions.
- **Securing dynamic virtual communities:** with incoming and outgoing members that communicate through networks, which are increasingly heterogeneous and mobile. Communities should be able to choose and implement their own security policies. Today's technologies such as virtual private networks are static and do not accommodate the required dynamism.
- **Securing critical infrastructures:** This has to be dealt with from a system perspective. Deregulation has created infrastructures whose dependability is unknown and the multiplicity of actors has created vulnerabilities. Furthermore, infrastructures such as communication, transport, energy, financial or such as an airport are increasingly interdependent. If things affect one, they affect many through cascading and/or escalating failures.

From the user perspective (as an individual or as a member of a "community"), multiparty end-to-end security has to be achieved. This means securing both the content at the application level and securing the infrastructure, that is, the various properties of the communication such as network and system architecture, routers, firewalls, devices, and access control. As more intelligence goes into the network, there will be more inherent vulnerabilities such as in protocols, which will therefore have to be secured. Furthermore, the architecture of the whole communication system becomes more complex and data in caches, routers, base stations, etc., will have to be secured. In this context, mobility introduces even more security challenges with seamless service provision. Security has to take into account the type of communication; the semantics of the application; and the type of content. The diverse facets of security should be built in the open—not in obscurity—and should be auditable. In this context, monoculture—same chip, same operating system, same router, same crypto, and so forth—introduces critical system vulnerabilities. In ad-

Copyright © 2007, Idea Group Inc. Copying or distributing in print or electronic forms without written permission of Idea Group Inc. is prohibited.

addition, "open source" may, therefore, have a role to play, provided it is effectively audited. End to end security means also providing security when crossing different security policies, different jurisdictions, and/or different interoperable trusted third parties to build a chain of trust.

DYNAMICS AND CHALLENGES

Building and providing trust and confidence in Ambient Intelligence scenarios would imply addressing and meeting specific needs and requirements at all levels--content, network, and device. This would mean to consistently express specific security policies, which describe the organisational and technical processes and mechanisms to manage security, at every level as well as to coherently enforce those policies, which would normally appear to be distinguished and independent. Enforcing the different security policies would, therefore, need technical capability to automatically understand the global security context and to efficiently mediate between the various policies. A given security policy can be implemented using various means, depending on the level and nature of trust and security it needs for its user communities. Those means need to offer a global service although built on a potentially broad and heterogeneous set of elements. This view (IRG Report) is sketched in Figure 1.

A different perspective from the system architectural one in Figure 1 is provided by taking the *user community angle* that would privilege the view of the value chain and all stakeholders involved. From a vertically integrated client server model, we move towards a horizontal model where producer and consumer of content dialogue via connectivity services and intermediaries, as indicated in Figure 2.

The main challenge is *to build dynamically the chain of trust between all stakeholders* involved at a certain point in time *in the service composition in order*

Figure 1. Expressing and enforcing security policies

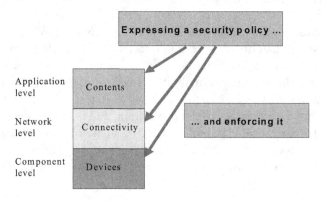

Copyright © 2007, Idea Group Inc. Copying or distributing in print or electronic forms without written permission of Idea Group Inc. is prohibited.

Figure 2. Horizontal model for information producers and consumers

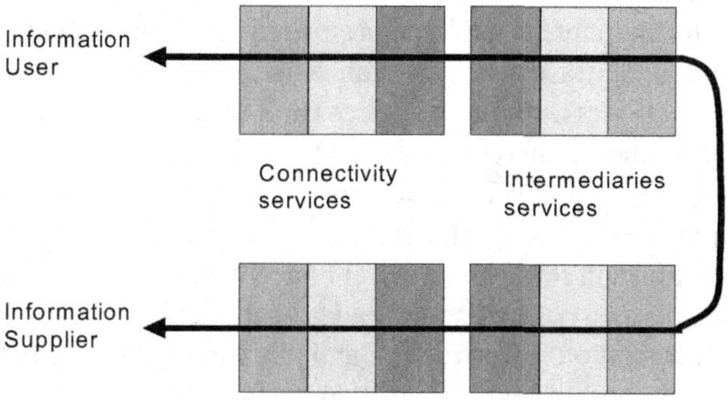

to deliver and support multiparty end-to-end security. This may entail mediation between different security policies when crossing the various intermediary domains. This perspective would become of greater importance as the interest in new architectures (i.e., GRID, P2P etc.) and Web Service composition grows.

Delivering security solutions that are technically and economically feasible and that ensure a proper balance between civil liberties and law enforcement is the challenge of this area.

THE RESEARCH AGENDA

The following sections will briefly present the security and dependability research priorities that have been identified for the domain on "Trust & Security" in the thematic priority Information Society Technologies (IST) (IST Web site, 2005) of the 6th Framework Programme. In this context, we emphasise that several security aspects touch on a number of IST domains among which are embedded systems and components, software technologies, wireless and fixed communication, networking, and knowledge technologies.

Securing the Information Infrastructure

There is a number of featuring trends that are important to scope the challenge of securing the information and communication infrastructure. First is the increasing heterogeneity which would emerge at all levels despite the push towards homogeneity (e.g., business consolidation) by convergence and de-regulation. Second is the tight interconnection, complexity and openness of large-scale communications and information infrastructures which imply (1) enhanced co-operation between a large number of different service providers and operators pertaining to different jurisdictions, and (2) new types of systemic vulnerabilities (e.g., due to interdependencies

Copyright © 2007, Idea Group Inc. Copying or distributing in print or electronic forms without written permission of Idea Group Inc. is prohibited.

between infrastructures) and proliferation of various threats of malicious as well as accidental natures.

In response to the unpredictable nature of infrastructures, new dynamic approaches to service and infrastructure assurance including risk-based and response-based methods at all layers of the service provision would be needed. This should, however, not discard the extensive deployment of content and knowledge services in industry, commerce, and consumer sectors, which implies increased criticality and higher economic value of digital assets as well as the need for appropriate information protection and for availability of underlying information services. The grand objective in this area is to holistically address the new security vulnerabilities, the flaws of the information infrastructure and its inherent heterogeneity in order to provide appropriate and auditable security properties, which are essential for the delivery of vital services for our society and our economy in general.

Key Target Technologies

- *Technologies and mechanisms* to knowingly enforce dynamic security policies (in particular with location based services and personalization) for heterogeneous, re-configurable and evolving processing/computing and network architectures (mobile, ad hoc, P2P, Bluetooth, etc.), network awareness technologies, disaster recovery technologies, network forensic technologies, and so forth.
- *Chaining trusted resources*, Security in clear, watermarking for identification/authentication/etc., encryption, security policy enforcing mechanisms and protocols, light PKI, temporal security, mobile code, and so forth.
- *Technology and mechanisms to virtually and dynamically configure* and use "platforms" for service development.

Dependability and Interdependencies in Information Society

By ensuring the dependable behaviour of the information infrastructure, we would protect our industry's wealth, its investments in information and communication technologies as well as its intangible assets. Furthermore, achieving a dependable behaviour of the infrastructure would mean ensuring flexible and co-operative management of large-scale computing and networking resources; establishing distributed early warning capability; and, last but not least, providing resources for effective prevention detection, confinement, and response to disruptions. The dependable behaviour of the information infrastructure depends on the behaviour of a growing number of players, systems, and networks. The interdependency among critical infrastructures (like the electric grid, e-commerce and e-business systems, the financial/banking systems, telecommunication, etc.) that are enabled and supported

Copyright © 2007, Idea Group Inc. Copying or distributing in print or electronic forms without written permission of Idea Group Inc. is prohibited.

by the information infrastructure can not be easily mastered by currently available technologies. These critical infrastructures are global and geographically distributed beyond any jurisdictional or governmental boundary. The overall goal of pursuing dependability and better understanding of interdependencies in Information Society will be to support innovative and multidisciplinary R&D to cope with and master scale issues of dependability associated to new business and everyday life application scenarios. Important aspects of the scale issues would be those associated with (1) the increasing volatility and growing heterogeneity of products, applications, services, systems and processes in the digital environment; (2) increasing interconnection and interdependency of the information and communication infrastructure and with other services and systems vital for our society and our economy.

Key Target Technologies

- **Technologies, architectures, and systems:** Robust open source software, advanced ubiquitous and wireless technologies, new architectures and computing paradigms (covering autonomy, self-adaptability, self-healing, real-time, etc.), distributed attack detection systems, modelling and synthetic environment for real-time dependability and continuity analysis, extensively deployed networked embedded system, assessing dependability properties of COTS, risk management, human related technologies and systems, and so forth.
- **Metrics and assurance:** Including plasticity and human aspects of systems, tools for real time patterns and analysis of open network traffic data, complexity issues, validation, verification, testing, certification, and so forth.
- **Interdependencies:** Micro and macro dimensions, large scale and composable modelling and simulation capabilities, network awareness technologies, emergent systems properties, time dimension, social and cultural dimension, risk perception, communication and awareness, risk management in open environments, and so forth.
- **International co-operation:** Focussing on technical domain of common interest and mutual benefits such as modelling interdependent utilities, dependability certification, reliability and security of computational GRIDs, trustworthy and dynamic information sharing, and so forth.

Managing Identity in Information Society

Identity management would be more of an area of growing interest and concerns. This trend is linked to the growing need to counterbalance the asymmetric capability provided by technology to transparently produce, record, and mining data. Furthermore, advanced communication, transmission, and browsing mechanisms rely more and more on automatically produced traces of transactions which may very easily be digested to build profiles at least linkable to users. Contextually,

Copyright © 2007, Idea Group Inc. Copying or distributing in print or electronic forms without written permission of Idea Group Inc. is prohibited.

such developments and trends are making privacy the highest priority concern for users who feel uncomfortable with e-tranaction embedding personal data. This situation gets even more complex by considering the likely increase of reliance on autonomous and detached entities (i.e., autonomous agents, mobile codes, portable trusted devices, intelligent and responsive devices, personal area networks, domotic devices, etc.) that, in a way, would carry some notion of "identity" which would have to be managed.

However, technology could equally be used by criminals to cover up illegitimate activities, and therefore the needs for privacy must be offset and balanced with security requirements for the benefit of the society, in particular the needs to ensure compliance and enforcement of the law mapping technology solutions to policy. A proper balance should be ensured in a transparent way and in full awareness of the users. The overall goal of research in this area would be:

- To develop new technologies, tools, trusted components and systems for identity management, privacy-aware authentication and authorisation schemes to meet the future needs as well as improve convenience and ease of their use via better user-interface, personal trusted device, smart cards, biometrics, etc.
- To stimulate and federate the research community in working various domains--technical, economics, legal, or societal—in order to promote an EU coherent approach to meet privacy needs.

Key Target Technologies

- Protection of personal identity vs. multiple and virtual identity management capability—including management of roles
- Anonymity, pseudonyms, unobservability, and unlinkability
- Information hiding
- Context-aware and location-aware services vs. privacy
- New paradigms and models for enforcing rights and fulfilling obligations which would leverage the full range of options from hard identification to minimal authentication and/or authorisation
- New access control techniques privacy-aware, role based, rule based, and so forth.
- Use of biometrics vs. identification and authentication needs
- Ability to trace and audit personal data
- Non-technical issues linked to the use of biometrics privacy concerns and the need of testing methods to assess non-technical aspects of biometrics (e.g., acceptability, usability, and trust in authorities handling biometric data doing so in a legal and open manner).

Copyright © 2007, Idea Group Inc. Copying or distributing in print or electronic forms without written permission of Idea Group Inc. is prohibited.

Security and Mobile Information Society

Another important element which contributes to change the horizon of security consideration and challenges is "mobility." This notion has to be articulated at all levels: from physical, to logical; from infrastructural to technological; from jurisdictional to contextual, and so forth. To date, the highest interest of technical developments is devoted to mobile communications with the main focus on basic networking architectures and technologies for wireless LANs, UMTS, Bluetooth, RFID, etc. However, not sufficient effort is put on security of the up to now fairly immune—towards attacks over the network—mobile communication networks (for instance the security for multi-hop ad-hoc networks is still in its infancy), which are running the risk of becoming as vulnerable as the fixed networks, especially into the perspective of having future mobile information devices given the ability to download software, negotiate resources, upgrade profiles, and applications, and so forth. Leveraging such development, a flourishing number of location-aware and context-aware services are emerging and more sophisticated ones are likely to develop. However, still unsatisfactory is the way in which mobility is being re-conciliated with privacy and data protection for which there is a need to develop more clearly defined policies from the perspective of user privacy. Lastly, another source of increasing vulnerabilities of mobile networks is their growing openness where mobile network functionality (e.g., location, charging/billing, messaging, etc.) is being made externally available to third-party service providers. There is a need to enhance the capability to analyse, model, simulate, or reason large heterogeneous networks with rapidly changing characteristics, ad-hoc formations and multiple security domains. Both fundamental theory and practical experience is lacking in modelling such systems. In addition, it is critical to develop integrated approaches to security (including scalable security policies) through all level of design, development, and evolution of systems for which dynamic and ad hoc networking constitutes a new challenge.

Key Target Technologies

- Security for mobile routers
- Security for multicast communication in mobile networks
- Efficient and transparent charging mechanisms in the presence of multiple payment schemes in mobile networks
- Security policy and authorisation issues associated with (potentially many) different administrative domains in mobile networks
- Specification of requirements for security and privacy specific to mobility.
- Development and integration of "trusted components."
- User Interface and usability of functionality for security and privacy choices
- Defining and managing privacy policies so as to permit access to location-sen-

Copyright © 2007, Idea Group Inc. Copying or distributing in print or electronic forms without written permission of Idea Group Inc. is prohibited.

sitive services or other advanced services (e.g., charging/billing information, personal setting/preferences, profiles of used services, etc.) without intrusion into the user's private life
- Biometrics and privacy implications
- New types of evaluation profiles for mobile devices
- Development of new applications on trusted devices, e.g. use of credentials
- Rich delegation/authorisation infrastructures that would support several levels of certificates and support the management of different roles, credentials and privileges

Securing Digital Assets

Due to pervasiveness and the increasing diversification of networks and content (multimedia content, software, platform, video stream, applets, autonomous agents …), securing storage, transfer, manipulation of digital assets becomes more and more complex. This implies that a much broader perspective needs to be considered by moving from more conventional digital right management systems to dynamic assets management so as to tackle future concerns and issue, like:

- The end-user needs to be empowered to access to his "digital assets" anywhere, anytime, from any type of platform (SW/HW) in a secure and transparent way
- The heterogeneity and the evolving propriety (dynamic configuration) of networks introduce vulnerabilities, especially at the interface between different portions of the infrastructure with different protocols/proprieties
- The end-user needs to be empowered to control his "digital assets" in an evolving environment adapting the properties of the content and of the system configuration to his needs in that specific environment. Active content might also be self-adapting to the specific environment, such autonomous components evolve in order to adapt to the needs linked to that environment.
- There is a great need from content industries for reliable technologies and protocols for protecting the rights of the works they own
- There is an increasing interest in manipulation recognition and ensuring data authentication
- Both the infrastructure and the content must be secured in order to ensure end-to-end protection
- Individual assets must be identified and linked to their owner and their associated security policy
- The technology must ensure end to end, the rights of the owner (ownership, privacy, confidentiality, etc.) intrinsically linked to the data security (integrity, authenticity, integrity, controllability, traceability, linkability, etc.).
- The technology must also ensure availability and accessibility of the secured content in a transparent way

Copyright © 2007, Idea Group Inc. Copying or distributing in print or electronic forms without written permission of Idea Group Inc. is prohibited.

In such a context, there is a need to promote and develop capability to efficiently manage dynamic and evolving digital assets by building on and enlarging the more conventional approach to digital right management.

Key Target Technologies

- Research in new security and cryptography protocols, authentication of users (biometrics) and of content (watermarking)
- Adapt security techniques to the type of network
- Secure the content and the container
- Tools to enable the user to trace and control the access right of his personal
- Improvement of watermarking robustness, in particular with respect to degradation, that are not so easily modelled in a theoretical framework
- Design of authentication technologies, both on the basis of watermarks and combinations of perceptual fingerprints and robust watermarks
- Design of reversible watermarking technologies (i.e., technologies where the original content can be completely restored)
- Development of watermarking for new 3D objects and multimedia composed scenes
- Development of watermarking applications that are not within the realm of copyright protection and security
- Establish reliable procedures to test the performance of robust watermarking systems

New Computing Architectures and Web Services Composition

Over the last few new models and architectures to enhance Internet computing, such as Grid, peer-to-peer, and Web services, have emerged. The move is away from the centralised Web client-server model towards collaborative resource sharing and user empowerment. The evolution is facilitated by advances in networking and middleware technologies and because a majority of computing platforms have sufficient power, Internet connectivity, and storage capacity to function as both client and server. This move triggers major security challenges. Up until now, grid computing was predominantly used in the big science world and peer-to-peer (P2P) in the academic and business world. Both are a manifestation of distributed computing and resource sharing. The Internet will transform itself into a ubiquitous fabric of grids and peers.

Web services are the technical standards that major computer companies are betting on to deliver a new generation of offerings on the Internet. Web services will

Copyright © 2007, Idea Group Inc. Copying or distributing in print or electronic forms without written permission of Idea Group Inc. is prohibited.

enable enterprises to employ component technologies across the Internet. "Edge" technologies are enabling enterprises to massively distribute content throughout the Internet. Content delivery networks are transforming the Internet into a persistent storage medium capable of delivering content from locations very close to those of the end user. Peer-to-peer networks link content stored on individual computers into communities that multiple users can access.

Key Target Technologies

- Security and trust
- Resource discovery and management, end-to-end issues, QoS
- Application integration. re-architecting business functions into modular network enabled components, legacy system integration
- Billing, accounting, content management, and migration
- Building industrial-strength computing environments
- Persistent infrastructure and network resilience
- Interoperability
- Knowledge sharing and digital rights management

NOTE

The content of this chapter is the sole responsibility of the author and in no way represents the view of the European Commission or its services.

This chapter builds on the conclusions and recommendation of report of the Internal Reflection Group on Trust and Security that was organised by the IST thematic priority in preparation of the 6th Framework Programme.

CONCLUSION

The advent of Ambient Intelligence and the increasing dependence of our society and economy on computer-based information and communication systems, networks, and information infrastructures pose new challenges for security and dependability technologies. These challenges call for innovative security models, technologies, and architectures as well as a better understanding of the implications of relying on technological systems. It is in this scenario that the domain on trust and security in the IST thematic priority in FP6 promotes innovative and multidisciplinary research on security and dependability in order to provide the capabilities needed to build a dependable information society that would be more secure, robust, and resilient to technical vulnerability, failures, and attacks.

Copyright © 2007, Idea Group Inc. Copying or distributing in print or electronic forms without written permission of Idea Group Inc. is prohibited.

REFERENCES

Ducatel, K. et al. (2001). Scenarios for Ambient Intelligence in 2001. *IPTS-Seville*. Retrieved from ftp://ftp.cordis.lu/pub/ist/docs/istagscenarios2010.pdf

FP5 ISTAG Web site. (2002). Retrieved from http://www.cordis.lu/ist/fp5-istag. htm

IST Web site. (2005). Retrieved from www.cordis.lu/ist

IRG Report on Trust & Security. Retrieved from ftp://ftp.cordis.lu/pub/ist/docs/irg-tc-v3.pdf

Copyright © 2007, Idea Group Inc. Copying or distributing in print or electronic forms without written permission of Idea Group Inc. is prohibited.

Chapter V

Biometric Authentication in Broadband Networks for Location-Based Services

Stelios C. A. Thomopoulos, National Center of
Scientific Research "Demokritos," Greece

Nikolaos Argyreas, National Center of
Scientific Research "Demokritos," Greece

ABSTRACT

Broadband communication networks have begun to spread rapidly over fixed networks, with wireless networks following at close distance. The excess capacity allows the offering of broadband services at competitive rates. Location-based services (LBS) over wireless broadband networks are becoming mainstream in an emerging ambient intelligence society. For LBS over broadband and, in particular, pier-to-pier networks, such as ad hoc networks, unambiguous user authentication is of paramount importance to user trust and safety, thus ultimately to the success of such service. Biometric authentication is an approach to providing irrefutable identity verification of a user, thus providing the highest level of security. This chapter addresses some of the issues associated with the use of biometric ID for user and apparatus authentication over broadband wireless networks (e.g., GPRS, UMTS, WiFi, LANs) and narrow band local networks (e.g., bluetooth, Zigbee, PANs, BANs).

Copyright © 2007, Idea Group Inc. Copying or distributing in print or electronic forms without written permission of Idea Group Inc. is prohibited.

INTRODUCTION

The spreading of broadband networks stimulates a wealth of Internet services over fixed and wireless networks with stationary and mobile devices. Combining accurate location information from enhanced GPS infrastructures, such as EGNOS, Galileo ..., with broadband wireless networks, provide the necessary infrastructure for delivering high quality and versatile location-based services (LBSs) ranging from travel information to entertainment, to crisis and incident management, to services on demand, to health care and peer-to-peer communications, to mention just a few.

In all these services, the common thread is the ability to unambiguously identify and authenticate the mobile user and customer to the LBS provider. Different LB services may have different authentication requirements. However, no matter what the application is all such services, the unambiguous authentication of the user is paramount to gaining the trust of the end user and thus achieving the success of the services. Unambiguous user authentication is paramount to the parties involved in an LB service and the trust upon which the service is built. If for example the LBS refers to the provision of transport services on demand, the ability to correctly identify and authenticate both parties involved in the transaction, that is the passenger (i.e., the user) and the driver (i.e., the service provider) build mutual trust and can be proved life-saving in the case of a car-jacking, criminal activity, or fraud.

User identification and authentication can be performed by a variety of means, ranging from a simple alphanumerical password to a more secure digital signature, to the ultimate in security biometric ID. Although a digital signature produced by an electronic device provides the convenience of a self-contained identification instrument, it does not prevent fraudulent use of a user ID. Since there is no unique and inherited connection between the user and the digital ID, any holder of the electronic device that produces the digital ID can produce a fraudulent authentication. The only means to eliminate such possibility is the use of biometric ID.

Biometric ID is a digital signature generated from the measurement of some bodily human characteristics that are unique, or different enough to be considered unique, from user to user. This Biometric ID, encoded properly, constitutes a unique signature for each user that cannot replicated by an impostor. This biometric ID can be used to meet the stringent requirements imposed by LB services and the necessary trust required by users and operators of such services alike. Examples of biometrics commonly used for user identification and verification include fingerprint identification, iris scan, face and voice recognition, signature recognition, hand geometry, and combinations thereof (Reisman & Thomopoulos, 1998; Thomopoulos & Reisman, 1993).

The use of biometric ID imposes certain restrictions and technological challenges that need to be addressed before biometric authentication becomes widely used as an enabling technology for irrefutable user authentication in LBS and other broadband services.

Copyright © 2007, Idea Group Inc. Copying or distributing in print or electronic forms without written permission of Idea Group Inc. is prohibited.

BIOMETRIC ID

A. Requirements for Biometric ID Usage

Biometric ID is the mathematical encoding of certain bodily features that are considered unique for each human being and differ enough from person to person so that this difference can be used safely enough to tell apart one person from another. For example, in the case of fingerprints, biometric features are the characteristic points that are formed from the endings or bifurcations of the finger ridges and/or the pattern of the ridges themselves. In the case of the iris scan, biometric features are the radial patterns of the iris. In the case of the face, biometric features are the relative location of the eyes, mouth, nose, and so forth.

The mathematical encoding of the biometric features constitutes what is referred to as biometric "template" or biometric ID (Thomopoulos, Reisman, & Papelis, 1996). No matter which biometric is used, the biometric features constitute unique and personal human characteristic and as such, they are protected by the Personal Information Protection Act (PIPA) (Personal Information Protection Act, S.A. 2003, c. P-6.5). This protection imposes a number of issues, concerns, and restrictions with the extraction (or capturing) of biometric features, their (electronic) storage, encoding into a biometric template and the subsequent retrieval and use of this template for user authentication. In addition to privacy, other concerns with the use of biometric features relate to the medical information that may be contained in and revealed by biometric features, the safety of the process and devices used in the extraction and verification process, and the protection of the user's privacy (ANSI:The American National Standards Institute, 2005; also ISO: International Organization for Standardization).

A biometric "template" constitutes a non-reversible mathematical transformation of the extracted biometric features (Thomopoulos, Reisman, & Papelis, 1996). In that respect, it cannot be used outside the specific device that is used to extract it (and subsequently verify it) as a means to identify one's identity without his or her consent, thus violating the PICA. However, it can be used indirectly through the use of the specific device and process used to extract it to coerce evidence about one's identity without his or her consent. In that regard, even the biometric template, albeit its mathematical irreversibility, constitutes private and personal data and as such it is mandatory that it is protected by the Private Information Protection Act (PIPA, S.A. 2003, c. P-6.5).

The restrictions imposed by the PICA reflect on the technological specifications for the processes and devices used for biometric ID verification. Hence, the requirement that any biometric information, including the biometric template, constitutes private data and requires that the biometric data be stored in a memory device that is only accessible by the owner of this data, either in the form of raw biometric data or a processed biometric template (Stapleton, 2003). Furthermore, any retrieval of such information from the storage device (memory) must be done over secure and

Copyright © 2007, Idea Group Inc. Copying or distributing in print or electronic forms without written permission of Idea Group Inc. is prohibited.

cryptographically protected communication links, and any subsequent processing of this information must be done by a secure processor. These restrictions lead to almost uniquely defined architectures for biometric verification (The BioAPI™ Consortium, 2005). The most readily available and seemingly universal architecture involves the use of a smart card as a memory device for storing the user biometric ID template and a local secure processor for capturing the biometric information, processing it to extract the biometric features, and comparing it against the stored template. Alternative storage technologies include memory chips or tokens. In this case, the biometrics data processor is part of the memory device, in a size that is not larger than a conventional memory stick. Using either technology, the PICA requirements can be met. The biometric template is always at the possession of the user, any processing is done locally, and over links and processors that are securely isolated from the WWW. However, in the process of enforcing PICA, one of the major advantages of biometrics and biometric ID, namely the convenience not to carry any type of ID other than one's self, is being lost. This is the trade-off between the convenience offered by the card-less biometric identification, and the restrictions imposed by PICA that translate in the need to carry and use a plastic card in order to store the biometrics template in a user-controlled memory.

The cartoon displays in Figures 1 and 2 show the typical registration and authentication processes for biometric ID. These processes have been implemented in the VeriEasy biometrics access control system that was developed in the context of the Bioathletics[1] project. The project aims at implementing a distributed biometrics

Figure 1. Registration process of the PICA-compliant smart card based biometrics (fingerprint) VeriEasy access control system for athletic events and installations

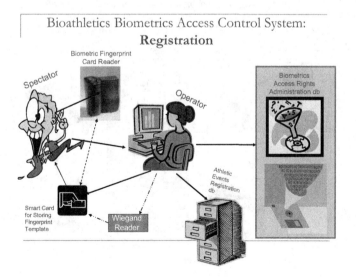

Copyright © 2007, Idea Group Inc. Copying or distributing in print or electronic forms without written permission of Idea Group Inc. is prohibited.

ID system to allow secure access to spectators, VIPs and the press in athletic installations and events using their biometric ID only.

BIOMETRICS IN ATHLETICS

Athletic events represent an ideal field of application and showcase test
beds for biometrics as they combine a usually large crowd, the need for speedy
but secure authentication, electronic ticketing, and overall security concerns by
potential troublemakers. VeriEasy™ was developed in the context of the funded
research program Bioathletics to provide a unified BioAPI compliant platform for
addressing the concerns of the athletic events industry in secure physical access to
stadium for athletes, spectators, and VIPs. In the VeriEasy™ system, the biometrics (fingerprint) template is stored directly from the card Verification and Access
Process as implemented in the VeriEasy access control system for athletic events
and installations reader in a smart card that stays with the template's owner at all
times. This way the PICA requirements are fulfilled in terms of both privacy and
protection against eavesdropping, since the template stays with his or her owner
at all times and processing is done locally over a trusted link. The user smart card
serial number is then linked to a back office legacy system database that contains
demographic (non-private and sensitive) information about the user and access
rights and athletic event attendance information.

During an athletic event, the user accesses the stadium or the equivalent athletic
installation using his or her biometric ID smart card. The stored user's biometric
ID is compared against his or her fingerprint live scan locally using the same secure local processor and communication link. If the authentication is positive, the

Figure 2. PICA-compliant smart card based biometrics (fingerprint).

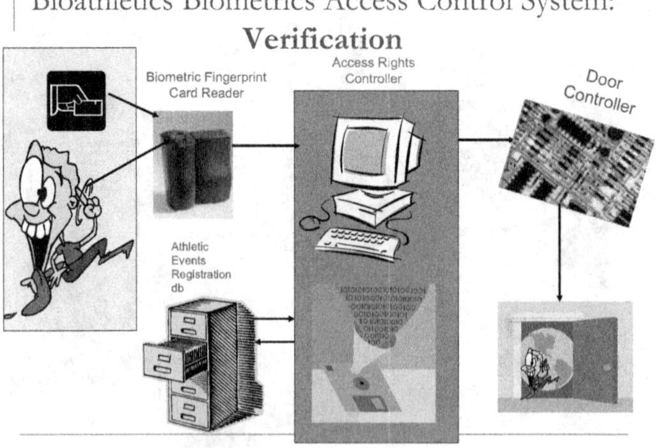

Copyright © 2007, Idea Group Inc. Copying or distributing in print or electronic forms without written permission of Idea Group Inc. is prohibited.

system is connected via a broadband connection to the back office athletic events database to acquire the appropriate access permissions for the specific event the user is attempting to gain access to. If the user has purchased the appropriate ticket for the event or has access rights to it, an authentication acknowledgment signal is returned to the device to enable access to the athletic premise. Alternative, a positive acknowledgment message can be displayed on a monitor, if the system operates with a human attendant. The verification and access process for VeriEasy is shown in a cartoon way in Figure 2.

Another restriction that is imposed on biometrics ID systems is the encryption of any biometrics data. Encryption in the VeriEasy system is achieved using a private key that is encrypted in the smart card. Other encryption methods are possible and can be used in conjunction with the smart card encryption. Another link that must be secured in the Verification and Access process is the physical electric connection from the door controller to the electric door latch.

This link can be secured by using an encryption-decryption hardware pair to encrypt the electric signal that commands the opening and closing of the gate. This way the entire local biometric authentication-access process is secured. It remains, however, to secure all long haul communication network links.

In order to make the biometrics ID registration-verification-access process entirely secure globally, all long hauls fixed or wireless communication network links must be secured as well. One way to achieve this is use VPN tunneling for data communication from the distributed access points to the centralized back offices database or databases that hold the athletic event schedules, ticket information, event schedules, athletic installations layout, access rights, and authorizations.

Finally, if the biometric authentication devices communicate with the local Access Rights Controller via a bluetooth or zigbee wireless link, this wireless link must be secured as well. Both bluetooth and zigbee protocols provide a security layer but the level of security of these layers is still not widely tested.

Hence, if a bluetooth or zigbee wireless link is used in the biometrics ID system, it may be required to use encryption on top of their security layer until their security is extensively tested and proven.

Figure 3 depicts the VeriEasy verification process as a generic secure verification process applicable to any biometrics ID authentication system operating over any broadband communication network. Hence, the biometrics authentication system architecture of VeriEasy, and thus Bioathletics, provides: a trusted and secure means of biometrics ID extraction and processing at the local level, compliant with the PICA specifications for personal data protection and privacy; a globally secure network architecture for data exchange and information communication; and a locally secure wireless network for the interconnection and networking of devices and signaling.

Any biometrics authentication system since the biometrics field is continually evolving and no standard has been reached yet.

Copyright © 2007, Idea Group Inc. Copying or distributing in print or electronic forms without written permission of Idea Group Inc. is prohibited.

Figure 3. Securing all communication links, fixed and wireless, either via a VPN, bluetooth, or zibgee, the security layer provides a globally secure and trusted, PICA-compliant smart card based biometrics (fingerprint) authentication for any broadband application with emphasis to LBS applications

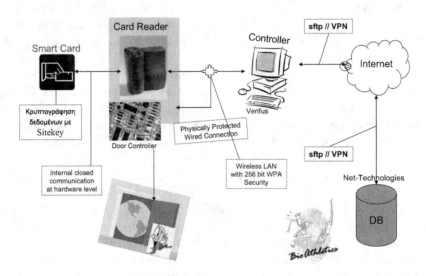

The Bioathletics paradigm can be generalized to other broadband applications that require biometrics ID authentication. A number of useful conclusions drawn from the Bioathletics project are summarized in Table 1. These conclusions are relevant and applicable to the implementation of any PICA-compliant biometrics ID authentication system that may be required for the unambiguous and trusted user authentication in broadband applications, with LBS being one of them.

In addition to the security requirements imposed on a biometrics ID authentication system, the system must also be Bio-API compliant. Compliance with the Bio-API allows to encapsulate all manufacturer dependent biometric and algorithm processes in callable DLLs. In this way, the core structure of the biometrics ID authentication system remains fixed, whereas new biometric feature extraction, encoding, and verification modules can be easily integrated in the system with minor modifications. This modularity is extremely important as it allows adaptation to new biometrics as time progresses. This adaptation is keen to the success of any biometrics authentication system since the biometrics field is continually evolving and standards have yet to be defined.

BioAPI™ and BSP Implementation

The BioAPI™ Specification version 1.1 0 is an ANSI 0 (INCITS 358-2002) standard and currently under ISO standardization process (ISO/IEC JTC1/SC37)

Copyright © 2007, Idea Group Inc. Copying or distributing in print or electronic forms without written permission of Idea Group Inc. is prohibited.

Table 1. Recommendations for the implementation of a biometrics ID authentication system

Process	Device	Communication Link	Security level	PICA requirements	PICA compliant
Biometrics feature extraction and template creation	Biometrics reader with local processor	Local and secure. Data encryption if necessary	Secure and trusted	Personal data protection	Yes
Biometrics template storage	Local with the user: Smart Card or Memory Stick with or w/out processor and built-in memory	Directly in a smart card or memory stick	Private and secure	Privacy and protection of personal data	Yes
Biometrics ID authentication	Biometrics reader with local processor & Local Card or Memory Stick reader	Local. Encryption of data may be required from smart card or memory stick to local processor.	Secure and trusted	Privacy and protection of personal data	Yes
Access of back office permission rights db	Secure Server	VPN with or without additional data encryption	Secure	N/A unless it carries private data info – to be avoided	N/A
Local devices and command signaling via wireless links	Biometric readers, controllers, actuators	Wireless local links: bluetooth or zigbee	bluetooth or zigbee Security protocol with or w/out additional data encryption	Secure personal data transfer if inevitable	Yes

Copyright © 2007, Idea Group Inc. Copying or distributing in print or electronic forms without written permission of Idea Group Inc. is prohibited.

specifying an Application Programming Interface (API), which was introduced to facilitate the implementation of Biometric applications (The BioAPI Consortium; and The BioAPI Consortium: BioAPI™ Specification version 1.1). BioAPI is a standard biometric technology interface, which is intended to provide a high-level generic biometric authentication model; one suited for any form of biometric technology. BioAPI supports, among other lower level functions, the basic functions of Enrollment, Verification, and Identification, and includes a database interface to allow a biometric service provider (BSP) to manage the Identification population for optimum performance in an application independent manner. There is a reference implementation for Microsoft® Windows® (early alpha) publicly available by the BioAPI™ Consortium 0, as well as two internally released beta implementations; one for Java (under Windows®, via JNI) by (Gens Software Ltd); and one for Unix™ / Linux™ by SAFLINK. There are several commercial implementations to date—mainly by members of the BioAPI™ Consortium—either in the form of BioAPI™ framework SDK or in the form of BSP Biometric Service Provider (BSP) SDK or specific BSP implementations for the vendors' Biometric Devices. However, market acceptance is still immature and market penetration of BioAPI™ compliant applications and biometric devices is speculated to significantly increase in the next two years (The BioAPI Consortium; and The BioAPI Consortium: BioAPI™ Specification version 1.1).

A BioAPI™ compliant application consists of at least two different modules, the application module, which could be seen as the "top" level application (Level H) and the BSP (Biometric Service Provider) module, which could be seen as the "bottom" level application (Level L). The application module would be the biometric application and the BSP module would be the service provider module, which should control the biometric hardware. The BSP could be seen as a black box from the side of the application developer, since the technical details of a given device will not concern him.

Access to the biometric mechanisms is through a set of standard interfaces defined by BioAPI™. The approach taken by the BioAPI™ is to hide, to the degree possible, the unique aspects of individual biometric technologies, and particular vendor implementations, products, and devices, while providing a high-level abstraction that can be used within a number of potential software applications.

One of the most important terms of the BioAPI™ standard is the BIR. The term Biometric Identification Record (BIR) refers to any biometric data that is returned to the application; including raw data, intermediate data, and processed sample ready for verification or identification, as well as enrollment data.

Theoretically, BSPs that are supplied by vendors and conform to the BioAPI™ interface specification, can be used by any application developed using the BioAPI™ framework.

The BioAPI™ Consortium claims, among other things, that the BioAPI™ will enable rapid development of application, flexible deployment between platforms, and simple application interfaces modularity of biometric applications.

Copyright © 2007, Idea Group Inc. Copying or distributing in print or electronic forms without written permission of Idea Group Inc. is prohibited.

For an application to be compliant with the BioAPI™ specification, a software application must perform that operation consistent with the BioAPI™ specification for each BioAPI™ function call made. That is, all input parameters must be present and valid. There is no minimum set of functions that must be called.

For a BSP to claim compliance to the BioAPI™ specification, it must implement mandatory functions for their category. They are categorized as either a Verification or Identification BSP. BSPs must accept all valid input parameters and return valid outputs. Additionally, they must provide all required module registry entries. Entries to the module registry must be performed upon BSP installation. Biometric data generated by the BSP must conform to the data structures defined in BioAPI™ Specification. A BioAPI compliant BSP must support all Module Management and Handle operations.

When an application is connected to a given BSP, the process initializes the BioAPI™ Framework, loads the BSP desired, and then attaches a module of the given BSP to the application. Once the application is connected to a BSP, it can perform BioAPI™ calls for several biometric operations as Capture, Enrollment, Verification, and Identification.

The BioAPI™ concept is very interesting, but some things in the implementation may get confusing. For instance, data exchange between the BSP and the application can be an issue. There is no asynchronous way to pass data from the BSP to the application. Also when it comes to communication of the application and the BSP, the rules of communication can be quite restraining.

In the given implementation of BioAPI™, when it comes to the BSP wanting to notify the application that some event has occurred, the API defines that the notifications that can be made are "on insertion" or "on removal" of a biometric device, "on fault" of a device and "on presence" or "on removal" of a biometric source (e.g., presence of a finger on a fingerprint device). In other words an application can only be notified if:

a.   A new device is plugged in the system.
b.   An existing device is unplugged from the system.
c.   An existing device doesn't work properly.
d.   A biometric source is presented to one of the biometric devices in the system, or is removed from it.

The application can command the BSP with commands such as BioAPI_Enroll(…) or BioAPI_Verify(…). The idea of BioAPI™ includes the idea that any attached device should be handled from the BSP so that different devices can be used if they provide a suitable BSP. However, as existing biometric devices may not be fully compliant to BioAPI™, there might be cases that it may be deemed necessary to command the device to perform something that is not foreseen by the BioAPI™ without violating the BioAPI™ standard. Otherwise, the application will

Copyright © 2007, Idea Group Inc. Copying or distributing in print or electronic forms without written permission of Idea Group Inc. is prohibited.

no longer be BioAPI™ compliant, since no other de vice is expected to work with the same command and the idea of the BSP module as a black box is lost.

Another problem exists with the data exchange between the application and the BSP. The API gives the application the right to use a payload as input on Enrollment and Create Template, or as output on Verification and Verify Match (Identification). In any other case the API does not provide the application the right to exchange data with the BSP. Two questions are raised then:

a.   What happens in the case that the application needs to send data to the BSP asynchronously and vise-versa?
b.   What should the payload data be, if the data that is exchanged through payload are not specified by the API?

The data exchange through payload might be anything, but since the API does not define what this data should be, then it is almost impossible to find two different BSPs passing the same data through payload and on the same form. This means that the application is highly impossible to be able to function with the BSP of a different device, thus a need for BSPs for devices from different manufacturers and vendors.

EXPANDING THE CAPABILITIES OF VERIEASY™

In many applications, in particular in high security/high authentication fidelity cases, more than one biometrics technology is required to exist and operate under different authentication scenarios in the same environment. Such a heterogeneous biometric devices network may consist of fingerprint scanners, voice recognition devices, and face and iris scanners, all working in various combinations for ID verification under various authentication scenarios. Using the VeriEasy™ client-server architecture, we can build BSPs for each type of biometrics device we intend to use in the security network and control them via a single application! This way the highest security standards are achieved without loosing any flexibility. For example, in a heterogeneous biometrics network, the Server BSP can grab the proper fingerprint template from the smartcard or request to the application for the right one when a centralized Template Database is in place.

The obvious advantage of this architecture is that it defines a middle layer between the application and the native BSPs, so that the native BSP programmer needs to know about his device and nothing more, the middle layer programmer (if any) needs to know about the biometric network and nothing more, and the application programmer needs to know nothing at all about biometrics!

Copyright © 2007, Idea Group Inc. Copying or distributing in print or electronic forms without written permission of Idea Group Inc. is prohibited.

Furthermore we can use plug and play BSPs (e.g., have a BSP installed, as a client one), and let the Server BSP to reconfigure itself in order to handle the new device.

MULTIFUNCTIONAL BSPS

Using more than one biometric technology may be a highly unprofitable venture, because of the cost of different kinds of devices coming from different hardware distributors. But even more, the maintenance of such a system could be proved a constant headache for our administration personnel (different contracts of maintenance). It is here where VeriEasy™ comes to provide the winning solution--the multifunctional BSP. That means that the same device can operate in many different ways so it is up to us to choose the proper way for the specific device, whenever we want to.

Hence, setting up the most complex biometric devices network to meet the security needs of an organization is only one click away! Moreover, if for security concerns changes are required in the security network design at run time (!), VeriEasy™ allows on the fly reconfiguration of the security network design without service interruption!

Biometrics Authetication in Broadband Networks and Location-Based Services

Advances in broadband, and in particular wireless broadband networks, enable the provision of personalized multimedia services, as well as location-based services (LBS's). Those services extend from electronic maps and navigation, to location sensitive tourist guidance, transportation, car-pooling, ad hoc networking, and ubiquitous computing, to incident management, emergency services, to make reference to just a few. In all LB services, the sensitive information is the user's location and the user's identity. Both these two pieces of information must be protected by the provided service or infrastructure the service is running on, and authenticated when necessary by means directly controlled by the user. Simply imagine how critical it is to authenticate the user's ID unambiguously when the LBS is a car pooling service provided over an ad hoc (peer-to-peer) network. In such an application where verification of the true identity of the user may be a life and death situation, it becomes imperative to have a bullet-proof biometrics authentication system to provide unambiguous user ID verification.

Such a system should protect the user ID from theft, forgery, and misuse.

CONCLUSION

The architecture and design of a distributed biometric ID verification system has been presented. The VeriEasy™ system provides protection of the user privacy

Copyright © 2007, Idea Group Inc. Copying or distributing in print or electronic forms without written permission of Idea Group Inc. is prohibited.

and ID, compliant with the sensitive personal data protection guidelines and legislations, and is BioAPI compliant using BSP compliant interfaces.

ACKNOWLEDGMENT

The research for the development of a BioAPI™/BSP compliant biometrics authentication system for ID verification in athletics events have been sponsored by the General Secretariat of Research & Technology, of the Greek Ministry of Development, under Contract No. ΣΠ/ΑΘ/17+32, Operational Program "Competitiveness" Oct. 2003.

REFERENCES

ANSI: American National Standards Institute. Retrieved from http://www.ansi.org

Gens Software Ltd. (n.d.). Retrieved from http://www.gensoft.com

ISO: International Organization for Standardization. Retrieved from http://www.iso.ch

Personal Information Protection Act, S.A. 2003, c. P-6.5. (n.d.). Retrieved from http://www.psp.gov.ab.ca/index.cfm?page=legislation/act/index.html

Reisman, J. G., & Thomopoulos, S. C. A. (1998). Data fusion architecture for automated fingerprint identification for very large databases. In *Proceedings SPIE* (Vol. SPIE-3374).

SAFLINK Corporation. (n.d.). Retrieved from http://www.saflink.com

Stapleton, J. (2003, June 23-26). *KPMG, State of Biometric Standards.* Presentation at the BiometricTech Conference, New York.

The BioAPI™ Consortium. (2005). Retrieved from http://www.bioapi.org

The BioAPI™ Consortium: BioAPI™ Specification version 1.1. (n.d.). Retrieved from http://www.bioapi.org

Thomopoulos, S. C. A., & Reisman, J. G. (1993). Fusion-based, high volume Automatic Fingerprint Identification System (AFIS). In *Proceedings of SPIE 93*, Innsbruck, Austria (Vol. SPIE-2093).

Thomopoulos, S. C. A., Reisman, J. G., & Papelis, Y. E. (1996). Ver-i-Fus: An integrated access control and information monitoring and management system. In *Proceedings of SPIE* (Vol. SPIE-2934, pp. 1991-200).

ENDNOTE

[1]   The project "Bioathletics" has been funded by the General Secretariat of Research & Technology (GSRT) of the Greek Ministry of Development under the Contract ΑΘ 17+32 / 2-10-2003.

Copyright © 2007, Idea Group Inc. Copying or distributing in print or electronic forms without written permission of Idea Group Inc. is prohibited.

Chapter VI

Secure Online Metering for a Liberalized Energy Market

Christoph Ruland, University of Siegen, Germany

ABSTRACT

The liberalisation of the energy market requires frequent online access to metering devices. That is not only necessary for exchanging meter data, but also for management reasons. The integration of strong security mechanisms is an essential requirement for the introduction of online meter device access. The project Secure Electronic Exchange of Metering Data (SELMA) supported the development of a concept, the implementation, and a field trial test of prototypes of such metering devices. This chapter focuses on the security aspects. It describes the security analysis, the required security services, and the security concept. The security concept includes the security mechanisms and cryptographic techniques applied to the metering data as well as the security management.

Copyright © 2007, Idea Group Inc. Copying or distributing in print or electronic forms without written permission of Idea Group Inc. is prohibited.

INTRODUCTION

The introduction of the liberalized energy market in Germany has lead to important changes in the energy economy. The role of the customer has altered from a simple energy subscriber to an energy customer. Now a customer is not only consuming energy but also influencing the actual market situation. The basic idea behind this new point of view is that it should be possible for every person or organisation not only to buy but also to sell energy. The liberalised energy market provides the concept that there has to be a separation between generation, selling, and trading as well as transportation and distribution of energy. Since the energy market is not a complete new contrivance, the consisting distribution network is a fixed object.

The customer may subscribe to different energy providers. It is possible to receive the energy during the day from one provider and during the night from a different provider, or to get the basic energy level from one provider and the energy during the peak hours from another one. Therefore, it will be necessary to frequently read the information about the delivered energy from the energy meter device. That should be performed online via any communication network (wired or wireless, public or private, etc.). A high security level has to be applied to the system to protect the interests of all parties (customers, providers, energy plants, etc.).

The project Secure Electronic Data Exchange of Metering Devices (SELMA) is a project, which is funded by the German Federal Ministry of Economics and Labour (BmWA). The communication between the participants of the energy market and the provision of energy data are independent on the transport medium. SELMA project partners are energy providers, manufacturers of metering devices (Electricity, Gas) and meter management systems, the verification administration, the national metrology institute, organisations for the protection of consumer rights, the national security agency, the University of Muenster for legal aspects and the University of Siegen. The University of Siegen is responsible for the achievement of the security analysis and the development of the security concept.

This chapter focuses on the security aspects of SELMA. It describes the results of the security analysis and deducts the needed security services. The requirements by different laws will be mentioned before the security and cryptographic concepts are explained. Management aspects will be described followed by a conclusion.

SECURITY ANALYSIS

Figure 1 shows the information flow of a transaction. The metering device performs the measurement and provides the raw data (primary or secondary data depending on the type of energy and mode of measurement). The data acquisition entity accesses the metering device online via any network and reads the measurement information, which is assigned to the customer. This information is stored

Copyright © 2007, Idea Group Inc. Copying or distributing in print or electronic forms without written permission of Idea Group Inc. is prohibited.

Figure 1. Transaction model

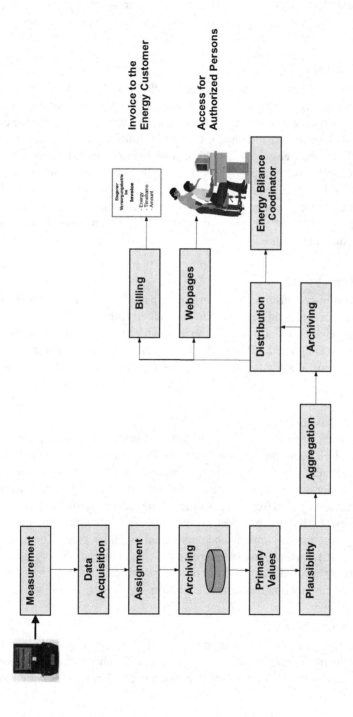

Copyright © 2007, Idea Group Inc. Copying or distributing in print or electronic forms without written permission of Idea Group Inc. is prohibited.

in an archive. Then so-called primary values are provided. Substitute information has to be added, if no data is available. All of the measurement data is checked for plausibility and corrected, if necessary. The next step supports the aggregation of measurement information. The measurement information of all locations is collected, for example, if a big customer has a general contract for all of its subsidiaries. After that phase, the information is archived again and then distributed to the energy circuit balance coordinator who plans and schedules the delivery of energy and compares the consumed energy with the energy schedules. It is also forwarded to the billing department, which issues the invoices, and to a Web server. From here, the customer can check its measurement data and the billing information. It is also the goal of the project that each customer should be able to check its bills and to build trust for the calculation of the energy costs. The original presentation and content of the measurement data can be used during their complete lifecycle.

In a first step of the security analysis, Figure 1 has been re-drawn to recognize the different interests of the engaged parties in the system. Following roles have been identified (see Figure 2).

Customer

The customer consumes the energy and pays for it. The consumed energy is recognized by a metering device, which is located at the site for the customer. The customer receives a bill from the energy provider(s) and releases some personal information to the provider. The customer may be an end customer, an energy provider, or an energy distributor. Therefore, Figure 2 can be cascaded in the horizontal direction.

Energy Provider

The energy provider purchases energy and sells it to its customers who then receive invoices about the delivered energy. The energy provider has to know the amount of delivered energy for each of its customers. The energy provider can itself collect the meter data or outsource this functionality to a third party. Therefore, the meter information is read from the customers meter device by a data acquisition party, and then forwarded to the provider. Optionally, they are summed up per customer. The billing functionality can also be outsourced to a third party. Therefore, we get additional parties, which may be interested to fraud the system.

The energy provider can also use other distribution partners. Therefore, Figure 2 can also be cascaded in the vertical direction.

Data Acquisition

Data acquisition is done by a third party. It is ordered by an energy provider to acquire the measurement information. It is double-checked; primary values are optionally calculated or replaced by substitute data. They are formatted to further

Copyright © 2007, Idea Group Inc. Copying or distributing in print or electronic forms without written permission of Idea Group Inc. is prohibited.

Figure 2. Roles in the energy market

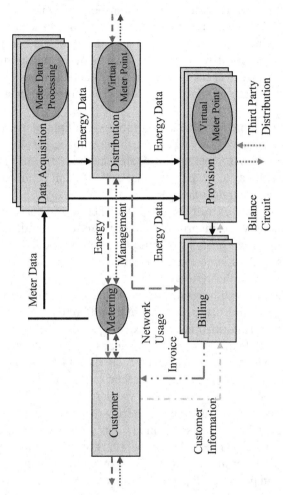

computations and forwarding. These data are now called energy data to differentiate them from the measurement data. They are normally given directly to the energy provider, sometimes also to the distributor network provider.

Billing

Billing is done by a third party. It is ordered by an energy provider to perform the billing. The invoices are printed and sent to the customer, and the customer can access the invoice and the information, which have been used for the invoice via the Internet.

Copyright © 2007, Idea Group Inc. Copying or distributing in print or electronic forms without written permission of Idea Group Inc. is prohibited.

Distribution Network Provider

The cable and pipeline system, which transports the energy, is owned by a different organization, for example, the energy provider of a municipality. The energy providers, which use these transport systems to deliver the energy to their customers, have to pay for that usage to the owners of the transport systems. The network administration can check the flow of energy and the plausibility of the sum of all energy of all energy providers of all different sources of energy, which use that transport system.

There can be multiple data acquisition entities, multiple energy providers, and multiple billing organisations serving one customer who receives the energy via one distributor. Some of the participating parties are competitors, some of them contract partners. Therefore, it has to be assumed that each of them could have an interest to enrich itself by cheating the other parties.

The next phase analyses the type of attacks. There are standard attacks by third parties on confidentiality and integrity of the transmitted or stored data. These attacks are not in the focus of this analysis because they can be encountered by standard security mechanisms. More interesting are active attacks, which can be performed by the regular partners of the system.

Such active attacks can be modifications at the site of the customer or during data transmission, or during data processing at the different locations of the partners where the measurement information is forwarded or processed (see Figure 1). Another attack is the masquerade of a system participant as a different system participant, for example, when a customer sends the data with the address of another customer. Finally, it is possible that the customers do not accept the billing because the measurement data is not authentic. These attacks are standard attacks in distributed systems mapped to the application of distributed metering devices. Nevertheless, there is a new type of attacks, which are possible in systems with different roles—federated attacks. Federated attacks are attacks by coalitions of two or more participants of the system to fraud one or more of the others. For example, a customer and a data acquisition party can perform a federated attack to cheat another customer, or two customers can build a coalition to cheat the energy provider. Therefore an in depth analysis has been achieved which partners can build coalitions with other partners to perform attacks.

These mentioned attacks are aimed on the metering information. The devices have to be remotely managed for operational and security parameters (access control, clock, logbook, etc.). Therefore, attacks on the management component and management commands and responses are also possible and have to be made impossible. Only authorized commands should be performed for management actions.

Considering all of these risks of attacks, the following security services are required:

Copyright © 2007, Idea Group Inc. Copying or distributing in print or electronic forms without written permission of Idea Group Inc. is prohibited.

- Confidentiality for personal related data
- Data integrity for measurement data and management information
- Availability of measurement data and billing information
- Authentication of Data Origin of measurement data, commands, and billing information
- Access control to measurement data and management information
- Non-Repudiation of measurement data and of receipts for measurement data

The security concept has to provide these security services. It has been decided by the project partners that it these should be based on following principles:

- Digital signatures of the measurement data are used. They should correspond technically to Qualified Signatures (according to the Digital Signature Law)
- The measurement records are extended by digital signatures, time variant parameters, additional identifications, etc.
- End-to-end authentication of the origin of the measurement data from generation until billing. End-to-end authentication implicates data integrity
- Verification of the measurement information should be possible for each of the authorized participants of the market
- Transport oriented confidentiality for transmission of personal information or sensitive data

LEGAL FRAMEWORK

The following laws have to be considered when a concept is designed for secure online measurement data exchange (the roman figures in brackets reference to the area in Figure 3, where that law is important):

- Federal Data Protection Act (BDSG) (I, II, III)
- Telecommunications Act together with Telecommunications Data Protection Ordinance (I, II, III)
- Teleservices Data Protection Act (TDDSG) (III)
- Digital Signature Act (SiG) (I, II)
- Verification Act (EichG) (I)
- Requirements of the Verification Administration/Authorities (for electronic, software controlled Metering Devices) (I)

Therefore, all domains are covered by at least one law.

Copyright © 2007, Idea Group Inc. Copying or distributing in print or electronic forms without written permission of Idea Group Inc. is prohibited.

Figure 3. Meaning of laws for the system domains

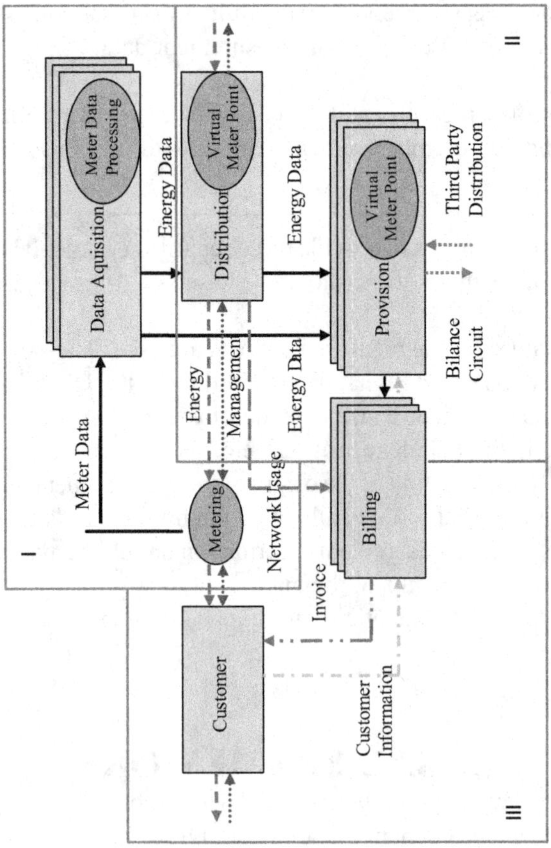

SECURITY CONCEPT

The security concept has to satisfy the requirements of the security analysis. The essential components of the security concept are:

- The metering devices are extended by a "Signature Generation Device" (MIM= Meter Identification Module). Such a "Signature Generation Device" has to be approved for the generation of "qualified digital signatures" according to the Digital Signature Law. The security level of the MIM has to be EAL 4 plus (Common Criteria) or E3 high (ITSEC)

Copyright © 2007, Idea Group Inc. Copying or distributing in print or electronic forms without written permission of Idea Group Inc. is prohibited.

- The measurement unit and the MIM are protected by a physical seal for the verification authority to prevent manipulations of the measurement unit and of the communication between the measurement unit and the MIM
- All Requests and Commands to the metering device are digitally signed and verified. They are verified the MIM using public keys which have been sent as certificates. The authorisation is checked by an Access Rights Management
- All messages from the metering devices are digitally signed by the metering device
- The metering devices should contain a real time clock, because timestamps play an important role to detect replay attacks
- Every MIM generates its own Cryptographic Key System. The private key never leaves the MIM
- Metering devices use elliptic curve cryptography (ECDSA) (ISO15946-2., 2002)
- A certified external Certification Authority delivers RSA key systems (Rivest, Shamir, & Adleman, 1978) for the verification authorities. The private key is stored on a smart card. This smart card has a similar functionality and security level as the MIM
- The verification authorities certify the (ECC) public keys of the metering devices by Qualified Signatures using as well approved digital signatures creation devices. These SELMA certificates as well as the CRL are constructed along X.509v3, rsp. X.509.2
- All certificates are published in a SELMA LDAP directory

The decision to use elliptic curve cryptography in the metering devices has been made because of many advantages of elliptic curve cryptography compared to RSA or DSA. These advantages are shown in Figure 4. The numbers have been taken from NESSIE Project IST-1999-12324 (2003). The main advantages are the size of the signatures, which are much smaller, and the speed to generate the signatures for the measurement information.

On one hand, the usage of elliptic curve cryptography in the metering devices complicates the overall cryptographic concept, because it requires a hybrid cryptographic concept. Actually, Certification Authorities issue only RSA keys and RSA based certificates, which contain public RSA keys and which are signed by the CA by using RSA. These RSA key systems are generated by the CA for the verification authorities and transported on smart cards to the owners of the keys (= verification authorities). On the other hand, it can be assumed for the future that the CAs will be able to issue also certificates for elliptic curve cryptography. Then the cryptographic concept can be simplified to a homogenous concept only using elliptic curve cryptography.

The verification authorities use their RSA key systems (received from the CA) to issue certificates about the public keys of all entities, which use elliptic curve cryptography to sign measurement or measurement equivalent data. Measurement

Copyright © 2007, Idea Group Inc. Copying or distributing in print or electronic forms without written permission of Idea Group Inc. is prohibited.

Figure 4. Comparison of RSA and ECDSA cryptography (According to NESSIE Project IST-1999-12324, 2003)

	ECDSA (GFp)	RSA 1024
System Parameter	576 Bit	.....
Private Key	192 Bit	2560 Bit
Public Key	384 Bit	1041 Bit (e=65537)
Length of Signature	384 Bit	1024 Bit
Longword Arithmetic	192 Bit	1024 Bit
Signature Time	2.6 ms	27 ms
Verification Time	6.5 ms	3 ms

equivalent data are substitute data, if no data are available, or aggregated data, for example.

All entities, which generate measurement data or measurement equivalent data like the meter device, the data acquisition, the unit of creating primary measurement data, plausibility unit, and measurement aggregation unit use a MIM (= certified digital signature generation unit) to generate the digital signature (see Figure 5).

All units, which verify measurement (equivalent) information, need a hardware or software component for the verification of digital signatures based on elliptic curves.

The billing information, which is available for customers on the Internet, is signed by using RSA, because software is available for all customers. Therefore, the departments, which create the invoices, are also equipped with RSA cryptography and RSA certificates from a CA.

There is a SELMA directory service, which publishes all certificates issued by the verifications authorities for all of the entities, which sign measurement or measurement equivalent information, so everybody is able to verify these signatures. The SELMA directory is stored on a LDAP server.

CONCEPT OF THE MANAGEMENT SYSTEM

There is an online management system to control the metering devices. There are two parts of the management system. One is responsible for parameters and information, which are under control of the verification authorities (management of verified components); the other is under control of the provider (management of non-verified components). The verification authorities are responsible for the security management and device management (parameters concerning the measurement); the provider may control the other parameters.

Copyright © 2007, Idea Group Inc. Copying or distributing in print or electronic forms without written permission of Idea Group Inc. is prohibited.

Figure 5. Cryptographic hybrid system of digital signature algorithms

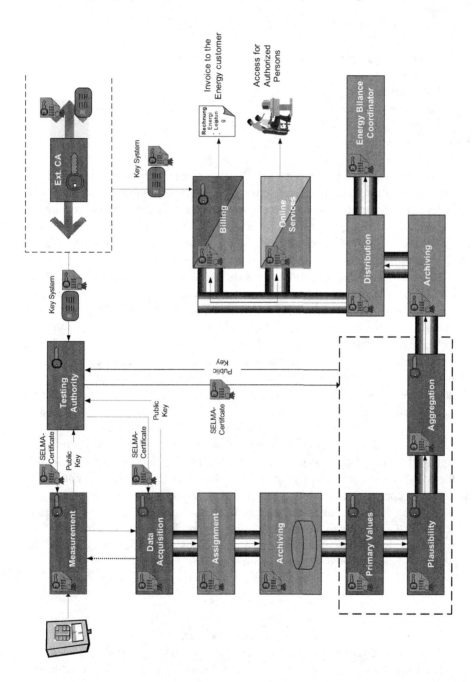

Copyright © 2007, Idea Group Inc. Copying or distributing in print or electronic forms without written permission of Idea Group Inc. is prohibited.

The security management of the verification authorities supports the following functions:

- Read the public key
- Initiate the generation of a new key system (ECDSA)
- Initiate the exchange of an old key by a new
- Load certificates
- Load access rights
- Set or adjust the clock
- Read/reset the logbook

The metering devices perform only elliptic curve cryptography. Therefore, the management stations have to also use elliptic curve cryptography. The management units for verified parameters also use a hardware-based unit (MIM) to generate the digital signatures. Management units for non-verified components may use software-based solutions. Therefore, certificates containing public elliptic curve keys signed by RSA keys have to also be issued for these management stations.

There exists a complex structure inside the MIM for the management of access rights. It is based on certificates which are loaded by authorized entities. The certificate is verified and the public key is stored inside the MIM. During the first initialisation of the metering device, which is done locally by a verification authority, two certificates of the organisation of the verification authorities are stored. These two certificates have a function like master certificates or root certificates, because all certificates of the different verification authorities have to be verified by one of these root certificates. The provider, who is generally the owner of the metering device, enlists itself as the provider to the metering device by loading its SELMA certificate, rsp. the public key. The provider enlists the verification authorities, which are ordered by the provider to achieve the verification actions. Therefore, a complete chain of public keys corresponding to the roles in the systems are loaded to the MIM. Each command has to be signed by the entity, which is entitled to achieve this command according to the access right management.

A strong focus has been put on practical management aspects, which may arise during the lifetime of a metering device. Examples are the sale of a provider organisation, the change of the ordered verifications authorities on behalf of the provider, and the change of data acquisition entities.

CONCLUSION

The liberalized energy market requires frequent and on time reading of metering information. All authorized participants should have easy access to measurement data, which are relevant for them. The measurement information presents a high

Copyright © 2007, Idea Group Inc. Copying or distributing in print or electronic forms without written permission of Idea Group Inc. is prohibited.

Figure 6. Management system

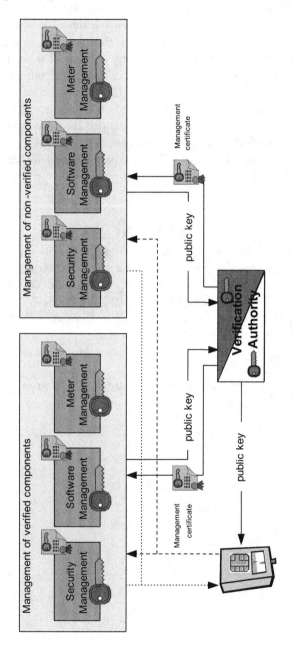

Copyright © 2007, Idea Group Inc. Copying or distributing in print or electronic forms without written permission of Idea Group Inc. is prohibited.

money equivalent value. A high security level is requested by all market participants as well as by verification authorities, metrological institute, national security agency, personal data protectors, and consumer rights protectors. The SELMA project has developed standards for a secure solution for metering devices in a liberalized energy market which are approved by all participating partners. The security solution is compatible to standard public key infrastructures and uses technologically qualified signatures according to the Digital Signature Law. A number of metering devices and management systems have been developed and tested in a field trial.

The concept is exemplary and can be extended for many other applications, which have to be verified by law (scales and pumping stations).

Further information about the project, the partners, and the technology can be found under www.selma-project.de.

REFERENCES

ISO15946-2. (2002). ISO/IEC JTC1/SC27–*Information technology—Security techniques—Cryptographic techniques based on elliptic curves, Part 2—Digital Signatures. Switzerland, International Standardisation Organi*sation.

NESSIE Project IST-1999-12324. (2003, February 20). *Public Report: Performance of Optimized Implementations of the NESSIE Primitives, (*Version 2.0.) Brussels, European Community.

Rivest, R., Shamir, A., & Adleman, L. (1978). *A method of obtaining digital signatures.* CACM, 21, 120-126.

SELMA. (2006). *Sicherer ELektronischer Messdaten-Austausch.* Retrieved February 20, 2006, from http://www.selma-project.de

Copyright © 2007, Idea Group Inc. Copying or distributing in print or electronic forms without written permission of Idea Group Inc. is prohibited.

Chapter VII

Deployment of E-Government Municipal Services:
Enforcement of Security Policies

Nikolaos Oikonomidis, University of Siegen, Germany

Sergiu Tcaciuc, University of Siegen, Germany

Christoph Ruland, University of Siegen, Germany

ABSTRACT

This chapter presents the research results on reliable enforcement of security policies for electronic services deployment in small- and medium-sized governmental organisations (SMGOs). Motivation for this research has been the fact that SMGOs interact frequently with citizens and/or businesses, to offer paper-based and electronic services, which utilize a limited number of resources, such as employees and funds. SMGOs also interact with each other in local or cross-border transactions, exchanging information on behalf of citizens, businesses or the organisation itself. There is an obvious need for a secure, interoperable, and cost-effective e-government platform that addresses the requirements of SMGOs, improves the quality of the citizens' involvement, and strengthens the fundamental structure of these organisations.

Copyright © 2007, Idea Group Inc. Copying or distributing in print or electronic forms without written permission of Idea Group Inc. is prohibited.

INTRODUCTION

Citizens interact regularly with the municipalities or the municipal organisations. Public administrations offer a variety of services like requests/processing of certificates, (local) tax payment, and promotion of city information. An effective and efficient service provision brings benefits to both municipalities and the involved citizens/customers of the particular services. Electronic services provide a unique opportunity to enhance and expand the offered services by making them more flexible, since they may provide location and time independent access for the citizens, enhancing their mobility. Rapid execution of services that might otherwise require a considerable amount of time and effort and a one-stop service provision are one of the main scopes of SMGOs. These benefits are not realisable where there is a lack of the proper infrastructure to serve citizens, such as in small municipalities with limited resources and/or large areas of responsibilities. Provision of such electronic services can be achieved with the use of multimodal access mechanisms (e-mayor Consortium, 2004). Due to the fact that exchanged data in forms and documents may contain private or sensitive data, it is imperative to introduce security mechanisms that guarantee to citizens and businesses a trustworthy means of communication via a network that may be insecure, such as the Internet. Trust is also a strong requirement in such an environment. It can be achieved through the use of cryptographic mechanisms (e.g., through the use of electronic signatures and timestamps) that assure the security requirements of confidentiality, authentication of data and users, integrity of content, and non-repudiation by the receiver. Appliance of such security mechanisms affords secure exchange of documents and identification between citizens/businesses and SMGOs. It is the base for trust toward the whole system (e-mayor Consortium, 2004). This chapter presents a subset of the mentioned security requirements, namely authentication and authorisation under the scope of access control policies.

Next, the e-mayor project is introduced as well a high-level description of the system architecture. The main chapter addresses the aspects of policy enforcement for local and cross-border municipal e-government services. At the end, conclusion, lessons learned and an outlook are given.

EMAYOR PROJECT

E-Mayor (IST-2003-507217) addresses the specific audience of SMGOs across Europe. This project looks especially at transactions that are performed on a European level. Such services typically handle the secure exchange of documents, forms, and other information across national borders. The terms of "SMGO" and "cross-border service" has been defined by the e-mayor consortium. All participating municipalities fall into the category of SMGOs. The target group for e-mayor comprises municipalities up to half a million citizens normally located in urban or metropolitan areas. e-mayor aims to contribute toward the provision of secure and

Copyright © 2007, Idea Group Inc. Copying or distributing in print or electronic forms without written permission of Idea Group Inc. is prohibited.

interoperable e-government services. The chosen approach results into a generic platform (e-mayor platform) hosting municipal services that are designed, adapted, and implemented considering specific stakeholder needs, and then validated within several municipalities. Related work can be found in other European projects like (Intelcities) and (RISER).

E-Mayor System Architecture

The system design resulted to the specification of an architecture, which is described at the top-level, as a set of components, each one comprising certain functionalities (Figure 1).

- User interface communicates with the service handling for the actual provisioning of the service to the users
- Policy enforcement encapsulates functionalities such as auditing, access control, and security mechanisms
- Service handling represents the core of the system and has dependencies to all other packages.
- Format transformation is responsible for transforming documents from a country-bound local format to a universal format and vice versa.
- Content routing provides forwarding functionality for requests and legal documents from one platform to another
- The Municipal systems adaptation is the linking point with the existing (legacy) systems of the municipalities
- The persistent storage modules handle storage to the file system or databases

Figure 1. E-mayor system components

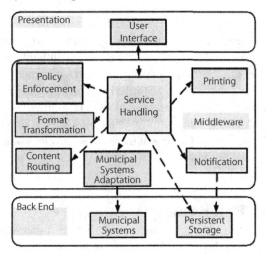

Copyright © 2007, Idea Group Inc. Copying or distributing in print or electronic forms without written permission of Idea Group Inc. is prohibited.

- Output notification and printing provide support for notification and printing services

POLICY ENFORCEMENT FOR LOCAL AND CROSS-BORDER E-GOVERNMENT SERVICES

Enforcement of security policies depends on many factors. Each governmental organisation maintains a set of security policies specifically for its internal assets. Security policies related to the interaction with other governmental organisations may be considered but often not implemented. Interoperability of governmental electronic services between different countries has been raised as an issue in the recent years. Frameworks exist partly as results of research projects and the initiative to provide common frameworks established from official supranational organisations has just been started. In this section, a conceptual architecture is presented that provides security policy enforcement for cross-border e-government services.

Platforms that enable the collaboration of e-government domains have a high geographical distribution which consequently leads to a high distribution of computational resources. Such a distribution includes:

- Interaction between a citizen who accesses the e-government platform from a private/public computer
- Interaction with the civil servant who is involved in the transaction of the service provision that the citizen requested
- Interaction of computational components in a national e-government platform
- Interaction of computational components between two e-government platforms (collaborating domains)

Depending on the specific requirements, the security of the transport layer can be enforced by the use of relevant protocols (e.g., transport layer security/secure socket layer) (Thomas, 2000). Each user should be authenticated before using the system as well as during the service execution. Deployment of authentication mechanisms fulfills this requirement. Similarly, domain protection against attacks is enforced by the use of appropriate technologies (e.g., firewalls that circumvent the e-government domains). Such requirements are gathered into rules that can be expressed in form of policies. Mapping of these rules into electronic format together with an architecture that enforces these electronic policies can provide the required security set by the SMGOs.

Security Policy Enforcement Architecture

The proposed architecture for security policy enforcement is depicted in Figure 2. In general, a multi-tier architecture can be considered. The presentation

Copyright © 2007, Idea Group Inc. Copying or distributing in print or electronic forms without written permission of Idea Group Inc. is prohibited.

layer is represented by the Web tier. The business layer comprises of the service handling, together with the policy enforcer, the policy enforcement points (PEPs), and the policy decision point (PDP). Since the focus in this section is on security policy enforcement, all components that interact with the service handling in order to provide e-government services are not shown in the diagram. However, they are considered to be present. Further, in order to provide a technical insight, the components that provide the underlying functionality for the platform architecture are shown in the figure. To describe them shortly, the Web application server provides the user interface to the client and is an access point to the e-government platform. Enterprise application server is used for the invocation of the platform functional components. Business process execution language server (BPEL Server) (Matjaz, Mathew, & Sarang, 2003) is used for the coordination of the platform functional components.

The protocol used to access the policy enforcer whenever this is required, starts with the client login procedure via the Web application server. The first policy that is applied in this step is the mutual (both server and client) authentication that is needed in order for the client to make use of the e-government services. In Figure 2, there is no direct connection from the Web application server to the policy enforcer; however, it is a valid option to provide a policy enforcer and consequently a PEP that lies in the Web application server and issues policy driven request to the depicted PDP. After successful authentication, the Web application server calls the Web tier component for providing the appropriate user interface to the e-government services. Web tier consequently calls the service handling to create an access session in order to keep track of the user's activities while he or she is logged in the platform. Service handling retrieves the profile of the user from the policy enforcer, according to the credentials provided by him or her. Policy enforcer checks the validity of the user credentials. It is assumed that the user credentials are valid. In that case, policy enforcer retrieves the user profile—or creates a new one if the user logged for the first time into the system—and returns it to the service handling.

After a successful user authentication and access session assignment, the user is presented with a list of possible services he or she is eligible to use. As in the previous case, the protocol of a service provision starts from the client who invokes one of the listed services. The Web tier signals the service handling to create a service session for the given access session. Service handling forwards a request for desired service access to the policy enforcer. Additionally, service handling forwards the user profile that was retrieved in the previous step again to the policy enforcer. After policy enforcement process is complete, the policy enforcer returns a statement on permission or denial for this service access. In the positive case, the user is permitted to proceed with the chosen e-government service. The interaction between Policy Enforcer, PEPs and PDP is based on the XACML principles and mechanisms (OASIS, 2003).

Copyright © 2007, Idea Group Inc. Copying or distributing in print or electronic forms without written permission of Idea Group Inc. is prohibited.

Figure 2. Security policy enforcement architecture in an e-government domain

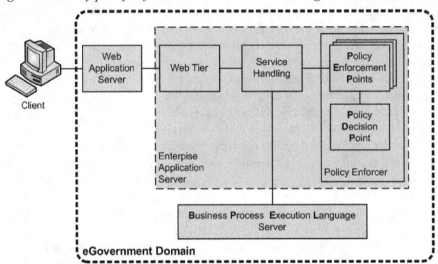

Figure 2 shows the policy enforcement architecture in a single e-government domain. In an environment of cross-border e-government services deployment, the proposed architecture should be present in each participating organisation. The distributed nature of this architecture has many advantages over a central conception of policy enforcement whereas the most significant advantage is the fact that there is no single point of failure due to the distribution of the policy enforcement components. The ability for each collaborating e-government domain to specify and implement its own policies is another major advantage. When common policies should apply, appropriate synchronisation protocols may be deployed to achieve that goal. Even in the case of synchronized policies, localized policies may apply. Figure 3 depicts a simplified view of the full architecture with the distributed policy enforcers. It should be noted that the service-handling component of each domain platform is the "steering wheel" for the interaction with the other domains. Policy enforcer makes use of policy information objects according to local, national, and /or supranational (e.g., EU) regulations.

Policy Information Object

A policy information object represents the constraints, conditions, and rules that will have to be respected and enforced by the platform. A policy will reflect any organisational policies that apply to service processing, computational, and human resources. The term policy is defined in ISO/IEC 15414 (ISO, 2002) as a "sentence" which consists of special "words." These words reflect obligation, authorisation, and permission or prohibition. Such a sentence has—as in the normal grammatical

Copyright © 2007, Idea Group Inc. Copying or distributing in print or electronic forms without written permission of Idea Group Inc. is prohibited.

Figure 3. Distributed policy enforcement architecture for collaborating e-government domains

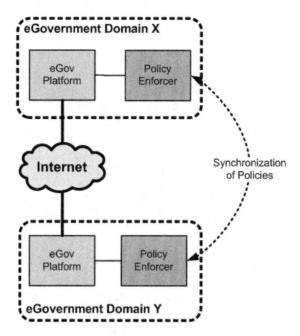

case—subjects, verbs, objects, and conditional adverbs. Additionally, constraints on possible actions are also introduced by verbs.

Putting these terms into the information model, the structure depicted in Figure 4 has been designed specifically for access control policies. The e-govAccessControl Policy consists of the following elements:

- **Target:** Which resource is accessed?
- **Subject:** Who wants to access the resource?
- **Condition:** What is required to access the resource?
- **Action:** What is asked to be done on/with the resource?
- **Evaluation Scheme:** Provides the result of the combination of the evaluation of all policy conditions

The E-GovPolicySubject represents the entity which will invoke one or more E-GovPolicyAction objects. An e-govPolicyAction takes effect on an E-GovPolicyTarget. One or more e-govPolicyCondition objects provide the conditions that allow or deny the invocation of the respective e-govPolicyAction objects. In the

Copyright © 2007, Idea Group Inc. Copying or distributing in print or electronic forms without written permission of Idea Group Inc. is prohibited.

Figure 4. Elements of a policy information object

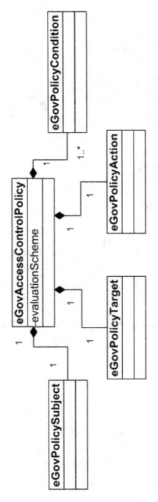

following sections, two examples of access control policies (i.e., authentication policy and authorisation policy) are presented. The depicted policies are enforced within the e-mayor platform.

Authentication Policy

The authentication policies set authenticates and identifies users according to their credentials (Figure 5). This policies set includes the authentication policies that apply to each collaborating e-government domain. The root policy is driven by an "all permit" combining algorithm, meaning that all other policies that exist in the

Copyright © 2007, Idea Group Inc. Copying or distributing in print or electronic forms without written permission of Idea Group Inc. is prohibited.

policy tree should evaluate with "Permit" in order for the e-government platform to provide successful user authentication and enable the user to proceed with the use of e-government services. The first level of policies consists of the CertificateTrustedPolicy, the RolePolicy, and the IssuerCAPolicy. CertificateTrustedPolicy deals with the trustworthiness of the cryptographic (PKI) certificate that the user has provided for authentication. Permission or denial of this policy depends on the evaluation of the user credentials including validation against CRL. The IssuerCAPolicy ensures the access of the users holding credentials issued by a specific CA or a list of CAs. Cross certification of CAs can be considered in this policy. The user role is checked in the RolePoliciesSet that specifies a policy for each user role. The policy names of the RolePoliciesSet are self-explanatory. The roles that exist in e-mayor are Citizen, Civil Servant, Administrator, and Server. Each of these roles has access to specific resources. Further, the presented platform is designed in such a way that only citizens of the country where each e-government platform is located can login. In this case, the country is Germany (DE), thus, a check of the country in the user certificate is also a rule that applies to the role policies.

The role Server is a special case that depicts a server certificate used for TLS/SSL mutual authentication between national and cross-border e-mayor platform instances. If the role is Server, the country of origin is not considered by this policy.

Authorisation Policy

After successful authentication, the policy applied is the one that provides authorisation to a specific service. Presented next is an example of an authorisation policy for a service that provides residence certification (Figure 6). ResidenceCertificationAuthorisationPolicy consists of three policies that apply to specific steps of the residence certification service. A certificate of residence is requested, approved, and finally issued. In some cases where cross-border issuance is desired, the approval of the request together with the request are forwarded from one platform instance to another. A request of a residence certificate can be initiated by a user with the role of citizen or civil servant. An approval of a pending request can be initiated only by a user with the role of civil servant.

After the process of the request by the municipal system, a document (certificate of residence) is generated. This document must be approved by a civil servant. ResidenceCertification-DocumentApprovalPolicy covers this step. Finally, an approved residence certification request can be forwarded only by an entity with the role of Server. This step is critical for the cross-border deployment of e-government services and enables the enforcement of cross-border policies. Cross-border policies are defined as the union of the policies that apply locally to each participating platform instance in a cross-border service deployment. Such policies are enforced in the case where the process that drives the service provision migrates from one platform instance to another. Cross-border policies can cover interregional as well as international cooperation policies, where applicable.

Copyright © 2007, Idea Group Inc. Copying or distributing in print or electronic forms without written permission of Idea Group Inc. is prohibited.

Figure 5. Authentication policies of e-mayor

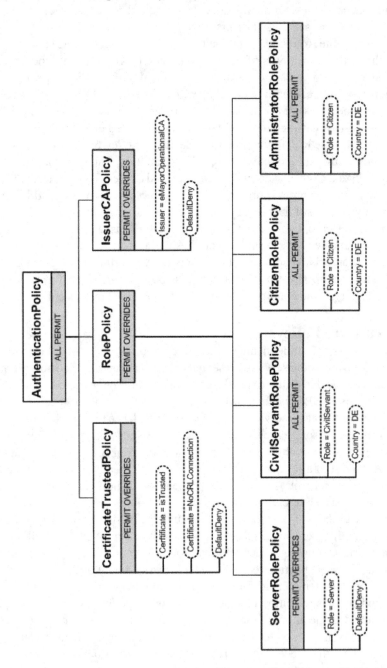

Copyright © 2007, Idea Group Inc. Copying or distributing in print or electronic forms without written permission of Idea Group Inc. is prohibited.

Figure 6. Authorisation policies of the e-mayor service "Residence Certifica-tion."

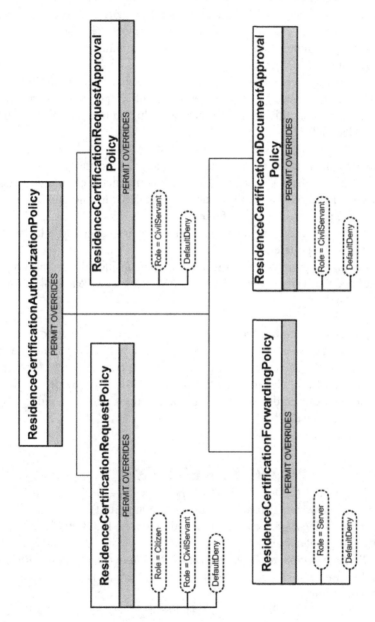

Copyright © 2007, Idea Group Inc. Copying or distributing in print or electronic forms without written permission of Idea Group Inc. is prohibited.

CONCLUSION AND OUTLOOK

The introduced architecture for security policy enforcement is a major research topic that addresses many problems which should be solved in order to achieve the desired provision of electronic governmental services. The e-mayor approach complies with government organisations' existing administrative infrastructure, enabling provision of new services.

Security policies synchronisation and management across multiple domains (national and supranational) are not required at the initial stage of e-government deployment but plays a significant role for achieving higher mobility of the citizens.

Lessons learned:

- E-government services must be based on end-to-end security.
- Security mechanisms provided by different components of an e-government platform should be in line with platform requirements and applied by units such as the presented policy enforcer.
- Security policy enforcement should be driven by interoperable, adaptable and synchronisable policies.
- Security provision in e-government should be considered as an accompanying service that can be adapted to the specific needs of each e-government application.

The approach that has been presented encompasses the intention to extend and continue the ongoing research and provide a reliable architecture that integrates security policy enforcement into municipal electronic environments. Further, the proposed architecture is planed to be enhanced in order to provide solutions to privacy issues in cross-border scenarios. These solutions will be integrated in the policy enforcement layer.

REFERENCES

E-mayor Consortium. (2004). D2.1 *Municipal services—analysis, requirements, and usage scenarios.* Brussels, European Community.

Intelcities. (2006). *Intelligent cities.* Retrieved February 15, 2006, from http://intelcities.iti.gr/intelcities

ISO. (2002). *Information technology—Open distributed processing—Reference model—Enterprise language.* Switzerland: International Organisation for Standardisation.

Matjaz, B., Mathew, B., & Sarang, P. (2004). *Business process execution language for Web services.* Birmingham, UK: Packt Publishing.

OASIS. (2003). *Core specification, eXtensible Access Control Markup Language (XACML) (Version 1.)* USA, OASIS.

Copyright © 2007, Idea Group Inc. Copying or distributing in print or electronic forms without written permission of Idea Group Inc. is prohibited.

RISER. (2006). *Trans-European e-government for business and citizen.* Retrieved February 15, 2006, from http://www.riser.eu.com/

Thomas, S. (2000). *SSL and TLS essentials securing the Web.* New York: John Wiley & Sons Inc.

Copyright © 2007, Idea Group Inc. Copying or distributing in print or electronic forms without written permission of Idea Group Inc. is prohibited.

Chapter VIII

E-Government and Denial of Service Attacks

Aikaterini Mitrokotsa, University of Piraeus, Greece

Christos Douligeris, University of Piraeus, Greece

ABSTRACT

The use of electronic technologies in government services has played a significant role in making citizens' lives more convenient. Even though the transition to digital governance has great advantages for the quality of government services it may be accompanied with many security threats. One of the major threats and hardest security problems e-government faces are the denial of service (DoS) attacks. DoS attacks have already taken some of the most popular e-government sites off-line for several hours causing enormous losses and repair costs. In this chapter, important incidents of DoS attacks and results from surveys that indicate the seriousness of the problem are presented. In order to limit the problem of DoS attacks in government organizations, we also present a list of best practices that can be used to combat the problem together with a classification of attacks and defense mechanisms.

Copyright © 2007, Idea Group Inc. Copying or distributing in print or electronic forms without written permission of Idea Group Inc. is prohibited.

INTRODUCTION

Since we live in a world where electronic and Internet technologies are playing an important role in helping us lead easier lives, local and state governments are required to adopt and participate in this technology revolution. Digital government or e-government technologies and procedures allow local and national governments to disseminate information and provide services to their citizens and organisations in an efficient and convenient way resulting in reducing waiting lines in offices and in minimizing the time to pick up and return forms and process and acquire information. This modernization of government facilitates the connection and cross cooperation of authorities in several levels of government—central, regional, and local—allowing an easy interchange of data and access to databases and resources that would be impossible otherwise.

E-government undoubtedly makes citizens' lives and communication easier by saving time, by avoiding and bypassing the bureaucracy, and by cutting down paper work. It also provides the same opportunities for communication with government not only to people in cities but also to people in rural areas. Moreover, e-government permits greater access to information, improves public services, and promotes democratic processes.

This shift to technology use and the transition to a "paperless government" is constantly increasing. According to Holden, Norris, and Fletcher (2003), in 1995 8.7% of local governments had Web sites, while in 2003 this number showed an increase that reached 83%. Despite these encouraging statistics, the adoption of digital government proceeds with a slow pace as security issues, like confidentiality and reliability, affect the fast progress of e-government. Since e-government is mainly based on Internet technologies, it faces the danger of interconnectivity and the well-documented vulnerabilities of the Internet infrastructure. The Institute for E-Government Competence Center (IFG.CC, 2002) states that in 2002, 36 government Web sites were victims of intrusions. Most of the e-government attacks have taken place in Asia (25%) and more precisely in China and Singapore (19%), as well as in the USA (19%).

According to the U.S. Subcommittee on Oversight and Investigations (2001), the FedCIRC incident records indicate that in 1998 the number of incidents that were reported was 376, affecting 2,732 U.S. Government systems. In 1999, there were 580 incidents causing damage on 1,306,271 U.S. Government systems and in 2000 there were 586 incidents having impact on 575,568 U.S. government systems. Symantec (2004) (Volume VI, released September 2004, activity between January 2004 and June 2004) gives information about Government specific attack data. In this report, one can see that the third most common attack e-government has faced, besides worm-related attacks and the Slammer worm, is the TCP SYN Flood denial of service attack.

So in order to have effective e-government services without interruptions in Web access as well as e-mail and database services, there is a need for protection

Copyright © 2007, Idea Group Inc. Copying or distributing in print or electronic forms without written permission of Idea Group Inc. is prohibited.

against DoS attacks. Only with reliable e-government services not threatened by DoS attacks governments may gain the trust and confidence of citizens.

Moore, Voelker, and Savage (2001) state that the denial of service (DoS) attacks constitute one of the greatest threats in globally connected networks, whose impact has been well demonstrated in the computer network literature and have recently plagued not only government agencies but also well known online companies. The main aim of DoS is the disruption of services by attempting to limit access to a machine or service. This results in a network incapable of providing normal service either because its bandwidth or its connectivity has been compromised. These attacks achieve their goal by sending at a victim a stream of packets in such a high rate so that the network is rendered unable to provide services to its regular clients.

Distributed denial of service (DDoS) is a relatively simple, yet very powerful, technique to attack Internet resources. DDoS attacks add the many-to-one dimension to the DoS problem making the prevention and mitigation of such attacks more difficult and their impact proportionally severe.

DDoS attacks are comprised of packet streams from disparate sources. These attacks use many Internet hosts in order to exhaust the resources of the target and cause denial of service to legitimate clients. DoS or DDoS attacks exploit the advantage of varying packet fields in order to avoid being traced back and characterized. The traffic is usually so aggregated that it is difficult to distinguish between legitimate packets and attack packets. More importantly, the attack volume is often larger than the system can handle. Unless special care is taken, a DDoS victim can suffer damages ranging from system shutdown and file corruption to total or partial loss of services.

Extremely sophisticated, "user-friendly," and powerful DDoS toolkits are available to potential attackers increasing the danger that an e-government site becomes a victim in a DoS or a DDoS attack by someone without a detailed knowledge of software and Internet technologies. Most of the DDoS attack tools are very simple and have a small memory size something that is exploited by attackers, who achieve easily implementation and manage to carefully hide the code. Attackers constantly modify their tools to bypass security systems developed by system managers and researchers, who are in a constant alert to modify their approaches in order to combat new attacks.

The attackers in order to have more devastating results change their tactics and the way they launch DoS attacks. One of these tactics is the silent degradation of services for a long period of time in order to exhaust a large amount of bandwidth instead of a quick disruption of network services.

The result of these attacks in government organisations among others include reduced or unavailable network connectivity and, consequently, reduction of the organisation's ability to conduct legitimate business on the network for an extended period of time. The duration and the impact of the attack depends on the number of

Copyright © 2007, Idea Group Inc. Copying or distributing in print or electronic forms without written permission of Idea Group Inc. is prohibited.

possible attack networks. It is also worth bearing in mind that even if an organisation is not the target of an attack, it may experience increased network latency and packet losses, or possibly a complete outage, as it may be used from the attacker in order to launch a DDoS attack.

In this chapter, we stress the severity that a DoS attack may have for e-government agencies. To this end, statistics and characteristic incidents of DoS attacks in e-government agencies are presented. Furthermore, we present a classification of DoS and DDoS attacks, so that one can have a good view of the potential problems. Moreover, we outline a list of best practices that can be used in government organisations in order to further strengthen the security of their systems and to help them protect their systems from being a part of a distributed attack or being a target of DoS/DDoS attacks. Long-term countermeasures are also proposed that should be adopted for more efficient solutions to the problem.

Following this introduction, this chapter is organised as follows. In the section "Denial of Service Attacks" the problem of DoS attacks is investigated, DoS incidents and results from surveys related to DoS attacks, and a classification of DoS attacks are presented. In the section "Distributed Denial of Service Attacks" the problem of DDoS attacks is introduced, giving the basic characteristics of well known DDoS tools, and presenting a taxonomy of DDoS attacks. In the section "Classification of DDoS Defense Mechanisms," we present the DDoS defense problems and propose a classification of DDoS defense mechanisms. In the section "Best Practices for Defeating Denial of Service Attacks" best practices for defeating DoS attacks that can be used by government organizations are presented, while in the section "Long Term Countermeasures" some long-term efforts against DoS attacks are presented.

DENIAL OF SERVICE ATTACKS

Defining Denial of Service Attacks

The WWW Security FAQ (Stein & Stewart, 2002) states that "a DoS attack can be described as an attack designed to render a computer or network incapable of providing normal services." In a DoS attack, a computer or network resource is blocked or degraded resulting in unavailable system resources but not necessarily in the damage of data.

The most common DoS attacks target the computer network's bandwidth or connectivity (Stein & Stewart, 2002). In bandwidth attacks, the network is flooded with a high volume of traffic leading to the exhaustion of all available network resources, so that legitimate user requests cannot get through, resulting in degraded productivity. In connectivity attacks, a computer is flooded with a high volume of connection requests leading to the exhaustion of all available operating system resources, thus rendering the computer unable to process legitimate user requests.

Copyright © 2007, Idea Group Inc. Copying or distributing in print or electronic forms without written permission of Idea Group Inc. is prohibited.

Denial of Service Incidents

Undoubtedly, DoS attacks are a threatening problem for the Internet, causing disastrous financial losses by rendering organisations' sites off-line for a significant amount of time as we can easily confirm by frequent news reports naming as victims of DoS attacks well-known large organisations with significant exposure in the e-economy.

Howard (1998) reports denial of service attacks' statistics where one can see the dramatic increase in such attacks even in the first years of the Web. The Internet Worm (Spafford, 1998) was a prominent story in the news because it "DoS-ed" hundreds of machines. But it was in 1999 when a completely new breed of DoS attacks appeared. The so-called distributed denial of service attacks stroke a huge number of prominent Web sites.

Criscuolo (2000) reports that the first DDoS attack occurred at the University of Minnesota in August 1999. The attack, flooding the Relay chat server, lasted for two days and it was estimated that at least 214 systems were involved in the attack launch. In February 2000, a series of massive denial-of-service (DoS) attacks rendered out of service several Internet e-commerce sites including Yahoo.com. This attack kept Yahoo off the Internet for 2 hours and lead Yahoo a significant advertising loss. In October 2002 (Fox News, 2002), 13 routers that provide the DNS service to Internet users were victims of a DDoS attack. Although the attack lasted only for an hour, 7 of the 13 root servers were shut down, something that indicates the potential vulnerability of the Internet to DDoS attacks. In January of 2001, Microsoft's (WindowsITPro, 2001) Web sites hosting Hotmail, MSN, Expedia, and other major services were inaccessible for about 22 hours because of a DDoS attack. Despite attacks on high-profile sites, the majority of the attacks are not well publicized for obvious reasons.

CERT (2001) reports that in July 2001, the Whitehouse Web site was the target of the Code Red worm. The attack on the Whitehouse lasted from about 8 a.m. to about 11:15 a.m. Between 1 p.m. and 2 p.m., page request continued failing, while after 2 p.m. the site was occasionally inaccessible. In order to alleviate the effects of the attack, the Whitehouse momentarily changed the IP address of the Whitehouse. gov Web site.

Sophos.com (2002) reports that in June 2002, the Pakistani's Government Web site accepted a DoS attack that was launched by Indian sympathizers. The attack was launched through a widespread Internet worm called W32/Yaha-E, which encouraged Indian hackers and virus writers to launch an attack against Pakistan Government sites. The worm arrived as an e-mail attachment and its subject was relative to love and friendship. The worm highlighted the political tensions between Indian and Pakistan and managed to render the www.pak.gov.pk Web site unreachable. The worm created a file on infected computers that urged others to participate in the attack against the Pakistani government.

Copyright © 2007, Idea Group Inc. Copying or distributing in print or electronic forms without written permission of Idea Group Inc. is prohibited.

ITworld.com (2001) reports that even the site of CERT was the victim of a DDoS attack on May 28, 2001. Although the CERT Coordination Center is the first place where someone can find valuable information in order to be prevented against malicious cyber attacks it was knocked offline for two days by a DDoS attack accepting information at rates several hundred times higher than normal.

Cs3.Inc (2005) reports that a DDoS attack was launched on the U.S. Pacific command in April 2001. The source addresses of the attack belonged to the People's Republic of China, although the exact origin of the attack has yet not been identified. Despite the fact that the internal networks of the command were not affected, in the long-term no one can deny the fact that critical government operations may be easily disrupted by attackers. After this incident, the political tension between the two countries increased considerably. The U.S. government worries that U.S. critical network assets may be a target of a DDoS attack as a digital continuation of the terrorist attacks against New York in September of 2001. But government systems can not only be victims of DoS attacks, but may also be used unwittingly in order for a DoS attack to be performed by hosting the agents of a DDoS attack, thus participating involuntarily in the conduction of the attack.

Moore et al. (2001) report that in February of 2001, UCSD network researchers from the San Diego Supercomputer Center (SDSC) and the Jacobs School of Engineering analyzed the worldwide pattern of malicious denial-of-service (DoS) attacks against the computers of corporations, universities, and private individuals. They proposed a new technique, called "backscatter analysis" that gives an estimate of worldwide denial of service activity. This research provided the only publicly available data quantifying denial of service activity in the Internet and enabled network engineers to understand the nature of DoS attacks.

The researchers used data sets that were collected and analyzed in a three-week long period. They assessed the number, duration, and focus of the attacks, in order to characterize their behaviour and observed that more than 12,000 attacks against more than 5,000 distinct targets, ranging from well-known e-commerce companies to small foreign Internet service providers and even individual personal computers on dial-up connections. Some of the attacks flooded their targets with more than 600,000 messages/packets per second.

In addition, they reported that 50% of the attacks were less than ten minutes in duration, 80% were less than thirty minutes, and 90% lasted less than an hour. Two percent of the attacks were longer than five hours, 1% is greater than ten hours, and a few dozen spanned multiple days. Furthermore, according to this research, 90% were TCP-based attacks and around 40% reached rates as high as 500 packets per second (pps) or greater. Analyzed attacks peaked at around 500,000 pps, while other anecdotal sources report larger attacks consuming 35 megabits per second (Mbps) for periods of around 72 hours, with high-volume attacks reaching 800 Mbps.

The Computer Security Institute (2003) in the 2003 CSI/FBI survey reported that denial of service attacks represent more than a third among the WWW site

Copyright © 2007, Idea Group Inc. Copying or distributing in print or electronic forms without written permission of Idea Group Inc. is prohibited.

incidents, where unauthorized access or misuse was conducted. Forty-two percent of respondents to the 2003 survey reported DoS attacks. In 2000, 27% reported such attacks. There appears to be a significant upward trend in DoS attacks. The Computer Security Institute (2004) in the 2004 CSI/FBI survey reported that the highest reported financial losses due to a single DoS attack increased from $1 million in 1998 to $26 million in 2004 and emerged for the first time as the incident type generating the largest total losses.

We should also keep in mind that many government organisations interpret DDoS attacks as simply being an experience of inadequate service from their ISP and are not aware that they are under attack. This has as result the fact that nine out of ten DDoS attacks go unreported. In spite of such evidence, most government organisations overlook the necessity of using preventive mechanisms to combat DoS attacks.

Although there is no panacea for all types of DoS attacks, there are many defense mechanisms that can be used in order to make the launch of an attack more difficult and provide the means to reach the disclosure of the identity of the attacker.

Denial of Service Attack Classification

DoS attacks can be classified into five categories based on the attacked protocol level. More specifically, Karig and Lee (2001) divide DoS attacks in attacks in the *Network Device Level*, the *OS Level*, *application based attacks*, *data flooding attacks*, and *attacks based on protocol features*.

DoS attacks in the Network Device Level include attacks that might be caused either by taking advantage of bugs or weaknesses in software, or by exhausting the hardware resources of network devices. One example of a network device exploit is the one that is caused by a buffer-overrun error in the password checking routine. Using this exploit, certain routers (Karig et al., 2001) could be crashed if the connection to the router is performed via telnet and entering extremely long passwords.

The OS level DoS attacks (Karig et al., 2001) take advantage of the ways protocols are implemented by operating systems. One example of this category of DoS attacks is the Ping of Death attack (Insecure.org, 1997). In this attack, ICMP echo requests having data sizes greater than the maximum IP standard size are sent to the victim. This attack often results in the crashing the victim's machine.

Application-based attacks try to take a machine or a service out of order either by exploiting bugs in network applications that are running on the target host or by using such applications to drain the resources of their victim. It is also possible that the attacker may have found points of high algorithmic complexity and exploits them in order to consume all available resources on a remote host. One example of an application-based attack (Karig et al., 2001) is the finger bomb. A malicious user could cause the finger routine to be recursively executed on the victim, in order to drain its resources.

Copyright © 2007, Idea Group Inc. Copying or distributing in print or electronic forms without written permission of Idea Group Inc. is prohibited.

In *data flooding attacks*, an attacker attempts to use the bandwidth available to a network, host, or device at its greatest extent, by sending massive quantities of data and so causing it to process extremely large amounts of data. An example is flood pinging.

DoS attacks *based on protocol features* take advantage of certain standard protocol features. For example, several attacks exploit the fact that IP source addresses can be spoofed. Moreover, several types of DoS attacks attempt to attack DNS cache on name servers. A simple example of attacks exploiting DNS is when an attacker owning a name server traps a victim name server into caching false records by querying the victim about the attacker's own site. If the victim name server is vulnerable, it would then refer to the malicious server and cache the answer.

DISTRIBUTED DENIAL OF SERVICE ATTACKS

Defining Distributed Denial of Service Attacks

The WWW Security FAQ (Stein & Stewart, 2002) states "A DDoS attack uses many computers to launch a coordinated DoS attack against one or more targets. Using client/server technology, the perpetrator is able to multiply the effectiveness of the DoS significantly by harnessing the resources of multiple unwitting accomplice computers, which serve as attack platforms." It is distinguished from other attacks by its ability to deploy its weapons in a "distributed" way over the Internet and to aggregate these forces to create lethal traffic. The main goal of a DDoS attack is to cause damage on a victim either for personal reasons or for material gain or for popularity.

Mirkovic, Martin, and Reiher (2001) state that the following Internet characteristics make DDoS attacks very destructive:

1. **Interdependency of Internet security:** When a machine is connected to the Internet, it is also connected to countless insecure and vulnerable hosts, making it difficult to provide a sufficient level of security.
2. **Limited resources:** Every host in the Internet has unlimited resources, so sooner or later its resources will be consumed.
3. **Many against afew:** If the attacker's resources are greater than the victim's resources then a DDoS attack is almost inevitable.

DDoS Strategy

A distributed denial of service attack is composed of four elements, as shown in Figure 1.

Copyright © 2007, Idea Group Inc. Copying or distributing in print or electronic forms without written permission of Idea Group Inc. is prohibited.

Figure 1. Architecture of DDoS attacks

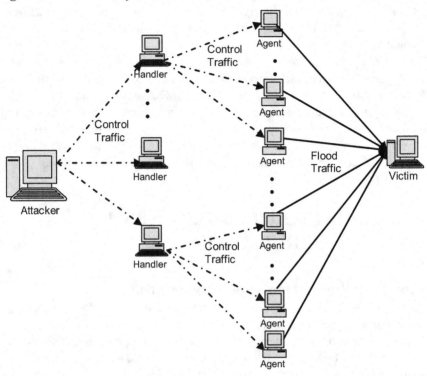

1.   The *real attacker*
2.   The *handlers or masters*, who are compromised hosts with a special program capable of controlling multiple agents, running on them (Cisco Systems, Inc., 2006)
3.   The attack daemon agents or zombie hosts, who are compromised hosts, running a special program and generate a stream of packets towards the victim (Cisco Systems, Inc., 2006)
4.   A *victim* or *target host*

The following steps take place in order to prepare and conduct a DDoS attack:

•   **Step 1. Selection of agents:** The attacker chooses the agents that will perform the attack. The selection of the agents is based on the existence of vulnerabilities in those machines that can be exploited by the attacker in order to gain access to them.

Copyright © 2007, Idea Group Inc. Copying or distributing in print or electronic forms without written permission of Idea Group Inc. is prohibited.

- **Step 2. Compromise:** The attacker exploits the security holes and vulnerabilities of the agent machines and plants the attack code. Furthermore, the attacker tries to protect the code from discovery and deactivation. Self-propagating tools such as the Ramen worm (CIAC Information Bulletin, 2001) and Code Red (CERT, 2001) soon automated this phase. When participating in a DDoS attack, each agent program uses only a small amount of resources (both in memory and bandwidth), so that the users of computers experience minimal change in performance The people who use the agent systems do not know that their systems are compromised and used for the launch of a DDoS attack (Specht & Lee, 2003). When participating in a DDoS attack, agent programs consume little resources this means that the users of computers experience minimal change in performance.
- **Step 3. Communication** (Specht et al., 2003): Before the attacker commands the onset of the attack, he communicates with the handlers in order to find out which agents can be used in the attack, if it is necessary to upgrade the agents and when is the best time to schedule the attack.
- **Step 4. Attack:** At this step, the attacker commands the onset of the attack (Mirkovic, 2002). The victim and the duration of the attack as well as special features of the attack such as the type, port numbers, length, TTL, and so forth can be adjusted.

In a new generation of DDoS attacks, the onset of the attack is not commanded by the attacker but starts automatically during a monitoring procedure of a public location on the Internet. For instance, a chat room may be monitored and when a specific word is typed the DDoS attack is triggered. It is even more difficult to trace the attacker and reveal its true origin in such an environment. We can understand the enormity of the danger if the trigger word or phrase is commonly used.

Specht et al. (2003) state that a multi-user, online chatting system known as Internetrelay chat (IRC) channels is often used for the communication between the attacker and the agents, since IRC chat networks allow their users to create public, private and secret channels. An IRC-based DDoS attack model does not have many differences computed to the agent-handler DDoS attack model except from the fact that an IRC server is responsible for tracking the addresses of agents and handlers and for facilitating the communication between them. The main advantage of the IRC-based attack model over the agent-handler attack model is the anonymity it offers to the participant of the attack.

DDoS Tools

There are several known DDoS attack tools. The architecture of these tools is very similar whereas some tools have been constructed through minor modifications of other tools. In this section, we present the functionality of some of these

Copyright © 2007, Idea Group Inc. Copying or distributing in print or electronic forms without written permission of Idea Group Inc. is prohibited.

tools. For presentation purposes, we divide them in *agent-based* and *IRC-based* DDoS tools.

Agent-based DDoS tools are based on the agent—handler DDoS attack model that consists of handlers, agents, and victim(s) as it has already been described in the section on DDoS attacks. Some of the most known agent-based DDoS tools are the following: *Trinoo, TFN, TFN2K, Stacheldraht, mstream, and Shaft.*

Trinoo (Criscuolo, 2000) is the most known and mostly used DDoS attack tool. It is a tool that is able to achieve bandwidth depletion and can be used to launch UDP flood attacks. *Tribe Flood Network (TFN)* (Dittrich, 1999a) is a DDoS attack tool that is able to perform resource and bandwidth depletion attacks. Some of the attacks that can be launched by TFN include Smurf, UDP flood, TCP SYN flood, ICMP echo request flood, and ICMP directed broadcast. *TFN2K* (Barlow & Thrower, 2000) is a derivative of the TFN tool and is able to implement Smurf, SYN, UDP, and ICMP Flood attacks. TFN2K has a special feature of being able to add encrypted messaging between all of the attack components (Specht et al., 2003). *Stacheldraht* (Dittrich, 1999b) (German term for "barbed wire"), that is based on early versions of TFN, attempts to eliminate some of its weak points and implement Smurf, SYN Flood, UDP Flood, and ICMP Flood attacks. *Mstream* (Dittrich, Weaver, Dietrich, & Long, 2000) is a simple TCP ACK flooding tool that is able to overwhelm the tables used by fast routing routines in some switches. *Shaft* (Dietrich et al., 2000) is a DDoS tool similar to Trinoo that is able to launch packet flooding attacks by controlling the duration of the attack as well as the size of the flooding packets.

Many IRC-based DDoS tools are very sophisticated as they include some important features that are also found in many agent-handler attack tools. One of the most known IRC-based DDoS tools is *Trinity* (Hancock, 2000). *Trinity v3* (Dietrich et al., 2000) besides the up to now well-known UDP, TCP SYN, TCP ACK, TCP NUL packet floods introduces TCP fragment floods, TCP RST packet floods, TCP random flag packet floods, and TCP established floods. In the same generation with Trinity is *myServer* (Dietrich et al., 2000) and *Plague* (Dietrich et al., 2000). MyServer relies on external programs to provide DoS and Plague provides TCP ACK and TCP SYN flooding. *Knight* (Bysin, 2001) is a very lightweight and powerful IRC-based DDoS attack tool able to perform UDP Flood attacks, SYN attacks and an urgent pointer flooder. A DDoS tool that is based on Knight is *Kaiten* (Specht et al., 2003). Kaiten includes UDP, TCP flood attacks, SYN, and PUSH+ACH attacks and it also randomizes the 32 bits of its source address.

DDoS Classification

To be able to understand DDoS attacks it is necessary to have a formal classification. We propose a classification of DDoS attacks that combines efficiently the classifications proposed by Mirkovic et al. (2001), Specht et al. (2003), and more recent research results. This classification is illustrated in Figure 2 and consists

Copyright © 2007, Idea Group Inc. Copying or distributing in print or electronic forms without written permission of Idea Group Inc. is prohibited.

Figure 2. Classification of DDoS attacks

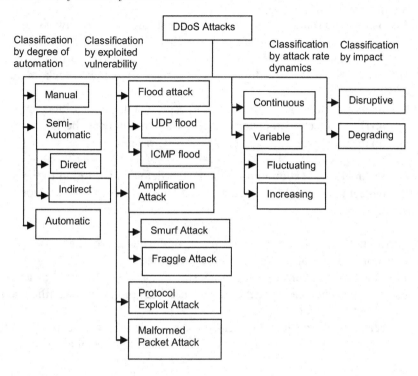

of two levels. In the first level, attacks are classified according to their degree of automation, exploited vulnerability, attack rate dynamics and their impact. In the second level, specific characteristics of each first level category are recognized.

CLASSIFICATION OF DDoS
DEFENSE MECHANISMS

DDoS attack detection is extremely difficult. The distributed nature of DDoS attacks makes them extremely difficult to combat or trace back. Moreover, the automated tools that make the deployment of a DDoS attack possible can be easily downloaded. Attackers may also use IP spoofing in order to hide their true identity. This spoofing makes the traceback of DDoS attacks even more difficult.

We may classify DDoS defense mechanisms using two different criteria. The first classification categorizes the DDoS defense mechanisms according to the activity deployed as follows:

Copyright © 2007, Idea Group Inc. Copying or distributing in print or electronic forms without written permission of Idea Group Inc. is prohibited.

1.   **Intrusion prevention:** Tries to stop DDoS attacks from being launched in the first place.
2.   **Intrusion detection:** Focuses on guarding host computers or networks against being a source of network attack as well as being a victim of DDoS attacks either by recognizing abnormal behaviours or by using a database of known.
3.   **Intrusion response:** Tries to identify the attack source and block its traffic accordingly.
4.   **Intrusion tolerance and mitigation:** Accepts that it is impossible to prevent or stop DDoS attacks completely and focuses on minimizing the attack impact and on maximizing the quality of the offered services.

The second classification divides the DDoS defenses according to the location deployment resulting (Mirkovic, 2002) into the following three categories of defense mechanisms:

1.   **Victim network mechanisms:** Helps the victim recognize when it is the main target of an attack and gain more time to respond.
2.   **Intermediate network mechanisms:** Are more effective than victim network mechanisms since they achieve a better handling of the attack traffic and an easier tracing back to the attackers.
3.   **Source network mechanisms:** Trys to stop attack flows before they enter the Internet core and facilitate the traceback and investigation of an attack.

The previous classification of DDoS defense mechanisms is described thoroughly in Douligeris and Mitrokotsa (2004).

BEST PRACTICES FOR DEFEATING DENIAL OF SERVICE ATTACKS

DoS attacks can lead to a complete standstill of entire government organisations, thereby costing millions of dollars in lost revenue and/or productivity and moving citizens away from e-services. Some governments do not understand the seriousness of the problem, resulting in vulnerable and easy to compromise systems. These systems pose a threat not only to the organisations themselves but also to anyone else targeted by a hacker through these systems. This means it is critical to take preemptive measures to reduce the possibility of these attacks and minimize their impact.

Since DoS attacks are extremely complicated one must note that there is no single-point solution and no system is secure proof. No one can deny though that with effective advance planning government agencies could respond efficiently and rapidly to security threats like denial of service. Below we list some practices that can be used in order to reduce these attacks and diminish their impact.

Copyright © 2007, Idea Group Inc. Copying or distributing in print or electronic forms without written permission of Idea Group Inc. is prohibited.

1. **Establish a security policy and educate:** As stated by Walters (2001), it is of great importance to establish and maintain a security policy. In addition to covering the basics of antivirus, user access, and software updates, on no account one should neglect to address ways to combat DoS/DDoS attacks in such a policy. Moreover, a security policy should be adequately communicated to all employees. It is important to verify that the knowledge skills of system administrators and auditors are current, something that can be achieved by frequent certifications. Of great importance is the continuous training of the organisation's personnel in new technologies and forensic techniques.

2. **Use multiple ISPs:** Government organisations should consider using more than one ISP, in order to make a DoS/DDoS attack against them harder to carry out. In the selection of ISPs, it is important to keep in mind that providers should use different access routes in order to avoid a complete loss of access in the case one pipe becomes disabled (Walters, 2001). It has also been proposed to set legislation to make it obligatory for ISPs to set up egress filtering.

3. **Load balancing:** Specht et al. (2003) state that a good approach in order to avoid being a victim of DoS attacks is to distribute an organisation's systems' load across multiple servers. In order to achieve this, a "Round Robin DNS" or hardware routers could be used to send incoming requests to one or many servers.

4. **Avoid a single point failure:** In order to avoid a single point failure the best solution is to have redundant ("hot spares") machine that can be used in case a similar machine is disabled (Householder, Manion, Pesante, Weaver, & Thomas, 2001). Furthermore, organisations should develop recovery plans that will cover each potential failure point of their system. In addition, organisations should use multiple operating systems in order to create "biodiversity" and avoid DoS attack tools that target specific Operating Systems (OSs).

5. **Protect the systems with a firewall:** Walters (2001) states that since the exposure to potential intruders is increasing, the installation of firewalls that tightly limit transactions across the systems' periphery government organisations should be built to provide effective defenses. Firewalls should be configured appropriately keeping open only the necessary ports. In addition, firewalls are able to carefully control, identify, and handle overrun attempts. Moreover, ingress filtering should be established in government Web servers so that they cannot be used as zombies for launching attacks on other servers. Government departments should also specify a set of IP addresses that could be used only by Government servers.

6. **Disable unused services:** It is important, that as Leng and Whinston (2000) state, organisations' systems remain simple by minimizing the number of services running on them. This can be achieved by shutting down all services that are not required. It is important to turn off or restrict specific services that might otherwise be compromised or subverted in order to launch DoS attacks.

Copyright © 2007, Idea Group Inc. Copying or distributing in print or electronic forms without written permission of Idea Group Inc. is prohibited.

For instance, if UDP echo or character generator services are not required, disabling them will help to defend against attacks that exploit these services.

7. **Be up to date on security issues:** As it is widely known the best way to combat DoS attacks is to try to be always protected and up-to-date on security issues (Householder et al., 2001). It is important to be informed about the current upgrades, updates, security bulletins, and vendor advisories in order to prevent DoS attacks. Thus, the exposure to DoS attacks can be substantially reduced, although one would not expect the risk to be eliminated entirely.

8. **Test and monitor systems carefully:** The first step in order to detect anomalous behaviour is to "characterize" what normal means in the context of a government agency's network. The next step should be the auditing of access privileges, activities, and applications. Administrators should perform 24x7 monitoring in order to reduce the exhausting results of DoS attacks that inflict government servers. Through this procedure, organisations would be able to detect unusual levels of network traffic or CPU usage (Householder et al., 2001). There are a variety of tools that are able to detect, eliminate, and analyze denial-of-service attacks.

9. **Mitigate spoofing:** An approach that intruders often use in order to conceal their identity when launching DoS attacks is source-address spoofing. Although it is impossible to completely eliminate IP spoofing, it is important to mitigate it (Singer, 2000). There are some approaches that can be used in order to make the origins of attacks harder to hide and to shorten the time to trace an attack back to its origins. System administrators can effectively reduce the risk of IP spoofing by using ingress and egress packet filtering on firewalls and/or routers.

10. **Stop broadcast amplification:** It is important to disable inbound directed broadcasts in order to prevent a network from being used as an amplifier for attacks like ICMP Flood and Smurf (Leng et al., 2000). Turning off the configuration of IP directed broadcast packets in routers and making this a default configuration is the best action that could be performed by network hardware vendors.

11. **DNS for access control should not be used:** Using hostnames in access list instead of IP addresses make systems vulnerable to name spoofing (Leng et al., 2000). Systems should not rely on domain or host names in order to determine if an access is authorized or not. Otherwise, intruders can masquerade a system, by simply modifying the reverse-lookup tables.

12. **Create an incident response plan:** It is important to be prepared and ready for any possible attack scenario. Government organisations should define a set of clear procedures that could be followed in emergency situations and train personnel teams with clearly defined responsibilities ready to respond in emergency cases (Householder et al., 2001). Any attacks or suspicious system flaws should be reported to local law enforcement and proper authorities (such

Copyright © 2007, Idea Group Inc. Copying or distributing in print or electronic forms without written permission of Idea Group Inc. is prohibited.

as FBI and CERT) so that the information could be used for the defense of other users as well.

LONG TERM COUNTERMEASURES

The variety and sophistication of DoS attacks are likely to increase, so despite the defensive measures that can be used now, we need to confront DoS attacks as a problem that requires a long-term effort in order to define and implement effective solutions. It is important to note here that governments should adopt a nonintrusive approach for the protection against DoS attacks while there is a fine line between limiting criminal activity and limiting economy, education, information, and personal freedoms.

Suns Institute (2000) identifies some actions that will help in defending against DoS attacks more effectively in the distant future. Among them one finds the accelerated adoption of the IPsec components of IPv6 and Secure DNS. It is important that the security updating process be automated. Vendors should be encouraged to implement this on behalf of their clients in order to make it easier to update their products and provide information on security issues. Furthermore, research and development of safer operating systems is necessary. Topics to be addressed should include among others anomaly-based detection and other forms of intrusion detection. In addition, governments should consider making some changes in their government procurement policies in a way that security and safety are emphasized.

A significant role in the fight against denial of service attacks would be the establishment of organisations that would be responsible for network security monitoring and incident handling. These organisations should encourage the public awareness about security issues, inform critical owners' infrastructures and government departments about threats, promote and encourage the adoption and production of security standards and maintain statistics and incident databases as well as cooperate with similar organisations (e.g., CERT).

Governments should also ensure that government agencies take all the necessary steps in order to ensure their IT security. Government departments should encourage a better investigation of computer attacks while respecting the privacy and personal rights of Internet users. Additional funding for the training of expert personnel in securing IT Technologies and educating citizens in order to be prevented from cyber crime is a must. It is also important to promote and encourage law enforcement authorities to prosecute perpetrators across national borders and examine the legal framework to facilitate this cooperation.

CONCLUSION

Undoubtedly, DoS attacks should be treated as a serious problem in the Internet. Their rate of growth and wide acceptance challenge the general public's view of

Copyright © 2007, Idea Group Inc. Copying or distributing in print or electronic forms without written permission of Idea Group Inc. is prohibited.

electronic transactions and create skeptical governments and businesses. No one can deny that DoS attacks will continue to pose a significant threat to all organisations including government organisations. New defense mechanisms will be followed by the emergence of new DoS attack modes. A network infrastructure must be both robust enough to survive direct DoS attacks and extensible enough to adopt and embrace new defenses against emerging and unanticipated attack modes. In order to ensure high resiliency and high performance in public and private networks efforts need to be concerted by administrators, service providers and equipment manufacturers. It is of great importance that citizens communicate with their government authorities online. No one should be allowed to shut down valuable e-government services. A more enlightened approach would be to ask all citizens to take responsibility for securing the Internet in their hands. Public awareness is the key in order to securely exist and succeed in the world of e-government.

REFERENCES

Barlow, J., & Thrower, W. (2000). *TFN2K—An analysis.* Retrieved from http://se-clists.org/lists/bugtraq/2000/Feb/0190.html

Bysin. (2001). *Knight.c Sourcecode.* Retrieved from http://packetstormsecurity.nl/distributed/knight.c

CERT. (2001). *CERT Coordination Center Advisory CA-2001-19 Code Red Worm Exploiting Buffer Overflow in IIS Indexing Service DLL.* Carnegie Mellon Software Engineering Institute. Retrieved from http://www.cert.org/advisories/CA-2001-19.html

CIAC Information Bulletin. (2001). L-040: The Ramen Worm. *Computer Incident Advisory Capability (CIAC).* Retrieved from http://www.ciac.org/ciac/bulletins/l-040.shtml

Cisco Systems, Inc. (2006). *Strategies to protect against distributed denial of service (DDoS) attacks* (Document ID: 13634). Retrieved from http://www.cisco.com/warp/public/707/newsflash.html

Computer Security Institute. (2003). *2003 CSI/FBI Computer Crime and Security Survey.* CSI Inc.

Computer Security Institute. (2004). *2004 CSI/FBI Computer Crime and Security Survey.* CSI Inc.

Criscuolo, P. J. (2000). *Distributed denial of service Trin00, Tribe Flood Network, Tribe Flood Network 2000, and Stacheldraht CIAC-2319* (Tech. Rep. No. , UCRL-ID-136939, Rev. 1.). Department of Energy Computer Incident Advisory Capability (CIAC), Lawrence Livermore National Laboratory. Retrieved from http://ftp.se.kde.org/pub/security/csir/ciac/ ciacdocs/ciac2319.txt

Cs3 Inc. (2005). *Defending government network infrastructure against distributed denial of service attacks.* CS3-inc.com. Retrieved from http://www.cs3-inc.com/government-ddos-threat-and-solutions.pdf

Copyright © 2007, Idea Group Inc. Copying or distributing in print or electronic forms without written permission of Idea Group Inc. is prohibited.

Dietrich, S., Long, N., & Dittrich, D. (2000). Analyzing distributed denial of service tools: The shaft case. In *Proceedings of the 14th Systems Administration Conference (LISA 2000)* (pp. 329-339), New Orleans, LA.

Dittrich, D. (1999a). *The tribe flood network distributed denial of service attack tool. University of Washington.* Retrieved from http://staff.washington.edu/dittrich/misc/ trinoo.analysis.txt

Dittrich, D. (1999b). *The Stacheldraht distributed denial of service attack tool. University of Washington.* Retrieved from http://staff.washington.edu/dittrich/misc/ stacheldraht.analysis.txt

Dittrich, D., Weaver, G., Dietrich, S., & Long, N. (2000). *The mstream distributed denial of service attack tool.* University of Washington. Retrieved from http:// staff.washington.edu/dittrich/misc/mstream.analysis.txt

Douligeris C., & Mitrokotsa, A. (2004). DDoS attacks and defense mechanisms: Classification and state-of-the-art. *Computer Networks, 44*(5), 643-666.

Fox News. (2002). *Powerful attack cripples Internet.* Retrieved from http://www. linux.security.com/content/view/112716/65/

Hancock, B. (2000). Trinity v3, A DDoS tool, hits the streets. *Computers & Security, 19*(7), 574-574.

Holden, S., Norris, D., & Fletcher, P. (2003). Electronic government at the local level: Progress to date and future issues. *Public Performance and Management Review, 26*(4), 325-344.

Householder, A., Manion, A., Pesante, L., Weaver, G. M., & Thomas, R. (2001). *Trends in denial of service attack technology* (v10.0). CERT Coordination Center, Carnegie Mellon University. Retrieved from http://www.cert.org/archive/pdf/DoS_trends.pdf

Howard, J. (1998). *An analysis of security incidents on the Internet 1989-1995.* PhD thesis, Carnegie Mellon University. Retrieved from http://www.cert. org/research/ JHThesis/Start.html

Insecure.org. (1997). *Ping of death.* Retrieved from http://www.insecure.org/sploits/ ping-o-death.html

Institute for e-government Competence Center (IfG.CC). (2002). *eGovernment: "First fight the hackers."* Retrieved from http://www.unipotsdam.de/db/elogo/ ifgcc/index.php?option=com_content&task=view&id=1450&Itemid=93 &lang=en_GB

ITworld.com. (2001). *CERT hit by DDoS attack for a third day.* Retrieved from http://www.itworld.com/Sec/3834/IDG010524CERT2/

Karig, D., & Lee, R. (2001). *Remote denial of service attacks and countermeasures* (Tech. Rep. No. CE-L2001-002). Department of Electrical Engineering, Princeton University.

Leng, X., & Whinston, A.B. (2000). Defeating distributed denial of service attacks. *IEEE IT Professional, 2*(4) 36-42.

Copyright © 2007, Idea Group Inc. Copying or distributing in print or electronic forms without written permission of Idea Group Inc. is prohibited.

Mirkovic, J. (2002). *D-WARD: DDoS network attack recognition and defense.* PhD dissertation prospectus. Retrieved from http://www.lasr.cs.ucla.edu/ddos/pro-spectus.pdf

Mirkovic, J., Martin, J., & Reiher P. (2001). *A taxonomy of DDoS attacks and DDoS defense mechanisms* (Tech. Rep. No. 020018). UCLA CSD.

Moore, D., Voelker, G., & Savage, S. (2001). Inferring Internet denial of service activity. In *Proceedings of the USENIX Security Symposium*, Washington, DC (pp. 9-22).

SANS Institute. (2000). *Consensus roadmap for defeating distributed denial of service attacks* (Version 1.10). Sans Portal. Retrieved from http://www.sans.org/dosstep/ roadmap.php

Singer, A. (2000). *Eight things that ISP's and network managers can do to help mitigate distributed denial of service attacks.* San Diego Supercomputer Center (SDSC), (NPACI). Retrieved from http://security.sdsc.edu/publications/ddos.shtml

Sophos.com. (2002). *Indian sympathisers launch denial of service attack on Pakistani government.* Retrieved from http://www.sophos.com/virusinfo/articles/yahae3.html

Spafford, E. H. (1998). *The Internet worm program: An analysis* (Tech. Rep. No. SD-TR-823). Department of Computer Science Purdue University, West Lafayette, IN.

Specht, S., & Lee R. (2003). *Taxonomies of distributed denial of service networks, attacks, tools, and countermeasures* (Tech. Rep. No. CE-L2003-03). Princeton University.

Symantec. (2004). *Symantec reports government specific attack data* (Article ID 4927). Symantec.com. Retrieved from http://enterprisesecurity.symantec.com/publicsector/ article.cfm?articleid=4927

WindowsITPro. (2001). *Microsoft suffers another DoS attack. WindowsITPro Instant Doc 19770.* Retrieved from http://www.windowsitpro.com/Articles/Index.cfm? ArticleID=19770&DisplayTab=Article

U.S. Subcommittee on Oversight and Investigations Hearing. (2001). *Protecting America's critical infrastructures: How secure are government computer systems?* Energycommerce.house.gov. Retrieved from http://energycommerce.house.gov/ 107/hearings/04052001Hearing153/McDonald229.htm

Stein, L. D., & Stewart, J. N. (2002). *The World Wide Web Security FAQ version 3.1.2. World Wide Web Consortium (W3C).* Retrieved from http://www.w3.org/Security/Faq

Walters, R. (2001). Top 10 ways to prevent denial-of-service attacks. *Information Systems Security, 10*(3), 71-72.

Copyright © 2007, Idea Group Inc. Copying or distributing in print or electronic forms without written permission of Idea Group Inc. is prohibited.

Chapter IX

Certificate Management Interoperability for E-Government Applications

Andreas Mitrakas, European Network and Information
Security Agency (ENISA), Greece

ABSTRACT

Secure e-government aims at supporting public administration in delivering enhanced public services. In e-government, electronic signatures and certification services are used to invoke trust and security in services and applications. Certification services, however, are often on offer in an apparent geographical or contextual isolation threatening to create new fault lines across e-government services that rely on them. As public administration often operates at multiple levels and in a compartmental manner, the risk is that limitations in the interoperability of certification services might hamper trust and security in the whole value chain of e-government. Drawing from the case of small public administrations, this chapter proposes a certification service architecture and approach to support interoperability in secure e-government services.

Copyright © 2007, Idea Group Inc. Copying or distributing in print or electronic forms without written permission of Idea Group Inc. is prohibited.

INTRODUCTION

The promise of e-government for a simplified and efficient Public Administration (PA) has been regarded by governments worldwide as a means to carry out public policy and enhance services to citizens and organisations. E-government aims at introducing to public administration, information, and communication technologies (ICT) at a mass scale in a way previously unknown and for tasks often impossible to carry out without ICT. Online citizens and organizations gain access to 24/7 services over an array of transactions with the PA and often in combination with private sector or other third party services. Cross-border interoperability is a critical aspect in delivering such services. Electronic signatures are an infrastructure technology upon which e-government applications rely to ensure authentication and non-repudiation of transactions. While electronic authentication is often associated with identity management, non-repudiation is essential for critical e-government applications that require the undisputed commitment of the signatory. Using electronic signatures in cross-border transactions across multiple application environments may become an awkward experience due to interoperability limitations that may lead to setbacks in trust. It is therefore becoming critical to allow for the seamless validation of electronic signatures in multiple application environments. This chapter addresses certain issues related to certification authority (CA) services across e-government infrastructures and it reviews prevailing models to assess their suitability for interoperability in e-government. Emphasis is placed on the suitability of these models for applications made available by e-government organizations, particularly small ones that typically rely on limited resources that cannot necessarily sustain demanding deployments in terms of technology used and organisational cost. In building trusted e-government services, grasping the trust requirements of each application is an essential prerequisite. Since trust is likely to be based on certificate-based services, ensuring interoperability across the board is a priority for administrations in the Member States but also for the European Union (EU) in an effort to enhance interoperability and encourage cross-border deployments. After providing a short overview of the state of art, the remainder of this chapter presents existing interoperability models. Furthermore, this chapter presents a proposed interoperability model that leverages on an overarching interoperability capability.

BACKGROUND:
TRUST AND E-GOVERNMENT

While the EU E-Europe initiative has focused on government services online, seamless access to government information services and decision-making procedures have also been seen as a priority (Prins, Eifert, Girot, Groothuis, & Voermans, 2001). The envisaged application environment for e-government seeks to meet the

Copyright © 2007, Idea Group Inc. Copying or distributing in print or electronic forms without written permission of Idea Group Inc. is prohibited.

expectations of citizens and businesses alike especially with regard to providing efficient and cost effective e-government services (UNCTAD, 2001). Applications of e-government aim at citizens and business with varying levels of involvement and service functionality. These applications may often rely on electronic signatures to safeguard the transmission of user and transaction data. Online e-government services that leverage upon electronic signatures for citizens include for example: taxation, social security, registration services, etc. Typical e-government applications that require the identification of organisations include social security contributions, corporate tax, VAT submissions, company registries, and electronic public procurement. More recently, the set up of official registries such as those required for accountants and companies, also rely on the use of electronic signatures. In certain areas a drive toward greater cooperation among PAs can be observed, that is often motivated by the need to service a larger population in the EU internal market or leverage upon a greater range of services. In some cases, cooperation may also be instantiated by interactions at a political level that have led to successful deployments, like for example, the European Digital Tachograph (see, Council regulation (EC) No 2135/98 of 24 September 1998 amending Regulation (EEC) No 3821/85 on recording equipment in road transport and Directive 88/599/EEC concerning the application of Regulations (EEC) No 3820/84 and (EEC) No 3821/85). As it can be expected in complex transaction areas such as electronic procurement, a combination of technologies and a multitude of interoperability options have to be taken into consideration to allow for the seamless cooperation among PAs and provide appropriate interactions with private sector services. In such environments, PA processes may require re-designing to ensure interoperability and accessibility.

While cross-border PA services are desirable, their need cannot always be justified by the way PAs work and the sort of services they offer. PA cooperation typically occurs in selected and clearly defined areas where there has been a manifestation of the need to cooperate. Sometimes PA cooperation can be instantiated through dedicated applications. Identification services have been singled out as a centerpiece in e-government efforts to provide personalized and efficient services to citizens (Mitrakas, 2002). In the EU, cross-border e-government services have been deemed essential to support the mobility of the citizens and stimulate competition among public administrations that is likely to lead to greater efficiency and better services for citizens and organizations (Blivet, Mitrakas, & Moyal, 2001).

In spite of the obvious benefits that interoperability presents, PAs in Member States often maintain a silo approach that sometimes constrains them from leveraging upon or offering cross-sector and cross-border services (Eymeri, 2001). Operating in isolation and setting up silo constraints can be well justified in a nation-centric PA that only serves internal needs. For a PA, however, that seeks to cooperate with other organisations and participate in the EU internal market, there is scope in opening up services to parties that do not necessarily reside in its own jurisdiction. The shift toward e-government is the means to effect this change. Therefore, public

Copyright © 2007, Idea Group Inc. Copying or distributing in print or electronic forms without written permission of Idea Group Inc. is prohibited.

interest can be interpreted as the need toward greater cooperation among PAs for the purpose of enhancing services rendered within the EU internal market by using electronic means.

Identity management is a critical application that evidences the shift toward e-government. By allowing the authentication of citizens and organizations across the board in a range of other e-government applications, identity management is a critical undisputed element in the e-government application lifecycle. Managing identities for e-government, a complex application area, requires a relatively high degree of interoperability to allow for the delivery of services across multiple PA platforms that can be accessible through e-government services. Opening up such functionality to other Member State PAs is an additional challenge to tackle.

Much like other application environments, e-government has also passed from a stage of one-sided communications to a performative level of transactions that involve multiple actors in both the private and public sector. The figure below illustrates the evolutionary stages of e-government stages that seek to add to cross-border functionalities.

Figure 1. Evolution of e-government transactions

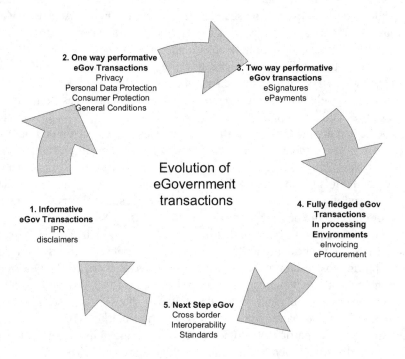

Copyright © 2007, Idea Group Inc. Copying or distributing in print or electronic forms without written permission of Idea Group Inc. is prohibited.

To date the role of PA is twofold acting as issuer of identities, like for example electronic identity or more often as a relying party, that validates and accepts electronic signatures that citizens use. Relying parties require mechanisms that permit the validation of electronic signatures from resources that the issuing authority makes available. This approach, as it can be expected, has significant merits within the domain of a single PA irrespectively of the level in which it might be applied, being local, regional, federal etc. Interestingly enough in private sector applications this challenge has largely been addressed through market oriented solutions. A challenge for PAs is how to leverage on market solutions to allow for interoperable identity management and other e-government applications made available through PA.

PAs face significant shortcomings when identity management centric e-government services are made available at a cross-border level. Currently the open question for a PA is how to access a validation resource especially in the case where that PA relies on a certificate that has been issued by a foreign CA that belongs to a PA in another Member State. Accessing that resource is a necessary step before validating and accepting that certificate. To date there has been no real life evidence of large-scale cooperation among EU Member State PAs to ensure the validation of electronic identities issued by various authorities. Pursuant to the increase in e-government deployments, future e-government services are likely to depend on the rate of interoperability at the certificate validation level in a way that ensures seamless services.

A critical question is whether information society beneficiaries, that include citizens, businesses, and other PAs, have a right to interoperability of information society services. Article 2 of the EU Treaty stipulates sustainable information society that establishes a right to information society services. While at a Member State level this right might be interpreted as granting access to and affording e-government services at the EU level, interoperability becomes critical to give effect to the sustainability of information society service. Within the EU, internal market rules that sometimes depend on information society services rely on the requirement for interoperability to assume a meaningful form. The ubiquitous business and private use of public open networks has resulted in a surge of regulation concerning an array of issues, among which certification services promise to tackle the issue of identity management and identity assurance in a hard to secure environment. It has been argued that citizens have political and moral rights against the state that are prior to the welfare of the majority. In this regard, legal rights can extend beyond those explicitly laid down (Dworkin, 1977). In terms of information society services, beneficiaries require access to meaningful services in a way that enhances the internal market and ensures other basic rights such as the protection of personal data. While interoperability of certification services is a viable means to exercise and enjoy the right to accessing e-government applications it should be encouraged and afforded protection in a meaningful way.

Copyright © 2007, Idea Group Inc. Copying or distributing in print or electronic forms without written permission of Idea Group Inc. is prohibited.

An additional question relates to whether the EU level is the most appropriate to address interoperability of e-government services especially in the certificate management area. With regard to e-government interoperability, it is necessary to underline the importance of adhering to the principles of proportionality and sub-sidiarity (Mousis, 2002). Especially for e-government certification services for the purpose of identity management, it is expected that cross-border deployments will observe the principle that regulation that can be regulated at a national level within a Member State does not have to be addressed at an EU level. From the conception of policy to its implementation, the level at which action is taken, like for example from the EU to local levels, and the selection of the instruments used, must be in proportion to the objectives pursued. Consequently, before launching an initiative, it is essential to check if public action at the EU level is really needed. Additionally it has to be established whether action at EU level is the most appropriate to address the issue at hand (Hix, 1999).

To enhance certificate management services for e-government interoperability, it is necessary to seek the appropriate level of cooperation as well as an operation model that is suitable with respect to the technical and operational features of the applications involved. In e-government, various trust models can be considered and implemented to meet the requirements of diverse types of applications. To date these models can mostly be based on bilateral agreements, cultural or orga-nizational preferences, and trust requirements. These models, however, often face limitations with regard to scalability and acceptance for mass deployments. To make e-government services evolve, a certain degree of national control might have to be substituted by a shared responsibility among e-government services. The released level of control can be entrusted to a mutually shared body that will be designate by the PAs involved. To enhance the EU internal market, by means of e-government services, it is critical to ensure that PAs share the vision and service the goal for e-government interoperability.

LEGAL CONSIDERATIONS

Electronic signatures and their subsequent regulation in the EU are a critical element in the question of certification services for identity management. With the EU Directive 99/93/EC, electronic signatures acquired a legal meaning next to the technical one that they already had. Directive 99/93/EC on a Common framework for electronic signatures has made a significant impact on e-government applica-tions by laying the ground rules and pro-actively encouraging the standardisation of certificate based signature services (Mitrakas, 2003). One important objective that this Directive has accomplished is averting the fragmentation of the internal market of electronic signatures within the EU that has spared a critical part of the internal market with regard to information society (Aalberts & van der Hof, 1999). While further steps are required to enhance interoperability levels across the EU, state of

Copyright © 2007, Idea Group Inc. Copying or distributing in print or electronic forms without written permis-sion of Idea Group Inc. is prohibited.

the art implementations in several application areas including identity management manifest the value of electronic signature standards.

Directive 99/93/EC introduces three classes of electronic signatures, namely a general class of electronic signatures, advanced electronic signatures, and advanced electronic signatures based on qualified certificates and created by a secure signature creation device. A specific type of electronic signatures, known as qualified signatures, meets certain formal requirements and is afforded the same legal effect as hand-written signatures, according to article 5.1 of the Directive. The effect of advanced electronic signatures, which are based on a qualified certificate and are created by a secure signature-creation device is that they meet the legal requirements of a signature in relation to data in electronic form in the same manner as a hand-written signature satisfies those requirements in relation to paper-based data; and that they are admissible as evidence in legal proceedings. Furthermore, an advanced electronic signature is a generic type of electronic signature that meets the conditions of uniquely identifying the signatory while the signatory remains associated with the signed data (Mitrakas, 2006).

Article 5.2 of the Directive 99/93/EC addresses the legal effect of signatures that do not meet the requirements of qualified signatures. These types of signatures are afforded significant recognition provided that supportive evidence ensures their trustworthiness.

The signatures of article 5.2 can also be used for identification and authentication, like when using S/MIME, for example. These types of signatures are within the focal area of organisations seeking to make available e-government applications available where hand-written signatures are not necessary for the purpose of non-repudiation of a transaction. In the EU, electronic signatures have in some cases epitomised the security requirements mandated for certain e-government applications. Since electronic signatures ensure already the non-repudiation of the transaction, the authentication of the transacting parties, the confidentiality of the communication, and the integrity of the exchanged data, they are also supported by a stringent set of audit and compliance rules that ensures the quality and level of services offered by a certification service provider (Caelli, Longley, & Shain, 1991; Pfleeger, 1997). Applications such as national electronic identity schemes based on electronic signatures provide the functionality and control that governments need to manage large populations of users of their electronic systems (Deprest & Robben, 2003). Electronic signatures for the purpose of authentication provide e-government services with the ability to centralise and focus their security requirements as well as complement additional security requirements that it might actually have.

An increasing number of deployments and applications make use of qualified signatures for the purpose of non-repudiation. In a paper-based environment, law requires hand-written signatures in a relatively small number of formal transactions, a tendency that might be projected in electronic transactions also. It can be argued that the assertions on qualified signatures have thus far paid little service to the general

Copyright © 2007, Idea Group Inc. Copying or distributing in print or electronic forms without written permission of Idea Group Inc. is prohibited.

use of electronic signatures. This tendency can be amended by improvements in the available technology and more importantly the drive toward raising the current rate of penetration of electronic transactions also for e-government.

Directive 99/93/EC permits Certification Service Providers (CSP) to make services available without seeking for ex ante authorisation by Member States' authorities prior to commencing operations. It remains at the Member States' discretion, however, to decide how they ensure supervision of CSPs according to the provisions of the Directive. The Directive does not preclude establishing private sector based supervision systems or oblige certification service providers to apply for supervision under any applicable accreditation scheme. The Directive therefore permits the split between the legally establishing a CSP in one Member State while the provision of services remains in another.

In deploying interoperable electronic signatures in the EU, standardisation has played a significant role especially in terms of the deliverables of the European Electronic Signatures Standardisation Initiative (EESSI) that hold a pivotal position. The EESSI standards have been promulgated by the European standardization organizations as the European Telecommunications Standards Institute (ETSI) and European Committee for Standardization/Information Society Standardization System (CEN/ISSS). The EESSI standards can be further extended to reflect the current and specific needs of industry and PAs. EESSI standards have also addressed the matter of electronic signature validation that is an essential requirement to establish trust in a chain of certificates that are used in e-government applications. To carry out cross-border public services it is necessary to have the ability to check the validity of the electronic signatures that are in use. Checking the validity of an electronic signature requires controlling a directory that contains status information of digital certificates. Such directory contains all certificates that have been revoked or suspended at the time a request is made. Information published on such directories must be kept up to date regularly or provided in real time.

TRUST MODELS FOR CERTIFICATE SERVICE MANAGEMENT

Several models are currently available to deploy validation authority services across multiple domains. While some of them are based on private sector experience from electronic commerce, others have evolved exclusively to serve e-government needs. A critical factor to the future deployment of these models is likely to be the applications they shall be called to support, the rate of technology use within the PA as well as the type and level of public e-government services on offer. Present day monolithic approaches of a single model per Member State are likely to be replaced by a tailor made model based on an application centric approach.

Documented and enforceable policy plays a significant role in determining the conditions in which certificate services are rendered. A certificate policy for

Copyright © 2007, Idea Group Inc. Copying or distributing in print or electronic forms without written permission of Idea Group Inc. is prohibited.

example is used to ensure the policy objectives for the CSP with regard to security requirements of certificate management. A certification practice statement is also used to ensure how such objectives are met (ETSI TS 101 456). At the application level, relying parties may use signature policies to assess the validity of electronic signatures. A signature policy describes the scope and the usage of electronic signature with a view to address the operational conditions of a given transaction context (ETSI 102 041). A signature policy is a set of rules under which an electronic signature can be created and determined to be valid (ETSI TS 101 733). A signature policy determines the validation conditions of an electronic signature within a given context. A context may include a transaction type, a legal regime, a role assumed by the signing party, etc. Policies are the means to invoke trust and convey information in electronic commerce by defining appropriately indicated trust conditions (Mitrakas, 2004). Additionally certificate policies and certification practices statements remain entirely under the domain of the application service provider and are, typically audited for compliance.

As validation of identities is a critical issue that e-government services address to enhance interoperability, the remainder of this section presents prevailing models for e-government validation authority interoperability.

Cross-Certification

Cross-certification aims at establishing a trust relationship between two CAs. Cross certification is carried out by setting an interoperability path for one or more applications between two discreet certificate management domains or two CAs within the same certificate domain (Lloyd, 2001). According to the IETF PKIX Group, "A Cross-certificate is a certificate issued by one CA to another CA which contains a CA signature key used for issuing certificates." This definition is consistent with the X.509 standard in which it stated that a certification authority can be the subject of a certificate issued by another certification authority. In this case, the certificate is called a cross-certificate whereby the issuer of a certificate and the subject are different CAs. CAs issue certificates to other CAs in order to authorise the subject CA, as is the case of strict hierarchies. Alternatively, cross certificates are used in order to recognise the existence of the subject CA as is the case in a distributed trust model. Cross-certification is a unilateral action that typically applies within a strict hierarchy where a superior CA issues a certificate to a subordinate one. Advantages associated with cross-certification include that each domain remains autonomous from any external trust considerations and the internal trust relationship between the relying parties and the trust anchor (i.e., hierarchically superior CA) within the domain are not affected. Open issues in cross-certification render its administration uneconomical due to the large number of bilateral agreements that have to be executed as well as potentially time-consuming negotiations

Copyright © 2007, Idea Group Inc. Copying or distributing in print or electronic forms without written permission of Idea Group Inc. is prohibited.

Cross-Recognition

A Task Group within the Telecommunications and Information Working Group of APEC (APEC TEL, 2001) defines cross-recognition as "An interoperability arrangement in which a relying party in one PKI domain can use authority information in another PKI domain to authenticate a subject in the other PKI domain, and vice versa" (APEC TEL, 2001). The CA accreditation schemes of the UK (tScheme) and The Netherlands (TTP.NL) follow a similar approach whereby an authority appointed by Law to accredit CSPs, grants approval on the basis of successfully passing an audit based on specific criteria. Some steps have already been taken for the mutual recognition between accreditation schemes that operate in various Member States.

Cross-recognition differs from cross-certification because there is no mutual or unilateral recognition between CAs. Cross-recognition is based on the notion that independent CAs would somehow be licensed or audited by a mutually recognized trusted authority (e.g., an accreditation authority or an independent auditor). A foreign CA is regarded as trustworthy if it has been accredited by a formal accreditation body or has been successfully audited by a trusted independent auditor. Accreditation can be accomplished on the basis of successful assessment according to specific mutually recognized criteria. Cross recognition requires cooperation between PA and private entities that are entrusted with the approval of the CA services. Deterrents for Cross-recognition include:

- A relying party is expected to make the trust decisions rather than the CAs but it is not yet clear how the relying party will gather the information necessary to make an informed decision
- Cross-recognition may not be acceptable in cases where high levels of assurance or trust are required especially where the control of the chained CAs must remain at arms length due to application constraints

Bridge CA

Bridge CAs use cross-certification as the basis for inter-domain interoperability. A bridge CA is effective in the diminution of the number of bilateral agreements required by the cross-certificate entities. The bilateral cross-certification agreements that are required in a fully meshed approach is: n*n, where n represents the number of participating CAs, making it a complicated and laborious endeavour that has limited ability to scale. Acting as an intermediary, a bridge CA introduces one organization to another. It is, therefore, no longer necessary for each organization to enter into a bilateral cross-certification with any other organization. Each participating CA gets cross-certified with the bridge CA. The conditions of trust are described in a certificate policy that prevails for the entire domain of cross certification. Where certificate policies overlap, participating organizations can have a trusted path to each other's resources via the bridge CA. A bridge CA can significantly reduce the

Copyright © 2007, Idea Group Inc. Copying or distributing in print or electronic forms without written permission of Idea Group Inc. is prohibited.

overhead required especially when the number of organizations that belong to the same policy is extended (ETSI TS 101 733, ETSI TS 102 042). Open issues for a bridge CA mostly associate with the policy (i.e., certificate policy or certification practice statement each CA applies and they include):

- Certificate Policy usage and assurance levels that might clash with application limitations and might require format and content mapping
- Certificate Profiles that might nurture conflicts related to key usage (i.e., authentication, non repudiation, or both)
- Client software configuration that might require building the trust path or that alternatively is required to rely on trust anchors included in one's own browser

Certificate Trust List and Bridge CA

A Certificate Trust List (CTL) is a signed PKCS#7 data structure that contains a list of trusted CAs. Within the CTL, a hash of the public key certificate of the subject CA identifies whether a CA is trusted. The CTL also contains policy identifiers and supports the use of extensions. From an inter-domain interoperability perspective, the CTL essentially replaces the cross-certificate pair. The relying party trusts the issuer of the CTL, who in return allows the relying party to trust the CAs conveyed within the CTL. The relying party can access a CTL by including one or more of the operational protocols defined within the IETF PKIX working group or via an out-of-band distribution mechanism. Like any of the other alternatives discussed in this chapter, acceptable practices and procedures are required in order for this mechanism to be a viable alternative to achieve inter-domain interoperability. Particularly important is to establish what constitutes a trusted CTL issuer and determine the criteria that the CAs must adhere to before they can be deemed "trusted."

A bridge CA enables organisations to communicate with one another on a secure and authenticated basis. Certificate management resources of discreet CAs are linked together by incorporating previously issued top root certificates into the Bridge-CA network. A CA that registers with a bridge CA can have its own certificates recognised by all other participating organizations without having to individually negotiate the reciprocal recognition of its root. The European Bridge-CA is an implemented model of the bridge CA concept carried out by the Teletrust association in Germany (www.teletrust.de).

The program Interoperable Delivery of European E-Government Services to public Administrations, Businesses, and Citizens (IDABC) of the European Commission has underlined the need for further interoperability in the area of certification services within the EU. The IDABC bridge CA has been deemed necessary to add trust to e-government applications. The IDABC CA model, however, does not necessarily seek to cross-certify participating CAs, by approving their policies (Certification Practice Statement—CPS) etc. The IDABC bridge CA distributes a

Copyright © 2007, Idea Group Inc. Copying or distributing in print or electronic forms without written permission of Idea Group Inc. is prohibited.

signed list of the root certificates of the CAs approved for use by the Member States for their respective PAs (ETSI TS 102 231, ETSI TR 102 030). By making the CA's root certificates available either through signed lists or via a repository, IDABC expects to act as a gateway so that relying parties establish trust with a CA within the PA originating from another Member State (Callens, 2003).

Root CA

A Root CA model is based on the assumption that trust derives from one trusted source that is organized in a strict hierarchical order. A root CA is the trust anchor for all relying parties within a given domain. Subordinate CAs may be deployed, however relying parties will not rely on any certificates issued by a subordinate CA, unless a valid certificate path can be traced back to the root CAs. In a strict hierarchy, a subordinate CA features one superior CA. Further, subordinate CAs are not permitted to have their own self-signed certificates while only the root CA has a self-signed certificate. Strict hierarchies:

- Comprise of one root CA and zero or more subordinate CAs
- Are appropriate for business cases where policy controls are to be enforced in a "top-down" approach
- Have been established to support specific vertical applications within an industry (e.g., Identrus)

In strict hierarchies, the consequences of compromise of a root CA private key could be severe. In addition, there is no single root CA that applies to every PKI domain, so it not possible to maintain a strict hierarchy across all conceivable domains. This means that one of the other methods previously discussed must be used to establish a trust relationship between these otherwise isolated domains. In specific implementations, an added benefit of the Root CA model permits the trusted root to undertake the operation of the directory of certificates if a CA fails to find a successor in case of ceasing operating, which is a clear benefit for the relying party. Open issues for cross-recognition include CA reluctance to accept subordination out of fear for the market or hierarchical position.

There are issues regarding the overlapping validity periods of the keys of the CAs.

Looking at the root CA model it is hard to avoid noticing the demanding security requirements, however justified they might be, that might limit scaling. Currently it is not conceivable to attain to the desired interoperability levels for multiple CAs operating across the EU under the root CA model. In this regard, the German regulator's view is that "Until such time, legally recognized digital signatures may only be used in international business transactions if the correspondent has been issued certificates by a German CA." The Digital Signature Act (see, Gesetz über Rahmenbedingungen für elektronische Signaturen (Signaturgesetz - SigG)1) of

Copyright © 2007, Idea Group Inc. Copying or distributing in print or electronic forms without written permission of Idea Group Inc. is prohibited.

May 16, 2001 (BGBl. I S. 876) as such does not prohibit the establishing of offices abroad by German CAs for the acceptance of certificate requests and the provision of signature components. However, this has been considered to be a mere temporary solution until a more suitable model is adopted.

AN INTEROPERABILITY ARCHITECTURE FOR E-GOVERNMENT

The e-mayor project aims at setting up and operating a platform for secure e-government exchanges of data for multiple applications of small e-government organisations. While typical of these organisations is the need to be cost effective due to the budgetary constraints the benefits from interoperating with counterparty organisations in other Member States can have a significant impact on citizen perception for e-government. Often e-government solutions might have to be made available by small PAs that face specific shortcomings in terms of resources and expertise. In such cases certificate management infrastructure must be adapted to the needs of small PAs and meet specific requirements such as scalability, simplicity in the use,

Figure 2. Certificate interoperability for small PAs

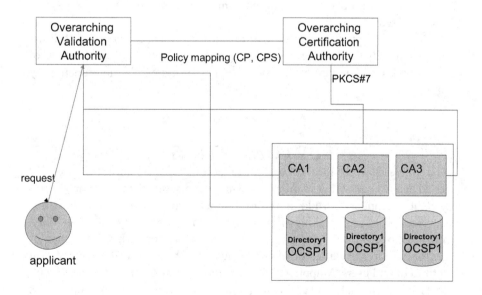

Copyright © 2007, Idea Group Inc. Copying or distributing in print or electronic forms without written permission of Idea Group Inc. is prohibited.

and low access to resources. While this section proposes an architecture that meets these objectives and fulfils the interoperability requirements among heterogeneous entities. Figure 2 presents an overview of the recommended architecture.

End entities such as citizens and small PAs that are entitled to request services within the proposed infrastructure must register locally within their certificate service of their own administration. To facilitate the interactions among various small PAs certificate services must become sufficiently interoperable in order to recognize each other's root and allow end entities carrying out end user transactions.

For the end-entity certificate validation, an overarching validation authority (oVA) makes available validation services by redirecting certificate validation requests to the appropriate validation service of a local CA. An oVA provides the end entity with the technical capability to check the certificate status through an appropriate application. Using a certificate trust list that is composed by a list of predefined and trusted CAs is a desirable add on. Browsers and other applications have the ability to allow users to add other root certificates besides the ones included therein by default as needed. The end user can therefore update the default lists of CA roots to match their individual requirements.

The potential risk is the ease in which root certificate updates can take place within end entity applications, could potentially be exploited by malicious actors to add false root certificates that can be further used to carry out bogus and fraudulent transactions with PAs. To overcome this problem, a list of trusted CAs is digitally signed by a dedicated Overarching Validation Authority (oCA). An oCA is a technical facilitator and is entrusted with the competence to set up a policy and a technical framework to support the cross-border recognition of certificates issued by the various local CAs that service the small PAs. An oCA can address the critical issue of the recognition of local CAs in a large number of contexts, being geographic, organizational, etc.

The previous represents a basic interoperability model for PAs. The following section expands this basic concept by elaborating certain elements that are of interest to the PA with regard to the application environment that interoperability is sought.

FURTHER STEPS

The policies that each local CA makes available may additionally be mapped and reconciled against each other in order to ensure organisational and legal interoperability. Policy mapping is an additional albeit optional step to complement the basic model presented before. By taking a flexible approach toward policy interoperability, the proposed model allows for an enhanced level of transactions in heterogeneous PA services that require the validation of certificates and subsequently the management of identities of end users. Mapping and reconciling policy frameworks in overlapping transactions might however threaten transactions, which are based on the use

Copyright © 2007, Idea Group Inc. Copying or distributing in print or electronic forms without written permission of Idea Group Inc. is prohibited.

and acceptance of varying terms. A typical hard case might involve for example overlapping policy conditions, which apply to certificates issued by different CAs. The situation is exacerbated when CAs that do not have the means to recognise one another issue certificates that can be used in the same transaction environments (ETSI TS 102 231). Although such certificates may well be complementary to a transaction framework the varying assurance levels they provide might threaten the reliability of the e-government application environment as a whole (Mitrakas, 2005a). Reconciling the methods used across various electronic signing environments is likely to contribute to creating trust in e-government services.

Besides policy mapping, setting up equivalence levels is a significant requirement that might also have to be introduced at a later stage in order to ensure compliance with prevailing rules and reconcile the differences among the approach toward voluntary accreditation conditions according to article 3.2 of 99/93/EC. To date the degree of equivalence among accreditation schemes across the EU Member States is unclear with the consequence of possibly inhibiting the use of certification services in cross-border transactions for PA purposes. Using intermediaries is recommended to ensure equivalence levels according to prescribed criteria. Intermediaries could collect applicable policies in a repository as well as specify audit conditions and provide advance notice concerning the legal status of the scheme or legal requirements under which a certificate has been issued or a root operates (Mitrakas & Bos, 1998). Policy mapping tools based on decision support systems could be developed in order to facilitate the management of disparate policies of participating CAs.

An additional issue associates with the way that operational requirements of an oCA are addressed. Based on present day experience whenever a new CA seeks recognition by the oCA its name and root certificate have to be added to the master trust list that is signed by the oCA and subsequently distributed to the implicated end entities. Distributing updated trust lists might face scalability shortcomings if there are more than a small number of CAs used by the various PAs across the EU. This problem could be addressed by setting up a single reference directory for CAs that seek the inclusion of the root in a given trust list. By accessing the directory of CA roots, an end entity that transacts with the PA enhances its ability to establish the trustworthiness of the CA issuing the certificate in question because it can directly validate the certificate path online. The role of the oCA can be limited to providing the secure publication of the directory as well as ensuring the inclusion of a pointer to the directory by all trusted local CAs. Including CAs in a directory however is likely to require a classification mechanism for the CAs included therein (ETSI TS 102 231).

Furthermore, an area of future attention could address policy frameworks related to the application layer in an e-government transaction. To respond to transparency requirements it is expected that online applications will increasingly become more demanding in explaining to the end user what they do and actually warranting the performance. Through a combination of dedicated legislation and policy (e.g., CPS)

Copyright © 2007, Idea Group Inc. Copying or distributing in print or electronic forms without written permission of Idea Group Inc. is prohibited.

part of this requirement has been addressed. It remains to be seen how providing comprehensive description of the technical features and functionality of the online e-government application might be tackled. In e-government it is still required to enhance the features that invoke trust and safety to the benefit of end users. Policies for the application layer are likely to become more in demand in e-government applications where the requirement for transparency in the transaction and accountability of the parties involved is higher than in electronic business (Mitrakas, 2005a). Finally, specifying policies further to meet the needs of particular application areas, groups or organisations are additional expectations, like for example in the area of eProcurement. In e-government it is expected that interoperability will be enhanced through best practices and standards regarding policy in specific vertical areas. Typical content for an application layer policy may include aspects associated with the kinds of underlying services that are involved, the profile of the providers that make these services available, architectural premises, disclosures with regard to databases, personal data, validation services as well as liability or warranty that might be offered to the end user. The scope of application layer policy is to contribute to the transparency of the application platform that might ultimately lead to trust and legal safety (Mitrakas, 2005b).

Further standardisation is a way to effect the desired changes to enhance interoperability in e-government CA services. A set of overarching rules has yet to emerge and be accepted for this architecture to become fully operational. While political support at the EU level is necessary for the set up and operation of an overarching infrastructure that is trusted by CAs more initiatives are necessary to contribute toward establishing a framework of best practices in cross-border CA service recognition for the PA. Applications for e-government are likely to provide the additional drive like for example in the area of identity management especially for such areas as electronic invoicing and electronic public procurement (CWA 15236:2005).

While interoperability remains a constant requirement for information society, e-government applications need to also benefit in a way that allows applications from various PAs to work together. Identity management is a key e-government application that has the ability to render interoperability requirements applicable across multiple functional applications such as e-procurement and e-invoicing. A much needed improvement would be to strive for a policy framework that meets the requirements of law and associated applications.

CONCLUSION

To date Member States' e-government services have developed certification services across multiple platforms. The Directive 99/93/EC does not necessarily address the issue of the cross-border recognition of CA services for the purpose of validating identities in an identity management environment that is leveraged upon

Copyright © 2007, Idea Group Inc. Copying or distributing in print or electronic forms without written permission of Idea Group Inc. is prohibited.

e-government applications. Furthermore, policy requirements of the e-government application layer remain fragmented. The EESSI standards and several PA and industry initiatives have strived to address this issue with some success. However, present date standards have but succeeded to provide entwined solutions that work well when a small number of strings of two or more strands are brought together. Lacing together however does not necessarily provide an answer to interoperability in a complex application area as e-government where multiple PAs originating from a vast number of contexts must trust each other to provide end-to-end services. As interoperability of services across EU Member States becomes ever more demanding additional efforts are necessary in order to set the guidelines required. New architecture elements including enhanced policy mapping tools, intermediaries to establish equivalence levels between CAs and one or more directories for trusted CA roots can provide the additional functionality needed in e-government. Failing to come up with a scalable interoperability solution is likely to put at risk sophisticated infrastructures and turn them yet again to modern day information silos for PAs that are able to merely operate in the local context alone. Failure to meet interoperability requirements risks impacting the beneficiaries of e-government services that typically seek to operate and contribute to the success of the EU internal market. The strong drive in support of applications, such as electronic identity for the movement of persons, as well as electronic public procurement, for public sector transactions are likely to provide the necessary impetus to achieve certificate service interoperability. Policy and Law must follow suit and facilitate the need of end users to rely on appropriate identity resources to carry out secure electronic transactions.

ACKNOWLEDGMENT

This chapter has been drafted within the framework of the e-mayor project (IST- 2003-507217) co-funded by the European Commission. While the views expressed herein are strictly personal and reflect the author's involvement in the e-mayor project on behalf of Ubizen NV (a Cybertrust company), in no way do they represent those of the author's employer past or present. The author wishes to thank Dr. Abdel Youssouf for his valuable insight.

REFERENCES

Aalberts, B. P., & van der Hof, S. (2000). *Digital signature blindness, Analysis of legislative approaches toward electronic authentication.* Deventer, The Netherlands: Kluwer.

APEC eSecurity Task Group. (2001). *Achieving PKI interoperability.* Canberra, Australia: APEC.

Blivet, L., Mitrakas, A., & Moyal, M. (2001). *Pre-inventory of smart card based PKI projects in the European Union.* Brussels: eEurope Smart Cards Report.

Copyright © 2007, Idea Group Inc. Copying or distributing in print or electronic forms without written permission of Idea Group Inc. is prohibited.

Caelli, W., Longley, D., & Shain, M. (1991). *Information security handbook*. London: Macmillan.

Callens, B. (2003). *Trust list usage recommendations for a bridge/gateway CA pilot for public administrations*. Brussels: Certipost report.

CWA 15236 :2005. (2005). *Analysis of standardization requirements and standardization gaps for eProcurement in Europe*. Brussels: European Committee for Standardisation.

Deprest, J., & Robben, F. (2003). *E-Government: The approach of the Belgian Federal Government*. Brussels: FEDICT and CBBSS.

Dworkin, R. (1977). *Taking rights seriously*. London: Duckworth.

ETSI TS 101 456. (2001). *Policy requirements for certification authorities issuing qualified certificates*. Sophia-Antipolis, France: European Telecommunications Standards Institute.

ETSI TS 101 733. (2001). *Electronic signature formats*. Sophia-Antipolis, France: European Telecommunications Standards Institute.

ETSI TS 102 042 v1.1.1. (2001). *Policy requirements for certification authorities issuing public key certificates*. Sophia-Antipolis, France: European Telecommunications Standards Institute.

ETSI TS 102 231 V1.1.1. (2001) *Provision of harmonized trust Service Provider status information*. Sophia-Antipolis, France: European Telecommunications Standards Institute.

ETSI TR 102 030 v.1.1.1. (2001) *Provision of harmonised trust Service Provider status information*. Sophia-Antipolis, France: European Telecommunications Standards Institute.

Eymeri, J. (2001, November 26-27). *The electronic identification of citizens and organisations in the European Union: State of Affairs*. Paper presented at the 37th Meeting of the Directors-General of the Public Service of the Member States of the European Union. Bruges.

Hix, S. (1999). *The political system of the European Union*. London: Palgrave.

Lloyd, S. (2001). *CA-CA interoperability*. Billerica, MA: PKI Forum.

Mitrakas, A. (2002). Citizen centric identity management: Chip tricks? *Network Security*. Winchester, UK: MCC International.

Mitrakas, A. (2003). *Electronic signatures in European and Greek Law: Application issues in banking transactions*. Hellenic Bankers Association Bulletin. Athens.

Mitrakas. A. (2004). Policy-driven signing frameworks in open electronic transactions. In G. Doukidis, N. Mylonopoulos, & N. Pouloudi (Eds.), *Information society or information economy? A combined perspective on the digital era*. Hershey, PA: Idea Group Publishing.

Mitrakas, A. (2005a). *Policy frameworks for secure electronic business—Encyclopedia of information science and technology* (Vol. I-III). Hershey, PA: Idea Group Publishing.

Copyright © 2007, Idea Group Inc. Copying or distributing in print or electronic forms without written permission of Idea Group Inc. is prohibited.

Mitrakas, A. (2005b). *Soft law constraints in e-government.* Paper presented at the Proceedings of the BILETA 2005 Conference, Belfast.

Mitrakas, A., & Bos, J. (1998). The ICC ETERMS repository to support public key infrastructure. *Jurimetrics, 38*(3) 473-496. Tempe, AZ.

Mitrakas, A., & Van Eecke, P. (2006). Commentary on Directive 1999/93 on a community framework for electronic signatures. In T. Dreier, C. Gielen, & R. Hacon (Eds.), *Concise commentary on European intellectual property law* (Vol. IV), *E-Commerce/DataProtection.* The Hague, The Netherlands: Kluwer.

Mousis, N. (2002). *Guide to European policies.* Rixensart, Belgium: European Study Service.

Pfleeger, C. (1997). *Security in computing.* Upper Saddle River, NJ: Prentice Hall.

Prins, C., Eifert, M., Girot, C., Groothuis, M., Voermans, W. (2001). *Taking administrative law to the digital era regulatory initiatives in France, Germany, Norway, and the United States.* The Hague, The Netherlands: Sdu Uitgevers.

UNCTAD. (2001). *E-commerce and development report 2001.* New York: United Nations.

Copyright © 2007, Idea Group Inc. Copying or distributing in print or electronic forms without written permission of Idea Group Inc. is prohibited.

Chapter X

Privacy-Enhanced Identity Management for E-Services

Claudio Agostino Ardagna, Università degli Studi di Milano, Italy

Marco Cremonini, Università degli Studi di Milano, Italy

Ernesto Damiani, Università degli Studi di Milano, Italy

Sabrina De Capitani di Vimercati, Università degli Studi di Milano, Italy

Fulvio Frati, Università degli Studi di Milano, Italy

Pierangela Samarati, Università degli Studi di Milano, Italy

ABSTRACT

This chapter introduces the concept of privacy-enhanced identity management for e-services supporting the user's needs to protect their privacy and sensitive information. Business activities are increasingly based on the use of remote resources and e-services as well as on the interaction between different, remotely-located, parties. In this context, the electronic execution of private and/or sensitive transactions must fully preserve information privacy by managing in a trustworthy and responsible way all identity and profile information that is released to remote parties. In this chapter, we investigate the main problems concerning identity management for e-services and outline the features that the next-generation of identity management systems should provide for. State-of-the-art technology in the field of privacy-enhanced identity management systems is also compared with traditional public key

Copyright © 2007, Idea Group Inc. Copying or distributing in print or electronic forms without written permission of Idea Group Inc. is prohibited.

infrastructure (PKI) solutions. The analysis of the benefits of these modern identity management systems is presented and discussed with references also to the results of some experiences in the area of e-government, whose objective is the development of public administration privacy-aware e-services.

INTRODUCTION

The widespread diffusion of online services provided by public and private organizations, mostly driven by e-commerce and more recently by e-government applications, has stressed the need of more secure ways to authenticate and authorize users who need to access online resources (Feldman, 2000).

In particular, we can define authentication as any process by which we can verify that the users are who they claim they are. The most common way to enforce authentication is based on the use of a pair username-password. However, many other techniques can be used such as digital certificates, smart cards, retina scans, voice recognition, or fingerprints. Access control is, instead, concerned with evaluating every request submitted by users who have entered the system, to access data and resources to determine whether the request should be allowed or denied based on a specified policy (Ardagna & De Capitani di Vimercati, 2004; Ashley, Hada, Karjoth, and Schunter, 2002; Ashley, Hada, Powers, and Schunter, 2003; De Capitani di Vimercati & Samarati, 2001). Basically, a policy defines the rights granted to users to exercise actions (e.g., read, write, create, delete, and execute) on certain objects.

In this chapter, we focus first on authentication technologies and architectures that address the growing needs of security requirements in the scenario of business-to-consumers applications. Kerberos (Kohl & Neuman, 1993) proposed at the beginning of the 90s, is an example of a successful technology for authenticating requests for network resources. The great expansion of Web-based systems led to application environments that crossed the boundaries of real organizations. Cross-domain digital identities are then required as well as new procedures for user authentication must be adopted, when online services, resource stakeholders, and users are geographically and organizationally distributed. In this context, new solutions need to be proposed to address interoperability and scalability challenges, among which single sign-on (SSO) (De Clercq, 2002) and credential-based authentication play an important role. The public key infrastructure (PKI) (Arsenault & Turner, 2002) is a well-known method for providing credential-based authentication and digital signatures solutions to electronic business and government applications by means of certification authorities hierarchies and the support of cross-certificates. When e-government systems were being designed, PKIs seemed to be the best answer to satisfy their requirements, such as the possibility for national or regional governments to establish root CAs aimed at improving the interoperability among

Copyright © 2007, Idea Group Inc. Copying or distributing in print or electronic forms without written permission of Idea Group Inc. is prohibited.

public agencies, guaranteeing correct procedures, and providing users of public services with a generalized token (e.g., identity certificate, smart card), that can be used as a credential for all possible requests. Also, PKIs usage was soon regulated by a number of international institutions. The European Commission, all European national governments, the U.S. federal government, many U.S. states and federal departments, as well as the Canadian and Australian governments, are significant examples of institutions that have regulated PKIs, each within its own jurisdiction. Today, however, a traditional PKI looks too complex as infrastructure for most e-government applications and several drawbacks have been identified. Deploying and operating PKIs involves considerable difficulties, due to management, administrative and regulatory reasons, which have ultimately limited the real diffusion and success of PKIs for public electronic services. For instance, interoperation between different CAs, although theoretically straightforward, proved awkward in practice, partly for technical problems, partly for increasing competition among authorities, market positioning of technology providers, and difficulties in the definition of all formal agreements needed to have common semantics, data format and system compatibility. However, despite the huge interest that PKIs generated when the first experimental systems were proposed to citizens of regional and local institutions and to professional categories, user interaction represents perhaps the most severe

Figure 1. A partial identity example (Source: Damiani, De Capitani di Vimercati, & Samarati, 2003)

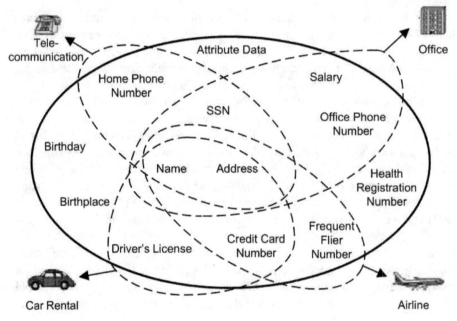

Copyright © 2007, Idea Group Inc. Copying or distributing in print or electronic forms without written permission of Idea Group Inc. is prohibited.

problem for an effective utilization of PKIs. PKI technologies usage was never fully understood by the majority of users, which, consequently, do not always fulfill all the duties that PKIs require.

Many researchers share the opinion that a more flexible and cost-effective solution could be achieved following the digital identity management (DIM) approach (Damiani, De Capitani di Vimercati, & Samarati, 2004). A comprehensive identity management solution should provide complete support for the definition and the life cycle management of digital identities and profiles, as well as an infrastructure for exchanging and validating this information. In the following, the term digital identity will be used to refer to two (non-disjoint) concepts (Damiani, De Capitani di Vimercati, & Samarati, 2003): nyms and partial identities. Nyms can be used to give a user a different identity under which operates at any interaction. A partial identity is any subset of the properties (e.g., name, age, credit-card, employment, and so on) associated with a user (see Figure 1).

Recently, some identity management solutions have been proposed, such as the Liberty Alliance's Identity Federation Framework (ID-FF), an open architecture and a set of specifications to enable federated identity management (www.projectliberty.org), the Sun Java System Identity Manager (www.sun.com), the Oracle Identity Management (www.oracle.com) (Miley, 2004), and the Microsoft .NET Passport (www.passport.com). Also, some research projects (e.g., Privacy and Identity Management for Europe [PRIME, 2005]) are being carried out aimed at providing breakthrough innovation concerning digital identity definition and management. The concept of digital identity is often associated with the concept of privacy. Users, in fact, are concerned about their private information and often they are likely to refuse to make use of services provided by the global information infrastructure since they prefer not to have their personal data under the control of anyone at any-

Figure 2. User log-on to multi-service domains

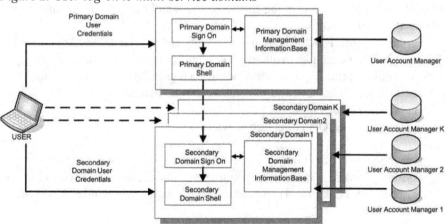

Copyright © 2007, Idea Group Inc. Copying or distributing in print or electronic forms without written permission of Idea Group Inc. is prohibited.

time. Hence, the request for privacy-enhanced digital identity management systems poses an entirely new set of challenges to access control systems.

The remainder of this chapter is organized as follows. First, we give an overview of SSO technology and describe our single sign-on implementation integrated with strong authentication technologies (i.e., smart card and biometric), able to improve and secure authentication processes and users profiles management. As we will see, this integration with smart cards fulfills the needs of protection against replay attacks. Then, we compare public key infrastructures and the concept of digital identity discussing the benefits that the newer approach can provide. Following, we depict our current effort within the PRIME European project, describing a privacy-enhanced access control system. Finally, we present our conclusions. Furthermore, in the "Appendix" we describe a proof-of-concept prototype within the PRIME project.

SSO AND IDENTITY MANAGEMENT

A major critical problem due to the huge amount of services available on the Net is the proliferation of user accounts and identities. Users, typically, have to log-on to multiple systems, each of which may require different usernames and authentication information. System administrators have to manage user accounts within each system to ensure the integrity of security policy enforcement. Figure 2 illustrates how log-on to multiple systems is performed usually. Each system acts as an independent domain. The user, first, interacts with a primary domain to establish a session by providing a set of applicable credentials. From this session, the user can require services from secondary domains providing another set of credentials applicable to each of these domains.

From the account management point of view, this approach requires independent management of profiles in each domain and the use of different authentication mechanisms. Several usability and security concerns have been recognized, leading to a newest approach to the log-on process aimed at coordinating and, where possible, integrating different user log-on mechanisms and user account management tools for different domains.

Furthermore, the Health Insurance Portability and Accountability Act (HIPAA) (HIPAA, 2005), for example, explicitly states that companies are required to assign a unique profile for tracking user identities to each user. A service/architecture that provides such a coordination and integration is called single sign-on (SSO) (Galbraith et al., 2002) (see Figure 3).

In particular, a SSO architecture provides:

- Reduction of (1) the time spent by the users during log-on operations to individual domains, (2) failed log-on transactions, (3) the time used to log-on to secondary domains, (4) costs and time used for users profiles administration.

Copyright © 2007, Idea Group Inc. Copying or distributing in print or electronic forms without written permission of Idea Group Inc. is prohibited.

Figure 3. User single sign-on to multi-service domains

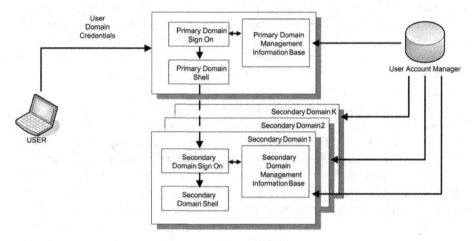

- Secure and simplified administration, because with a centralized administration point, system administrators reduce the time spent to add and remove users to the system or modify their access rights (authorization).
- Improvement to (1) users security, the user has to manage only one pair username/password, (2) system security, through the enhanced ability of system administrators to maintain the integrity of user account configuration including the ability to change an individual user's access to all system resources in a coordinated and consistent manner, and (3) services usability.

In the SSO approach, the primary domain is responsible for collecting and managing all user credentials and information used during the authentication process. This information is then used by single sign-on services, within the primary domain, to support the transparent authentication to each of the requested secondary domains (Ardagna, Damiani, De Capitani di Vimercati, Frati, & Samarati, 2006).

CAS++ Architecture:
A Certificate-Based Open-Source SSO Implementation

We give, as an example, an overview of an open-source SSO system, called CAS++, developed as an extension to Yale University's CAS (Aubry, Marchal, & Mathieu, 2004; Central Authentication Service [CAS], 2005) by our group at the University of Milan in the context of a joint research project with Siemens Mobile. This solution is based on the use of certificates, integrated with the JBoss security layer (JBoss, 2005; Scott, 2003) and with the authentication mechanism implemented by a public key infrastructure (PKI).

Copyright © 2007, Idea Group Inc. Copying or distributing in print or electronic forms without written permission of Idea Group Inc. is prohibited.

CAS++ implements a fully stand-alone server that provides a simple, efficient, and reliable SSO mechanism through HTTP redirections, focused on user privacy (opaque cookies) and security protection. It permits a centralized management of user profiles granting access to all services in the system with an unique pair username/password. The profiles repository is stored inside the SSO server application and it is the only point where users' credentials/information are accessed, thus reducing information scattering.

CAS++ uses standard protocols, such as HTTPS, for secure communications between parties, and X.509 digital certificates for credentials exchange (ITU-T, 2000). It enriches the traditional CAS authentication process through the integration of biometric identification (by fingerprint readers) and smart card technologies. Our authentication process flow (see Figure 4) starts from a user request for an identity certificate to a CA. Then, the user receives a smart card that contains a certificate, signed with the private key of the CA, that certifies the user identity. This certificate is only decrypted by mean of a key represented by her fingerprint (KFingerprintUser). When the user wants to access a service, first of all, she decrypts the information inside the smart card and sends the certificate in encrypted form (KPu-CAS++) to the CAS++ server. The latter decrypts the certificate with its private key and verifies its validity by interacting with the CA. If the certificate is valid, CAS++ extracts the information and authenticates the user.

For every further access in the session, the user is authenticated by the service providing only the ticket returned by the CAS++ server (TGC, ticket granting cookie). The advantages of this mechanism are that the account management is centralized and separated by the real application, and the user does not have to

Figure 4. Single sign-on authentication with certificate

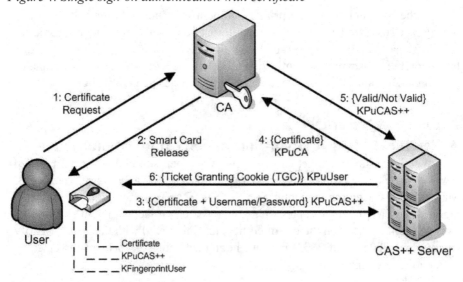

Copyright © 2007, Idea Group Inc. Copying or distributing in print or electronic forms without written permission of Idea Group Inc. is prohibited.

remember the pair username/password because they are logically contained in the certificate used during the authentication phase. The introduction of smart cards and fingerprint readers does not affect the system performance and does not require huge additional costs.

PKI AND IDENTITY MANAGEMENT

In today's e-government systems, conventional PKI's basic privacy and authentication techniques (Ford, Housley, Polk, & Solo, 2002) have been straight-forwardly applied to bilateral communications, such as a citizen paying a local tax or a fine to a local administration. PKI authentication has also been used for multilateral communications, where a citizen signs a document or an application that several people will read. In many e-government applications, PKI is also used as a way to enhance privacy, by having the citizen encrypting the information she is submitting to the remote service with the recipient's public key. However, this approach is only suited to two-way communications. In the multilateral scenario, where multiple recipients share a message that should be kept private, current PKI technology does not provide a simple answer. Another drawback is the possibility for a citizen to lose the support (floppy, smart-card, or others) holding her private key, which is required for decryption of information that the public administration sends to her.1 Moreover, if a private key is compromised, the PKI certificate must be revoked and a new one issued, along with a new private key. Normally, private keys are split into several pieces, called shares. Shares must be stored in different trusted locations, or encrypted with each of their public keys and held by the key's owner, making it impossible for one person alone to reconstruct the private key.

E-government applications, relying on PKI on a large scale and over a significant period of time, need advanced capabilities of managing end-users' keys life cycle, including share management and provisions for recovering lost keys.

Privacy Issues

Besides the drawbacks previously outlined, some major privacy-related concerns have been raised about PKI as it does not provide a comprehensive solution for avoiding unauthorized disclosure of personal information. Indeed, personal credentials provided by users to service providers should be used for the sole purpose of granting access to the specific online service they are submitted to. Instead, they have been often used to profile users for marketing campaigns. Discriminatory and even criminal actions against users have been reported as consequences of personal information leakage. To keep unauthorized disclosure of personal information in check, besides the adoption of specific legislations, the notion of digital identity itself is evolving beyond PKI. An environment for managing digital identities should support at least the following basic requirements.

Copyright © 2007, Idea Group Inc. Copying or distributing in print or electronic forms without written permission of Idea Group Inc. is prohibited.

- **Privacy:** A digital identity solution should be respectful of the users rights to privacy and should not disclose personal information without explicit consent.
- **Minimal disclosure:** Service providers must require the least set of credentials needed for service provision, and users should be able to provide credentials selectively, according to the type of online service they wish to access.
- **Anonymity support:** Many services do not need to know the real identity of a user. Pseudonyms, multiple digital identities, and, even, anonymous accesses must be adopted when possible.
- **Legislation support:** Privacy-related legislation is becoming a powerful driver towards the adoption of digital identities. The exchange of identity data must not then violate government legislation such as the HIPAA or Gramm-Leach-Bliley Act (GLB) (Gramm-Leach-Bliley Act, 2005; HIPAA, 2005).

With respect to these requirements, the usual way of designing PKI-based authentication and authorization systems is not satisfactory. In particular, selective disclosure of credentials is normally not implemented, because users attributes, either inserted into X.509 identity certificates or collected as attribute certificates (Farrell & Housley, 2002), are defined according to functional needs, making it easier to collect all credentials in a row instead of iteratively asking for the ones strictly necessary for a given service only.

Pseudonymity, multiple identities and anonymity are also usually not supported in PKI-based architectures. Also, extensibility of the X.509 certificate format has encouraged the practice of encapsulating information needed for authorization within the identity certificate, making it difficult to cleanly separate the two sets of information. Furthermore, even when identity certificates and attribute certificates are disjoint, there has been a trend towards designing authorization architectures that strictly integrate the two types of certificates by referencing identity certificates inside attribute certificates (Essiari, Mudumbai, & Thompson, 2003; Farrell et al., 2002).

PRIME Overview

These new requirements regarding digital identities have driven a number of research projects. The PRIME project (PRIME, 2005) is a large-scale research effort aimed at developing an identity management system satisfying the requirements expressed for protecting users personal information and providing, at the same time, a framework that can be smoothly integrated with current architectures and online services. The main objectives of the PRIME project are the following. First, PRIME is aimed at giving the users the maximum control on their personal data and to allow anonymous interactions. Users should then be able to use pseudonyms with support of unlinkability during interactions with other parties. Second, it should be possible

Copyright © 2007, Idea Group Inc. Copying or distributing in print or electronic forms without written permission of Idea Group Inc. is prohibited.

to define privacy rules governing the system usage. The rules should establish how to use the system and, in particular, allow the definition of policies for defining trust relationships, privacy preferences, and authorization policies (see section "A New Vision of Privacy and Digital Identity"). The final policies that govern the interactions should be the result of a policy negotiation by parties. Third, PRIME should provide a powerful and flexible mechanism (Ardagna & De Capitani di Vimercati, 2004; Ardagna, Damiani, De Capitani di Vimercati, & Samarati, 2004; Jajodia, Samarati, Sapino, & Subrahmanian, 2001) for enforcing privacy rules together with the evidence that policies are effectively enforced at the receiving parties. The enforcement of privacy policies is a more complicate task than the enforcing of traditional access control policies, because they have several additional features such as obligations, policy combination, and refinement. Finally, PRIME should provide an integrated approach where all privacy-enhancing technical components will be integrated into tools for privacy-enhanced digital identity management.

A NEW VISION OF PRIVACY AND DIGITAL IDENTITY

To define a privacy-enhanced access control system based on the concept of digital identity, we first need to identify the main characteristics that it should fulfill.

- **Anonymity and end-user control:** The access control system should enable full end-user control over the digital identities to be used. In other words, access control needs to operate even when interacting parties wish to remain anonymous or to disclose only specific attributes about themselves.
- **Flexible and expressive access control rules:** The access control rules should be able to refer to the different partial identities associated with users. Also, it is important to be able to specify access control rules about subjects accessing the information and about resources to be accessed in terms of rich ontology-based metadata (e.g., Semantic Web-style ones), increasingly available in advanced e-government applications (Corallo, Damiani, & Elia, 2002).
- **Client-side restrictions:** In addition to traditional server-side access control rules, users should be able to specify restrictions on how the released information can be used by their remote counterpart.

To take these issues into account, a new privacy-aware access control model is needed together with an access control protocol for the communication of policies and of identity information among parties (De Capitani di Vimercati, Paraboschi, & Samarati, 2003). Specifically, we have introduced the definition of four different types of privacy policies.

Copyright © 2007, Idea Group Inc. Copying or distributing in print or electronic forms without written permission of Idea Group Inc. is prohibited.

- Access control policies govern access/release of data/services managed by the party, as in traditional access control (De Capitani di Vimercati & Samarati, 2001).
- Release policies govern release of properties, credentials, personal identifiable information (PII) of the party and specify under which conditions they can be disclosed (Bonatti & Samarati, 2002).
- Sanitized policies provide filtering functionalities on the response to be returned to the counterpart to avoid release of sensitive information related to the policy itself.
- Data handling policies define how the personal information disclosure will be (or should be) dealt with at the receiving party.

In the following, we deal with access control policies, outlining their structure and underlying model.

A Privacy-Aware Access Control Policy

Although the specific syntax of the access control rules will depend on the language used to define a policy, the policy will contain the following basic elements.

- **Subject expression:** To provide expressive power and flexibility, a rule should specify the entities against which access must be controlled through expressions. Each expression identifies a set of subjects having specific properties. Each user is then associated with a profile that defines the name and value of some properties that characterize the user.
- **Object expression:** The characterization of the entities to be protected should be specified through expressions. As for subjects, each object is associated with a profile which defines the name and value of some properties that characterize the object.
- **Actions:** Policies must be able to make distinctions based on the type of actions being performed (e.g., read, write, execute, and so forth).
- **Purposes:** Data access requests are made for a specific purpose or purposes, which represent how the data is going to be used by the recipient.
- **Conditions:** Rules can include additional conditions, in the same way as legislation often makes statements based on specified conditions.
- **Obligations:** To improve privacy, users can define some obligations attached to the data.

Therefore, when a certain access is allowed, the parties involved must take some additional steps, following the defined obligations.

Copyright © 2007, Idea Group Inc. Copying or distributing in print or electronic forms without written permission of Idea Group Inc. is prohibited.

Each access request submitted to the system results in an access decision notifying that the request is granted, denied, or undefined. More precisely, the system can return three different responses:

- **Yes:** Request is granted
- **No:** Request is denied
- **Undefined:** Current information is insufficient to determine whether the request can be granted or denied. Additional information is needed and it is requested by communicating the sanitized policy. Additional information may be either sufficient or simply necessary for the counterpart to eventually have its request satisfied.

An undefined decision corresponds to the case where the conditions specified in the access control rules cannot be evaluated neither as yes nor as no. For instance, suppose that a user can access a service if he or she is at least eighteen and can provide a credit card number. Two cases can occur: (1) the system knows that the user is not yet eighteen and therefore returns a no response; (2) the user has proved that he or she is eighteen and the system returns an undefined response together with the request to provide the number of a credit card.

Finally, in the "Appendix" is described an implementation of privacy-aware access control system, developed within the PRIME project.

CONCLUSION

The protection of privacy and digital identity in today's global infrastructure requires application solutions combining technology (technical measures), legislation (law and public policy), and organizational and individual policies and practices. Emerging scenarios of user-service interactions in the digital world are also pushing towards the use of multiple and dependable identities. While some preliminary DIM-based systems have been designed and implemented, a general solution to the identity management issue is still underway. This chapter has illustrated the main characteristics of the current solutions for authorization process and identity management in e-services and it has presented the preliminary results of our ongoing activity in the context of a joint research project with Siemens Mobile and in the framework of the PRIME project.

ACKNOWLEDGMENTS

This work was supported in part by the European Union within the PRIME Project in the FP6/IST Programme under contract IST-2002507591 and by the Italian MIUR within the KIWI and MAPS projects.

Copyright © 2007, Idea Group Inc. Copying or distributing in print or electronic forms without written permission of Idea Group Inc. is prohibited.

REFERENCES

Ardagna, C. A., & De Capitani di Vimercati, S. (2004). A comparison of modeling strategies in defining XML-based access control languages. *Computer Systems Science & Engineering, 19*(3), 141-149.

Ardagna, C. A., Damiani, E., De Capitani di Vimercati, S., & Samarati, P. (2004, September). A Web service architecture for enforcing access control policies. In *Proceedings of the 1ˢᵗ International Workshop on Views on Designing Complex Architectures (VODCA 2004)*, Bertinoro, Italy (Electronic Notes in Theoretical Computer Science, Vol. 142, pp. 47-62).

Ardagna, C. A., Damiani, E., De Capitani di Vimercati, S., Frati, F., & Samarati, P. (2006). Single sign on for open source application servers: A comparative approach. In *Proceedings of the 21ˢᵗ IFIP International Information Security Conference "Security and Privacy in Dynamic Environments,"* Karlstad, Sweden.

Arsenault, A., & Turner, S. (2002). *Internet X.509 public key infrastructure: Roadmap.* Internet Draft, Internet Engineering Task Force.

Ashley, P., Hada, S., Karjoth, G., & Schunter, M. (2002). E-P3P privacy policies and privacy authorization. In *Proceedings of the ACM Workshop on Privacy in the Electronic Society (WPES 2002),* Washington, DC, USA.

Ashley, P., Hada, S., Powers, C., & Schunter, M. (2003). *Enterprise Privacy Authorization Language (EPAL).* IBM Research.

Aubry, P., Marchal, J., & Mathieu, V. (2004). ESUP-Portal: Open source single sign-on with CAS (Central Authentication Service). In *Proceedings of EUNIS04 -IT Innovation in a Changing World*, Bled, Slovenia.

Bonatti, P., & Samarati, P. (2002). A unified framework for regulating access and information release on the Web. *Journal of Computer Security, 10*(3), 241-272.

Buell, D. A., & Sandhu, R. S. (2003). Guest editors' introduction: Identity management. *IEEE Internet Computing, 7*(6), 26-28.

Central Authentication Service (CAS). (2005). Retrieved from http://jasigch.princeton.edu:9000/display/CAS

Corallo, A., Damiani, E., & Elia, G. (2002). A knowledge management system enabling regional innovation. In *Proceedings of the VI International Conference on Knowledge-Based Intelligent Information & Engineering Systems (KES 2002),* Crema, Italy. Damiani, E., De Capitani di Vimercati, S., & Samarati, P. (2003). Managing multiple and dependable identities. *IEEE Internet Computing, 7*(6), 29-37.

De Capitani di Vimercati, S., & Samarati, P. (2001). Access control: Policies, models, and mechanisms. In R. Focardi & R. Gorrieri (Eds.), *Foundations of Security Analysis and Design* (LNCS 2171). Berlin, Germany: Springer-Verlag.

Copyright © 2007, Idea Group Inc. Copying or distributing in print or electronic forms without written permission of Idea Group Inc. is prohibited.

De Capitani di Vimercati, S., Paraboschi, S., & Samarati, P. (2003). Access control: Principles and solutions. *Software—Practice and Experience, 33*(5), 397-421.

De Clercq, J. (2002). Single sign-on architectures. In *Proceedings of International Conference on Infrastructure Security (InfraSec 2002)*, Bristol, UK.

Essiari, A., Mudumbai, S., & Thompson, M. R. (2003). Certificate-based authorization policy in a PKI environment. *ACM Transactions on Information and System Security, 6*(4), 566-588.

Farrell, S., & Housley, R. (2002). *An Internet attribute certificate for authorization.* Request For Comments 3281, Internet Engineering Task Force.

Feldman, S. (2000). The changing face of e-commerce. *IEEE Internet Computing, 4*(3), 82-84.

Ford, W., Housley, R., Polk, W., & Solo, D. (2002). *Internet X.509 public key infrastructure: Certificate and Certificate Revocation List (CRL) profile.* Request For Comments 3280, Internet Engineering Task Force.

Galbraith, B., Hankinson, W., Hiotis, A., Janakiraman, M., Prasad, D. V., Trivedi, R., et al. (2002). *Professional Web services security.* Birmingham, UK: Wrox Press.

Gramm-Leach-Bliley Act. (2005). Retrieved from http://www.epic.org/privacy/glba/

HIPAA (Health Insurance Portability and Accountability Act). (2005). Retrieved from http://www.hipaa.org/

ITU-T (ITU Telecommunication Standardization Sector). (2000). *Information technology—open systems interconnection—the directory: Authentication framework.* Recommendation X.509 (03/00), International Telecommunication Union.

Jajodia, S., Samarati, P., Sapino, M., & Subrahmanian, V. (2001). Flexible support for multiple access control policies. *ACM Transactions on Database Systems, 26*(2), 18-28.

JBoss, Open Source Application Server. (2005). Retrieved from http://www.jboss.org

Kohl, J., & Neuman, B. C. (1993). *The Kerberos network authentication service* (version 5). Request For Comments 1510, Internet Engineering Task Force.

Miley, M. (2004). Know who, know how: Using oracle technologies to manage identities. *Oracle Magazine,* n.8.

PRIME (Privacy and Identity Management for Europe). (2005). Retrieved from http://www. prime-project.eu.org

Scott, S. (2003). *The JBoss Group: JBoss administration and development third edition* (3.2.x Series). JBoss Group, LLC. Indianapolis, IN: Sams Publishing.

Copyright © 2007, Idea Group Inc. Copying or distributing in print or electronic forms without written permission of Idea Group Inc. is prohibited.

APPENDIX
A SAMPLE IMPLEMENTATION

In this appendix, we describe a proof-of-concept prototype developed to show how access control can work with minimal client-side information disclosure. Our prototype supports only a subset of the requirements illustrated in the chapter. In particular, our current prototype deals with resource protection only and does not yet take into account obligation and purpose, which will be added in future releases. Compared to early commercial implementations of identity management systems, like the one being developed at Lawrence Livermore National Laboratory (Miley, 2004), our approach provides the general notion of a policy language and of controlled release of personal information. On the other hand, at this stage we did not address engineering issues regarding scalability and backward compatibility with current standards. More precisely, our prototype supports access control rules based on the specification of generic conditions (boolean expressions of properties/credentials) on subjects and objects. The prototype provides features for the specification of the ontologies and profiles of subjects and resources and of the access control rules for protecting resources. Upon the submission of an access request from a client (possibly anonymous or non authenticated), which is characterized by the *subject* making the request, the *action* being requested, and the *object* (resource) on which the subject wishes to perform the action, the system returns the conditions (properties/credentials) that, according to the specified policies, the client should satisfy to gain access (partial policy evaluation). Access control rules supported by the prototype have the following form:

> *subject* WITH *subject expression* CAN *action* ON *object*
> WITH *object expression* IF *conditions*

where: (1) *subject* identifies the subject to which the rule refers, (2) *subject expression* is an expression that allows the reference to a set of subjects depending on whether they satisfy given conditions, (3) *action* is the action to which the rule refers, (4) *object* identifies the object to which the rule refers, (5) *object expression* is an expression that allows the reference to a set of objects depending on whether they satisfy given conditions and (6) *conditions* is a boolean expression of conditions that an access request, to which the rule applies, has to satisfy.

Our prototype recognizes users/objects specified in a subject/object ontology and for which there is a subject/object profile (i.e., a set of properties associated with users such as name, address, occupation, and so on, and a set of properties associated with objects such as owner, creation date and so forth). The subject ontology contains terms that can be used to make generic assertions on subjects while the object ontology contains domain-specific terms that are used to describe the resource content and to make generic assertions on objects. The field conditions allows only credential-based conditions based on a credential ontology that defines

Copyright © 2007, Idea Group Inc. Copying or distributing in print or electronic forms without written permission of Idea Group Inc. is prohibited.

abstractions and how these abstractions are implied by a combination of different credential types. A credential ontology is a set of facts of the form abstraction IM-PLIEDBY expression, where expression can be a boolean formula of abstractions and/or credential types. We assume that credential-based conditions are intended to be evaluated against the subject's profile. For instance, a credential ontology can include the fact photo-id IMPLIEDBY driver-licence OR passport OR id-card meaning that any of credentials driver-licence, passport, and id-card is considered to contain photo-id.

The prototype includes four Prolog modules and a Java application interface. A Prolog module contains the evaluation engine, the other three modules contain the declarations of the ontologies, policies, and profiles, respectively, as described previously. The Java application interface (see Figure 5) is structured as follows: on the top, there are three text boxes, labeled User, Action, and Object, used to insert an access request. By clicking the button labeled Evaluate, the access request is evaluated against the defined access control policies. The output of the evaluation is shown in the box labeled Results. It contains a 3-colors traffic light (on the left): red means access denied, green means access granted, and yellow means undefined. In the latter case the text area on the right shows a list of alternatives (conditions) that must be fulfilled to gain the access. By mean of the tabs named ontologies, profiles and policy is possible to define the overall environment in which the access control engine acts.

As an example, consider a movie rental scenario that simulates the case of a user that wants to book a movie; Figure 6 illustrates an example of subject ontology and object ontology suitable for this scenario.2

Figure 5. Java application interface

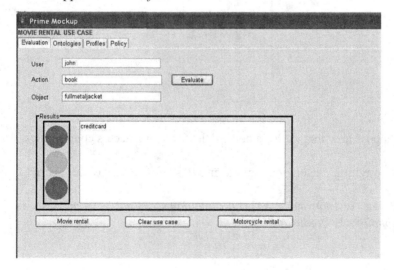

Copyright © 2007, Idea Group Inc. Copying or distributing in print or electronic forms without written permission of Idea Group Inc. is prohibited.

Figure 6. An example of subject ontology and object ontology

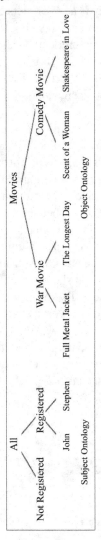

Suppose now that we have defined the following access control rules:

- Anonymous users can book movies if they provide a credit card.

   RULE 1: *Anonymous* WITH *nocondition* CAN *book* ON *movies* WITH *nocondition* IF *creditCard*

Copyright © 2007, Idea Group Inc. Copying or distributing in print or electronic forms without written permission of Idea Group Inc. is prohibited.

- War movies available on a Web interface can be booked by registered users who live in Italy if they provide a credit card.

  RULE 2: *RegisteredUsers* WITH *nationality*="Italian" CAN *book-online* ON *War Movie* WITH *availability*="online" IF *creditCard*

Consider the access request submitted by user John to book movie fullmetaljacket and assume that we only know that John is Italian (from his user profile). RULE 1 is not applicable. The evaluation of condition creditCard in RULE 2 against the profile associated with user John is undefined. This means that user John has never provided a credit card credential. The system then returns to John the information that is necessary to take a yes or no decision (see Figure 5). If John provides a valid credit card, the access is granted, otherwise it is denied.

ENDNOTES

[1]   This problem is even worse with PKI than with traditional symmetric encryption, because the citizen is the only one who has access to her private key.

[2]   For simplicity, our prototype supports only assertions of the form subject1 (object1, resp.) ISA subject2 (object2, resp.) corresponding to the traditional abstractions that can be defined within the domain of the users and objects, respectively. ISA is the basic hierarchical relation. If one item ISA another item then the first item is more specific in meaning than the second item.

Copyright © 2007, Idea Group Inc. Copying or distributing in print or electronic forms without written permission of Idea Group Inc. is prohibited.

Chapter XI

A Protocol for Anonymous and Accurate E-Polling

Danilo Bruschi, Università degli Studi di Milano, Italy

Andrea Lanzi, Università degli Studi di Milano, Italy

Igor Nai Fovino, Joint Research Centre, Italy

ABSTRACT

E-polling systems are a fundamental component of any e-democracy system as they represent the most appropriate tool for fostering citizens' participation to public debates. Contrarily to e-voting protocols, they are characterized by less stringent security requirements and they can also tolerate errors affecting a small percentage of votes, without compromising of the final result. Thus, their realization can be effectively pursued supporting the diffusion of e-democracy. In this chapter, we propose a simple protocol for an accurate and anonymous e-polling system. Such a protocol satisfies, among the others, the following properties: a vote cannot be altered, duplicated, or removed without being detected and votes remain anonymous. Moreover, voters will be able to measure the level of trust of the process by verifying that their own votes have been correctly counted.

Copyright © 2007, Idea Group Inc. Copying or distributing in print or electronic forms without written permission of Idea Group Inc. is prohibited.

INTRODUCTION

The milestone of any democracy is participation. Obviously, such a postulate holds even in the case of e-democracy. In such a context, the model of direct democracy, which is hindered by nowadays population sizes and state organizations, would become possible through the adoption and diffusion of electronic polling systems. Whereby electronic polling systems we mean a set of hardware and software devices, which enable people to express their opinion on specific issues, provide a mean for gathering, and concentrate opinions from many participants. The main objective of e-polling systems is to capture general trends and people orientation on some specific issue. Generally speaking, polling systems, are one of the most appropriate tool for fostering citizens participation to public debates, and their online version enables more people to voice their views with less effort, because electronic polling can be performed from distributed locations at different times. Even if polling systems resemble voting systems, they are strongly differentiated by their final scopes. In fact, votes impose decisions while opinions expressed in a poll can only influence decisions. Such a difference has a huge impact on the security requirements, which characterize the two systems. In particular, the most critical security requirements, which so far compromised the realization of complete e-voting protocols only have a minor relevance in the construction of a polling system. For example, while a perfectly correct output has to characterize a voting process, an almost correct output can be tolerated by a polling process. Again, coercion and vote buying is a huge problem for voting systems but it has no relevance for polling systems. Thus even if we still do not have a complete solution to e-voting in either theoretical nor practical domains, we strongly believe that the current state of knowledge enables the construction of reliable and efficient polling systems, which in the short term could become a very important component of any e-democracy system, and significantly contribute to the diffusion of this new form of democracy. Starting from this consideration we devised a polling system which is: anonymous, sufficiently reliable (i.e., reproduce the opinions expressed by voters only with a marginal error), individually verifiable, and it is quite efficient and cost-effective. We believe that the adoption of our protocol and of similar ones, will greatly improve the state of the art on e-democracy, and contribute to its diffusion. This chapter is organized as follows: in "Related Works," we will provide a brief overview on e-voting protocols, which can be adopted as well for building e-polling system; in "Voting vs. Polling,"we formally define an e-polling system underlying the differences with traditional e-voting systems. In "Preliminaries," we describe the notation adopted throughout the chapter and we provide the definitions of peculiar concepts used for designing our protocol. In "The E-Polling Protocol," a detailed description of the credential system and of our e-polling protocol is provided. The section "Correctness Analysis" contains a correctness analysis of our protocol, followed of our final considerations.

Copyright © 2007, Idea Group Inc. Copying or distributing in print or electronic forms without written permission of Idea Group Inc. is prohibited.

RELATED WORKS

As just mentioned, we are not aware of specific papers that address the construction of e-polling protocols, as all of the efforts in such a field has been concentrated on the construction of e-voting protocols. Historically, three main approaches have been adopted to solve the challenges of electronic vote:

- Chaum's Mix-nets scheme (Chaum, 1981)
- Chaums's Blind signature (Chaum, 1985)
- Homomorphic schemes (Elgamal, 1984)

In the following, we report some of the attempts performed in devising voting systems, which constituted a point of reference for our research on e-polling systems. The first electronic voting protocol was published by Chaum (1981). It relies upon public key cryptography as most electronic voting protocols, however it does not guarantee voters' privacy. Chaum then proposed a protocol which unconditionally conceals voters' identity (Chaum, 1988), but the entire voting procedure could be disrupted by a single voter. A solution to this problem was suggested by Cohen (1986), but the protocol proposed is neither simple (college level mathematics is required for voters to independently verify election results) nor efficient. Benaloh and Tuinstra (1994) proposed a voting protocol, which allows voters to easily verify the results but voting booths must be used, thus violating the mobility property. Nurmi, Salomaa, and Santean (1991) designed a protocol known as Two Agency Protocol, that preserves the ease of verification properties and relax the "booth" constraint, thus yielding a protocol where voters can easily verify the results. However, it lacked voters' anonymity.

A breakthrough in the design of electronic voting protocols was realized by Fujioka, Okamoto, and Ohta (1992), who solved the privacy problem of the Two Agency Protocol using the blind signatures technique introduced in 1982 by Chaum. The Fujioka et al. protocol is generally indicated in the literature as the first practical electronic voting scheme. It still does not address the problem of preventing administrators from casting votes for abstained voters. The problem could be solved if abstained voters were forced to cast blank votes, which is clearly a hardly practical solution. Moreover, in this scheme the voter's preference is encrypted before to be sent to the vote recipient. This implies during the counting phase that the voter anonymously sends the key to decrypt the vote. The presence of this additional phase in the usual voting scheme is really not practical.

Horster, Michaels, and Petersen in (1995) maintaining the original schema of Fujioka, eliminate this phase adopting a blind multi signature scheme. In this work, the presence of more than one administrator (who has the task to sign the vote according to the blind scheme) is required. The security in this case is based on the concept that at least one of the administrators is honest. The SENSUS pro-

Copyright © 2007, Idea Group Inc. Copying or distributing in print or electronic forms without written permission of Idea Group Inc. is prohibited.

tocol (Cranor & Cytron, 1997), which was implemented and tested with simulated elections, overcomes the abstained voter problem.

Karro and Wang (1999) proved that SENSUS also suffers from some drawbacks such as the lack of accuracy and proposed another protocol that solves the identified problem. However, from our perspective, neither this protocol satisfies the accuracy property since it is possible to impersonate voters. Furthermore, we note that both protocols (Cranor & Cytron, 1997; Karro & Wang, 1999) make some impractical assumptions such as the existence of three or four trusted third parties, which must not collude in order to guarantee the correctness of the protocol, and the existence of a trusted third party that generates the cryptographic keys, which enable the voters to vote but not to cheat.

The design of a flawless electronic voting protocol is very difficult, and no protocols have been designed yet that completely satisfy all the requirements. A fairly exhaustive overview of the state of the art regarding voting protocols and their implementations can be found in the work of Cranor (2004).

To our knowledge, very little software is available that implements such protocols. Two systems are available, both explicitly written for non-government elections: Sensus and Evox. Sensus is an electronic polling system developed by Lorrie Cranor (Cranor & Cytron, 1997), but after the initial implementation, it was never deployed nor maintained. Evox, is under development at MIT, it is based on the work of Fujoka et al. (1992), and unlike Sensus, it is continuously maintained and improved.

For sake of completeness, we note that some electronic polling systems recently appeared on the Internet (http://www.epoll.com, http://www.misterpoll.com). However, such systems are not designed to maintain the level of security and privacy that we would expect, for example there is no way to express an opinion anonymously and there is no way for verifying the accuracy of the results. Moreover, no scientific paper apparently supports these polling systems.

VOTING vs. POLLING

In this section, we will define the requirements which, from our point of view, should characterize a polling protocol with respect to a voting protocol. Such a characterization is obtained by critically evaluating the most important requirements, which so far have been defined for voting protocols. We however underline that as time progressed, more and more requirements have been defined for voting protocols, and the general opinion is that new requirements still have to be discovered, in order to completely define an electronic voting protocol. Following Lee and Kim (2002), the requirements of electronic voting can be classified into the following two categories (see also Benaloh, 1994; Fujioka et al., 1992; Lee & Kim, 2000; Michels & Horster, 1996; Niemi & Rendall, 1994):

Copyright © 2007, Idea Group Inc. Copying or distributing in print or electronic forms without written permission of Idea Group Inc. is prohibited.

- **Basic requirements:**
  - ° **Privacy:** Nobody can get any information about the voter's vote.
  - ° **Completeness:** All valid votes should be counted correctly.
  - ° **Soundness:** Any invalid vote should not be counted.
  - ° **Eligibility:** No one who is not allowed to vote can vote.
  - ° **Fairness:** Nothing can affect the voting.
  - ° **Unreusability** (prevent double voting): No voter can vote twice.
- **Extended requirements:**
  - ° **Robustness:** The voting system has to work properly regardless of partial failure of the system.
  - ° **Receipt-freeness:** A voter neither obtains nor is able to construct a receipt proving the content of his vote.
  - ° **Individual verifiability:** Each eligible voter can verify that his vote was really counted.
  - ° **Universal verifiability:** Anyone can verify the fact that the election is fair and the published tally is correctly computed from the ballots that were correctly cast.
  - ° **Incoercibility:** A voter cannot be coerced into casting a particular vote, by a coercer. This is a stronger requirement than receipt-freeness. If we assume that the coercer cannot observe the voter during the very moment of voting, receipt-freeness gives incoercibility and vote buying is prevented.

The basic requirements are satisfied in most electronic voting systems, while the extended requirements are hard to implement and in many cases they require large amount of computation and communication. In the case of a polling scheme, it is reasonable to require that it will satisfy the following security requirements:

- **Privacy:** Nobody can get any information about the voter's vote.
- **Completeness:** All valid votes should be counted correctly.
- **Eligibility:** No one who is not allowed to vote can vote.
- **Soundness:** Any invalid vote should not be counted.
- **Unreusability:** No voter can vote twice.
- **Individual verifiability:** Each eligible voter can verify that his vote was really counted.

In the following we will describe a protocol which satisfies all the previously mentioned properties but the eligibility one, which as previously described, we preferred to sacrifice in order to get a more easy and efficient protocol. However, the solution proposed, satisfies a weaker form of eligibility which we denoted by Weak Eligibility and can be defined as follows: "Only eligible voters can get voting credentials from trusted authorities."

Copyright © 2007, Idea Group Inc. Copying or distributing in print or electronic forms without written permission of Idea Group Inc. is prohibited.

PRELIMINARIES

In this section, we define the notation which will be adopted throughout the chapter, and we recall the main properties of some technological components which we will use for building our solution, which is based on the RSA public key cryptosystem. Throughout the chapter:

- **n $A{\rightarrow}B$: data:** Indicates that in the n-th step of the protocol, the player A sends the message data to player B. The message data in general is composed by parts concatenated together. The compound messages may follow these forms:
  - ○ **$n.m$:** Denotes the text n followed by the text m
  - ○ **$\{data\}_k$:** Denotes the data encrypted or signed under the key k
- **PK_i:** Denotes i's public key
- **SK_i:** Denotes i's private key
- **$H(|M|)$:** Denotes the digest of the message M
- **SSL_F :** Denotes an ssl connection on a mutually authenticated channel (Full)
- **SSL_{HK}:** Denotes an ssl connection on a half authenticated channel, using the digital certificate K

In our protocol we will use a blind signature scheme based on the RSA algorithm, as introduced by Chaum (1982). We briefly recall that through the blind signature operation a party A can obtain a digital signature on a message m from a party B without revealing the content of m. The blind signature of a message m by B is computed as follows. Initially A chooses a random number $rand$ and sends the following quantity M to B:

$$M = (m * \{rand\}_{PK_B}) \tag{1}$$

Once B receives M it signs M with its own private key and sends the result to A, i.e.,:

$$\{M\}_{SK_B} = \{(m * \{rand\}_{PK_B})\}_{SK_B} \tag{2}$$

Once A receives $\{M\}_{SK_B}$ it performs the following transformations, which will enable him to obtain a "packet" containing the original message m digitally signed by B:

$$\{M\}_{SK_B} = \{(m * \{rand\}_{PK_B})\}_{SK_B} \tag{3}$$

$$= \{m\}_{SK_B} * \{\{rand\}_{PK_B}\}_{SK_B} \tag{4}$$

Copyright © 2007, Idea Group Inc. Copying or distributing in print or electronic forms without written permission of Idea Group Inc. is prohibited.

$$= \{m\}_{SK_B} * rand \tag{5}$$

At this point, the player A is able to compute the result using the random number chosen in the first step.

$$\{m\}_{SK_B} = \frac{\{m\}_{SK_B} * rand}{rand} \tag{6}$$

Our e-polling protocol will make use of anonymous credentials. The notion of anonymous credential was originally introduced by Chaum and Evertse (1986) as a mean for enabling access controls to system and applications, without revealing the identity of the subjects performing such operations. In such an approach, a user is provided by some credentials released by trusted organizations, which have to be exhibited in anytime he or she wants to access some protected service. Camenisch and Lysyanskaya (2001) propose a practical anonymous credential system based on the strong RSA assumption and the DDH assumption, which is a good example of implemented anonymous credential schema. For securing the communications among the various agents which constitute our protocol, we will use the TLS protocol. TLS (Transport Layer Security) previously known as the secure socket layer (SSL) (Dierks & Allen, 1999) is a standard originally developed by Netscape in order to provide confidentiality and integrity on the network traffic, as well as authenticity of the involved peers. TLS works in terms of connections and sessions between clients and server. It is designed to authenticate the server and optionally the client. It provides communication privacy through symmetric encryption and integrity through message authentication codes. The protocol we devised provides user anonymity at application level, but in order to have a fully anonymous communication channel, anonymity needs to be provided also at network layer. We achieve such a goal by referring to the notion of Mix introduced by Chaum (1981). A Mix is an HW appliance which can anonymizes communication between senders and recipients by means of cryptography, scrambling the messages, and normalizing them (padding to constant size, fixing a constant sending rate by sending dummy messages). A Mix-Net can be defined then as a set of Mix, with Mix net the anonymity property is enforced by the presence of more than a mix.

THE E-POLLING PROTOCOL

In the following we describe the polling protocol we devised. During the description of the protocol the following terms will be used:

- **Voters:** The subjects interested in participating in a polling.
- **Polling server:** The host that collects the voter's opinions.

Copyright © 2007, Idea Group Inc. Copying or distributing in print or electronic forms without written permission of Idea Group Inc. is prohibited.

- **Trusted third party (TTP):** An entity which guarantees the eligibility of a voter and releases the vote certificates.
- **Credential authentication token:** Any kind of digital token used to lock the vote credential.
- **Vote certificate:** A digital certificate, which witness the eligibility of a user to participate to a polling session.

The Credential System

In this section, we describe the credential system which we devised for our protocol based on the notion of anonymous credential. Our protocol assumes that for participating in a polling session, a voter has to be previously enrolled by the TTP. The enrollment is performed as follows: any eligible voter contacts the TTP off-line, which after a face to face authentication, releases to the voter a secret random number rand (credential authentication token), stored by the TTP in a suitable database, and a vote certificate such as the SHA1 of a password or of a X.509 certificate. Once a voter has performed such "preliminaries," he is entitled to get vote credentials, a vote credential for any ballot. In order to get a vote credential, a voter contacts the TTP and sends it his or her Vote certificate, and then he or she chooses a random number (for efficiency reasons an hash value of m is used) and performs a blind signature on it. The TTP, according to the blind signature scheme signs the quantity received by the voter, multiply the result by the credential authentication token, and sends it to the voter. We call such a quantity pseudo credential. The message exchange among the entities involved in this phase is shown in Figure 1.

Figure 1. Get vote credential phase

Get vote credential phase

r = random number used to perform the blind signature scheme

$rand$ = Credential authentication token

m = random number which represent the vote credential

$c = H(|\,voting\_certificate\,|)$

$M = H(|\,m\,|) * \{r\}_{PK_{TTP}}$

1. User → TTP: c
2. TTP → User: ACK
3. User → TTP: M
4. TTP → User: $\{M\}_{SK_{TTP}} * rand$

Copyright © 2007, Idea Group Inc. Copying or distributing in print or electronic forms without written permission of Idea Group Inc. is prohibited.

Once the pseudo credential has been received, the client unlocks the pseudo credential dividing it by random number rand:

$$\{M\}_{SK_{TTP}} = \frac{\{M\}_{SK_{TTP}} * rand}{rand} \tag{7}$$

Then the voter performs the last phase of blind signature scheme, (equation 3):

$$\{M\}_{SK_{TTP}} = \{(H(|m|) * \{r\}_{PK_{TTP}})\}_{SK_{TTP}} \tag{8}$$

$$= \{(H(|m|)\}_{SK_{TTP}} * \{\{r\}_{PK_{TTP}}\}_{SK_{TTP}} \tag{9}$$

$$= \{H(|m|)\}_{SK_{TTP}} * r \tag{10}$$

At this point, the *Voter* can verify the TTP signature on the voting *credential* (equation 11). Finally, the user builds the anonymous voting credential that is equal:

$$= H(|m|) * \{H(|m|)\}_{SK_{TTP}} \tag{11}$$

Such *voting credential* has some important properties, first of all it does not contain any information about the identity of the voter as it contains only the random number *m* chosen by the *Voter*; secondly it can be used as one time credential, in fact when the *e-polling* server receives the credentials, it stores them into a database, and discard any new attempt to reuse them.

The Protocol Architecture

In this section, we provide an overview of our e-polling protocol, which we assume will be implemented as a Web service. The protocol can be divided into three main phases: (1) The credential request phase, (2) The voting phase, and (3) The vote receipt phase. The key components of the whole architecture are:

- **The validation proxy:** This is a software component installed on the polling server, its main tasks are to detect request vote and to validate anonymous vote credentials.
- **The credential proxy:** This is a software component which is installed on the voter's computer and it performs the communication between the voter's browser and TTP in order to obtain the pseudo credential and to compute the anonymous credential.

Copyright © 2007, Idea Group Inc. Copying or distributing in print or electronic forms without written permission of Idea Group Inc. is prohibited.

- **The TTP database:** This database contains the *Credential Authentication Tokens* released to the voters during the "enrollment phase."
- **The polling server database:** This database contains the vote credentials which have already been used.
- **Connections memory structures:** This software component holds the state of every pending SSL connections. These memory structures are used by the e-polling system in the voting phase, their main scope is to maintain the state of every SSL connection in order to check the appropriate states of vote authorization phase. They hold a different state for each connection, the possible states are:
  - **Pending:** The voter has performed the SSL authentication but he or she doesn't send the anonymous credential.
  - **Anonymous:** The voter has performed the SSL authentication and he or she sent the right anonymous vote credential.
  - **Vote:** The voter has performed the SSL authentication, he or she sent the right anonymous credential and he or she has performed the vote.
- **Web server:** This component is installed on the server machine which provides the polling service.
- **Anonymizer layer:** The scope of this component is to provide the anonymity channel, hiding the network identity of the initiator of the communication towards the other end of the communication and towards network observers. In order to achieve this, we adopted the *Chaum mixes* (Chaum, 1981) which lies in the middle of the communication between the voter and the *polling server*. These mixes machines are routers whose task is to hide the correspondence between the inputs and outputs, altering the flow of messages, in order to prevent the timing attack. Every time the client communicates with the e-polling server, the mix, which lies in the middle of the communication, masquerades the IP source of every input network packets with its own IP, and send them out in random order.

The connections among the architectural components just described are depicted in Figure 2. In the following, we describe the different phases throughout which the protocol evolves.

The Request Credential Phase

A client requests access to a generic Web service via the browser. The *Credential Proxy* forwards it to the *polling server*. If the requested server does not involve any polling operation, the communication follows the path of a standard Web connection, otherwise, in the case the user requested the access to a polling server, the *Validator proxy* returns to the *Credential Proxy* the request for the credential. At this point, the *Credential Proxy* begins the communication with the *TTP*, sending

Copyright © 2007, Idea Group Inc. Copying or distributing in print or electronic forms without written permission of Idea Group Inc. is prohibited.

Figure 2. Get vote Credential phase

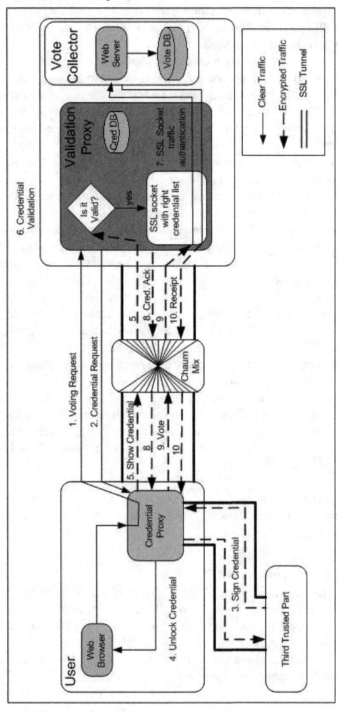

Copyright © 2007, Idea Group Inc. Copying or distributing in print or electronic forms without written permission of Idea Group Inc. is prohibited.

Figure 3. Request credential phase

Request credential phase

C = *client*

S = *polling server*

VP = *Validation Proxy*

CP = *Credential Proxy*

TTP = *Trusted Third Party*

r = *random number used to perform the blind signature scheme*

$rand$ = *random number used to lock the credential*

m = *random number which represent the vote credential*

$c = H(|voting\ certificate|)$

$M = H(|m|) * \{r\}_{PK_{TTP}}$

1. $C \rightarrow S$: *request vote page*
2. $VP \rightarrow CP$: *request vote credential*
3. $CP \rightarrow TTP$: $SSL_F\{c\}$
4. $TTP \rightarrow CP$: $SSL_F\{ACK\}$
5. $CP \rightarrow TTP$: $SSL_F\{M\}$
6. $TTP \rightarrow CP$: $SSL_F\{\{M\}_{SK_{TTP}} * rand\}$

the digest of the vote certificate and requiring a vote credential. More formally all steps are shown in Figure 3.

The Voting Phase

Once the credential vote has been received, the voter can perform the "voting phase." In such a phase the Credential Proxy establishes an encrypted communication channel with the Validation Proxy (only server side authentication to preserve its anonymity) and sends it the anonymous credential; the Validation proxy sets the state of the connection as pending and checks the TTP's validity of the credential, if it is valid, it checks if it has been already used, if this is the case the connection will be closed. Otherwise, it stores the credential into the Polling server database and sets the authorized state on the connection, now the voter casts his or her vote through the Web client and sends it to the Polling server. The communication between the client and the polling server is protected by Chaum mixes. All steps performed in this phase are depicted in Figure 4.

Copyright © 2007, Idea Group Inc. Copying or distributing in print or electronic forms without written permission of Idea Group Inc. is prohibited.

Figure 4. Voting phase

Voting phase
$Credential = H(\mid m \mid) * \{H(\mid m \mid)\}_{SK_{TTP}}$
$PA = proxy\ anonymizer\ (Chaum\ Mix)$
1. **CP → PA**: $SSL_{H_{SK}}\{credential\}$
2. **PA → VP**: $SSL_{H_{SK}}\{credential\}$
3. **VP → PA**: $SSL_{H_{SK}}\{ACK\}$
4. **PA → CP**: $SSL_{H_{SK}}\{ACK\}$
5. **C → PA**: $SSL_{H_{SK}}\{Vote\}$
6. **PA → S**: $SSL_{H_{SK}}\{Vote\}$

The Receipt Phase

The last phase of the protocol is performed in order to obtain the vote receipt which will be used by the voter for verifying that his or her own vote has been correctly counted. Afterwards the voter has performed his or her vote, the *Credential Proxy* computes the digest of the vote (that will be used as control ticket) and sends this number a nonce (The nonce is used in order to build a unique receipt vote) to the *Validation Proxy*, which sends a signed receipt to the Credential proxy. At this point, the *Credential Proxy* checks the sign on the back of the ticket, stores it into its hard disk, and closes the connection.

Ballot Publication Phase

At the end of the polling session, a Web page containing all the votes received associated with the relative *control ticket* will be published. The voter, in order to control if the vote has not changed during the vote operation can control if the vote associated to the ticket is right. All steps of this phase are shown in Figure 5.

CORRECTNESS ANALYSIS

In this section we perform a security analysis of our e-polling protocol by showing that it satisfies the requirements defined in "Related Works," which we recall are:

1. **Unreusability:** A voting credential can be used only once
2. **Completeness:** All valid votes must be counted correctly
3. **Privacy:** All votes must be kept secrets
4. **Soundness:** Invalid votes are not accepted.

Copyright © 2007, Idea Group Inc. Copying or distributing in print or electronic forms without written permission of Idea Group Inc. is prohibited.

Figure 5. Receipt phase

> **Request credential phase**
>
> C = *client*
>
> S = *polling server*
>
> VP = *Validation Proxy*
>
> CP = *Credential Proxy*
>
> TTP = *Trusted Third Party*
>
> r = *random number used to perform the blind signature scheme*
>
> *rand* = *random number used to lock the credential*
>
> m = *random number which represent the vote credential*
>
> $c = H(|voting\ certificate|)$
>
> $M = H(|\ m\ |) * \{r\}_{PK_{TTP}}$
>
> *1.* **C → S:** *request vote page*
>
> *2.* **VP → CP:** *request vote credential*
>
> *3.* **CP → TTP:** $SSL_F\{c\}$
>
> *4.* **TTP → CP:** $SSL_F\{ACK\}$
>
> *5.* **CP → TTP:** $SSL_F\{M\}$
>
> *6.* **TTP → CP:** $SSL_F\{\{M\}_{SK_{TTP}} * rand\}$

5. **Weak eligibility:** Only eligible voters can get voting credentials from trusted authorities.
6. **Single verifiability:** The voter is able to verify if its vote has be counted correctly.

In order to provide such proof, we will define the threat model for a polling protocol, subsequently we will describe the strategy adopted for making our protocol resilient to these threats and finally we will show how such a strategy contributes to the satisfaction of the previously mentioned requirements.

Threat Model

An attacker may be interested in maliciously interact with a polling system in order to:

*   **Influence the final tally:** For example for influencing trading and marketing decision
*   Capture information on individuals or group of individuals to guess preferences, behaviors and other kind of information normally classified as sensible related to individuals (e.g., potential costumers), or to blackmail people

Copyright © 2007, Idea Group Inc. Copying or distributing in print or electronic forms without written permission of Idea Group Inc. is prohibited.

We classify the threats aimed at obtaining the first objective as *Integrity Threats* and as *Privacy Threats* the others. We note that for Integrity we identify here not only the Vote integrity but even the entire voting protocol integrity (i.e., also the violation of requirements 1, 2, 4, 5, and 6 falls in this class)

Integrity Threats

In this class, we group all the threats whose ultimate scope is the modification of the final tally. Such an objective can be obtained in the following ways:

1.   **Multiple use of credential:** This is a well-known scenario, in which a credential is used more than once. In this way, an attacker could modify the final result of a ballot by simply adding more than a preference. The preconditions of this attack are:
     •   The attacker is able to obtain a certain number of valid credentials
     •   A valid credential can be used more than once or can be changed in order to be used more than once
     In our protocol such an attack is not possible because the polling server stores the code of all the used credentials in order to discover and deny the multiple use of a credential. Moreover, the use of a signature scheme avoids the use of a modified version of credential. Furthermore it is not possible to obtain more than one credential per ballot, since the TTP flags any user which receives a vote credential.

2.   **Vote modification:** In this scenario the attacker modifies an authorized vote. This result can be theoretically done in two ways. Either performing a man in the middle attack on the channel connecting the client to the polling server or compromising the polling server itself. The preconditions necessary to perform these attacks are the following:
     •   The attacker needs a physical access to the network between the client and the polling server (first attack)
     •   The attacker must be able to compromise the polling server (second attack)
     The man in the middle scenario, cannot be performed as we adopted an encrypted channel with mutual authentication. Moreover, the second scenario, is avoided by the release of a receipt (digest of the vote), that is the proof that a correct vote operation is performed; thus the voter has the possibility to control in an anonymous way if his vote has been correctly counted.

3.   **Vote stealing:** An attacker obtain from the TTP server the credentials of a set of authorized voters that have not already express their vote. In our protocol, an attacker is not able to obtain valid credential from TTP due to the authentication and lock mechanisms adopted.

4.   **Vote selling:** An attacker pays an authorized voter in order to obtain a valid credential or to convince a voter to express a particular vote. This is a well-known problem of all the voting system (even of the physical voting systems).

Copyright © 2007, Idea Group Inc. Copying or distributing in print or electronic forms without written permission of Idea Group Inc. is prohibited.

At the present, to our knowledge a real solution to this threat does not exist. In electronic voting literature, some protocols tried to solve this problem linking for example the credential, to some sensible information (credit card number etc.) of the authorized user, in order to discourage the credential sale. Such a strategy, however, is useful only in the case in which the credential is set to the attacker (may be more appropriate to call him corrupter), and can be easily circumvented by simply let the voter vote and asking him some proof of the expressed vote (in our case it could be simply the receipt of the polling server). We believe that if this is a big problem in the case of voting protocols, it is not so relevant in the case of e-polling. In such a case, the number of voter which have to be corrupted and consequently the economical effort to undertake in order to significantly modify the final ballot is too high.

Privacy Threats Class

In this class, we group all the attacks whose ultimate scope is the voter privacy violation. As explained before, we only consider the information that an attacker can obtain trying to corrupt our protocol. In this case, a malicious user can exploit only two points of attack:

1. **The network between client(voter) and polling server:** The attacker, who has physical access to this network portion, can capture the traffic between the client and the polling server. Then analyzing such a traffic he can become aware of the vote expressed by the voter. Our protocol is resilient to the described attack, as it adopts an encrypted channel (e.g., TLS) avoiding the possibility of a successful network sniffing.
2. **The polling server:** If the polling server (or the machine that hosts the server) has some security hole, an attacker may be able to obtain the control of such a server. Thus, an attacker may be able subvert the privacy property. Our protocol preserves such a property by the use of the anonymous credential scheme. Moreover, the protocol even guarantee the network privacy (e.g., IP address) adopting between client and polling server a Chaum Mix (Chaum, 1981).

The following cases, for sake of completeness, even need some discussion:

• If we assume that the TTP is not really trusted, a collaboration between the TTP and the polling server (to break the voter privacy) must be taken in account. In our system the TTP does not know the credential that it signs (a blind signature scheme is adopted), then the collaboration between the two servers cannot product any type of information that can violate the privacy of the voter.
• The corruption of the Chaum Mixer, is not sufficient to compromise the privacy of the system (we remember that the vote is encrypted, and the Mix is not able

Copyright © 2007, Idea Group Inc. Copying or distributing in print or electronic forms without written permission of Idea Group Inc. is prohibited.

to decipher it). An attacker that has the control of the Mix can only say that a User on machine A has performed a vote operation. However, if the attacker has the control of both the mix and the polling server, a timing analysis can be performed in order to guess the vote expressed by a certain user. This, however, is a scenario extremely complicated considering the normal target of polling systems. An expensive but good solution (in term of complexity of implementation) to this problem can be obtained with a substitution of the mix with a crowd architecture (Reiter & Rubin, 1999).

- Finally a lack of privacy can happen if we the client machine is not properly protected. In this case a remote attacker could be able to obtain exactly the information related the vote expressed by the voter, but this problem is not related with the e-polling protocol.

Requirements Analysis

We are now ready to prove that our protocol satisfies the following require-ments:

- **Unreusability:** This requirement is normally not satisfied if a credential ob-tained from the TTP can be used more than once. As explained before, our protocol avoids the multiple use of a credential, in fact the polling server stores the code of every used credential and deny the voting operation to all the us-ers that show an already used credential. For this reason, this requirement is satisfied.

- **Completeness:** This requirement can be violated only if it is possible to modify the vote (forcing then the polling server to count the vote in a wrong way). As shown in the previous section this in our protocol is not allowed and then the requirement is satisfied.

- **Soundness:** Every vote sent to the polling server in our protocol is signed and only the votes correctly signed are accepted. This implies that every invalid vote is not accepted by the e-polling system. Consequently, it is not possible to count invalid votes.

- **Privacy:** The violation of this requirement implies that an attacker can guess the vote expressed by a user, based on some information obtained breaking the e-polling protocol. In our protocol, as explained before, this is possible only if both the mix and the polling servers are simultaneously corrupted and collaborate in order to obtain such an information. This is too expensive a task (in term of time spent and knowledge necessary) to be justifiable for the typi-cal target of a polling system. However if this is the case, the problem can be solved by adopting a crowd scheme, which is based on the notion of blending into a crowd. As said previously, crowd is more complex than Chaum Mix, but has the advantage to guarantee a strong privacy protection.

Copyright © 2007, Idea Group Inc. Copying or distributing in print or electronic forms without written permis-sion of Idea Group Inc. is prohibited.

- **Weak eligibility:** In our protocol, the satisfaction of such a requirement is strictly connected to the robustness of the authentication phase. The protocol can be easily adapted to either weak or strong authentication mechanisms, depending on the level of security which has to be reached by the process.
- **Individual verifiability:** The single verifiability allows a user to control his or her vote has been correctly counted. In our protocol, the polling server releases a receipt to the voter at the end of the voting operation. Moreover, this receipt is signed so it cannot be modified on the fly by an attacker. A voter is then able to verify his or vote and then this requirement is satisfied.

CONCLUSION

The current state of the art in cryptography as well as in computer science makes it difficult to foresee a realistic data for design and implementation of secure and reliable e-voting service, thus hindering one of the most attractive applications of e-government. On the other hand, cryptographic and communication protocols are available for the construction of secure and reliable e-polling systems (i.e., tools aimed at capturing the general orientation of significant size populations) on issues of specific interests. It is our strong believe that a major emphasis on e-polling instead of e-voting by the scientific community as well as the decision makers and media will contribute to boost e-democracy and e-government applications. This work represents a contribution in such a direction. In this chapter we have shown how that current state of the art can be used for building an e-polling protocol which besides being secure and reliable, is also efficient and cost effective.

REFERENCES

Benaloh, J., & Tuinstra, D. (1994). Receipt-free secret-ballot elections. In *Proceedings of the 26th Symposium on Theory of Computing (STOC94)* (pp. 544-553).

Camenisch, J., & Lysyanskaya, A. (2001). An efficient non-transferable anonymous multishow credential system with optional anonymity revocation. In *Proceedings of Eurocrypt 2001* (LNCS 2045). .

Camenisch, J., & Van Herreweghen, E. (2002). Design and implementation of the idemix anonymous credential system. In *Proceedings of the 9th ACM Conference on Computer and Communications Security (CCS '02)*.

Chaum D. (1981). Untraceable electronic mail, return addresses, and digital pseudonyms. *Communications of the ACM, 24*(2), 84-88.

Chaum, D. (1982). Blind signatures for untraceable payments. Advances in cryptology. In *Cripto '82* (LCNS, pp. 199-203).

Chaum, D. (1985). Security without identification: Transaction systems to make big brother Obsolete. *Communication of the ACM, 28*(10), 10-30.

Copyright © 2007, Idea Group Inc. Copying or distributing in print or electronic forms without written permission of Idea Group Inc. is prohibited.

Chaum, D. (1988). *Elections with unconditionally-secret ballots and disruption equivalent to breaking RSA*. (LNCS 330, pp. 177-182), Springer-Verlag.

Chaum, D., & Evertse, J. (1986). A secure and privacy-protecting protocol for transmitting personal information between organizations. In *Crypto '86* (LNCS 263).

Cohen, J. D. (1986). *Improving privacy in cryptographic elections* (Tech. Rep. No. YALEU/DCS/TR-454). Yale University.

Cranor, L. F. (2004). *State of the art of e-voting protocol*. Retrieved from http://lorrie.cranor.org/voting/hotlist.html

Cranor, L. F., & Cytron R. K. (1997). Sensus: A security-conscious electronic polling system for Internet. In *Proceedings of the Hawaii International Conference on System Sciences*.

Dierks, T., & Allen, C. (1999). *The TLS protocol Version 1.0*. Retrieved from http://www.ietf.org/rfc.rfc2246.txt

ElGamal, T. (1984). A public key cryptosystem and a signature scheme based on discrete logarithms. In *Crypto '84* (LNCS 196, pp. 10-18). Springer-Verlag.

Fujioka, A., Okamoto, T., & Ohta, K. (1992). A practical secret voting scheme for large scale election. In *Advances in Cryptology Auscrypt '92* (LNCS 718, pp. 244-260), .

Horster, P., Michels, M., & Petersen, H. (1995). Blind multi-signature schemes and their relevance to electronic voting. In *Proceedings of the 11th Annual Computer Security Applications Conference*, New Orleans (pp. 149-155). IEEE Press.

Karro, J., & Wang J. (1999). Towards a practical, secure, and very large scale online election. In *Proceedings of the 15th Computer Security Applications Conference* (pp. 161-169).

Lee, B., & Kim, K. (2000). Receipt-free electronic voting through collaboration of voter and honest verifier. In *Proceeding of JW-ISC2000* (pp. 101-108).

Lee, B., & Kim, K. (2002). Receipt-free electronic voting scheme with a tamper-resistant Randomizer. In *Proceedings of ICISC* (LNCS 2587, pp. 389-406), Springer-Verlag, 2003.

Michels, M., & Horster, P. (1996). *Some remarks on a receipt-free and universally verifiable mix-type voting scheme*. Advances in Cryptology Asiacrypt 96 (LNCS 1163, pp. 125-132), Springer Verlag.

Niemi, V., & Rendall, A. (1994). How to prevent buying of votes in computer elections. In *Advances in Cryptology Asiacrypt '94* (LNCS 917, pp. 141-148), Springer Verlag.

Nurmi, H., Salomaa, A., & Santean, L. (1991). Secret ballot elections in computer networks. *Computers & Security, 36*(10), 553-560.

Reiter, M. K., & Rubin, A. D. (1999). Anonymous Web transactions with crowds. *Communications of the ACM, 42*(2), 32-48.

Copyright © 2007, Idea Group Inc. Copying or distributing in print or electronic forms without written permission of Idea Group Inc. is prohibited.

Chapter XII

Secure Multiparty/ Multicandidate Electronic Elections

Tassos Dimitriou, Athens Information Technology, Greece

Dimitris Foteinakis, University of Thessaly, Greece

ABSTRACT

In this chapter, we present a methodology for proving in Zero Knowledge the validity of selecting a subset of a set belonging to predefined family of sets. We apply this methodology in electronic voting to provide for extended ballot options. Our proposed voting scheme supports multiple parties and the selection of a number of candidates from one and only one of these parties. We have implemented this system and provided measures of its computational and communication complexity. We show that the complexity is linear with respect to the total number of candidates and the number of parties participating in the election.

Copyright © 2007, Idea Group Inc. Copying or distributing in print or electronic forms without written permission of Idea Group Inc. is prohibited.

INTRODUCTION

With the explosion of growth of the World Wide Web, the increase of computational power, computer memory, and the storage capacity, we have the ability to communicate more information faster, cheaper, and more reliably. The general trend toward a paperless society has affected the area of voting. Many attempts have been made to create systems that would allow modern computer-based technology to emulate the secure desirable properties valued in centuries of public voting.

Remote electronic voting refers to an election process whereby people can cast their votes over the internet, from the comfort of their home, or possibly any other location where they can get internet access. There are many aspects of elections besides security that bring this type of voting into question. The primary ones are:

- **Coercibility:** The danger that outside of a public polling place, a voter could be coerced into voting for a particular candidate
- **Vote selling:** The opportunity for voters to sell their vote
- **Vote solicitation:** The danger that outside of a public polling place, it is much more difficult to control vote solicitation by political parties at the time of voting
- **Invalid registration:** The issue of whether or not to allow online registration, and if so, how to control the level of fraud

The possibility of widely distributed locations where votes can be cast changes many aspects of our carefully controlled elections, as we know them. The relevant issues are of great importance and could very well influence whether or not such election processes are desirable. However, in this chapter, we do not discuss issues like the vulnerability of the internet to denial of service attacks, the unreliability of the Domain Name Service, or the various threats the supporting hosts are liable to, but we focus instead on the security considerations of the *voting process*.

Thanks to the advances in the fields of cryptography, an electronic voting system can satisfy the requirements that are considered self-evident for paper-based systems and at the same time be efficient and reduce the cost of large-scale elections. Fujioka, Okamoto, and Ohta (1992) define the properties of a secure, secret election:

- **Completeness:** All valid votes must be counted correctly
- **Soundness:** The dishonest voter cannot disrupt the voting process
- **Privacy and integrity:** All votes must be and remain secret and cannot be altered in transit. Hence, effective encryption must be used to protect the votes from being disclosed to third parties during transmission
- **Anonymity:** The voting system must support the voters' right to secrecy of their vote. Hence, the vote recording mechanism must not identify the individual voter.

Copyright © 2007, Idea Group Inc. Copying or distributing in print or electronic forms without written permission of Idea Group Inc. is prohibited.

- **Unreusability and eligibility:** No voter can vote twice and no one who isn't allowed to vote can vote
- **Fairness:** Nothing must affect the voting process. Voters must not be able to affect the system if the supply invalid ballots, colluding or fault authorities must not alter the voting process's results.
- **Verifiability:** Any external party can verify that the result of the election is correct. In particular, this means that votes are recorded as captured and cannot be manipulated when transferred from vote collection to tabulation.

The previous properties are taken for granted in all paper-based electoral systems. After a voter drops the ballot in the box, he or she leaves the voting area without any concern or doubt. Clearly, there is some authentication through ID cards and signatures, but the voter cannot be sure about various issues: Maybe the election officials stuffed the ballot box after the end of the elections or simply miscounted the ballots. Most systems rely heavily on the trust placed on the government appointed officials overseeing the elections.

On the other hand, there is significantly less trust when computers are involved in the election process. Almost everyone has seen a computer crash and the flaws discovered everyday in security applications weakens people's trust in computer-based election systems. Such problems, in conjunction with the general public's lack of understanding about computers and about the security that a carefully designed system can provide, result in distrust of electronic voting schemes. Any electronic voting scheme that can be applied to real life elections must satisfy the above requirements. Additionally, there is another set of requirements that an electronic voting scheme may or may not possess (Schneier, 1996).

- **Receipt-freeness:** The voter cannot construct any proof of the contents of his or her vote
- **Non-duplication:** A voter cannot duplicate the vote of another voter
- **Public participation:** Everyone knows who did and who did not vote
- **Private error correction:** A voter can prove that his or her vote was miscounted, without revealing how he or she voted

Many voting schemes have been proposed so far that satisfy the previous set of requirements, but they are limited by the ballot options they can support. Initial voting systems (Benaloh, 1997) allowed the voter to select one of two candidates ("yes/no" paradigm) and later systems can accommodate the selection of "t out of n" candidates (Baudron, Fouque, Pointcheval, Pouparde, & Stern, 2001; Cramer, Frankel, Schoenmakers, & Yung, 1996, Cramer, Gennaro, & Schoenmakers, 1997; Damgard et al., 2001). Such electoral systems are encountered in the United States and electronic voting systems have already been applied in various state elections. These systems however, cannot be used for elections whose structure is more

Copyright © 2007, Idea Group Inc. Copying or distributing in print or electronic forms without written permission of Idea Group Inc. is prohibited.

complicated than a selection of "*t* out of *n*" candidates like many electoral systems throughout Europe.

Our Contribution

In this work, we present an election system that will accommodate *multiple parties*, which in turn consist of *multiple candidates* and will allow a voter to select "*t* out of *n*" candidates within a *single party* and prove that this selection is valid. We do this by showing in a Zero Knowledge manner the validity of selecting a subset of a set belonging to a predefined family of sets. More specifically, we show how to prove that the voter's selection consists of t elements (candidates) all belonging to the *same* set (party) out of *k* sets of at most *n* elements each.

We apply this methodology in order to construct an election scheme that will accommodate multiple parties and the selection of *t* candidates *from one and only one* of those parties. Such election systems are common throughout the world, like in many European countries. Electoral systems with the previously mentioned structure are referred to "open party list" systems and are used in many countries, among which are the Netherlands, Norway, Greece, Spain, and Slovenia. Electronic voting schemes proposed up to now were limited to the selection of "*t* out of *n*" candidates and could not accommodate such a complex system. Our proposal extends existing voting schemes and can be applied to elections which have those requirements.

Furthermore, we have implemented a voting system that uses our proposed protocol in order to run an election. Our scheme guarantees the necessary requirements of a voting system mentioned in the introduction: privacy of voters, public verifiability, fairness and soundness, eligibility and reusability. *Privacy of voters* guarantees that a vote will be kept secret from any collusion of *t* or less authorities, where *t* is a system parameter. *Public verifiability* ensures that any external party can verify that the election is fair and that the published tally was computed correctly from the ballots that were correctly cast. *Fairness* and *Soundness* ensure that the system can tolerate up to *t* faulty or colluding authorities without its operation being affected. The existence of the bulletin board and of secure channels via public key cryptography ensures *eligibility* and *unreusability*.

Finally we performed a set of experiments to measure the time taken for creation and verification of the Zero Knowledge proofs, the size of produced ballots as well as the total time needed for a voter to cast a vote in our system, including user and server authentication, ballot creation, transmission and verification, for various system parameters. We prove and validate experimentally that the running time of the algorithm for the creation of the ballot and the zero knowledge proofs is linear with respect to the total number of candidates in the elections. Hence, our system not only fulfills the basic security requirements, but it is also user friendly and practical, an essential characteristic of any voting system that is to be used for public elections.

Copyright © 2007, Idea Group Inc. Copying or distributing in print or electronic forms without written permission of Idea Group Inc. is prohibited.

RELATED WORK

An electronic voting scheme consists of a set of protocols which allow voters to cast ballots while a group of authorities collect the votes and output the final tally. Election schemes in (Benaloh & Tuinstra, 1994; Benaloh, 1997; Cramer et al., 1996; Cramer et al., 1997) were first described by Benaloh (1997). All these schemes mainly discuss the "yes/no" vote scenario. Such schemes utilize a cryptosystem that has the *homomorphic* property (see section about the Paillier Cryptosystem), which allows the computation of the tally without the decryption of individual ballots. Two different election models have been proposed so far.

In Benaloh schemes, a voter shares his or her vote between n authorities so that any t of them can recover it. Each authority computes its encrypted share of the tally and finally t of them needs to collaborate to compute the actual tally.

In schemes like the one described by Cramer et al. (1997), the voters send their encrypted votes to a single combiner. Using the *homomorphic* property of the cryptosystems the combiner computes the encrypted tally in a public verifiable way. Then t authorities need to collaborate in order to recover the tally by running a threshold cryptosystem.

Systems described by Cramer et al. (1996, 1997), which are implemented in commercial electronic voting applications, use a variant of the El Gamal cryptosystem exhibiting the homomorphic property and having a threshold version (Pedersen, 1992). This cryptosystem requires exponent search in order to compute the final tally from the ballot product, an operation that is computationally *expensive* and may render the system inefficient when the number of voters increases.

Our system uses the Paillier Cryptosystem (Paillier, 1999) which exhibits the homomorphic properties needed by the election scheme and more importantly provides an efficient decryption algorithm as well as the largest bandwidth among all cryptosystems using a trapdoor to compute the discrete logarithm. A threshold version of the cryptosystem that was presented by Damgard et al. (2001) and Fouque, Poupard, and Stern (2000) allow its usage in the case of multiple authorities to jointly run a threshold cryptosystem and collaborate in order to decrypt the final tally.

CRYPTOGRAPHIC TOOLS

In this section, we present the various cryptographic tools and primitives that we use throughout this work. We start with an overview of the Paillier Cryptosystem which we will use for encrypting the voter's selections. We present its encryption, decryption, and key generation algorithms as well some significant properties that make this cryptosystem ideal for our purpose.

Copyright © 2007, Idea Group Inc. Copying or distributing in print or electronic forms without written permission of Idea Group Inc. is prohibited.

The Paillier Cryptosystem

Paillier (1999) proposes a new probabilistic encryption scheme based on computations in the group $Z^*_{N^2}$, where N is an RSA modulus. This scheme has some very attractive properties: It is homomorphic, it allows encryption of many bits in one operation with a constant expansion factor and allows for efficient decryption. This cryptosystem is based on the *Decisional Composite Residuosity Assumption* (DCRA).

Description of Paillier Scheme

- **Key Generation:** Let N be an RSA modulus $N = pq$, where p and q are prime integers. Let g be an integer of order a multiple of N modulo N^2. The public key is $PK = (N, g)$ and the secret key is $SK = \lambda(N)$ where $\lambda(N)$ is defined as $\lambda(N) = \text{lcm}[(p-1)(q-1)]$. We should note that Damgard and Jurik (2001) propose that $g = N+1$ can be used without degrading security. Then the public key will only consist of N.
- **Encryption:** To encrypt a message $M \in ZN$ choose a random $r \in Z^*_N$ and compute the ciphertext $c = g^M r^N \bmod N^2$.
- **Decryption:** To decrypt a ciphertext c, compute:

$$M = \frac{L(c^{\lambda(N)} \bmod N^2)}{L(g^{\lambda(N)} \bmod N^2)} \bmod N^2$$

where the L-function receives input from the set $S_N = \{ u < N^2 \mid u = 1 \bmod N\}$ and $L(u) = (u - 1)/N$.

Homomorphic Property

The encryption function has an "algebraic property" which allows computations with the encrypted values without knowing the contents of the ciphertexts. More precisely the encryption function has the following property:

for every $M_1, M_2 \in Z_N$, $E(M_1 + M_2) = E(M_1) E(M_2)$.

This property is necessary to achieve anonymity as well as universal verifiability since the tally can be computed without the decryption of individual votes by all interested parties. The decryption is performed on the final tally, guaranteeing the privacy of the voters.

In Table 1, we provide a trivial example in order to demonstrate how we utilize the homomorphic property of the Paillier cryptosystem. In this example, we assume that we have n candidates and 4 submitted ballots. An encryption of 1 denotes a "Yes" while of 0 denotes a "No." As it can be seen, by multiplying ballots and decrypting the final product, we find that Candidate 1 received 2 votes, Candidate 2 received 3 votes, and so forth.

Copyright © 2007, Idea Group Inc. Copying or distributing in print or electronic forms without written permission of Idea Group Inc. is prohibited.

Table 1. Example of Paillier Homomorphic encryption

	Candidate 1	Candidate 2	...	Candidate n
Ballot 1	$g^0 r_{11}^{\,N}$	$g^1 r_{12}^{\,N}$	...	$g^1 r_{1n}^{\,N}$
Ballot 2	$g^1 r_{21}^{\,N}$	$g^1 r_{22}^{\,N}$	...	$g^0 r_{2n}^{\,N}$
Ballot 3	$g^1 r_{31}^{\,N}$	$g^0 r_{32}^{\,N}$	...	$g^0 r_{3n}^{\,N}$
Ballot 4	$g^0 r_{41}^{\,N}$	$g^1 r_{42}^{\,N}$	...	$g^1 r_{4n}^{\,N}$
Ballot Product	$g^2 r_{1}^{\,N}$	$g^3 r_{2}^{\,N}$	...	$g^3 r_{n}^{\,N}$

In the scheme described by Cramer et al. (1996) as well as in other voting schemes a variant of the El Gamal encryption scheme is used. In this variant in order to encrypt a message m we need to compute ($g^k \bmod p$ and $g^m y^k \bmod p$) instead of ($g^k \bmod p$ and $my^k \bmod p$). In this manner, the scheme gains the homomorphic property needed for the election schemes. The negative side of this encryption scheme is that no trapdoor exists to compute m given $g^m \bmod p$. Therefore, this scheme is only used in "yes/no" schemes, where the message m is either 0 or 1 and therefore g^m lies in limited subset of messages and can be computed using exhaustive search. However, this scheme has been used in several voting systems including some commercial ones. In the case of elections with many candidates and a large number of voters the modified El Gamal scheme becomes inapplicable since exhaustive search or more efficient methods like index calculus cannot efficiently compute the final tally.

Threshold Version of Paillier Cryptosystem

A (t,n) threshold scheme does not reveal a secret S unless any t out of the n participants work together. In order to prevent authorities to learn the contents of submitted votes and to ensure the privacy of the voters a threshold version of the Paillier Cryptosystem can be used. In this case, instead of having a single authority decrypt the encrypted tally, n authorities share the secret, so that at least t are needed to perform the decryption operation. Such versions of the cryptosystem are presented by Damgard et al. (2001) and Fouque et al. (2000). A general description of a threshold decryption model follows.

The scheme includes the following participants: a combiner, a set of n authorities A_i and users.

- In the initialization phase, the authorities run a distributed key generation protocol to create the public key *PK* and the secret shares *SKi* of the private key *SK* with or without a trusted dealer (Damgard & Koprowski, 2001; Fouque & Stern, 2001). Next, the authorities publish the verification keys *VK*, *VK$_i$*.
- The user encrypts a message using the private key *PK*.
- To decrypt a ciphertext c, the combiner forwards c to all the authorities. Using the shares of the secret key *SK$_i$* and the verification keys *VK* and *VK$_i$* each

Copyright © 2007, Idea Group Inc. Copying or distributing in print or electronic forms without written permission of Idea Group Inc. is prohibited.

authority runs the decryption algorithm and produces a partial decryption c_i, providing a proof of validity for the partial decryption. The combiner can then produce the decryption of ciphertext c, if enough partial decryptions (t or more) are valid.

Zero Knowledge Proofs

Central to our results is the way to achieve an efficient proof of validity for ballots. The proof of validity shows to any interested party including the tabulation authorities that a ballot actually represents a valid vote. To maintain the privacy of the voters this proof of validity will be a zero knowledge proof. In general, a Zero Knowledge proof allows a prover to convince a verifier about the validity of statement without leaking any information other than its correctness.

The efficiency of the entire voting scheme depends greatly on the efficiency of the zero knowledge proofs in terms of computational effort and in terms of the required bandwidth. Our goal is to create a zero knowledge proof that the submitted ballot is a selection of t candidates from a *single* party. Since this a complex proof we will use as building blocks the zero knowledge proofs presented by Damgard et al. (2001) which we include here for completeness. We note that the following protocols are not zero knowledge as they stand, only honest verifier zero knowledge. However, zero knowledge protocols for the same problems can be constructed using standard methods and secondly in our applications we will always use them in a non-interactive variant based on the Fiat and Shamir (1987) heuristic. We use a pseudorandom function in order to produce the random challenge, without the prover interacting with the verifier, but also ensuring that the prover cannot cheat while creating the random challenge. More specifically we use a secure hash function h (*e.g.*, SHA-1) of the voter's name and parts of the proof to generate the random challenge the Verifier sends to the Prover.

In order for prover P to prove a statement S to verifier V, P selects the appropriate proof from the ones described below. It computes the first message a in this protocol and then computes: $e = h(a, S, ID(P))$, where $ID(P)$ is the prover's identity in the system. In our case, we use the username of the voter. The inclusion of $ID(P)$ in the input of h is done in order to prevent vote duplication.

In the following protocols, P denotes the prover and V denotes the verifier.

Proof for Power of N

Input: N and u

Private input for P: v such that $u = v^N \bmod N^2$.

This protocol proves that u is a power of N modulo N^2. The sequence of steps is:

1. P chooses a random $r \bmod N^2$ and sends to V: $a = r^N \bmod N^2$.

Copyright © 2007, Idea Group Inc. Copying or distributing in print or electronic forms without written permission of Idea Group Inc. is prohibited.

2. V chooses a random k bit number e and sends e to P.
3. P sends $z = rv^e$ mod N^2 to V and V checks that $z^N =$ aue mod N^2 and accepts only if and only if this is the case.

Proof for 1-out-of-2 power of N

Input: N, u_1, u_2
Private input for P: v_1 such that $u_1 = v1^N$ mod N^2

This protocol proves that either u_1 or u_2 is a power of N modulo N^2. The sequence of steps is:

1. P chooses a random r_1 mod N^2. It invokes M on input N, u_2 to get a conversation a_2, e_2, z_2. It sends $a1 = r_1^N$ mod N^2, a_2 to V.
2. V chooses s, a random t bit number and sends s to P.
3. P computes $e1 = s - e_2$ mod 2^t, $z^1 = r_1 v_1 e_1$ mod N^2 and sends e_1, z_1, e_2, z_2 to V.
4. V checks that $s = e_1 + e_2$ mod 2^t, $z_1^N = a_1 u_1^{e1}$ mod N^2 and, $z_2^N = a_2 u_2^{e2}$ mod N^2, and accepts if and only if this is the case.

In the previous protocol, M denotes the honest-verifier simulator for *proof for power of N* protocol above. Using these proofs as building blocks, we present our construction for selecting in Zero Knowledge a subset of candidates belonging to one and only one party.

VOTING PROTOCOL

The purpose of the vote is to select t candidates from a single party. Suppose there are K parties participating in the election and let each party have L candidates. The purpose of such an election would be to select a governing party as well as the members of the parliament, or elect a mayor of a municipality and the members of the council. The voter has to prove that the vote is valid, which means that it contains at *most t* positive selections and that all those selections are from the *same* party since one should not be able to vote for candidates belonging to deferent parties.

Since the total number of candidates is $K \times L$ we will hold $K \times L$ parallel "yes/no" votes. In this sense, the voter will select "yes" for t candidates and "no" for the rest. If we represent "yes" with "1" and "no" with "0", then the encrypted selection for candidate i will be $E_i = g^1 r^N = g r^N$ if the selection is "yes" or $E_i = g^0 r^N = r^N$ if the selection is "no", for some random $r \in Z^*_N$.

Along with the encryptions of the "yes/no" selections for the $K \times L$ candidates, the voter needs to send proof of the validity of those encryptions. For this purpose the protocol for *1-out-of-2 power of N* is utilized. Using this protocol, the user proves that either E_i or $E_{i/g}$ is a power of N modulo N^2, essentially proving that the

Copyright © 2007, Idea Group Inc. Copying or distributing in print or electronic forms without written permission of Idea Group Inc. is prohibited.

vote is either an encryption of "0" or "1". Most importantly, however, the voter has to prove that the t selected candidates come from the same party. For this purpose the voter needs to generate K proofs, one for each party, proving that either E_{P_i} or E_{P_i}/g^t is a power of N modulo N^2 using the protocol for 1-out-of-2 power of N. E_{P_i} is the product of the encrypted selections for party i:

$$E_{P_i} = \prod_{Party_i} E_i$$

In this manner, the voter proves that he or she has either selected 0 or t candidates from this party. This is due to the homomorphic property of the cryptosystem, since E_{P_i} will either be an encryption of 0 or t. Notice that the voter reveals no information about the party she has voted for, since she proves for *each* party that she has either selected 0 or t candidates from it, which is essential for the validity of the submitted ballot.

Finally, the voter needs to prove that he or she has selected exactly t candidates. In order to do that, the voter uses the *protocol of N power* in order to prove that $\prod_i E_i/g_t$ is a power of N modulo N^2, where $\prod_i E_i$ is the product of all the encrypted selections. Due to the homomorphic property of the cryptosystem $\prod_i E_i$ will be an encryption of "t" and $\prod_i E_i/g_t$ will be a power of N.

Having proven the previous properties for the submitted encrypted selections the user successfully shows that he or she has selected exactly t candidates from a single party and no candidates from the rest of the parties. This is the case since he or she proves that for every party he or she has selected t or 0 candidates and that he or she has selected t candidates in total.

It is easy to generalize the above protocol to allow up to t selections from a single party by adding t "dummy candidates" to the L candidates of each party. The voter will then place the selections she does not wish to use on the "dummy candidates." In the same manner, we can accommodate for blank votes be creating a dummy party with t candidates on which the selection will be placed.

VOTING SYSTEM IMPLEMENTATION

We will use a hash function h in order to make the proofs used by the above protocol non-interactive according to the Fiat-Shamir (1987) heuristic. We will also assume that an instance of threshold version of Paillier's scheme with public key (N, g) has been set up, with A_i's being the decryption servers. We will also assume that $N_2 > M$, where M is the number of voters, since N can always be chosen large enough to satisfy this inequality.

As we have mentioned in the introduction, we will use a general model for election described by Cramer (1997), which we mention briefly: We have a set of voters $V_1, V_2, \ldots, V_M$, a bulletin board B and a set of tallying authorities $A_1, A_2, \ldots$,

Copyright © 2007, Idea Group Inc. Copying or distributing in print or electronic forms without written permission of Idea Group Inc. is prohibited.

A_M. The bulletin board operates as follows: Every voter can write to B and no message can be deleted from B once it has been written there. Everyone can access the messages in B and can identify the origin of each message. This can be implemented in a secure way using existing public key infrastructure. Also assume that we have K parties $P_1, P_2, \dots, P_K$.

The Bulletin Board

Central to the operation of the election model is the Bulletin Board, whose operation is previously described. There have been various proposals about the implementation of the bulletin board in the literature, but these have been purely theoretical ones. These proposals include usage of the public key infrastructure or Write Once Read Many drives (WORM).

We have implemented the Bulletin Board as a server with access to a database where the ballots submitted by the users are stored. In order for a ballot to be written in the Bulletin Board, it must be signed by the authentication authorities. This signature ensures the users right to vote. Additionally the ballot must have a valid signature of the voter who submits it. If both conditions hold, the ballot is stored in the database, unless an entry for the same voter is found.

Voting Procedure

The voting procedure can be summarized with the following steps:

1. Each voter Vi decides on her votes (0 for "no" 1 for "yes") for the $K*L$ candidates, calculates $E_{ij} = E(v_{ij})$ and creates proofs:

    *   Proof that E_{ij} or E_{ij}/g is an N power modulo N^2 for all $j \in \{1 \dots K* L\}$.
    *   Proof that $\prod_j E_{ij}$ or $\prod_j E_{ij}/g_t$ ($j \in P_k$) is an N power modulo N^2 for all $k \in \{1 \dots K\}$.
    *   Proof that $\prod_{j=1}^{K \times L} E_{ij}/g'$ is an N power modulo N^2.

    She writes the encrypted votes E_{ij} and all the proofs in B.

2. Each authority A_k sets $\prod E_j = 1$ for all $j \in \{1 \dots K*L\}$.

    Then for all voters i

    *   Checks the proofs in B for voter Vi and if they are valid sets $\prod E_j = (\prod E_j)* E_{ij} \bmod N^2$.
    *   Executes its part of the threshold decryption protocol, using $\prod E_j$'s as input ciphertext and writes its result to the bulletin board B.

Copyright © 2007, Idea Group Inc. Copying or distributing in print or electronic forms without written permission of Idea Group Inc. is prohibited.

Figure 1. Structure of ballots

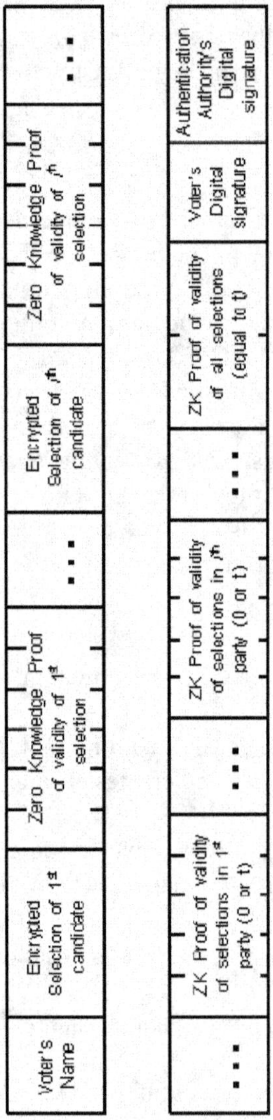

3. From the messages written by the tabulation authorities in B one can now reconstruct the final tally $\prod E_j$ for $j \in \{1 \ldots \underline{K} * L\}$. Clearly $\prod Ej = \prod_i E(v_{ij}) = E(\sum_i v_{ij})$. Therefore the decryption results will be $\sum_i v_{ij} \bmod N^2$ for candidates $j \in \{1 \ldots K * L\}$ which is $\sum_i v_{ij}$ since $N^2 > M$. One can also easily calculate the votes for each party by summing the votes that the candidates of each party have received and divide them by t: $Votes_{Party\,k} = \sum_j v_{ij} / t$, where $j \in$ Party K.

Copyright © 2007, Idea Group Inc. Copying or distributing in print or electronic forms without written permission of Idea Group Inc. is prohibited.

Figure 2. Proof creation time vs. total number of candidates participating in the election

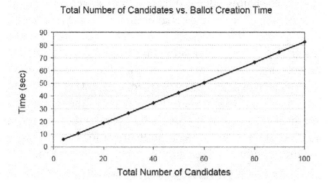

The security of this protocol follows from the security of the sub-protocols used and the semantic security of Paillier's Cryptosystem.

Ballot Structure

The structure of the ballots is shown in Figure 2. The ballot consists of the voter's name (or user ID, depending on system implementation). Then follows the voter's encrypted selection for the first candidate (either "yes" or "no"). After that the Zero Knowledge proof of the selection's validity is inserted. When the selections for all candidates in a party are inserted, the Zero Knowledge proof of validity for the number of "yes/no" votes in that party follows (which proves that the voter has selected either 0 or exactly t candidates from that party). The corresponding data for the rest of parties are appended to ballot. Finally, we append the Zero Knowledge proof that the voter has made t positive selections in total. Then the ballot is digitally signed by the voter and the authentication authorities, and the signatures are appended to the ballot.

Complexity Analysis

In the analysis that follows we will denote with C the total number of candidates that participate in the election. Without loss of generality we examine the case of K parties with L candidates each and an election that allows up to t selections within a party, so C will be equal to $K * (\underline{L} + t)$.

The voter generates C proofs of *1-out-of-2 power of N*, one for each candidate and K proofs of *1-out-of-2 power of N*, one for each party. Thus the voter needs to generate $C+K$ proofs in total, which is clearly O(C). If k is the bitlength of N then evidently the size of a vote in this voting protocol is $O(C*k)$. The same holds for the time needed for the computation and verification of the proofs.

Copyright © 2007, Idea Group Inc. Copying or distributing in print or electronic forms without written permission of Idea Group Inc. is prohibited.

We have implemented a system using the previous protocol and made measurements of the running time on a Pentium 4, 2.53GHz machine. In Figure 2, the time needed to create the Zero Knowledge proofs is displayed versus the total number of candidates in the elections. The system behaves linearly to the number of candidates and the computation time is acceptable even when a much larger number of candidates (>100) is used. For the implementation Java was used, which means that native code will reduce the computation time even further. For the tally computation $O(C * M)$ verifications of proofs need to be performed, where M is the number of voters as well as $O(C)$ decryption operations on the products of the individual votes. The time to verify the proofs for a single voter is less than that of the proofs' creation time. These operations, as well as the decryption operation can be done offline after the end of the elections without increasing the voter's waiting time.

The size of the ballots created, as we mentioned above, increases linearly to the number of candidates in the elections. In Figure 3, we show how the ballot size varies with respect to the total number of candidates in our system. As we expected the ballot size doubles when the number of candidates doubles.

We should note that our proposal is not limited to parties that have the *same* number of candidates each. We have used this model so far to simplify the description of the system and not to complicate the notations used in the Zero Knowledge proofs. Our proposal can be applied to elections *with parties that have an arbitrary number of candidates}* each and the analysis of the system complexity we previously made still holds.

Finally, we provide a formula for the ballot size in our system. In what follows, C is the number of candidates in the system, which are distributed (in any manner) in K parties. Let $|H|$ denote the size of the hashed commitments and $|N2|$ the size of the modulus used in the Paillier cryptosystem. The size of a vote is then:

Figure 3. Ballot size (in Kbytes) vs. total number of candidates participating in the election

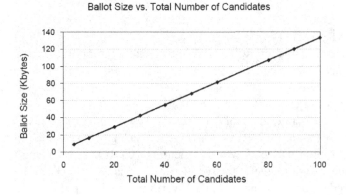

Copyright © 2007, Idea Group Inc. Copying or distributing in print or electronic forms without written permission of Idea Group Inc. is prohibited.

$$(5|N^2|+2|H|) * C +(4|N^2|+2|H|) * (K+1)$$

Evidently the ballot length is $O(C+K)$ and since in most cases $C>>K$ we can say that our system behaves linearly to the number of candidates. In practical applications we may choose $|H| = 80$ and $|N^2| = 2048$. For an election with 20 candidates and 3 parties the size of a vote is about 30Kbytes.

SECURITY ANALYSIS

In this section, we analyze the security properties of our design, and we show how our proposal satisfies the properties that a secure voting system should have (Section 1).

Privacy and Anonymity of Voters

The privacy of the voters' selections is guaranteed even if up to t authorities collude with each other. The use of a threshold cryptosystem guarantees that no faulty or malicious authority can decrypt the ballot submitted by a voter. Additionally, our election protocol uses the homomorphic property of the cryptosystem in order to compute the final tally without decrypting individual votes. This strengthens the voter's privacy, since at no point in the election process, will his vote be decrypted.

Privacy is also ensured by the utilization of Zero Knowledge proofs for showing the validity of the contents of a ballot. Such proofs, as we mentioned in the Zero Knowledge Proof Section, do not reveal any information to the prover about the contents of the secret. They just prove its validity.

Finally, all communications between voters and authorities are made though secure channels. An external attacker or eavesdropper can convey no information about the contents of the ballot since this is sent encrypted over the communication channel.

Public Verifiability

In our election system, anyone can verify the result of the lection and be convinced of its correctness. Any external party can verify that the election is fair and that the published tally as computed correctly from the ballots that were correctly cast. This is achieved with the use of a storage server (Bulletin Board).

Since a ballot posted on the Bulletin Board includes the proofs of correctness, anyone can verify the validity of the individual ballots, proving that only correct ballots where included in the computation of the final tally. Then one can compute the encrypted tally on its own by using the homomorphic property of the Paillier cryptosystem and running the same protocol run by the tallying authorities, thus proving that all ballots where counted by the authorities.

Copyright © 2007, Idea Group Inc. Copying or distributing in print or electronic forms without written permission of Idea Group Inc. is prohibited.

Furthermore, the partial decryption results produced by the tallying authorities are published in the bulletin board, along with the proofs of validity. An external party can verify these proofs and be convinced that the final result is correct.

Fairness and Soundness

We will prove that no malicious party, voter, or authority, can affect the voting process, or alter its results. A malicious user cannot affect the voting process by submitting invalid ballots or by not following the protocol. If a user tries to submit an invalid ballot, maybe by using its own custom-made software, the proofs of correctness will not be valid and the vote will be discarded by the authentication authorities. If the user tries to send the ballot directly to the Bulletin Board, the ballot would still be discarded since it would not have a valid signature. Finally, a user that does not follow the designated protocol in its communication with either of the servers will have its connection terminated or timed out.

The use of secure communication channels (e.g., SSL) provides security against an active attacker that is one that would not only record communications, but also try to alter the messages sent. Therefore, no external party can alter the messages sent by a user to the authorities and alter the integrity of the ballot.

As far as authorities are concerned, a malicious Authentication server cannot inject ballots in the system. The Authentication server can certainly sign whatever ballot it wishes, but these ballots will not have a valid signature by an eligible voter and will be discarded. The same holds for the Storage server. If it operates maliciously and writes invalid ballots or inserts ballots for absentees, these will be rejected at the counting phase by the tallying authorities, since they check the validity and signatures of each ballot before including it in the final tally.

The fairness and soundness of the elections is also guaranteed against colluding tallying authorities, as long as no more than t of them cooperate. This is achieved from the properties of the threshold cryptosystem, which prevents the decryption of a ciphertext unless there are more than t valid shares available. Therefore, no authority can miscount the ballots or inject some of its own during the computation.

Eligibility and Unreusability

Our system guarantees that only eligible voters are allowed to cast a vote. This is achieved by having the ballot signed by the authentication authorities who have a list of registered users and their public keys. A non-registered voter can vote by breaking the authentication protocol which uses a public key signature scheme (e.g., RSA, DSA). This hard and conventional wisdom says that the authentication protocol is secure. Another way is to acquire a registered user's public key and username and vote in their place. But this is not something we can take measures against electronically. A way to avoid such cases would be to have public voting areas, where an election official would perform standard authentication using an ID card.

Copyright © 2007, Idea Group Inc. Copying or distributing in print or electronic forms without written permission of Idea Group Inc. is prohibited.

Furthermore, the authentication authorities guarantee that no user is allowed to vote more than once since they maintain a list of who has voted and who has not.

Vote Duplication

Vote duplication is not allowed in our election system. This means that no user can copy the vote of another. This is an important property of an election system since one could then coerce or pay a voter so that the voter submits a copy of its vote. Vote duplication is prevented in our system, by having the username of the voter included in the construction of the Zero Knowledge proofs of validity of the ballot. Therefore, one cannot submit a vote without going though the creation of the Zero Knowledge proofs.

Public Participation

We chose to implement an election model that makes the information about who voted and did not public. Any external party can check the bulletin board and see the list of voters that submitted a ballot. This property has value depending on the particular society. For instance, in Greece, participation in the election process is required by the legislation and this property would be highly valued.

CONCLUSION AND FUTURE RESEARCH

We have presented a methodology for proving in Zero Knowledge the validity of a selection of t elements from one out of k sets of n elements each. We have used this methodology in order to construct an election scheme that can provide more complex ballot options than current existing ones. In particular, our implementation can host elections involving a number of parties each consisting of an *arbitrary number* of candidates with the voter having to select a subset of the candidates from a *single party*, without degrading security or efficiency. Furthermore, the computational and communication complexity is linear with respect to the number of candidates and the proposed voting system satisfies all necessary security requirements.

In our current research, we are examining the possibility to make the complexity of our system (ballot size and computations) proportional to the number of parties *plus* the number of selections the voter is requested to make. This may be achieved possibly by representing a selection as described by Baudron et al. (2001) and coming up with a new set of Zero Knowledge proofs, which can correlate the selection with a single party.

Additionally, we are examining the implementation of a distributed system architecture that will feature fault tolerance and load balancing by having multiple servers. This will not only improve the performance of the system when multiple users are handled, but will also shield the system against node failures, network failures and denial of service attacks which could make some of the servers inaccessible but not all.

Copyright © 2007, Idea Group Inc. Copying or distributing in print or electronic forms without written permission of Idea Group Inc. is prohibited.

REFERENCES

Baudron, O., Fouque, P. A., Pointcheval, D., Pouparde, G., & Stern, J. (2001, August). Practical multi-candidate election system. In *Proceedings of the ACM Conference on Principles on Distributed Computing*, Philadelphia.

Benaloh, J., & Tuinstra D. (1994). Receipt-free secret ballot elections. In *Proceedings of the 26th Symposium on the Theory of Computing (STOC)* (pp. 544-553). ACM.

Benaloh, J. (1997). *Verifiable secret ballot elections.* PhD thesis, Yale University.

Cramer, R., Frankel, Y., Schoenmakers, B., & Yung, M. (1996). Multi-authority secret-ballot elections with linear work. In *Eurocrypt '96* (LNCS 1070, pp. 72-83). Springer-Verlag.

Cramer, R., Gennaro, R., & Schoenmakers, B. (1997). A secure and optimally efficient multi- authority election scheme. In *Eurocrypt '97* (LNCS 1233, pp. 113-118). Springer-Verlag.

Damgard, I., & Jurik, M. (2001). A generalization, a simplification and some applications of paillier's probabilistic public-key system. In *PKC '01* (LNCS 1992, pp. 119-136). Springer-Verlag.

Damgard, I., & Koprowski, M. (2001). Practical threshold RSA signatures without a trusted dealer. In *Eurocrypt '01* (LNCS). Springer-Verlag.

Fiat, A, & Shamir, A. (1987). How to prove yourself: Practical solutions of identification and signature problems. In *Crypto '86* (LNCS 263, pp. 186-194). Springer-Verlag.

Fouque, P., & Stern, J. (2001). *Fully distributed RSA signatures under standard assumptions.*

Fouque, P. A., Poupard, G., & Stern, J. (2000). Sharing decryption in the context of voting or lotteries. In *Financial Crypto '00* (LNCS). Springer-Verlag.

Fujioka, A., Okamoto, T., & Ohta, K. (1992). A practical secret voting scheme for large-scale elections advances in cryptology. In *AUSCRYPT '92.*

Paillier, P. (1999). Public-key cryptosystems based on discrete logarithm residues. In *Eurocrypt '99* (LNCS 1592). Springer-Verlag.

Pedersen, T. P. (1992). Non-interactive and information-theoretic secure verifiable secret sharing. In *Advances in Cryptology—Crypto '91* (LNCS 576, pp. 129-140). Springer-Verlag.

Schneier B. (1996). *Applied cryptography.* New York: John Wiley and Sons.

Copyright © 2007, Idea Group Inc. Copying or distributing in print or electronic forms without written permission of Idea Group Inc. is prohibited.

Chapter XIII

Requirements on Cross-Agency Processes in E-Government:
The Need for a Reference Model

Jeffrey Gortmaker, Delft University of Technology, The Netherlands

Marijn Janssen, Delft University of Technology, The Netherlands

Rene W. Wagenaar, Delft University of Technology, The Netherlands

ABSTRACT

A big challenge for governments all over the world is to deliver secure, reliable, transparent, and accountable services to their citizens and businesses. Effective and efficient service delivery requires the orchestration of business processes going beyond the border of single agencies. Little is known about how to orchestrate these cross-agency service-delivery processes, and consequently governmental decision-makers are looking for support in designing such processes. This chapter investigates the applicability of two existing reference models, the workflow reference model, and the extended SOA reference model, to guide the development of cross-agency process orchestration. Although these reference models contain important elements, we found that these models do not provide support for issues like ensuring correct and in-time service-delivery processes, secure information sharing, and transparent and accountable processes.

Copyright © 2007, Idea Group Inc. Copying or distributing in print or electronic forms without written permission of Idea Group Inc. is prohibited.

INTRODUCTION

A big challenge for governments all over the world is to improve the service provisioning to their clients, citizens, and businesses, and to reduce the administrative burdens for citizens and businesses (Dutch Government, 2003, 2004). Citizens and business' expectations regarding service delivery is likely to rise as they get more and more accustomed to online trading and communicating at any time of the day (McIvor, McHugh, & Cadden, 2002).

A first step to satisfy this demand is offering access to governmental information and services online via the Internet. A next step is the provisioning of services using a "one-stop-shop" concept (Wimmer, 2002), where services of different governmental agencies are combined or integrated. An example is a virtual business counter that functions as a single point of contact for interaction with different kinds of governmental agencies.

Both steps in improving the governmental service-delivery processes have to deal with the fragmentation of governments (Wimmer, 2002), as roles and functions are distributed over many agencies. Service-delivery processes often include activities or sub-processes performed by different public agencies (Castellano, Pastore, Arcieri, & Summo, 2004; Contenti, Termini, Mecella, & Baldoni, 2003; Gortmaker & Janssen, 2004). Consequently, effective governmental service delivery requires the coordination of (parts of) service-delivery processes that involve multiple agencies. In this chapter, we will call this process orchestration.

Due to the fact that these processes span multiple governmental agencies, requirements for orchestrating cross-agency service-delivery processes differ from single-agency service-delivery processes. This becomes clear when realizing that information is passed from one system to another system using a communication network. Mechanisms to enable inter-agency communication and information-exchange are necessary, but also the coordination of the different process-steps becomes more difficult.

This problem of coordinating cross-agency service-delivery processes is not specific to the public sector; also in the private sector, businesses are looking for ways on how to coordinate their inter-organizational processes. Specific for the public sector is, however, the strong emphasis on transparency, consistency, reliability, security, and non-discrimination of the service-delivery processes. As many public service-delivery processes are largely determined by law, these aspects are of vital importance. Ensuring and maintaining secure and transparent processes is particularly important when service-delivery processes run across multiple, semi-autonomous agencies. The involvement of a large number of more or less autonomous agencies in service-delivery processes is a typical public sector characteristic.

Web service orchestration is a relatively new technology that can be applied to the problem of coordinating sub-processes that run across different agencies. Within governments, little is known about how to coordinate cross-agency service-delivery processes, the advantages of Web service orchestration-technology (Gortmaker,

Copyright © 2007, Idea Group Inc. Copying or distributing in print or electronic forms without written permission of Idea Group Inc. is prohibited.

Janssen, & Wagenaar, 2004), and how Web service orchestration-technology can be applied for coordinating secure, transparent, reliable, and accountable cross-agency service-delivery processes. Consequently, there is a need for a reference model that can support governmental decision-makers in implementing process orchestration in e-government.

The goal of this chapter is to investigate the extent to which existing reference models are able to support governmental decision-makers in implementing process orchestration in e-government. We do this by investigating two existing reference models and evaluating these models using requirements derived from practice. First, we discuss Web service orchestration technology, the workflow reference model, and the extended SOA reference model. Thereafter we investigate a case study, derive the main requirements on cross-agency coordination, and cluster these requirements in three categories. Next, we evaluate the reference models using these requirements and draw conclusions.

WEB SERVICE ORCHESTRATION

Web service orchestration is based upon the notion of a service-oriented architecture (SOA). Due to its loosely-coupled nature, SOA is very suitable for orchestrating service-delivery processes that run across relatively autonomous agencies (Stojanovic & Dahanayake, 2005). In a SOA, application functionality is not provided by one large monolithic application, but is provided by relatively small-grained services that are offered by different independent providers. Service requesters can search for services published in a service-directory, select the needed services, and thereafter invoke the services offered by the service-requesters. A SOA makes it possible to quickly assemble new compound services out of existing sub-services.

Although various middleware technologies can be used to achieve SOA, Web service standards satisfy the universal interoperability needs better (Pasley, 2005). Web Services enable the provisioning of functionality, both on application and business level, by means of a standardized interface in a way that they are easily invoked via Internet-protocols. Web services are modular, accessible, well-described, implementation independent, and interoperable (Fremantle, Weerawarana, & Khalaf, 2002). Using Web services, existing legacy applications can be reused by encapsulating them using a Web service interface.

Web service orchestration builds upon Web service technology and the concept of a SOA and is aimed at coordinaing different Web services using an executable business process. Wohed, Van der Aalst, Dumas, and Hofstede (2003) define an executable business process as "… [specifying] the execution order between a number of constituent activities, the partners involved, the messages exchanged between these partners, and the fault and exception handling mechanisms." In Web service orchestration, these activities are typically performed by Web services by means of their standardized Web service interface.

Copyright © 2007, Idea Group Inc. Copying or distributing in print or electronic forms without written permission of Idea Group Inc. is prohibited.

The standard language for Web service orchestration is the Business Process Execution Language for Web Services, BPEL4WS, or BPEL for short (Andrews et al., 2003). A process that is specified in BPEL consists of two types of activities: basic activities, such as receive, reply, wait, and structured activities as switch, while, and sequence. The structured activities determine the structure, or the sequencing of the process, and the basic activities determine what happens in the process, for example the invocation of a WS, receiving a message from a Web service, and so forth.

EXISTING REFERENCE MODELS

A Reference Model can be defined as "[a] generally accepted abstract representation that allows users to focus on establishing definitions, building common understandings, and identifying issues for resolution. [...]" (The Open Systems Joint Task Force, 1999). A reference model for process orchestration in e-government should guide the design process and provide support for the implementation of process orchestration by recommending and addressing certain issues. As such, a reference model should not describe technologies or protocols, but should give guidance for using them.

As workflow technology also concerns the automation of processes, its resemblance with Web service orchestration is clear (Zhao & Cheng, 2005). Moreover, some researchers claim that Web service orchestration should take more notice of the lessons coming from workflow-research (Piccinelli & Williams, 2003; Van der Aalst, 2003). For this reason, the existing workflow reference model may be relevant to decision-makers facing the problem of implementing process orchestration in e-government. As Web services and Web service orchestration are the main technologies for realizing a SOA, we will also investigate the extended-SOA reference model.

The Workflow Reference Model

The Workflow Management Coalition (WFMC) developed a reference model for workflow management systems (WFMS) to promote standardization of, and interoperability and connectivity between the WFMS that have arisen over the years (WFMC).

Figure 1 shows the workflow reference model that defines the generic components and interfaces that make up a WFMS. This model aims at promoting the interoperability between different WFMS. Central in the reference model is the workflow "enactment service" that consists of one or more workflow-engines. These engines execute the workflows, start new processes, select the people or applications that have to perform a task, send the necessary documents to the right people or applications, and so forth. The figure shows that the workflow reference model has five interfaces.

Copyright © 2007, Idea Group Inc. Copying or distributing in print or electronic forms without written permission of Idea Group Inc. is prohibited.

Figure 1. Workflow reference model

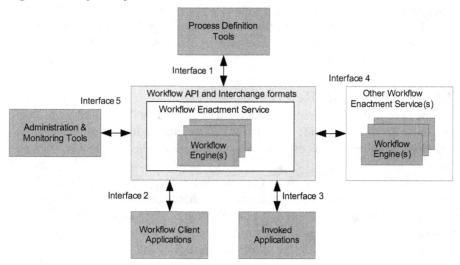

The first interface concerns the process definition tools. The processes that are executed by the WFMS can be defined "at design time" by means of a graphical process-editor for the process-flow, and with program-code or scripting for invoking external applications. This interface is implemented by means of XPDL, the XML Process Definition Language (WFMC, 2002). This is a standard language for defining and interchanging processes designed by the WFMS. WFMS can implement process-definitions that are designed by third party process definition tools by means of XPDL.

The second interface is with the workflow client applications. A client application is usually implemented by a graphical interface that consists of a "worklist" with the work items that have to be performed by the employee. The workflow engine does the assignment of tasks to the employees.

The third interface allows the WFMS to start external applications, either to perform automated tasks, or to support employees in executing their own tasks. A standard template with the address of a customer filled in can be started to support the employee task of sending a letter.

The fourth interface allows different WFMS to communicate with each other (i.e., that at a certain point in the process, the WFMS can start a (sub-) process on another WFMS). Complex interoperability scenarios in which a number of different WFMS, possibly of different vendors, cooperate to deliver a single enactment service are difficult to realize, as it requires that all engines can interpret common process definitions and maintain a shared view of process states across the different WFMS (Lawrence, 1997). More realistic is a form of cooperation where parts

Copyright © 2007, Idea Group Inc. Copying or distributing in print or electronic forms without written permission of Idea Group Inc. is prohibited.

of the process are transferred to another WFMS. The interfaces 1, 2, and 4 can be implemented by means of Wf-XML, a standard by the WFMC (WFMC, 2001).

A last interface with the workflow engine is used by different administrative and monitoring tools. These tools can be used to control issues like status, progress, and workload, and to add new users and roles.

The Extended SOA Reference Model

The extended-SOA reference model was developed by Papazoglou and Georgakopoulos (2003) to provide support for service composition and management to the basic SOA operations of publishing, discovering, selecting, and invoking a service.

Figure 2 gives an overview of the extended-SOA pyramid. The basic SOA-functionality is depicted at the bottom, and the higher-level functionality is depicted at the top of this figure. Whereas in the basic notion of a SOA only the roles of service-provider, service-requester, and service-directory were involved, the extended SOA adds the more advanced roles of service aggregator and operator, and replaces the service-directory with the more advanced role of a market-maker.

Composite services are services that are composed out of other services, which on their turn also can be provided as services themselves. Web service orchestration

Figure 2. Extended SOA reference model

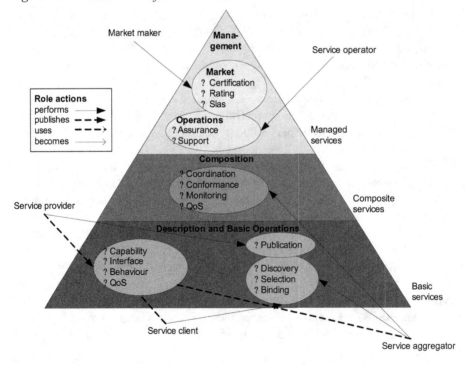

Copyright © 2007, Idea Group Inc. Copying or distributing in print or electronic forms without written permission of Idea Group Inc. is prohibited.

concerns process-based composition, and realizes a composite service by invoking the different sub services in a sequence according to a predefined process-flow.

Service aggregators bundle services and make them available to service request-ers. As such, they become service providers themselves. Typical tasks performed by a service aggregator are controlling the execution of the component services and managing the dataflow (coordination), subscribing to events or information produced by the component services, and publishing higher level composite events (monitoring), ensuring the integrity of the composite service (conformance) and leveraging, aggregating, and bundling the component's quality of service (QoS) to derive the composite QoS.

On top of these aggregated services, the extended-SOA reference model iden-tifies managed services in the service management layer depicted at the top of the SOA pyramid of Figure 2. At this level, the higher-level functionality concerning the management of all the different (aggregated) services is situated.

The functionality in the managed-service-layer can be divided into two catego-ries: market and operation. Certification of services, rating services, and guarding and monitoring service-SLA's are typical management activities performed by a market maker, supporting the buying and selling of services on a market. Another kind of managed services concerns operation management activities such as provid-ing assurance and support are performed by the service operator.

Security aspects are not directly mentioned, but implicitly included in all layers of the e-SOA pyramid. Service-certification and QoS composition, in the service management, and service composition layer, for example, both deal with different security-aspects of a service-oriented architecture. Service-certification can pro-vide a means to make sure that only services from "trusted" service-providers are included in governmental service-delivery processes, whereas QoS composition is functionality that derives composite QoS on several aspects, such as security from component Qos's.

Although it is outside the scope of reference models, it should be noted that the e-SOA model is based on the Web service protocol stack, which includes ws-security and other related protocols. WS-Security provides quality of protection through message integrity, message confidentiality, and single message authentication and can be used to accommodate a wide variety of security models and encryption technologies.

Comparing the Reference Models

We compared the reference models on their purposes, subject, and level of aggre-gation and found that they were heterogeneous and did hardly have any overlap.

The *purpose* of the workflow reference model was "to promote standardiza-tion of and interoperability and connectivity between the WFMS that have arisen over the years" (WFMC, n.d.). The purpose of the extended-SOA reference model is more to de-mystify the concept of service-oriented computing (SOC) and to list

Copyright © 2007, Idea Group Inc. Copying or distributing in print or electronic forms without written permission of Idea Group Inc. is prohibited.

and categorize all the needed functionality that is needed in successfully building systems using the SOC-paradigm. This explains why the workflow reference model consists of parts of a WFMS, and the extended-SOA reference model consists of layers, roles, and functionality.

The *subject* of the workflow reference model is the WFMS. The reference model prescribes the components it should be made of, and the interfaces between the components and the central workflow engine. The subject of the e-SOA reference model is the whole constellation of services, service-users, service-suppliers, and different kinds of third parties. This is a huge difference, but not so surprising when we consider that in a SOA, systems are built out of many small functional services.

The workflow reference model has components and interfaces as its objects; the e-SOA reference model has roles and functionality as its objects. Functionality and roles are situated on a business-level, whereas components and interfaces are situated on the implementation-level. This difference in *level of aggregation* is also apparent from the fact that the workflow-reference-model does not address security-aspects at all, where the e-SOA reference model does address some security-related functionality that needs to be performed in a SOA.

Although both reference models differ tremendously, both may contain important elements for a reference model that supports decision-makers in implementing process orchestration in e-government. The following section will present a case study at a business counter, where a prototype of process orchestration using Web-service orchestration was built.

CASE STUDY: THE BUSINESS COUNTER

General Description of the Business Counter

We investigated a case study to research the need for support for implementing process orchestration and to identify some main areas in which a reference model should be able to provide support. We selected the business counter as it is regarded as a best practice in The Netherlands and it wanted to orchestrate their cross-agency processes and was willing to cooperate.

The business counter provides all municipal services that are provided to the hotel-and catering industry. Typical examples are services specific to the hotel-and catering industry, such as a liquor license, a license to operate gaming machines, and a pavement café license, but also more generic business-permits, such as a parking permit, and an environmental permit. As these permits and licenses require the input from many different municipal departments and governmental agencies, their service-delivery processes are cross-agency processes that need to be orchestrated. Figure 3 provides a high-level overview of the business counter.

Although the business counter is viewed as a best practice, there was hardly

Copyright © 2007, Idea Group Inc. Copying or distributing in print or electronic forms without written permission of Idea Group Inc. is prohibited.

Figure 3. High-level overview of the business counter

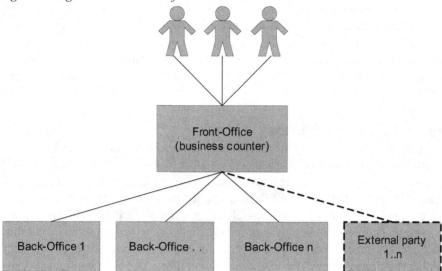

any ICT support at the time of investigation. For almost all services, the requester has to schedule an appointment with the business counter, after which the account manager coordinates the interactions with the back-office and the other agencies. Processing the permit-application, asking other departments for advice, and drafting the final permit are for most processes all done without the support of information systems other than traditional office applications.

Case-Study Approach

The case study at the business counter was conducted between July 2003 and May 2004, and in total we interviewed nine different persons at the municipality and also some representatives of the businesses in hotel and catering industry. At the municipality we interviewed persons at the business counter itself, employees at the different functional departments, and key ICT-staff to get an overview of the information systems in place.

We studied five processes at the business counter in detail: a license to open a café, a liquor license, a permit to organize special events, a permit to operate gaming machines, and an environmental permit. These processes were chosen, as the permit to open a café, the liquor license, and the gaming license processes together represent most of the work for the business counter and is the most complex cross-agency process. During the case study we found that these processes all ran largely in parallel and the organization of the process over different departments and agencies was very similar. For this reason, the permit to organize special events, and the environmental permit were also analyzed, as the first is almost completely being

Copyright © 2007, Idea Group Inc. Copying or distributing in print or electronic forms without written permission of Idea Group Inc. is prohibited.

taken care of by the licenses team, and the second is almost completely performed by the team environment supervision.

The issues that are defined in the next section are based on the analysis of all five processes that were analyzed at the business counter and the different departments involved in the service-delivery processes. This chapter uses the example of the liquor licensing process to illustrate the issues that are identified in the remainder of this chapter.

Liquor Licensing Process

A liquor license is one of the most important permits for the hotel and catering industry. Every restaurant or café that pours alcohol is obliged to apply for a license. For requesting a license, an entrepreneur contacts the business counter. After an initial intake meeting, the entrepreneur fills in an application form and returns it, together with the needed official documents, such as, for example, a floor plan. Hereafter, the name and address of the applicant are checked, the justice department and the police are asked for advice whether the applicant has a criminal record. Finally, the building department checks whether the building meets all legal requirements and the application for a liquor license is published in the municipal newspaper. Based on these advices, the back-office employee draws up a license or a letter stating the reasons for refusing the license.

Short lead-times on license-request are crucial to entrepreneurs. Also, the data provided to the government by the entrepreneurs often contains privacy-sensitive information. The cross-agency aspect and the nature of the liquor-licensing process put high requirements on security throughout the whole process. The sensitivity of the information involved (e.g., information on criminal record of applicant) requires secure communication and strict information-access-control. Moreover, the importance of giving thorough advice on granting a license or not requires strict control on who performs these process-steps. These issues are already difficult enough to deal with in a single-agency setting, but are even more difficult in a cross-agency setting, where responsibilities are scattered over different agencies, and are not always known beforehand. Too rigid access control on information may also lead to rigid inflexible processes, where agencies cannot anticipate customer needs.

Requirements on Cross-Agency Business Processes

This section discusses the main requirements on cross-agency processes. These requirements represent the areas in which a reference model should provide support. We derived the requirements from the case study and clustered the requirements into three main categories: (1) ensuring the correct and in time execution of business processes, (2) secure information-sharing, and (3) accountability.

Copyright © 2007, Idea Group Inc. Copying or distributing in print or electronic forms without written permission of Idea Group Inc. is prohibited.

Correct and In-Time Execution of Business Processes

As the process orchestrator is responsible for the overall service-delivery-process, one of the main tasks a process orchestrator must perform is to ensure that every sub-service in the cross-agency service-delivery process is completed in the right way, performed by the right person, and in time.

Service-levels can help in ensuring correct and in-time execution of every sub-service, but simply agreeing beforehand upon service-levels between the business counter and the different agencies alone is not enough. The service-levels need to be constantly monitored and mechanisms that respond when a service fails, when a service does not produce the required answer, or does not answer in-time, should be put in place.

At the business counter, the correct and in-time execution of cross-agency processes is very important, as the entrepreneurs requesting a liquor license, want information about whether the license will be granted or not as soon as possible. Often, entrepreneurs have to wait for the completion of the licensing process before they can open their café or restaurant. For the entrepreneur, each delay results in losing money. For the business counter, there are legal deadlines on the liquor-licensing process that must be met. As the business counter depends on other agencies or departments to perform certain tasks, it cannot completely control the lead-times of these sub-processes. For example, the sub-process of checking the identity of an entrepreneur that has its residence in another municipality can take a lot of time and repeated requests before it is finally completed. The business counter bases its decision to grant or deny a liquor license on the tasks performed by other agencies, for example the check for a criminal record at the business counter. It is therefore important that these tasks were executed correctly (i.e., by someone having the right responsibility, by not skipping certain checks, etc.) before an answer is sent back.

Secure Information Sharing

The secure sharing of information among different governmental agencies is crucial. When different agencies are all involved in one service-delivery process, they should all have access to the customer-data that is relevant to them. Authorization of users and especially the ability to present only the information that is relevant for them is a key issue. Within a single organization this may be solved relatively easy, for example by means of a large data warehouse, but in a governmental setting where many of the involved agencies have their own autonomy, this is much more complex. As the responsibilities are fragmented among many governmental agencies, so are its information-systems, making information sharing between multiple agencies far from straight forward.

Agencies that perform sub-services need the business counter to provide them with information about the customer, as they need this data in performing the process. At the business counter, the building-department, for example, needs information about the applicant of the liquor license; about the kind of restaurant it is request-

Copyright © 2007, Idea Group Inc. Copying or distributing in print or electronic forms without written permission of Idea Group Inc. is prohibited.

ing the liquor license for, and so forth. This "one-way" sharing of data is relatively straight forward, but when different agencies start updating data that is required by other agencies, there is a need for robust information-sharing mechanisms.

The issues of secure information-sharing will become even more important when the law comes into effect requiring that citizens cannot be asked to provide personal data that is already given to the government in general, which could be another agency (Dutch Government, 2003). Another major issue with information sharing is privacy. Not all agencies need all available customer information. For privacy reasons, every agency should only have access to the information they needs. An example is the information resulting from the check of the criminal record at the justice department. This data is not relevant and therefore should not be provided to other parties, such as the building department.

At the business counter, different departments and agencies that are involved in the liquor licensing and related processes all have different information-systems that are not able to communicate with each other. An entrepreneur mentioned that the tax office, the municipality, and the chamber of commerce identified his restaurant using three different names. Entrepreneurs had to fill in forms which requested the same information over and over again, for different, but also for the same departments and agencies. Not sharing information also makes enforcement more difficult. The lack of an integrated customer view makes it difficult to get an overview of all the permits a specific café or restaurant has been granted.

Accountability

Accountability is an important requirement for the whole public sector. For governmental service-delivery processes, it is especially important that the processes are transparent, non-discriminating, and consistent, and that the decisions made in the process are well motivated and made by the right person. Citizens and businesses no longer accept a black-box view of the service delivery process, but want to know what steps have to be taken in order to reach the final decision.

Ensuring accountability for governmental service-delivery processes that run across different organizations is especially difficult, as it has to cope with different (semi-) autonomous agencies that are involved in the process. For example, the decision not to grant a liquor license, because the police have strong suspicions against the applicant, should be very well motivated.

Ensuring accountability of cross-agency service-delivery processes requires specialized coordination mechanisms that ensure that the outcome of every process step is recorded, and that the overall process has run the way it was supposed to. No one should be able to change the stored information, as the information might be used as evidence.

At the business counter, for the process of granting a liquor license, account-ability is an important requirement in different ways. Entrepreneurs want the business counter to account for their acceptance/rejection decisions. When a license is rejected

Copyright © 2007, Idea Group Inc. Copying or distributing in print or electronic forms without written permission of Idea Group Inc. is prohibited.

based on "soft" evidence by the police that the person wanting to open a café may be a criminal, the business counter needs to be able to account for not granting the permit based on this information. Next to the entrepreneurs, the citizens also want the business counter to account for their decisions on the granting of liquor licenses. For example, when a license for a café in a residential area is granted, the business counter will have to account for their decision. In this case, it is important to show that all procedures have been followed rigidly.

APPLICABILITY OF EXISTING REFERENCE MODELS

The case study at the business counter provided the requirements for a reference model supporting governmental decision-makers in implementing process orchestration in e-government. The coordination issues that were identified in the previous section are the main issues that governmental decision-makers are facing in our case study, but might not be exhaustive as they are based on a single case study. This section will evaluate whether the two existing reference models meet the requirements that were identified in the previous section.

Workflow Reference Model

To evaluate applicability of the workflow reference model, it will have to be translated into orchestration-concepts. The obvious link is on the level of with Web service orchestration, instead of process orchestration. Analogous to workflow management, in Web service orchestration there also exists a central "orchestration server" to enact the process-flow. Examples are Oracle's BPEL Process Manager (Oracle, 2004), Microsoft Biztalk 2004 (Microsoft, 2004), and IBM Websphere Business Integration Server Foundation (IBM, 2004). Analogous to workflow, process definition and monitoring tools are also needed. External applications can be invoked by means of their Web service interface and human tasks can be supported by invoking a Web service interface to someone's e-mail client. Web service orchestration also relies on invoking Web services for interfacing with other orchestration servers. A process that is defined in BPEL can be made available as a Web service itself, and thus be called by a process on another orchestration server.

From this translation of the workflow reference model into cross-agency Web service orchestration-terms, it can be concluded that there is quite a large resemblance between workflow and Web service orchestration. The requirements that need to be addressed in cross-agency processes, including accountability, secure information sharing, and correct and in-time execution of the process remain unaddressed by this model. The reference model provides no support for guarding lead-times, or how to facilitate information-sharing. Instead, the reference model focuses on technical components, and technical interfaces. This is, analogous with the initial goal of the

Copyright © 2007, Idea Group Inc. Copying or distributing in print or electronic forms without written permission of Idea Group Inc. is prohibited.

workflow reference model, more relevant to vendors of orchestration technology, than to governmental decision-makers.

Extended-SOA Reference Model

The extended-SOA reference model is focused on providing roles and functionality for Web-services market (i.e., the selling and buying of Web-services). The model identifies a service-provider, service-requester, service-aggregator, service-operator, and even a market maker. Several of these roles can of course be performed by the same organization, but the model seems to be more tailored to situations where service requesters buy or rent services from service-providers on a services market.

Nevertheless, large parts of this reference model are still relevant to the situation of implementing process orchestration at the business counter. Especially the composite services layer is very relevant, as offering a service as a liquor license where sub-processes at different agencies are incorporated into the overall service-delivery process, is an example of composition. The managed-services-level appears to be less relevant in the case of the business counter, but may become so in the future, when Web service orchestration is adopted on a larger scale.

The business counter corresponds to the role of service aggregator in the reference model. It aggregates services that are provided by other agencies (service-providers), and provides these aggregated services to the customer. The reference model does address many of the issues that the decision-makers are facing by means of the tasks that the service-aggregator must perform.

The functionality in the composite services layer: coordination, monitoring and conformance checking, and agreeing on service levels of the incorporated services matches with the requirements that were identified at the business counter. Although it does address issues like the monitoring of component service, the calculation of QoS on aspects like security, cost, and performance, it does not provide any guidelines about how to fill them in. Decision-makers can use this reference model only to identify the roles and functionality that they need to consider, but will have find ways to implement these roles themselves.

CONCLUSION

The goal of this chapter is to investigate the applicability of two existing reference models to support governmental decision-makers for implementing process orchestration in e-government. We investigated the two models, derived requirements from practice and evaluated the models using these requirements.

The case study shows that cross-agency processes need to satisfy requirements that can be clustered in three categories: the correct and in-time execution of business processes, secure information sharing, and accountability.

Copyright © 2007, Idea Group Inc. Copying or distributing in print or electronic forms without written permission of Idea Group Inc. is prohibited.

We evaluated the two reference models using these requirements. Neither of the models can provide governmental decision-makers with enough support to design cross-agency processes satisfying the requirements. The workflow reference model is too much focused on technology implementations, and therefore fails to address the non-technical coordination issues, and although the e-SOA reference model does address many of the issues, the model remains rather abstract, only pinpointing the required functionality, but not indicating how this should be filled in. Moreover, this reference model aims at supporting Web services markets and not cross-agency processes.

To support governmental decision-makers in implementing process orchestration in e-government, a new reference model is needed meeting the above-mentioned requirements. Further research will focus on designing such a reference model.

REFERENCES

Andrews, T., Curbera, F., Dholakia, H., Goland, Y., Klein, J., Leymann, F., et al. (2003). *Business process execution language for Web services* (Version 1.1). Retrieved February 13, 2006, from http://www.ibm.com/developerworks/library/ws-bpel/

Castellano, M., Pastore, N., Arcieri, F., & Summo, V. (2004, June 17-18). *An e-government interoperability framework for cooperation among public administrations*. Paper presented at the 4th European Conference on e-government, Dublin Castle, Ireland.

Contenti, M., Termini, A., Mecella, M., & Baldoni, R. (2003). An eService-based framework for inter-administration cooperation. In M. A. Wimmer (Ed.), In *Proceedings of the 4th IFIP International Working Conference on Management in Electronic Government: KMGov 2003*, (Vol. 2645/2003, pp. 13-24). Rhodes, Greece: Springer-Verlag Heidelberg.

Dutch Government. (2003). Actieprogramma Andere Overheid (in Dutch).

Dutch Government. (2004). Meer ruimte voor ondernemers door minder lasten—Van lastenproductie naar lastenreductie (In Dutch).

Fremantle, P., Weerawarana, S., & Khalaf, R. (2002). Enterprise services. *Communications of the ACM, 45*(10), 77-82.

Gortmaker, J., & Janssen, M. (2004). *Business process orchestration in e-government: A gap analysis*. Paper presented at the 15th IRMA International Conference, New Orleans, LA.

Gortmaker, J., Janssen, M., & Wagenaar, R. W. (2004). *The advantages of Web service orchestration in perspective*. Paper presented at the 6th International Conference of Electronic Commerce, ICEC 2004, Delft, The Netherlands.

IBM. (2004). *Websphere business integration server foundation*. Retrieved July 13, 2004, from http://www-306.ibm.com/software/integration/wbisf/features/

Copyright © 2007, Idea Group Inc. Copying or distributing in print or electronic forms without written permission of Idea Group Inc. is prohibited.

Lawrence, P. (1997). *Workflow handbook 1997*. Chichester, UK: John Wiley & Sons LTD.

McIvor, R., McHugh, M., & Cadden, C. (2002). Internet technologies: Supporting transparency in the public sector. *International Journal of Public Sector Management, 15*(3), 170-187.

Microsoft. (2004). *Microsoft biztalk server home*. Retrieved July 13, 2004, from http://www.microsoft.com/biztalk/

Oracle. (2004). *Oracle BPEL process manager*. Retrieved July 13, 2004, from http://otn.oracle.com/products/ias/bpel/index.html

Papazoglou, M. P., & Georgakopoulos, D. (2003). Service-oriented computing. *Communications of the ACM, 46*(10), 24-28.

Pasley, J. (2005). How BPEL and SOA are changing Web service development. *IEEE Internet Computing, 9*(3), 60-67.

Piccinelli, G., & Williams, S. L. (2003). *Workflow: A language for composing Web services*. Paper presented at the Business Process Management: International Conference, BPM 2003, Proceedings, Eindhoven, The Netherlands.

Stojanovic, Z., & Dahanayake, A. (2005). *Service-oriented software system engineering: Challenges and practices*. Hershey, PA: Idea Group Publishing.

The Open Systems Joint Task Force. (1999). *Common lexicon and acronym dictionary*. Retrieved September 28, 2004, from http://www.acq.osd.mil/osjtf/html/terms.htm

Van der Aalst, W. M. P. (2003). Don't go with the flow: Web services composition standards exposed. *IEEE Intelligent Systems, 18*(1), 72-76.

WFMC. (2001). *Workflow management coalition workflow standard—interoperability Wf-XML Binding* (No. WFMC-TC-1023).

WFMC. (2002). *Workflow process definition interface—XML process definition language* (No. WFMC-TC-1025).

WFMC. (n/a). *About the WFMC—Introduction to the workflow management coalition*. Retrieved July 12, 2004, from http://www.wfmc.org/about.htm

Wimmer, M. A. (2002). A European perspective towards online one-stop government: The eGOV project. *Electronic Commerce Research and Applications, 1*(1), 92-103.

Wohed, P., Aalst, W. M. P. V. D., Dumas, M., & Hofstede, A. H. M. T. (2003). Analysis of Web services composition languages: The case of BPEL4WS. In *Web application modeling and development, conceptual modeling—ER 2003* (LNCS 2813, pp. 200-215), Berlin-Heidelberg: Springer-Verlag.

Zhao, J. L., & Cheng, H. K. (2005). Web services and process management: A union of convenience or a new area of research? *Decision Support Systems, 40*(1), 1-8.

Copyright © 2007, Idea Group Inc. Copying or distributing in print or electronic forms without written permission of Idea Group Inc. is prohibited.

Chapter XIV

Model Driven Security for Inter-Organizational Workflows in E-Government

Michael Hafner, Universität Innsbruck, Austria

Barbara Weber, Universität Innsbruck, Austria

Ruth Breu, Universität Innsbruck, Austria

Andrea Nowak, Austrian Research Center Seibersdorf, Austria

ABSTRACT

Model driven architecture is an approach to increase the quality of complex software systems by creating high-level system models and automatically generating system architectures and components out of these models. We show how this paradigm can be applied to what we call model driven security for inter-organizational workflows in e-government. Our focus is on the realization of security-critical inter-organizational workflows in the context of Web services, Web service orchestration, and Web service choreography. Security requirements are specified at an abstract level using UML diagrams. Out of this specification security, relevant artifacts are generated for a target reference architecture based on upcoming Web service security standards. Additionally, we show how participants of a choreography use model dependencies to map the choreography specifications to interfaces for their local workflows.

Copyright © 2007, Idea Group Inc. Copying or distributing in print or electronic forms without written permission of Idea Group Inc. is prohibited.

INTRODUCTION

E-government refers to the use of the Internet and other electronic media to improve the collaboration within public agencies and to include citizens and companies in administrative processes. A core aim of e-government is to bring about a digital administration in order to enhance quality of service (e.g., additional online information or service offerings) as well as efficiency (e.g., reduced case processing times, fewer errors or using fewer resources to accomplish the same task).

The implementation of e-government solutions is a very complex task that can only succeed if IT-experts and domain experts cooperate with each other at a high level of abstraction right from the beginning. Security issues rooted in provisions and regulations play a very critical role. These include security requirements of public law (i.e., Austrian Signature Act [1999] and the Austrian e-government Act [2004] as well as the Federal Act concerning the Protection of Personal Data [1999]), the Austrian Security Manual [n.d.], the OECD Guidelines for the Security of Information Systems and Networks [n.d.], and internal security requirements of the municipalities.

Security requirements must not be considered as an isolated aspect, except during all stages of the software development cycle (Devanbu & Stubblebine, 2000; Ferrari & Thuraisingham, 2000). As the engineering of security into the overall software design is often neglected, different approaches for integrating security in the system development cycle have been proposed (Hall & Chapman, 2002; Breu, Burger, Hafner, & Popp, 2004). Nevertheless, they do not yet exploit the potential of a model driven approach.

Model driven software development is particularly appealing in the area of security as many security requirements adhere to certain categories (e.g., integrity) and can be described in implementation-independent models. In most cases, the development of security-critical systems is based on a set of well-known protective measures (i.e., protocols, algorithms) for which the correctness has been proved.

In this chapter, we give an overview of our approach to the model driven realization of security-critical inter-organizational workflows in the context of Web services security, Web service orchestration, and Web service choreography. The description of security requirements is performed at a high level of abstraction. Security relevant artifacts are generated for a target architecture. A description of the target architecture can be found in Hafner, Breu, and Breu (2005) and Brue, Hafner, and Web (2004).

Our approach provides a specification framework for the design of collaborating systems in the context of the platform-independent Web service technology. It also supports the systematic transition from security requirements, via the generation of security artifacts, to a secure solution based on a Web services platform. The specification of security requirements is performed in a platform-independent way and can thus be applied by domain experts without in-depth technical knowledge.

The structure of the subsequent sections is as follows. After providing an overview on Web services composition, Web services security, and Model Driven

Copyright © 2007, Idea Group Inc. Copying or distributing in print or electronic forms without written permission of Idea Group Inc. is prohibited.

Architecture in Section 2, we present a case study in Section 3, and describe our model driven approach in Section 4. In Section 5, we describe our component-based Target Reference Architecture. Finally, Section 6 gives an overview of related work before Section 7 closes with a conclusion.

Backgrounds

This section briefly sketches the standards, technologies, and methodologies our approach is based upon.

Web Services Standards

The growing popularity of emerging Web services standards and technologies pushes the specification and implementation of powerful infrastructures based on platform-independent technology. The goal is to foster interoperability between partners who plan the realization of collaborations over networks (e.g., governmental and local authorities). Figure 1 provides a (partial) overview of existing Web services standards. The specifications and drafts cover various aspects related to the implementation of collaborations based on Web services.

Figure 1. Web services standards technology stack

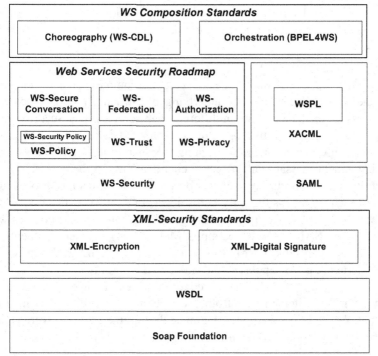

Copyright © 2007, Idea Group Inc. Copying or distributing in print or electronic forms without written permission of Idea Group Inc. is prohibited.

Web Services Composition

Beginning at the top of the technology stack, we have the composition of Web services. Businesses provide value-added services through composition of basic or elemental Web services using service composition languages. Very often different companies offer the services. A Web services composition consists of multiple invocations of other Web services in a specific order. A composition can either take the form of an orchestration or of a choreography. An orchestration describes how Web services interact with each other at the message or application level, including the business logic and the execution order of the interactions from the viewpoint of the partner controlling the workflow execution. A choreography or a business protocol describes the interaction between business partners in terms of the sequence of messages that are exchanged in a "peer-to-peer" fashion. There is no central control of workflow execution.

WS-BPEL (2003) is a workflow orchestration language for Web services. It supports the definition of executable business processes and provides partial support for abstract business protocols. BPML (Arkin, 2002) is quite similar to WS-BPEL as it supports Web services standards, but it is considered as semantically weaker.

While an executable business process models the behavior of a partner in a specific business interaction, a business protocol standard like WS-CDL (2004) specifies the public message exchange between parties and abstracts from how they are internally processed. Alternative standards to describe business protocols are WSCI (n.d.) and ebXML (Bernauer, Kramler, & Kappel, 2003). ebXML additionally comprises a powerful set of standards for the specification of B2B protocols but it is not compatible to the Web services concept.

Web Services Security

As Web services are often aggregated to carry out complex business transactions, not only the Web service itself or the underlying infrastructure has to be secured, but also the message exchange between different Web services. WS-Security (n.d.) is based on XML-Encryption (Eastlake, 2002) and XML-Digital Signature (Eastlake, 2002) and specifies a mechanism for signing and encrypting SOAP messages. It is used to implement message integrity and confidentiality at the application level. WS-Security also supports the propagation of the authentication information in the form of security tokens (e.g., Kerberos tickets or X.509 certificates). XACML (Godik & Moses, 2003) provides access control mechanisms and policies within documents, while SAML (Cantor, Kemp, & Maler, 2004) represents authentication and authorization decisions in XML format and is used to exchange this information over the Internet (e.g., to support single sign-on and log-out).

WS-Policy (Bajal et al., 2004) is used for the specification of requirements for Web services in their interaction with other services in a standardized, machine-readable format. Web services endpoints negotiate the parameters and advertise the set of requirements potential service requesters have to comply with when they want

Copyright © 2007, Idea Group Inc. Copying or distributing in print or electronic forms without written permission of Idea Group Inc. is prohibited.

to access the service (e.g., quality-of-service). WS-Security Policy (Della-Libera et al., 2002) is a complementary standard to WS-Policy and specifies how actors can assert to potential partners their policies with respect to specific WS-Security mechanisms. WS-Trust (Anderson et al., 2005) enables token interoperability. It provides a request/response protocol for the exchange, the issuance, and the validation of security tokens by a trusted third party.

Model Driven Architecture and Security

Model driven architecture (MDA) is an approach for the design and implementation of applications that aims at cost reduction and application quality improvement (Lodderstedt, 2003). At the very core of MDA is the concept of a model (i.e., abstraction of the target system). MDA defines two types of models, a Platform Independent Model (PIM), describing the system independently from the intended platform, and a Platform Specific Model (PSM) describing the system in terms of its technical infrastructure (e.g., J2EE or .NET). The process of converting a PIM into a PSM is called transformation. Models are described using a well-defined modeling language such as UML. Model Driven Security is based upon MDA in the sense that security requirements are integrated into design models, leading to security design models. Transformation rules of MDA are extended to generate security infrastructures (Lodderstedt, 2003).

CASE STUDY

Our methodology for the systematic design and realization of security-critical inter-organizational workflows is illustrated by a portion of a workflow drawn from the use case "Processing of an Annual Statement" (Figure 2) describing the interaction between a citizen (the Client), a business agent (the Tax Advisor), and a public service provider (the Municipality).

The use case was elaborated within the project SECTINO, a joint research effort between the research group Quality Engineering at the University of Innsbruck

Figure 2. Processing of an annual statement (global view on workflow)

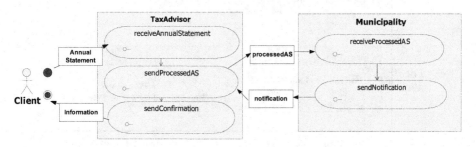

Copyright © 2007, Idea Group Inc. Copying or distributing in print or electronic forms without written permission of Idea Group Inc. is prohibited.

and the Austrian Research Center Seibersdorf. It is based on a case study involving a major Austrian municipality. The project aims at the development of a framework supporting the systematic and efficient realization and management of innovative e-government related workflows with a special focus on security requirements.

In Austria, all wages and salaries paid to employees of an enterprise are subject to the municipal tax. Businesses have to send the annual tax statement via their tax advisor to a municipality which is responsible for collecting the tax by the end of March of the following year. The municipality checks the declaration of the annual statement and calculates the tax duties. A notification with the amount of tax duties is then sent to the tax advisor by mail. Ultimately, the workflow should allow the declaration of the municipal tax via the internet.

One of the project goals is to analyze security issues that may stem from the migration of the workflow to an e-government based solution and create the necessary run-time artifacts for the target architecture through model transformation.

MODEL DRIVEN SECURITY FOR INTER-ORGANIZATIONAL WORKFLOWS

In this section, we present our approach to the management of security related aspects within the development process. We first present the model views, then proceed to the description of the models: the global workflow model, the local workflow model, and the interface model. We move on to describe model dependencies before giving an example on how to perform a risk and threats analysis and how to specify security requirements for the topmost level (global workflow) following a five step approach for security analysis called micro process for security engineering.

Figure 3. Two orthogonal views

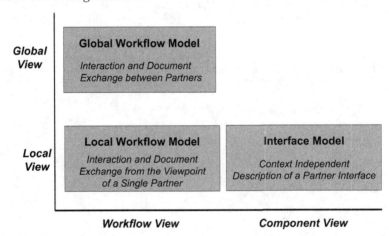

Copyright © 2007, Idea Group Inc. Copying or distributing in print or electronic forms without written permission of Idea Group Inc. is prohibited.

The requirements are transformed into run-time artifacts for the target reference architecture in Section 5.

Model Views

In the context of this chapter, a *workflow* describes a network of partners cooperating in a controlled way by calling services and exchanging documents. Our method of designing security-critical inter-organizational workflows is based on two orthogonal views: the *interface view* and the *workflow view* (Figure 3). The latter is further divided into the *global workflow model* (GWfM) describing the message exchange between cooperating partners, and the *local workflow model* (LWfM) describing the behavior of each partner.

The *interface view* represents a contractual agreement between the parties to provide a set of services based on the minimum set of technical and domain level constraints and thereby links the GWfM to the LWfM. The application of these orthogonal perspectives allows us to combine the design of components offering services that may be called in different contexts. From a security perspective, the Interface View deals with security requirements from the components' point of view, while the GWfM deals with the secure exchange of documents between different partners.

Global Workflow Model

The GWfM describes an integrated abstract view of the workflow involving partners in autonomous organizations. The global workflow describes the interaction of partners abstracting from internal processing steps and does not contain any connection to the business logic.

Figure 4. A sample document flow with security requirements (global workflow model)

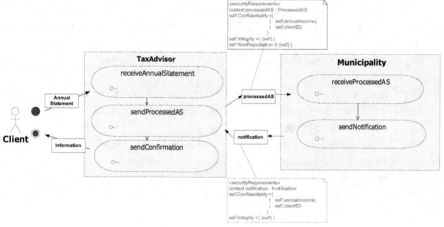

Copyright © 2007, Idea Group Inc. Copying or distributing in print or electronic forms without written permission of Idea Group Inc. is prohibited.

The details of the global workflow are captured and visualized with a UML 2.0 Activity Diagram (www.uml.org) as in Figure 4 and can optionally be mapped to WS-CDL.

Since we strongly focus our approach on Web services technology, which is the most widespread technology with strong vendor support, we consider WS-CDL and WS-BPEL as appropriate top-layer standards to the Web services protocol stack (including WSDL [Christensen, Curbera, Meredith, & Weerawarana, 2001], SOAP, UDDI, and related security standards). Although we use WS-BPEL to model local, executable processes, we decided to rely on UML 2.0 for the specification of inter-organizational collaboration protocols instead of using an "official" standard like WS-CDL. There are multiple reasons why we decided to rely on UML 2.0 instead of a specific choreography standard for the specification of the global workflow. UML 2.0 is a widespread modeling language with a comprehensive formal grounding and an intuitive visual notation. It provides all the means for modeling orchestration and choreography, it can easily be extended in various ways to provide complex workflow semantics, like security requirements at the global workflow level in our case. For a critical discussion of WS-CDL, please refer to Barros, Dumas, and Oaks (2005). In Hafner and Breu (2005) we provide a detailed account on how to map the UML 2.0 activity diagram to a choreography standard like the WS-CDL (2004).

In our example (see Figure 4), parts of the document sent from the Tax Advisor to the Municipality are meant to comply with confidentiality, integrity and non-re-pudiation. At runtime, the Policy Enforcement Point, acting as a security gateway, will have to sign and encrypt the document at the company's boundary according to a security policy configuration file containing the previously mentioned require-ments (Section 5).

The Process of Modeling a Global Workflow

We assume that there is no central control of the inter-organizational workflow. The workflow is de The distributed process involves three actors: the local govern-mental authorities (e.g., municipalities), the citizens and/or the companies, and a group of tax advisors, which were mapped to generic roles: Client, Municipality, and Tax Advisor. Additionally, the process had to be realized in a peer-to-peer fashion and should ultimately integrate security requirements.

The collaboration process was roughly specified as follows:

1.   The Client sends his Annual statement to his Tax Advisor
2.   The Tax Advisor does some internal processing on the document (e.g., format-ting, complement legal data, etc.)
3.   The Tax Advisor forwards the processed annual statement on behalf of his Client to the Municipality
4.   The Municipality calculates the amount of tax duties
5.   The Municipality returns a notification to the Tax Advisor

Copyright © 2007, Idea Group Inc. Copying or distributing in print or electronic forms without written permis-sion of Idea Group Inc. is prohibited.

6.   The Tax Advisor processes the notification
7.   The Tax Advisor informs his Client about his tax duties

Steps 1, 3, 5, and 7 correspond to interaction activities in the choreography, involving a peer-to-peer message flow between participants, whereas steps 2, 4, and 6 can be identified as being the "links" to the actors' local orchestrations, which would later be realized as an executable local workflow.

This first step leads to a common understanding of the structure of the "virtual" or the global workflow. Ideally, this includes the format, the structure and the sequence of the messages that are exchanged, the interfaces to the "business" or workflow logic each partner agreed to contribute to the composition, to operation semantics and to run-time constraints specification, information that is typically published in WSDL files and technical models (tModels) of UDDI Registries. From here on the participants have all information necessary to implement "interface"-compliant functionality at their nodes.

In practice, it is almost impossible to impose a straight top-down realization process on the participants for various reasons. First, it is very improbable that the partners will implement their logic from scratch. Very often partners have already implemented some kind of application logic, maybe even made it accessible to customers as a Web service. They probably want to reuse functionality of existing components running on a working infrastructure. The components reuse and their integration is a matter of cost-efficiency and requires some in-depth expertise of the technical staff.

Nor is it very likely that the partners will completely redesign the interfaces to their business logic to make them compliant to the naming conventions specified in the global workflow. Businesses and administrations can have organizational structures that may thwart a top-down approach from the very beginning (e.g., every business unit has its own IT-infrastructure, administrative units may have different reporting hierarchies, etc.).

This is why the participants of a choreography will proceed according to a hybrid approach projecting some of the interfaces of their local business logic to operations in the *interface model*, and, in turn, maybe wrap some of their local applications in order to comply with operations signatures of the *interface model*, which conforms to a uniform technical, syntactical, and semantic specification the partners agreed upon. If, for example, the partners agree to implement the global workflow based on Web services, some partners will have to provide a Web services wrapper for their application logic.

Local Workflow Model

The LWfMs define the portion of the global workflow each partner is responsible for. They are developed for each partner type. The LWfM is an executable process description that considers service calls from the outside and contains internal

Copyright © 2007, Idea Group Inc. Copying or distributing in print or electronic forms without written permission of Idea Group Inc. is prohibited.

Figure 5. A sample orchestration (local workflow model)

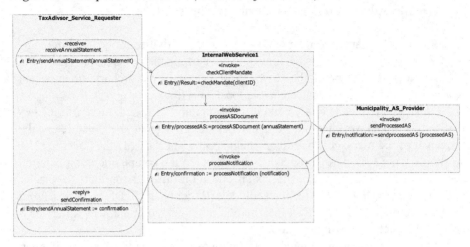

actions as well as connections to the business logic. It is a direct input for a local workflow management system and is typically developed internally by partners. Referring to the sample process, the GWfM captures the protocol between the on-line municipal tax component and the involved partners like the Municipality and the Tax Advisor, while the LWfM describes the sequence in which the component accepts and processes incoming messages based on the services described in the interface model.

The LWfM describes the necessary processing steps to calculate the tax duties. These steps are performed internally and are invisible to the outside.

Figure 5 shows an activity diagram capturing some aspects of the Tax Advisor's LWfM. The parts where the local workflow interacts with partners can be generated from the GWfM (receiveAnnualStatement sendConfirmation, and sendProcessedAS). Every actor will have to complement the part accessing his local logic (corresponding to the port InternalWebServices). With some additional specifications every actor can then generate WS-BPEL and WSDL files for his execution environment (e.g., using MDA tools like UML2BPEL [Anderson et al., 2005]).

Interface View

The *Interface View* describes the interface of every partner independently of its usage scenario and consists of four sub-models (Figure 6): the *Role*, the *Interface*, the *Access,* and the *Document Model*.

The *Document Model* is a UML class diagram describing the data type view of the partner. We talk of documents in order to stress that we do not interpret this class diagram in the usual object-oriented setting but in the context of XML schema. The *Interface* Model contains a set of abstract (UML) operations representing services the component offers to its clients. The types of the parameters are either basic types or classes in the document model. Additionally, pre- and post-conditions (in OCL

Copyright © 2007, Idea Group Inc. Copying or distributing in print or electronic forms without written permission of Idea Group Inc. is prohibited.

Figure 6. The sub-models of the workflow and the interface view

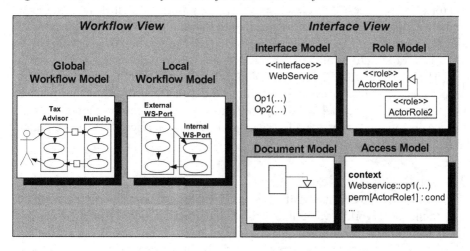

Figure 7. Model dependencies

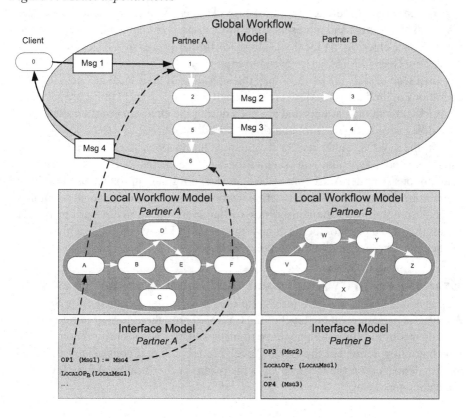

Copyright © 2007, Idea Group Inc. Copying or distributing in print or electronic forms without written permission of Idea Group Inc. is prohibited.

style) may specify the behavior of the abstract services. The *Role Model* describes the roles having access to the services. The *Access Model* describes the conditions under which a certain role has the permission to call a given service. The permissions are written in SECTET-PL (Alam, Breu, & Hafner, 2006) in a predicative style over the structures of the Document Model.

The Interface Model describes a component offering a set of services with given properties and permissions. Security requirements at this level of abstraction involve the support of a role model and the specification of access rights for particular Web service operations. A more detailed description of the Interface View can be found in Hafner, Breu, and Breu (2005).

Model Dependencies

Security requirements specified in the GWfM have to be mapped in a consistent way to the local workflows of all cooperating partners, which reflect the business logic in their local environment.

Partner A in Figure 7 is responsible for the implementation of the business logic covering Actions 1, 2, 5, and 6 in the GWfM. This can be seen as an abstract functional specification of the application logic a partner has to contribute to the global workflow. All the partners together agree on the signature format and naming conventions for the interfaces they provide to each other. These interfaces are visible to all partners and represent entry or exit points for data, messages or documents, either entering the local workflow for further processing or leaving it after processing (e.g., OP_1 (Msg1):= Msg4 in Figure 7).

In a second step, the partners map the interfaces of their local business logic to operations in the Interface Model (e.g., $LocalOP_B$ (LocalMsg1) in Figure 7). They are not visible to the partners and are used during the execution of their own local workflows in order to perform additional workflow actions.

In the GWfM, either one or two actions are mapped to an operation in the Interface Model depending on whether the message exchange is asynchronous or synchronous. Van der Aalst et al. (2001) present a formal approach based on Petri nets for the design of inter-organizational workflows guaranteeing local autonomy without compromising the consistency of the overall process. In our terms, this means that—in a peer-to-peer fashion—the local workflows should exactly realize the behavior as specified in the global workflow.

Example Security Analysis at the Global Workflow Level

In this section, we give an example of how a first iteration of a Security Analysis is performed at the level of the GWfM. Throughout further iterations, the participants of the choreography have to make sure that the security requirements, which are first defined at the GWfM level, are reliably and consistently modeled and implemented on the lower levels (this means at the local workflow level and the component level).

Copyright © 2007, Idea Group Inc. Copying or distributing in print or electronic forms without written permission of Idea Group Inc. is prohibited.

Figure 8. The micro process for security analysis

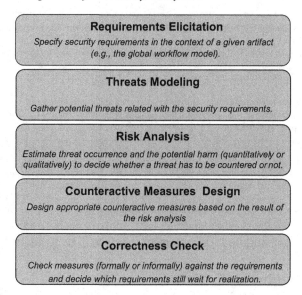

Security related aspects within the development of inter-organizational workflows are tackled by a five-step approach as illustrated in Figure 8 (Breu, Burger, Hafner, & Popp, 2004). The Micro Process for Security Analysis is performed iteratively at three levels of abstraction (at the global workflow level, the local workflow level, and the component level).

Requirements and measures are explored and described at the appropriate level of detail based on the corresponding artifacts (e.g., the GWfM). Table 1 illustrates the security analysis process using a sample scenario (Section 3).

In the early phases of design, security requirements are expressed in a textual way (e.g., by a security relevant section within the use case specification). In the context of the UML notation, we provide extended notation techniques. Security requirements are related to each other so that they can be traced from one level of abstraction to the next (i.e., each requirement is transformed into one or several requirements or into some protective measures at the abstraction level underneath).

TARGET REFERENCE ARCHITECTURE

In this section, we present our target reference architecture for a partner, which offers a portion of a distributed workflow. We give an overview of how the various standards are integrated into the architecture.

The basic component architecture is based on the data-flow model of XACML, which is an XML based OASIS standard for a policy and access control decision

Copyright © 2007, Idea Group Inc. Copying or distributing in print or electronic forms without written permission of Idea Group Inc. is prohibited.

Table 1. Sample scenario of a security analysis at the global level

1.	The data exchange within the "Processing of an Annual Statement" has to comply with the requirements of integrity and confidentiality.
2.	This workflow is open to the threat that a third unauthorized party may try to read and to modify the exchanged data.
3.	The probability of occurrence is estimated as medium, the possible damage is estimated as substantial.
4.	The measures to counter the threats involve encryption and digital signatures.
5.	The proposed measures are checked. There remains the requirement that the two partners have to authenticate each other.

language as described in Godik and Moses (2003). Figure 9 shows the target reference architecture in the view of a partner who implements his portion of the global workflow as a local workflow and offers an interface to its partners.

Workflow Engine

The core component is the workflow engine (1), which implements an orchestration language such as WS-BPEL (BEA, 2003) or BPML (Arkin, 2002) and aggregates and controls the sequence of existing Web services (2) to a composition that may be offered as a Web service of its own to external business partners. We use BPWS4J as a WS-BPEL engine (IBM, n.d.). In order to provide a trusted domain the elemental (2) and composite Web services (2) are wrapped by security components.

External Policy Enforcement Point

The external policy enforcement point (PEP) represents a single point of entry and acts as a security gateway (3). It intercepts incoming SOAP messages and applies basic security processing to the message structure. It extracts tokens from the inbound SOAP messages, decrypts elements, and checks the validity of signatures. Accordingly, the PEP adds tokens to, encrypts, and signs elements in outbound messages. This basic security-message-structure processing functionality implements standards like XML-Encryption, XML-Digital signature and WS-Security.

In case "non-repudiation-of-reception" was specified as a security requirement, the PEP returns a time-stamped and signed notification of receipt to the sender. In case of a specified "non-repudiation-of-submission," the PEP forwards a time-stamped copy of the signed message he received from the sender to the logging unit. The PEP interacts with other security components before forwarding an inbound message to the end-recipient (e.g., back-end application).

Copyright © 2007, Idea Group Inc. Copying or distributing in print or electronic forms without written permission of Idea Group Inc. is prohibited.

Figure 9. Target software architecture

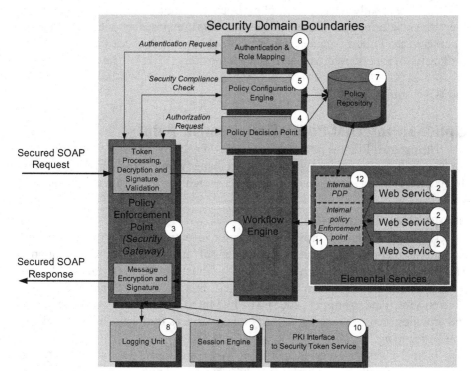

Authentication and Role Mapping Unit

The PEP first makes an authentication request to the Role Mapping Unit (6), which assigns a role to the caller. The request/response protocol is based on XACML.

Policy Configuration Engine

In a second step, the PEP checks the inbound message for compliance with security requirements by querying the Policy Configuration Engine (5). Alternatively, for outbound messages, the PEP queries the Policy Configuration Engine for security requirements to integrate into the message structure. The requirements for inbound and outbound messages are specified in a policy file based on the standards WS-Policy, XACML, and WS-Security. The security requirements, which were specified in the global workflow model, are directly translated into policy files for the configuration engine.

Copyright © 2007, Idea Group Inc. Copying or distributing in print or electronic forms without written permission of Idea Group Inc. is prohibited.

Policy Decision Point

The PEP finally queries the Policy Decision Point (4) for Authorization. It checks invocation requests from workflow partners to exposed services and forwards requests to the Policy Decision Points (4) or (12)—which check the requests according to some policy stored in the Policy Repository (PR) (7). The query protocol is based on XACML, whereas the policy files are based on WS-Policy, XACML, and WS-Security.

Optional: Internal Policy Enforcement Point

The external PEP (3) implements security objectives like user authentication, confidentiality, and integrity regarding data exchange with external partners, whereas the internal PEP (11) maps and enforces access rights to the local environment.

Supporting Components

The Logging Unit (8) provides application level tracing and error logging and basically implements the security requirement of "non-repudiation-of-reception." The Session Engine (9) implements a security context engine that works at the application layer and relies on WS-Trust (Della-Librera et al., 2002) and WS-Secure Conversation (Anderson et al., 2005). The PKI Interface (10) is based on WS-Trust and provides access to external security token services for token issuance, validation, or mapping.

Table 2 gives an overview of the security components, the functionality the components provide, the underlying standards and technologies, and the security requirements that are covered.

Related Work

Related work can be found in several areas. A number of approaches deal with secure document exchange and workflow management in a centrally organized environment. Among these are the Author-X system (Bertino, Castano, & Ferrari, 2001), PERMIS (Chadwick, 2002), and Akenti (Thompson, Essiari, & Mudumbai, 2003). Often a central control is appropriate, but there are also many application domains requiring a local organization.

A whole community deals with inter-organizational workflow management systems (Leyman & Roller, 2000; van der Aalst, 2000, 1999; Luo, Shet, Kochut, & Miller, 2000; Grefen, Aberer, Hoffner, & Ludwing, 2000; Casati & Shan, 2002). We do not aim to contribute a novel approach to this field. Instead, we rely on UML models for modeling workflows and existing workflow management systems based on Web services technology.

Bernauer et al. (Bernauer, Kramler, & Kappel, 2003) analyse security and workflow semantics related issues that arise when modeling B2B protocols. The chapter provides a methodical comparison of WSDL- and ebXML-based approaches.

Copyright © 2007, Idea Group Inc. Copying or distributing in print or electronic forms without written permission of Idea Group Inc. is prohibited.

Table 2. Security objectives and their implementation in the PEP component

Security Component	Provided Functionality	Implemented Technologies & Standards	Security Requirement
Security Gateway			
External PEP	SOAP Message Structure Processing	WS-Sec, XML-Encr.,XML-Sign, XACML	**Integrity** **Confidentiality** **Non-repudiation** *(Message Processing)*
Internal PEP	Internal Role Mapping Sate Dependent Permissions	XACML, XML	**Authorization**
Authentication Unit	Role Mapping	XACML, WS-Policy	**Authentication**
Policy Decision Point	Authorization Request Processing	XACML, WS-Policy, WS-Security	**Authorization**
Policy Repository	Policy Archive	XACML, WS-Policy, WS-Security	
PEP Configuration Engine	Check of Compliance to Security Requirements	XACML, WS-Policy, WS-Security	*(Security Compliance)*
Suporting Components			
Logging Unit	Message Level Tracing	XML, BPEL4WS	**Non-repudiation** **Of Sender**
	Error Logging	XML, BPEL4WS	
Session Engine	Security Context Management	WS-Secure Conversation, WS-Trust	**Authentication**
PKI Interface	Access to Securtiy Token Services	WS-Trust, SAML	*(Interface STS)*

SAML	Security Assertion Markup Language
XACML	Extensible Access Control Markup Language
XML-Sign.	XML Digital Signature
XML-Encr	XML Encryption
WS-Sec	Web-Services Security Specification
XML	Extensible Mark up Language
PKI	Public Key Infrastructure
STS	Security Token Service

Security extensions at a low level of abstraction for workflow management systems are treated in Atluri and Huang (1996), Gudes, Oliveir, and van de Riet (1999), Huang and Atluri (1999), Wainer, Barthelmess, and Kumar (2003).

Model driven approaches that are close to the idea of our framework are Basin, Dose, and Lodderstedt (2003), Lang (2003), and Lodderstedt, Basin, and Doser (2002). Lodderstedt (2003) introduced the notion of Model Driven Security for a software development process that allows for the integration of security requirements into system models and supports the generation of security infrastructures. These approaches deal with business logic, our approach deals with workflow management.

Mantell (2003) describes an implementation, where a local workflow is modeled in a case-tool, exported via XMI-files to a development environment, and automatically translated into executable code for a WS-BPEL engine-based on Web services. Nevertheless, the approach does not provide any facilities for the integration of security requirements at the modeling level nor does it support the specification of global workflows by means of peer-to-peer interactions as suggested by the concept of abstract processes in BEA (2003).

CONCLUSION, CURRENT, AND FUTURE ACTIVITIES

In this chapter, we have presented our approach to model driven security for inter-organizational workflows. Our framework is based on the idea of specifying security requirements at the abstract level of UML models and generating executable

Copyright © 2007, Idea Group Inc. Copying or distributing in print or electronic forms without written permission of Idea Group Inc. is prohibited.

software artifacts for the configuration of a target reference architecture, which is based on Web services technologies and (upcoming) standards.

By now, we have developed a code generator as proof-of-concept prototype, which implements the transformation functions taking the UML models and producing XML-based configuration files for some basic scenarios (confidentiality, integrity, and non-repudiation).

Current efforts are directed into several directions. We aim at the extension of the list of security requirements that can be expressed within our syntactic framework by considering additional features for basic security requirements (e.g., the distinction of documents signed by actors or by systems according to various legal requirements) and by introducing new types of complex, domain specific security requirements (e.g., transactional security requirements for electronic banking, message-level security context, and trust propagation, privacy in a distributed environment, etc.), which will be realized through "pluggable" components in the target architecture.

Our case studies in the field of e-government show us an increasing demand for high-level development of secure workflow realizations. This pushes us to tackle more complex workflow issues, like the "Qualified Signature," which requires a natural person's signature instead of a system's, the delegation of rights (e.g., a tax advisor acting on behalf of his client), and timing constraints on transactions (e.g., a notification has to returned within a two-weeks delay.

REFERENCES

Anderson, S. et al. (2005, February). *Web Services Secure Conversation Language* (WS-SecureConversation). Retrieved from ftp://www6.software.ibm.com/software/developer/library/ws-secureconversation.pdf

Anderson, S. et al. (2005, February). *Web Services Trust Language* (WS-Trust). Retrieved from ftp://www6.software.ibm.com/software/developer/library/ws-trust.pdf

Arkin, A. (2002). *Business Process Modeling Language.* San Mateo, CA, BPMI.org, 2002. Proposed Final Draft.

Alam, M., Breu, R., & Hafner, M. (2006). Modeling permissions in a (U/X)ML world. Accepted to *ARES 2006*, Vienne, Austria.

Atluri, V., & Huang, W. K. (1996). Enforcing mandatory and discretionary security in workflow management systems. In *Proceedings of the 5th European Symposium on Research in Computer Security.*

Austrian Security Manual. Retrieved from http://www.cio.gv.at/securenetworks/sihb/

Austrian Signature Act (Signaturgesetz - SigG). (1999). Art. 1 of the Act. *Austrian Federal Law Gazette*, part I, Nr. 190/1999.

Copyright © 2007, Idea Group Inc. Copying or distributing in print or electronic forms without written permission of Idea Group Inc. is prohibited.

Bajal S. et al. (2004, September). *Web Services Policy Framework* (WS-Policy). Retrieved from ftp://www6.software.ibm.com/software/developer/library/ws-policy.pdf

Barros, A., Dumas, M., & Oaks, P. (2005). A critical overview of the Web Services Choreography Description Language (WS-CDL). *BPTrends Newsletter,* Vol. 3. Retrieved from http://www.bptrends.com/publicationfiles/03%2D05%20WP%20WS%2DCDL%20Barros%20et%20al.pdf

Basin, D., Dose, J., & Lodderstedt, T. (2003). *Model driven security for process-oriented systems.* Paper presented at the 8th ACM Symposium on Access Control Models and Technologies.

BEA, IBM, Microsoft, SAP AG, Siebel Systems. (2003, May). *Specification: Business Process Execution Language for Web Services* (Version 1.1). Retrieved from http://www.ibm.com/developerworks/library/ws-bpel

BEA, Intalio, Sun Microsystems, SAP: Web Service Choreography Interface (WSCI) 1.0. (n.d.). Retrieved from http://www.w3.org/TR/wsci/

Bernauer, M., Kramler, G., & Kappel, G. (2003). Comparing WSDL-based and ebXML-based Approaches for B2B Protocol Specification. In *Proceedings of the 1st International Conference on Service-Oriented Computing (ICSOC).*

Bertino E., Castano S., & Ferrari E. (2001). *Securing XML Documents with Author X.* IEEE Internet Computing.

Breu R., Burger K., Hafner M., & Popp G. (2004). Towards a systematic development of secure systems. *Information Systems Security.*

Breu R., Hafner M., & Weber B. (2004). Modeling and Realizing Security-Critical Inter-Organizational Workflows. In W. Dosch & N. Debnath (Eds.), *Proceedings IASSE 2004, ISCA.*

Cantor, S., Kemp, J., & Maler, E. (2004, July 13). *Assertions and Protocols for the OASIS Security Assertion Markup Language (SAML)* (V2.0, Last-Call Working Draft 17). Retrieved from http://www.oasis-open.org/committees/download.php/7737/sstc-saml-core-2.0-draft-17.pdf

Casati, F., & Shan, M. (2002). Event-based interaction management for composite e-services in e-flow. *Information Systems Frontiers.*

Chadwick, D. W. (2002). RBAC Policies in XML for X.509 based privilege management. In *Proceedings of the IFIP TC11 17th International Conference on Information Security: Visions and Perspectives.*

Christensen, E., Curbera, F., Meredith, G., & Weerawarana, S. (2001). *Web Services Description Language (WSDL) 1.1.* Retrieved from http://www.w3.org/TR/wsdl

Della-Libera, G. et al. (2002, December). *Web Services Security Policy Language* (WS-SecurityPolicy). Retrieved from http://msdn.microsoft.com/Webservices/default.aspx?pull=/library/en-us/dnglobspec/html/ws-securitypolicy.asp

Devanbu, P., & Stubblebine, S. (2000). *Software engineering for security: a roadmap.* In A. Finkelstein (Ed.), *The future of software engineering* (pp. 227-239). ACM Press.

Copyright © 2007, Idea Group Inc. Copying or distributing in print or electronic forms without written permission of Idea Group Inc. is prohibited.

Eastlake D. et al. (Ed.) (2002, December 10). *XML Encryption Syntax and Process-ing. W3C Recommendation.* Retrieved from http://www.w3.org/TR/2002/REC-xmlenc-core-20021210/

Federal Act on Provisions Facilitating Electronic Communications with Public Bodies (E-Government Gesetz - E-GovG). (2004, March 1). Art. 1 of the Act. *Austrian Federal Law Gazette,* part I, Nr. 10/2004.

Federal Act concerning the Protection of Personal Data (Datenschutzgesetz - DSG2000). (1999, August 17). *Austrian Federal Law Gazette,* part I No. 165/1999.

Ferrari E., & Thuraisingham B. (2000). *Secure database systems.* In M. Piattini & O. Díaz (Eds.), *Advanced databases: Technology Design.* London: Artech House.

Godik, S., & Moses, T. (2003, February 18). *eXtensible Access Control Markup Language (XACML)* (Version 1.0 3 OASIS Standard). Retrieved from http://www.oasis-open.org/committees/xacml/repository

Grefen, P., Aberer, K., Hoffner, Y., & Ludwig, H. (2000). CrossFlow: Cross-organi-zational workflow management in dynamic virtual enterprises. *International Journal of Computer Systems Science & Engineering.*

Gudes, E., Olivier, M., & van de Riet, R. (1999). Modelling, specifying and imple-menting workflow security in cyberspace. *Journal of Computer.*

Hafner, M., & Breu, R. (2005). Realizing model driven security for inter-orga-nizational workflows with WS-CDL and UML 2.0: Bringing Web services, security and UML together. In L. Briand & C. Williams (Eds.), *Proceedings of the 8th International Conference MoDELS 2005,* Montego Bay, Jamaica: Model Driven Engineering Languages and Systems.

Hafner M., Breu R., & Breu M. (2005). *A Security Architecture for Inter-Organi-zational Workflows: Putting Security Standards for Web Services Together.* In C. S. Chen, J. Filipe, et al. (Eds.), *Proceedings ICEIS 2005.*

Hafner, M., Breu, R., Breu, M., & Nowak, A. (2005). Modeling inter-organizational workflow security in a peer-to-peer environment. In R. Bilof (Ed.), *Proceed-ings of the 2005 IEEE International Conference on Web Services, ICWS 2005,* Orlando, FL.

Hall A., Chapman R. (2002). Correctness by construction developing a commercial secure system. *IEEE Software, 19*(1) 18-25.

Huang, W. K., & Atluri V. (1999). *SecureFlow: A secure Web-enabled Workflow Management System.* Paper presented at the ACM Workshop on Role-Based Access Control.

IBM: BPWS4J. Retrieved from http://www.alphaworks.ibm.com/tech/bpws4j

IBM, Microsoft, VeriSign: Web services security (WS-Security). (n.d.). Retrieved from http://www-106.ibm.com/developerworks/Webservices/library/ws-secure/

Lang, U. (2003). *Access policies for middleware.* PhD thesis, University of Cam-bridge.

Copyright © 2007, Idea Group Inc. Copying or distributing in print or electronic forms without written permis-sion of Idea Group Inc. is prohibited.

Leyman, F., & Roller, D. (2000). *Production workflow: Concepts and techniques.* Prentice-Hall. Retrieved from http://www.uml.org

Lodderstedt, T. (2003). *Model driven security: From UML models to access control architectures.* Dissertation, University of Freiburg.

Lodderstedt, T., Basin, D., & Doser, J. (2002) SecureUML: A UML-Based Modeling Language for Model-Driven Security. In J.-M. Jézéquel, H. Hussmann, & S. Cook (Eds.), *Proceedings of the 5th International Conference on the Unified Modeling Language.*

Luo, Z., Shet, A., Kochut, K., & Miller, J. (2000). Exception handling in workflow systems. *Applied Intelligence.*

Mantell, K. (2003). *From UML to BPEL. IBM-developerWorks.*

OECD Guidelines for the Security of Information Systems and Networks. URL: http://www.ftc.gov/bcp/conline/edcams/infosecurity/popups/OECD_guide-lines.pdf.

Thompson M., Essiari A., & Mudumbai S. (2003). Certificate-based authorization policy in a PKI environment. *ACM Transactions on Information and System Security.*

Van der Aalst, W. M. P. (1999). Process-oriented Architectures for Electronic Commerce and Interorganizational Workflow. *Information Systems.*

Van der Aalst, W. M. P. (2000). Loosely coupled interorganizational workflows: Modeling and analyzing workflows crossing organizational boundaries. *Information and Management.*

Van der Aalst, W. M. P., & Weske, M. (2001). The P2P approach to interorganizational workflows. In K. R. Dittrich, et al. (Eds.), *Proceedings of the 13th International Conference on Advanced Information Systems Engineering (CAiSE'01).* Springer, Berlin.

W3C: Web Services Choreography Description Language (Version 1.0). (2004, December 17). W3C Working Draft. Retrieved from http://www.w3.org/TR/2004/WD-ws-cdl-10-20041217/

Wainer, J., Barthelmess, P., & Kumar, A. (2003). W-RBAC—A workflow security model incorporating controlled overriding of constraints. *International Journal of Cooperative Information Systems.*

Copyright © 2007, Idea Group Inc. Copying or distributing in print or electronic forms without written permission of Idea Group Inc. is prohibited.

Chapter XV

A Formalized Design Method for Building E-Government Architectures

Alexandros Kaliontzoglou, National Technical University of Athens, Greece

Basilis Meneklis, University of Piraeus, Greece

Despina Polemi, University of Piraeus, Greece

Christos Douligeris, University of Piraeus, Greece

ABSTRACT

E-government has the main goal of simplifying governmental processes and the interaction between citizens and state organizations. It therefore has to solve the problem of efficient and secure electronic exchange and processing of governmental documents and data across administration domains and boundaries, even crossing country borders. This is a difficult task that imposes a strict set of requirements to the design and modelling of e-government systems and demands the application of standardized architectural frameworks. This chapter demonstrates how the ISO/RM-ODP, in combination with the UML notation, supports the design and development of an open distributed e-government system, by addressing these requirements. It further presents a high-level case study of how RM-ODP has been applied in the case of the e-mayor platform to build a system supporting cross-border transactions between small to medium sized European municipalities.

Copyright © 2007, Idea Group Inc. Copying or distributing in print or electronic forms without written permission of Idea Group Inc. is prohibited.

INTRODUCTION

During the last decade, governmental organizations at all levels have invested considerable effort and financial resources in the development and adoption of e-government services.

E-government aims to simplify governmental processes and improve the interaction between citizens and state organizations through the use of electronic communications. The first era of e-government activities included Web site hosting and management. The more sophisticated of these efforts even allowed a limited transaction to be performed online. The next generation of e-government applications demand interactive service delivery, secure transactions, cross-border interactions, and a homogenous framework for e-government systems communication. In order to sustain the quality of their services, governmental organizations need to solve the problem of efficient and secure electronic exchange and processing of governmental documents and data. It is of utmost importance that these services are provided in a way that is easily adoptable and accessible by all citizens, businesses, and other public bodies.

Since public organizations may be distributed within a small area (e.g., a town hall and other municipal offices) or a larger one (across a wider geographical area--even across country boundaries), they need distributed system architectures. The development of an e-government distributed processing system needs to first have a clear understanding of the functionalities to be offered and then represent and structure the system's fundamental information in a way that will be effective and efficient in the final implemented system.

This is a difficult task that imposes a strict set of requirements to the design and modelling of e-government systems and demands the application of standardized architectural frameworks. This chapter demonstrates how the ISO Reference Model for Open Distributed Processing systems (RM-ODP) standard, in combination with the UML notation (OMG–UML, 2004), can support the design and development of an open distributed e-government system. It further presents a high-level case study of how RM-ODP has been applied in the case of the e-mayor platform to build a system supporting cross-border transactions between small- to medium-sized European municipalities.

The chapter is structured as follows: "Related Work in the Area of Architecture Modeling for Distributed Systems" gives a presentation of related work in the field of modelling frameworks for IT architectures. "Architectural Requirements of E-Government Systems" presents the specific requirements of governmental organizations that have to be addressed by a system architecture tuned to this environment. "An Overview of the RM-ODP Standard" gives an overview of the RM-ODP standard and presents its fundamental characteristics. "Suitability of RM-ODP for E-Government" shows how RM-ODP and its features fulfil these requirements. "The e-Mayor Case Study" presents a high-level case study of how the RM-ODP standard is being used for the design of a system targeting municipalities and, finally, the section "Conclusion" draws conclusions.

Copyright © 2007, Idea Group Inc. Copying or distributing in print or electronic forms without written permission of Idea Group Inc. is prohibited.

RELATED WORK IN THE AREA OF ARCHITECTURE MODELLING FOR DISTRIBUTED SYSTEMS

As shown in Tang, Han, and Chen (2004), there are a number of architectural frameworks that can be used in architecture modelling that provide a structured and systematic approach to designing systems. Such systems include the Zachman Framework for Enterprise Architecture (Zachman, 1987), the 4+1 View Model of Architecture (Kruchten, 1995), the U.S. Federal Government Federal Enterprise Architecture Framework (CIO–Council, 1999), the International Standard Organization/Reference Model of Open Distributed Processing (ISO/RM-ODP, ITU-T, 1996-98), the Open Group Architectural framework (The Open Group, 2003) and the DoD Architecture Framework from the U.S. Department of Defense (U.S. Department of Defense, 2003).

Furthermore, as discussed in Costa, Harding, and Young (2001), ISO/RM-ODP, OMG/CORBA (Object Modelling Group/Common Object Request Broker Architecture, OMG- CORBA, 2004), and OSF/DCE (Open Software Foundation/Distributed Computing Environment, The Open Group, 1997) are examples of standards for open distributed processing that cope with distributed systems heterogeneity and openness.

One can argue after a careful review of the systems previously mentioned that RM-ODP offers both a general framework and a reference model for the design of systems based on five different viewpoints and at the same time, its primary objective is to allow the benefits of distribution and information processing services to be realized in an environment of heterogeneous IT resources and multiple organization domains. Therefore, RM-ODP has received an increasing acceptance by the scientific and commercial community over the last years (Akerhurst, Waters, & Derrick, 2004; Blinov & Patel, 2003; Costa et al., 2001; Kande, Mazaher, Prnjat, Sacks, & Wittig, 2004; Nankman & Nieuwenhuis, 1996; Traore, Aredo, & Ye, 2004).

Based on the previous text, RM-ODP may thus be considered as a valid candidate for the modelling of an e-government specific architecture (German Federal Ministry of Interior, 2003). Nevertheless, in order to better support this claim, we demonstrate the feasibility of RM-ODP as such a framework in two ways. At first, we conduct an analysis of the basic requirements of e-government systems and then, after briefly presenting the standard and its concepts, we directly map these requirements to the characteristics and qualities that an RM-ODP designed system has. Secondly, we present a snapshot of the actual design of such an e-government system. This system is currently under development as part of the European Commission e-mayor project (e-mayor, 2004).

Although RM-ODP is deemed suitable for the design of architectures, it does not explicitly endorse a specific notation to be used along with its viewpoints. As

Copyright © 2007, Idea Group Inc. Copying or distributing in print or electronic forms without written permission of Idea Group Inc. is prohibited.

discussed in Kande et al., (2004) there are several (semi) formal languages and notations that can be considered for the purpose of specifying ODP viewpoints. Among them, the notation that best fulfils the requirement of being able to check the consistency of the different viewpoint specifications in the system is the Unified Modelling Language (UML). Among other languages, the Specification and Description Language (SDL) is also object-oriented and has a graphical notation, but it lacks the richness of concepts of UML and does not support extension mechanisms such as UML's stereotype. LOTOS and Z are other formal languages but have a limited set of basic concepts and also lack extension mechanism to overcome that disadvantage.

ARCHITECTURAL REQUIREMENTS OF E-GOVERNMENT SYSTEMS

In order to demonstrate the suitability of any modelling and architectural framework for e-government, we first need to outline the specific architectural and organizational requirements that have to be satisfied by the systems of governmental organizations wishing to engage themselves in e-government. The suitability of a framework can be proven by showing how systems built with this framework address these requirements.

Interoperability

It is hard to achieve interoperability in a governmental organization system due to various forms of heterogeneity that exist in governmental environments. The interconnection of governmental organizations that use various platforms and systems is a difficult task requiring easily identifiable and publishable e-services, as well as clear interfaces for the establishment of secure and reliable connection points. Furthermore, even within the boundaries of a single public organization, a system may be spread across a geographical area. For example, in the case of a municipality, the administrative offices may be located further away from the cultural centre or the town hall. The fact that there are a large number of smaller public organizations makes interoperability between these systems even more challenging.

Scalability

Enhanced scalability is also a requirement that must be met by the infrastructure of governmental organizations due to the large number of citizens that need to be served with acceptable levels of quality of service. Furthermore, public administrations are continuously in the process of deploying electronically traditional paper-based services as well as new services. An e-government system should be able to host an increasing number of e-services.

Copyright © 2007, Idea Group Inc. Copying or distributing in print or electronic forms without written permission of Idea Group Inc. is prohibited.

Security and Trust

E-government services have to be secure so that government employees and users trust the system and feel confident in using it. Governmental organizations need to design, implement, and operate a secure electronic environment for the exchange and processing of governmental e-documents, accessing the repositories of information for authorized public servants and hosting of shared applications.

User-Friendliness and Accessibility

A governmental organization environment has to be easily accessible by civil servants and citizens alike, with user-friendly interfaces covering the needs of various types of users. These requirements stem from the fact that governmental organizations have to serve a large number of citizens with diverse information technology training. It is very important that any complex operations be transparent to the end user. A governmental environment should also offer good international support for foreign citizens as well as support for disabled citizens.

Cost Considerations

Minimization of costs, both of deployment and operation, is a very important requirement for the successful deployment of e-government services. This issue is of even greater importance to smaller public organizations, which frequently do not have the same resources as their larger counterparts in terms of finances and personnel.

Transparent Automated Processing

Automated processing is linked to the operational costs of e-government services for governmental organizations since they have to satisfy the requests of many people with only a handful of personnel under normal operation.

Cross-Border Characteristics

An ever-increasing number of European citizens change their location to work in other countries. This means that there is a definite demand to support them in administrative procedures that include cross-border communication. In cross-border services, there is exchange of information, data, or documents between citizens and public administrations (C2G, G2G) in an international context and across administrative boundaries.

Limited Training

There is always a need for training of government employees during and after the deployment of e-services. This is especially true in the case of larger governmental organisations that employ hundreds or thousands of people. Training could prove to be an extremely costly and complicated procedure. The provision of limited

Copyright © 2007, Idea Group Inc. Copying or distributing in print or electronic forms without written permission of Idea Group Inc. is prohibited.

required training is of utmost importance for the minimisation of time that has to be invested by the staff before they operate any new system.

Compatibility with Existing Infrastructures

Citizens and governmental organisations have already established software, hardware, and network infrastructures. These infrastructures nevertheless can seldom interoperate within a distributed architecture comprising of several organizations. Therefore, such an architecture must provide a compatibility layer with existing and legacy systems so that their current data can be used, since the complete replacement of legacy systems is usually prohibitively costly.

Mobility Aspects

Mobile access affords citizens the use of services detached from strict office hours and independent of locations. Mobility and independence add real value to these services. Services with mobile aspects are of interest to facilitate access to the era of mobile internet services for governmental organizations, which means in particular a device-independent access to services (by cellular phone, PDA, etc.).

AN OVERVIEW OF THE RM-ODP STANDARD

ISO, IEC, and ITU-T have joined efforts to produce a common framework for developing ODP systems that benefit from the distribution of information processing services in environments of heterogeneous technology resources and multiple domains. The RM-ODP is the result of this effort. RM-ODP creates an architecture that integrates support for distribution, interworking, and portability and describes systems that support heterogeneous processing and information exchange between groups within an organization as well as between cooperating organizations (ITU-T, 1996-98).

RM-ODP defines the basic concepts of distributed processing, identifies the characteristics that qualify a system as an ODP system, and introduces five viewpoints, which are used in order to specify an ODP system. A viewpoint on a system is an abstraction of that system (or a part of it) that gives a specification of the whole (or part) of the system related to a particular set of concerns. RM-ODP also defines a viewpoint language that is used to describe each viewpoint. Each viewpoint language provides a set of definitions of concepts and rules enabling the specification of the system from its corresponding viewpoint. Furthermore, RM-ODP provides a framework for checking the system's conformance to the specification and the consistency between the different viewpoints and defines certain functions that are required to support an ODP system. Finally, it presents a system architecture, which provides distribution transparencies between system applications. Distribution transparencies enable complexities associated with system distribution to be hidden from applications when they are irrelevant to their purpose (ITU-T, 1996-98).

Copyright © 2007, Idea Group Inc. Copying or distributing in print or electronic forms without written permission of Idea Group Inc. is prohibited.

The five viewpoints and their corresponding languages, as defined in RM-ODP that are used to specify an ODP system are the following:

- **Enterprise viewpoint:** A viewpoint of an ODP system and its environment that focuses on the policies, which define the behaviour of an object in the system as well as the system's purpose of operation and scope. This viewpoint describes the system from the aspect of what it is required to do. The Enterprise Language is used to describe the Enterprise Viewpoint.
- **Information viewpoint:** A viewpoint which specifies and describes the information entities that are communicated, stored and processed in the system. The Information Language is used to describe the Information Viewpoint.
- **Computational viewpoint:** A viewpoint which focuses on the way distribution of processing is achieved. The Computational Language is used to describe the Computational Viewpoint.
- **Engineering viewpoint:** A viewpoint which focuses on the way different objects of the system use to communicate with each other and the resources that are needed to accomplish this communication. The Engineering Language is used to describe the Engineering Viewpoint.
- **Technology viewpoint:** A viewpoint which focuses on the selected technology of a system. The Technology Language is used to describe the Technology Viewpoint.

An ODP function is a function that is required to support Open Distributed Processing. RM-ODP specifies the functions that are required to support Open Distributed Processing and categorizes them into the following four areas:

- Management functions
- Coordination functions
- Repository functions
- Security functions

The distribution transparencies introduced in RM-ODP are the following:

- **Access transparency:** It is a distribution transparency which masks differences in data representation and invocation mechanisms to enable interworking between objects.
- **Failure transparency:** It is a distribution transparency which masks from an object the failure and possible recovery of other objects (or itself), in order to enable fault tolerance.
- **Location transparency:** It is a distribution transparency which masks the use of information about location in space when identifying and binding to interfaces. Location transparency allows objects to access interfaces without using location information.

Copyright © 2007, Idea Group Inc. Copying or distributing in print or electronic forms without written permission of Idea Group Inc. is prohibited.

- **Migration transparency:** It is a distribution transparency which masks from an object the ability of a system to change the location of that object.
- **Persistence transparency:** It is a distribution transparency which masks from an object the deactivation and reactivation of other objects.
- **Relocation transparency:** It is a distribution transparency which masks the relocation of an interface from other interfaces bound to it.
- **Replication transparency:** It is a distribution transparency which masks the use of a group of mutually behaviourally compatible objects to support an interface.
- **Transaction transparency:** It is a distribution transparency which masks the coordination of activities among a configuration of objects, to achieve consistency.

The system specification of RM-ODP is based on an object modelling approach. This approach provides a formalization of well-established design practices of abstraction and encapsulation.

SUITABILITY OF RM-ODP FOR E-GOVERNMENT

The use of RM-ODP as a standard for designing a distributed system enables and supports the development of systems with certain desired characteristics. These characteristics, which are depicted in Table 1 and described below, satisfy all the requirements of a distributed governmental organization system.

Table 1. RM-ODP features against e-government requirements

	Openness	Integration	Flexibility	Modularity	Federation	Manageability	QoS	Security	Transparency
Interoperability	√	√			√				
Scalability	√					√	√		
Security/Trust								√	
User Friendliness/Accessibility							√		√
Cost Considerations		√		√					
Transparent Automated Processing			√						√
Cross-border Characteristics	√				√				
Limited Training						√			
Compatibility with Existing Infrastructures		√	√						
Mobility Aspects			√						

Copyright © 2007, Idea Group Inc. Copying or distributing in print or electronic forms without written permission of Idea Group Inc. is prohibited.

Openness

Openness in a system makes possible the change of the processing node at which a component is situated without the need for modification. This feature supports the scalability needs of governmental organization applications. Such applications must satisfy the demands of a continuously expanding group of citizens and so the machines that are used to host these applications should be upgraded on a regular basis. Openness of the system's design ensures that the migration of the applications to the new hardware and software will be achieved in a smooth fashion.

Openness also ensures the meaningful interaction between components effectively covering the needs for interoperability and cross-border characteristics. The basis for interoperability is the communication and interaction between the different parts of the system. Furthermore, in order to achieve a satisfying interworking level between the different systems, cross-border characteristics must be integrated into them. The meaningful interaction of all components and the freedom to setup applications at any given node of the system (which are both provided by the system's openness) are essential in satisfying this goal.

Integration

Integrated systems incorporate various other systems and resources into a whole without costly ad hoc solutions. Systems with different architectures and different resources are fine-tuned to work together. Integrated systems deal with the problem of heterogeneity and thus satisfy the governmental organization applications' demands for interoperability and compatibility with existing infrastructures. Furthermore, effectively incorporating existing systems and resources into new architectures lowers the cost of the migration procedure to the new solutions. This last feature is of great importance to governmental organizations since their financial resources are very often extremely restricted.

Flexibility

Flexible systems are capable both of evolving and of accommodating the existence and the continuous operation of existing legacy systems. A major requirement of a governmental organization is the reuse of the major part of its existing infrastructure when a new IT solution is introduced. Flexibility addresses the requirement of compatibility with existing infrastructure. Furthermore, changes in the system's architecture and topology are easily adopted when a system is flexible. The majority of modern e-government solutions focus on the interaction with the citizens through more contemporary and widely available media (such as palmtop PCs or cellular phones) (German Federal Ministry of Interior, 2003; NECCC, 2004), which is a feature that requires mobile interfaces. Thus, flexibility helps to deal with transparent automated processing and mobility.

Copyright © 2007, Idea Group Inc. Copying or distributing in print or electronic forms without written permission of Idea Group Inc. is prohibited.

Modularity

The parts of a modular system are autonomous but interrelated. Modularity supports the reuse of previously developed software modules, which in turn lowers the cost of system development. Governmental organizations can benefit dearly from this option since it satisfies their need for low cost solutions, especially when upgrading an existing system or trying to develop a completely new application for newly introduced services.

Federation

A federated system can be combined with other systems from different administrative or technical domains in order to achieve a single objective. Federated systems are satisfying the needs for interoperability and cross-border characteristics. Oftentimes, a governmental organization's offices and departments are not located in the same building or even the same area, however the system must interoperate effectively. Federation addresses this need successfully.

Manageability

ODP-based systems are highly manageable. This means that they allow easy monitoring, control, and management of resources and processes in order to support configuration, QoS, and accounting policies. This directly affects the scalability of the system, since it allows easier management of the increasing number of users and helps with keeping the system operational in spite of the limited skilled and trained personnel available in governmental organizations.

Quality of Service (QoS)

Systems designed and implemented based on ODP must take into serious account several quality of service needs. These needs cover the timeliness, availability, and reliability in the context of resources (local and remote) and interactions, together with fault tolerance, that allows the remainder of a distributed system to continue to operate in the event of failure of some part. This means that ODP systems offer high availability, dependability, and accessibility, which is very important when the system has to be continuously up and running to cover the diverse needs of a large number of citizens throughout the day. QoS directly affects how users perceive their interaction with the services and finally the adoption of these services.

Security

ODP proposes a strong security framework for architectures ensuring that system facilities and data are protected against unauthorized access and respect privacy. Certain functions are defined that are fundamental and widely applicable to the development of ODP systems. More specifically, ODP defines security functions (such as access control function, authentication function, integrity function and

Copyright © 2007, Idea Group Inc. Copying or distributing in print or electronic forms without written permission of Idea Group Inc. is prohibited.

key-management function) which help organize and orchestrate the development and application of security policies within an ODP system. Security requirements posed by governmental organizations are generally strict and they are made often more difficult to be met in modern governmental infrastructures given the increasing needs for remoteness of interactions and for mobility of system components and the system users.

Transparency

ODP has as a primary goal--the integration of transparency in systems. Transparency hides the details and differences in mechanisms used to overcome problems caused by the distribution of applications. Aspects of distribution, which should be masked (totally or partially) include heterogeneity of supporting software and hardware and location and mobility of components and mechanisms to achieve the required level of QoS in the face of failures (e.g., replication, migration, check pointing, etc.). RM-ODP introduces a set of distribution transparencies in order to support this need. Transparency is critical for a number of governmental organization requirements: user friendliness in order to hide application and processing details from users and automated processing so that a small number of civil servants and public workers can manage systems successfully.

THE E-MAYOR CASE STUDY

The practical suitability of RM-ODP in e-government is demonstrated in this chapter through an implementation in the IST e-mayor project (e-mayor, 2004), where we have opted to use RM-ODP in the design and implementation of an e-government platform attuned to the environment of European Small- to Medium-Sized Governmental Organizations (SMGOs) (Kaliontzoglou, Sklavos, Karantjias, & Polemi, 2004), which in the e-mayor case includes several European municipalities. During the design phase, we have applied RM-ODP concepts and principles in combination with UML to define a system that addresses the various needs of the municipalities, as they have been identified during the analysis and user requirements collection phase of the project (e-mayor Consortium, 2004). An initial approach of the design specification concepts for the first three viewpoints have been presented in Meneklis, Kaliontzoglou, Polemi, and Douligeris (2005). This section presents the full design concepts with examples from all the RM-ODP viewpoints (Enterprise, Information, Computational, Engineering, and Technology).

Enterprise Viewpoint

As part of the Enterprise Viewpoint, e-mayor has identified the main stakeholders in the municipality community domain and the roles they assume in the environment, such as the citizens and their delegates and the civil servants working

Copyright © 2007, Idea Group Inc. Copying or distributing in print or electronic forms without written permission of Idea Group Inc. is prohibited.

Figure 1. The e-mayor community

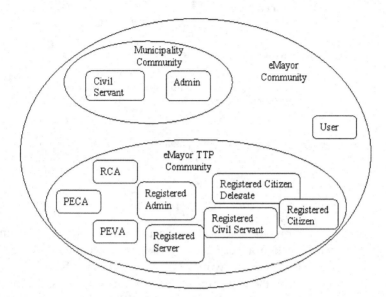

in the municipalities or other organizations. Furthermore, we have identified the business processes that take place in the communities along with the activities of the various roles in them and we have described the policies and constraints related to the processes. This has led to the definition of Enterprise objects. One example is the TTP sub-community within the wider e-mayor community that comprises of the Regional CAs, a Pan-European CA, a Pan-European Validation Authority and the various registered Users (registered Civil Servant etc.) as shown in Figure 1.

The Enterprise Viewpoint defines all the relationships between the entities and the processes they follow (e.g., for the PKI framework setup of an end-entity or the Certificate Validation). The specifications utilize free-form diagrams as well as UML diagrams (Use Case, Class, Collaboration, and Activity diagrams) for the representation of the previous concepts.

Information Viewpoint

The Information Viewpoint presents and analyzes various information objects that will be used by the e-mayor platforms and communicated between them. The information objects that have been identified are the e-documents, Service Requests, Credentials, Policies, User Profiles, various Registries, Notifications, Log Files, and Routing Objects. In order to represent the information objects, UML class diagrams are used.

Copyright © 2007, Idea Group Inc. Copying or distributing in print or electronic forms without written permission of Idea Group Inc. is prohibited.

Figure 2. E-document states and transitions

A characteristic information object is the e-document. The e-mayor e-document is a basic document information object, which represents any electronic document that is used in transactions inside one e-mayor platform, or between different platforms. e-documents are created by the platform to represent request forms, certification documents etc., and all their intermediate states. There have been defined various different states (formats) for all types of available e-documents. These states are used in different phases of an e-document's life cycle. An e-document may be in one of the following states: e-mayor Universal Format (eUF), e-mayor Local Format (eLF), Municipality Raw Format (MRF), or e-mayor Presentation Format (ePF).

Furthermore, methods for transforming an e-document from one format to another have been developed. The possible states and transitions for an e-document within the e-mayor system are presented in the diagram of Figure 2.

An e-document may start its life cycle in the MRF or eUF states based on whether the information contained in it has to be retrieved by an existing municipal system or not. The final states of an e-document can be the eLF or ePF based on whether it will be downloaded by the user to be stored (in eLF) or just presented on a graphical user interface (in ePF).

An information object crucial to the functionality of the platform is the Certification Document. The Certification Document represents the certificates (e.g., residence certificate) issued by the municipalities through the e-mayor platform. It is a direct descendant of the e-document information object as shown in Figure 3.

Another descendant of the e-document information object is the Service Request. The Service Request object represents requests made for a specific service offered by the e-mayor system such as certificate issuance, registration to the taxes services, or a notification about the state of processing of another request. As can be seen in Figure 4, the subclasses of the Service Request Information Object are Certificate Request, Registry Request, and Notification Request.

Copyright © 2007, Idea Group Inc. Copying or distributing in print or electronic forms without written permission of Idea Group Inc. is prohibited.

Figure 3. A certification document as an e-document subtype

Information objects presented thus far were all subtypes of the e-document information object. This is not the case for every object used by the platform. Another kind of information object is the Policy information object. A Policy object represents the constraints, conditions, and rules that will have to be respected and enforced by the e-mayor system. A Policy will reflect any organizational policies that apply to service processing, computational and human resources. Four categories of policies have been identified:

- A **legal policy** manifests the legal rules that have to be applied during the provision of a requested service
- A **security services policy** defines the steps that will be taken during the system's operation regarding the required security (cryptographic) services
- An **access control policy** regulates access control to resources and processes
- An **audit policy** controls how actions are recorded in the system for accountability purposes

The Policy object and its forms are depicted in the diagram of Figure 5. Information objects pass from various states as part of their life cycle and the

Figure 4. Service request types

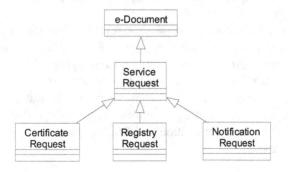

Copyright © 2007, Idea Group Inc. Copying or distributing in print or electronic forms without written permission of Idea Group Inc. is prohibited.

Figure 5. Policy types

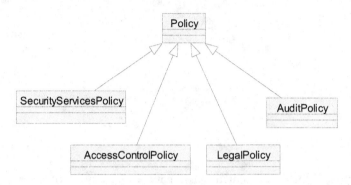

state transitions of the information objects are depicted in the Information Viewpoint using UML StateChart diagrams.

Computational Viewpoint

The Computational Viewpoint divides the computational functionalities in distinct packages and depicts their interconnection and collaboration based on the interfaces exposed. The packages are elaborated with further details showing the interfaces exposed by each package, as well as the internal mechanisms and modules. The computational packages identified in the e-mayor architecture are User Interface, Service Handling, Policy Enforcement, Format Transformation, Existing Systems Adaptation, Content Routing, Notification, Printing, and Persistent Storage. The overall deployment of the packages is specified in the engineering viewpoint and shown later in the chapter.

User Interface communicates with the Service Handling for the actual processing of the service. Policy Enforcement encapsulates a series of functionalities such as auditing, access control, security mechanisms, and the policies of the municipalities' legal frameworks. Service Handling represents the core of the system and has dependencies to all other packages. It communicates with the Policy Enforcement (e.g., for access control, encryption, and digital signature of documents and messages, etc.).

Format Transformation is responsible for transforming legal documents from a country-bound local format to a universal format for transport within the e-mayor environment and vice versa. Content Routing provides the routing functionality for forwarding requests and legal documents to another municipality(s). Municipal Systems Adaptation is the linking point with the municipal systems of the municipalities. Persistent Storage modules handle storage to the file system or databases. Finally, Output Notification and Printing provide support for printing and notification services.

Copyright © 2007, Idea Group Inc. Copying or distributing in print or electronic forms without written permission of Idea Group Inc. is prohibited.

Figure 6. Service Handling components and interfaces

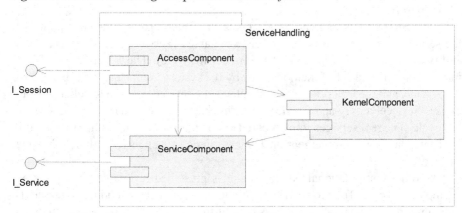

The specifications are supported by UML Component and Class diagrams for the presentation of interfaces and classes and Sequence diagrams for the presentation of sequences of actions involving multiple computational objects.

The Service Handling object is responsible for a major part of the system's functionality. The root component diagram for the Service Handling object is depicted in Figure 6.

The main components of the Service Handling object are the Access Component, the Kernel Component, and the Service Component. Furthermore, Service Handling exposes two interfaces: I_Session and I_Service.

The Access Component will realize the concepts of access session for service users, uniform administration of the system internal user representation, and profiles. For each user, a specified amount of personal data, authentication information, and service-specific preferences are stored. The personal data is collected as part of the registration process; the service-specific profile is installed within the framework of service usage. The Access Component is responsible for the identification and authentication of users. It supports the administration of the active access sessions and the service sessions.

The Kernel Component is a kind of universal framework for the administration of services and users. It administers information about:

- All registered users (UserProfile).
- All offered (available) services.

The Kernel Component includes internally required information and a service profile that contains user specific settings (UserServiceProfile). The Kernel Component directly uses interfaces exposed by other components, for example, Policy

Copyright © 2007, Idea Group Inc. Copying or distributing in print or electronic forms without written permission of Idea Group Inc. is prohibited.

Enforcer (AccessPolicyEnforcer, SecurityPolicyEnforcer) or Persistent Storage (SearchUserInterface).

The Service Component encapsulates the functionality (business logic) of the service and essentially consists of two classes (ServiceFactory and Service) and two interfaces (I_Service and I_ServiceLifeCycle). The I_ServiceLifeCycle interface specifies a set of methods used by the system to manage the life cycle of the service, and the I_Service interface allows the service usage to the clients. Both classes ServiceFactory and Service provide a basic implementation of the service life cycle. The real services implemented on the platform should inherit from both the basic classes and implement the business logic as well as extend the life cycle methods.

Another computational object, which is presented in this case study as an example, is Format Transformation. This computational object and its components will support the information processing and the state transitions of e-documents from one format to another. The root component diagram for Format Transformation components is shown in Figure 7.

The main components of the Format Transformation object are the Transformation Controller and the Template Manager. The Format Transformation object exposes two interfaces: the Transform Interface and the Management Interface.

The Transformation Controller accomplishes all tasks related to the transformations from one format to another, including all security processing and transferring within a platform and between different platforms. Documents are handled by

Figure 7. Breakdown of the Format Transformation object

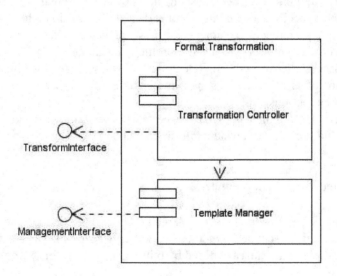

Copyright © 2007, Idea Group Inc. Copying or distributing in print or electronic forms without written permission of Idea Group Inc. is prohibited.

the e-mayor platform at the eUF and eLF formats. Failure of the Transformation Controller will result in inconsistencies and communication problems between the municipalities only when the forwarding of legal document(s) is invoked.

The Template Manager manages specialized profiles, which include the transformation mechanisms for municipalities that participate in e-mayor and their business documents. The idea behind these specialized templates is to decentralize the transformation rules and mechanisms. Each municipality possesses one or more localized templates for use in transformation. In this way, the Template Manager provides the rules and functionality for converting the documents from one format to another in order to present the same document in a concise manner to entities that may even reside in different countries. Due to this decentralized nature, the system is easily maintainable and changes to the eLFs or MLFs of a municipality do not affect the other municipalities. Failure of a Template Manager will affect the presentation of documents to the platform's end users.

Engineering Viewpoint

The engineering viewpoint of the ISO RM-ODP standard presents the interactions and communication between *Engineering Objects*. The various types of engineering objects that are defined by the standard are specified in (ITU-T, 1996-98).

Figure 8, Mapping of e-mayor architectural elements to engineering objects

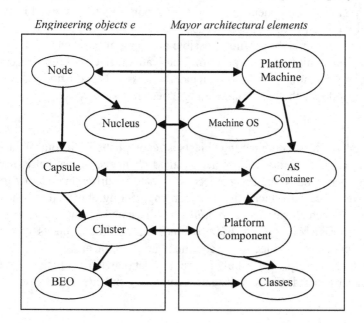

Copyright © 2007, Idea Group Inc. Copying or distributing in print or electronic forms without written permission of Idea Group Inc. is prohibited.

Mapping of e-mayor Architectural Elements to RM-ODP Concepts

The mapping of e-mayor architectural elements to engineering objects as defined in RM-ODP is demonstrated in Figure 8.

Nodes and Nuclei

An e-mayor platform comprises of a number of platform machines. Each machine corresponds to a certain tier of the e-mayor platform. A platform machine is mapped to the concept of a node in the engineering language. A platform machine is an integrated and independently managed computing system that manages and allocates the communication resources of the basic engineering objects that it contains. As a node, each platform machine contains capsules. The actual interaction and communication between the nodes are left to the capsules responsible for such processes. Every node is controlled by a special engineering object, the nucleus. The role of the nucleus is credited to the operating system of each node.

Capsules and Capsule Managers

Two of the five nodes of each e-mayor platform contain application servers for the initialization and handling of the Java beans and the resources needed for them to operate. The application server containers for these servers play the role of the capsules. Every capsule owns storage and a portion of the platform's processing resources. Each capsule is controlled by interactions with the capsule manager. The capsule manager of the e-mayor node is the application server of each tier.

Clusters and Basic Engineering Objects

The platform components, as they are introduced and described in the computational viewpoint, correspond to the clusters of each node in the engineering viewpoint. A cluster is the smallest possible grouping of basic engineering objects forming a single unit for the purposes of deactivation, check pointing, reactivation, recovery, and migration. On the other hand, the classes that constitute each component of the node are the basic engineering objects.

Channels

The interaction of engineering objects is accomplished and controlled through supporting communication mechanisms called channels. A channel is necessary whenever interacting engineering objects are located in different nodes (*distributed binding*). In the case of interaction between engineering objects that reside in the same node or even cluster a *local binding* is utilised and no channel is required.

A channel is a configuration of stubs, binders and protocol objects interconnecting a set of engineering objects. The communicating engineering objects are locally bound to stubs. A stub provides the conversion of data carried by interactions, applies controls, keeps records (for security and accounting), and interacts with engineering

Copyright © 2007, Idea Group Inc. Copying or distributing in print or electronic forms without written permission of Idea Group Inc. is prohibited.

objects outside the channel if required (for security reasons).

A binder manages the end-to-end integrity of that channel, provides relocation transparency and may interact with engineering objects outside the channel in order to perform its functions.

A protocol object provides communication functions, handles whatever peer protocols are in use and provides access to supporting services, such as directory services for translating addresses, when necessary.

The engineering language references three types of channels that correspond to the types of interfaces that computational objects in the computational viewpoint use: operation, stream, and signal channels. The e-mayor architecture comprises only of operation channels.

Overall Engineering Viewpoint of the E-Mayor Architecture

In accordance with the rest of the viewpoints that have been designed, the engineering viewpoint uses UML to represent the e-mayor architecture. This has been accomplished by following the guidelines published in (D. Frankel Consulting, 2003), where the engineering viewpoint is mapped to UML deployment diagrams.

As an example application of the RM-ODP concepts, Figure 9 presents the overall engineering viewpoint of the e-mayor architecture. The various components of the architecture and their interfaces correspond to the respective components in the computational viewpoint specification.

Platform Tiers

The e-mayor engineering viewpoint is divided into five nodes, each one representing one tier of the architecture. The various types of tiers are represented as UML stereotypes. These are:

*   **Node A:** The Client Tier, comprising of the browser components
*   **Node B:** The Interaction Tier, comprising of the Web server and its components
*   **Node C:** The main Enterprise Tier, comprising of the main application server and the platform main components that run as Web Services and EJBs
*   **Node D:** The secondary Enterprise Tier, comprising of another application server managing the choreography of the main platform services in order to implement the business logic of e-mayor
*   **Node E:** The Integration Tier, comprising of the Adaptation Layer components that sit "on-top" of any municipal existing/legacy system

Each one of these nodes contains either components or basic engineering objects (BEOs). The components or BEOs communicate with each other through channels. As it has already been stated, all channels in the e-mayor architecture are operation channels (i.e., there are no signal or streaming channels).

Copyright © 2007, Idea Group Inc. Copying or distributing in print or electronic forms without written permission of Idea Group Inc. is prohibited.

Figure 9. Overall engineering viewpoint

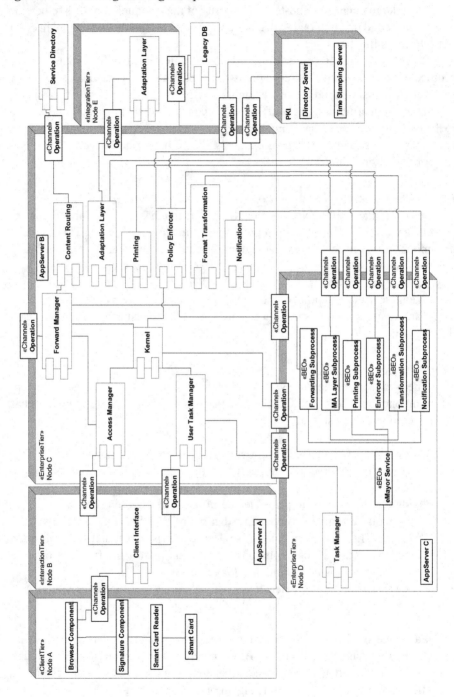

Copyright © 2007, Idea Group Inc. Copying or distributing in print or electronic forms without written permission of Idea Group Inc. is prohibited.

Figure 10. Format Transformation engineering object

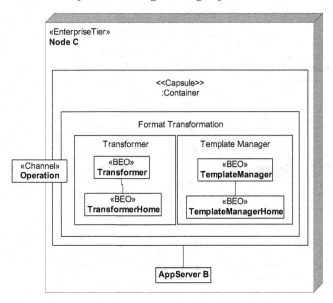

Engineering Objects

One example of the further deconstruction of the engineering viewpoints is given for the Format Transformation engineering object. The goal, based on RM-ODP, is to capture the objects within the object and the channels supported (along with any interfaces used to communicate through the channels). The rest of the engineering objects are analyzed based on this methodology.

The Format Transformation engineering object runs in a container provided by the application server A of Node C. It communicates with Node D through an operation channel, as depicted in Figure 10.

The Format Transformation object is divided in two distinct engineering objects: the *Transformer* that implements the main transformation engine, and the *Template Manager* that handles transformation templates. Each one of these engineering objects exposes a pair of interfaces to the rest of the architecture:

- Transformer exposes the remote Transformer interface and the local Trans-formerHome interface
- Template Manager exposes the remote TemplateManager interface and the local TemplateManger interface

All interfaces are BEOs.

Copyright © 2007, Idea Group Inc. Copying or distributing in print or electronic forms without written permission of Idea Group Inc. is prohibited.

Figure 11. Sample operation channel between the Printing component on Node C and the Printing subprocess on Node D

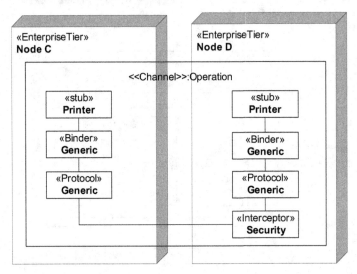

Channels

In the Use Case of the e-mayor engineering viewpoint, there is one type of channel and this is the operation channel. An example of the generic engineering viewpoint of such a channel is depicted in the following figure, as established between nodes C and D.

Each channel connects different nodes and in its fullest form comprises a stub, a binder, and a protocol object on each side of the node, as described in 0. Details for the technology specific types of the channels that exist in the e-mayor architecture are given in the technology viewpoint.

Technology Viewpoint

The RM-ODP technology viewpoint is directly related to the engineering viewpoint where specific technology choices for the objects are shown. This section demonstrates the technology choices adopted in the e-mayor architecture that have been incorporated into the technology viewpoints specification.

Overall Technology Viewpoint of the E-Mayor Architecture

The technology viewpoint also uses UML following the guidelines (ITU-T, 1996-98), where the technology viewpoint is mapped directly to the engineering viewpoint deployment diagrams, with specific technologies.

The overall technology viewpoint of the platform is depicted in Figure 12. This figure shows a choice of technology for each one of the engineering objects presented in the engineering viewpoint.

Copyright © 2007, Idea Group Inc. Copying or distributing in print or electronic forms without written permission of Idea Group Inc. is prohibited.

Figure 12. Overall technology viewpoint

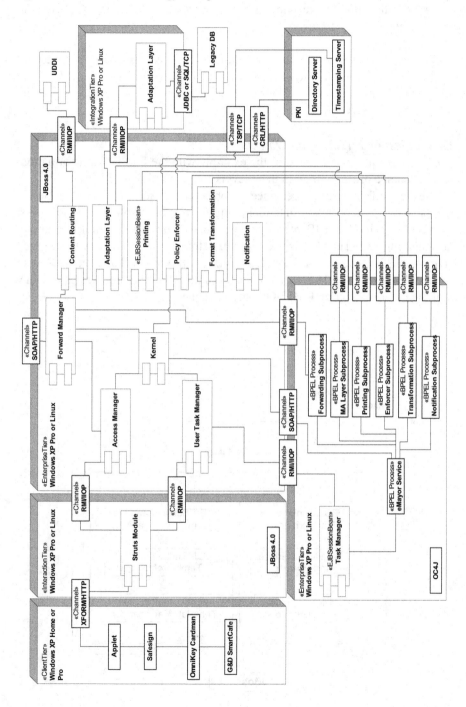

Copyright © 2007, Idea Group Inc. Copying or distributing in print or electronic forms without written permission of Idea Group Inc. is prohibited.

Technologies for Application Servers

As far as the choice of technologies for the application servers is concerned, the specifications are as follows:

- The application servers A and B (identified in Nodes B and C respectively in the engineering viewpoint), are JBoss 4.0
- The application server C (in Node D of the engineering viewpoint), is an Oracle Application Server (OC4J)

Technologies for Engineering Objects

Continuing the specification of the example with the Format Transformation object the choice of technology in this view is shown in Figure 13.

The Format Transformation engineering object comprises two EJB session beans that expose the transformation functionality to the rest of the platform objects. As shown, the object has four EJB interfaces (a pair for each one of the beans): the remote EJBRemoteInterface Transformer, the local EJBHomeInterface TransformerHome, the remote EJBRemoteInterface TemplateManager, and the local EJBHomeInterface TemplateManagerHome. The Format Transformation object communicates with the rest of the platform over an RMI/IIOP based channel.

Figure 13. Format Transformation detailed technology viewpoint

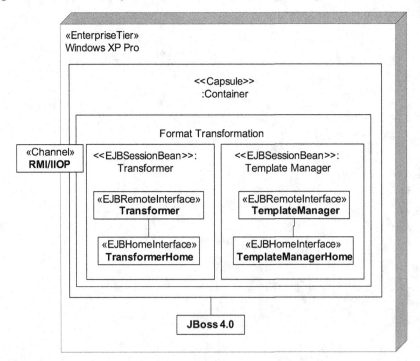

Copyright © 2007, Idea Group Inc. Copying or distributing in print or electronic forms without written permission of Idea Group Inc. is prohibited.

Figure 14. Sample technology viewpoint of a SOAP-based channel

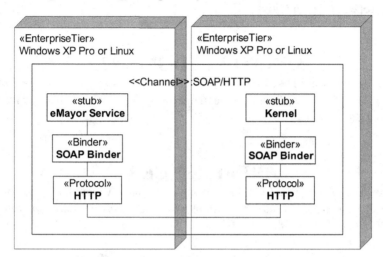

Technologies for Channels

Although in e-mayor we have only one type of channel in the engineering viewpoint, the actual technologies supporting the channels might be different. This has to be shown in the technology viewpoint in our specific use case. One example is a SOAP over HTTP channel as shown in Figure 14.

The figure is an example of the detailed representation of the technology viewpoint of the channel established between the Kernel engineering object on Node C and the e-mayor service engineering object on Node E.

In the case of Web Services and SOAP communication, the fragment of code that will be responsible for the marshalling and unmarshalling of data into the SOAP format is the corresponding stub of the communication channel between two engineering objects. The binder is the fragment of code that binds SOAP to the HTTP protocol in order to accomplish communication. Lastly, the protocol object is the fragment of code that implements HTTP.

CONCLUSION

In this chapter, we have demonstrated the suitability of the RM-ODP standard in the design of open distributed architectures attuned to e-government environments. The use of RM-ODP as the preferred framework encourages a clear separation of concerns (through the different viewpoint specifications), which in turn leads to a better understanding of the problems being addressed during the design of such a system. In the context of the e-mayor project, we have applied RM-ODP concepts

Copyright © 2007, Idea Group Inc. Copying or distributing in print or electronic forms without written permission of Idea Group Inc. is prohibited.

in order to design an e-government platform covering the needs of small to medium sized European municipalities.

ACKNOWLEDGMENTS

The authors would like to thank the E.C. for its support in funding the e-mayor project (IST-2004-507217), and all the members of the project consortium for valuable discussions.

REFERENCES

Akerhurst, D. H., Waters, A. G., & Derrick, J. (2004). A viewpoints approach to designing group based applications. *Design, Analysis, and Simulation of Distributed Systems 2004, Advanced Simulation Technologies Conference,* Arlington, VA (pp. 83-93).

Blinov, M., & Patel, A. (2003). An application of the reference model for open distributed processing to electronic brokerage. *Computer Standards and Interfaces* (pp. 411-425). Elsevier Science.

CIO-Council. (1999). *Federal enterprise architecture framework* (Version 1.1). Retrieved from http://www.cio.gov/archive/fedarch1.pdf

Costa, C. A., Harding, J. A., & Young, R. I. M. (2001). The application of UML and an open distributed process framework to information system design. *Computers in Industry* (pp. 33-48). Elsevier Science.

D. Frankel Consulting. (2003). *Applying EDOC and MDA to the RM-ODP engineering and technology viewpoints: An architectural perspective* (Vol. 01-00).

e-mayor, C. (2004). Sixth framework programme—*Electronic and secure municipal administration for European citizens—E-mayor* (IST-2004-507217). Retrieved from www.emayor.org

e-mayor consortium. (2004). Deliverable D2.1: Municipal services—Analysis, requirements, and usage scenarios. *E-mayor project* (IST-2004-507217). Retrieved from www.emayor.org

German Federal Ministry of Interior. (2003). *SAGA—Standards and Architectures for e-government Applications* (Version 2.0).

ITU-T. (1996-98). *Reference Model for Open Distributed Processing—Part 1: Overview, Part 2 Foundations, Part 3 Architecture. ITU-T Rec. X.901 | ISO/ IEC 10746 - 1,2,3.*

Kalontzoglou, A., Sklavos, P., Karantjias, T., & Polemi, D. (2004). A secure e-government platform architecture for small- to medium-sized public organizations. *Electronic Commerce Research & Applications*, 4(2), 174-186. Elsevier Science.

Copyright © 2007, Idea Group Inc. Copying or distributing in print or electronic forms without written permission of Idea Group Inc. is prohibited.

Kande, M., Mazaher, S., Prnjat, O., Sacks, L., & Wittig, M. (2004). *Applying UML to design an inter-domain service management application* (LNCS 1618, pp. 200-214). Springer-Verlag GmbH.

Kruchten, P. (1995, November). The 4+1 view model of architecture. *IEEE Software, 12*(6), 42-50.

Meneklis, B., Kaliontzoglou, A., Polemi, D., & Douligeris, C. (2005, March 2-4). Applying the ISO RM-ODP standard in e-government. *E-government: Towards Electronic Democracy: International Conference, TCGOV 2005, Proceedings,* Bolzano, Italy (LNCS 3416/2005, pp. 213). Springer-Verlag GmbH.

Nankman, M. A., & Nieuwenhuis, L. J. M. (1996). Specification of a distributed storage system. *Computer Communications* (pp. 30-38). Elsevier Science.

National Electronic Commerce Coordinating Council (NECCC). (2004). *mGovernment: The convergence of wireless technologies and e-government.* Retrieved from http://www.ec3.org/Downloads/2001/m-Government_ED.pdf

OMG. (2004). *Common Object Request Broker Architecture (CORBA) Specifications 3.0.3.* Retrieved from http://www.omg.org

OMG. (2004). *The Unified Modeling Language (UML) 2.0.* Retrieved from http://www.uml.org/

Tang, A., Han, J., & Chen, P. (2004). A comparative analysis of architecture frameworks. *Swinburne University of Technology SUTIT-TR2004.*

The Open Group. (1997). *Distributed computing environment 1.2.2.* Retrieved from http://www.osf.org

The Open Group. (2003). *The open group architecture framework* (Version 8.1 Enterprise Edition). Retrieved from http://www.opengroup.org/architecture/togaf/#download

Traore, I., Aredo, D., Ye, H. (2004). An integrated framework for formal development of open distributed systems. In *Information and Software Technology* (pp. 281-286). Elsevier Science.

U.S. Department of Defense. (2003). *Department of defense architecture framework Version 1.0* (Vol. 1). *Definition & guideline and volume 2 product descriptions.* Retrieved from http://www.aitcnet.org/dodfw

Zachman, J. (1987). A framework for information architecture. *IBM Systems Journal, 26*(3), 276.

Copyright © 2007, Idea Group Inc. Copying or distributing in print or electronic forms without written permission of Idea Group Inc. is prohibited.

Chapter XVI

Towards Building
E-Government on the Grid

Ying Li, Shanghai Jiao Tong University and Soochow University, China

Yue Chen, Soochow University, China

Minglu Li, Shanghai Jiao Tong University, China

ABSTRACT

This chapter introduces the goal of ShanghaiGrid and its sub-project e-government on the grid. It first presents the main achievements of the e-government in Shanghai, points out that one of problems of the e-government is how to integrate each government agency's resources to form cross-agency services for citizens, and argues why grid technique is an ideal way to solve that problem: grid can enable municipal government to integrate its information resources dispersed in different organizations in secure way with open standards and strengthen collaboration and information sharing. Then it gives a conceptual framework of e-government on the grid. Based on the GT3 core services, some core middlewares are developed to support the e-government infrastructure (i.e., workflow, transaction). OGSA-DAI is used to integrate data from different government agencies. The real-name citizen mailbox along with the MyProxy is the basic authentication method used in e-government.

Copyright © 2007, Idea Group Inc. Copying or distributing in print or electronic forms without written permission of Idea Group Inc. is prohibited.

BACKGROUND

Shanghai is a municipality of eastern China at the mouth of the Yangtze River. Today, it has become the largest economic center and important port city in China, with a land area covering 6,340 square kilometers and a population of 16 million people. Household PC penetration rate reached 70% and the Internet subscriber rate reached 47% in 2004. It is the entrepreneur city of the 2010 Shanghai World Expo. The municipal government is working toward building Shanghai into a modern metropolis and into a world economic, financial, trading, and shipping center by 2020. It has always been paying attention to the development and establishment of information industry and society. ShanghaiGrid is a long-term project sponsored by the Science and Technology Commission of Shanghai Municipality. It aims to construct a metropolitan-area Information Services Grid (ISG) and establish an open standard for widespread upper-layer applications from both communities and the government.

With the development of Information Technique, the e-government in Shanghai is rapidly developing and steps into the period of interactive government administration. The main achievements in official publication are listed below (Shanghai, 2005):

- The e-government network platform has been basically established. The public affairs network mainly transmits confidential information and connects 300 government agencies. The external network, mainly operating governmental general management and services, has been currently connected to 19 districts and counties and 72 municipal government agencies. Shanghai Public Affairs Network has been established and put into operation.
- The government's portal Web site of Shanghai-China (http://www.shanghai. gov.cn) as shown in Figure 1 offers 2379 forms in 707 service items, which can be downloaded via the portal. The daily portal visits reached 180,000 times in 2003 and 340,000 times in 2004. Users can personalize their portal and subscribe the information they want.
- Four major databases (population, legal identity, geographical information, and macro-economics) have taken shape and been put into use.

Although Shanghai's e-government is at the one of the top positions in China, it still has some weakness.

Current e-government infrastructure can not effectively solve the problem of "isolated island of information." The portal Web site provides more than 700 services, but most of them only provide simple tasks in certain areas; cross-domain and cross-department services are rarely found. For the security and policy issue, the information and data can not be shared directly by each agency of the government, which leads to something that could be done online must be done manually through each department agency. In some situations, citizens may file more than ten different

Copyright © 2007, Idea Group Inc. Copying or distributing in print or electronic forms without written permission of Idea Group Inc. is prohibited.

Figure 1. Chinese simplified Shanghai e-government portal

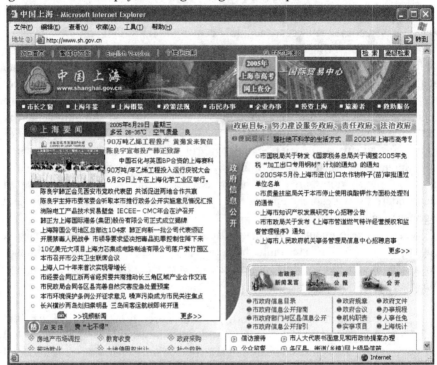

forms which download from the portal and manually hand in to several government agencies using the traditional approach, and each form contains similar data. The first reason that caused this situation from technique view is each government agency has it own database and for security and policy reasons, the data can not be shared directly from each other. That is what we call "isolated island of information." The second reason is the trust. How can the government agency identify that the one who filled out the form online is the right person?

The current Web portal service is citizen-centered, which means through the Web portal, and citizens can get the information they need and give feedback to the government. Using the Web portal simplified the delivery of services to citizens. However, the Web portal service now mainly serves individuals, the government-to-business and the government agency to agency should be further stressed. e-government is not just good for citizens-business benefits too. Like citizens, companies want governments to deliver information and services in an easier, cheaper, more accessible way (e-government, 2003).

So how to provide coordinated, seamless, and secure access to massive amounts of data held across various agencies in a government in heterogeneous environment is a big problem in developing e-government. Another problem is how to build a shared platform to deliver all kinds of services to the user in the city.

Copyright © 2007, Idea Group Inc. Copying or distributing in print or electronic forms without written permission of Idea Group Inc. is prohibited.

THE SHANGHAIGRID PROJECT

Grids offer us a new infrastructure and trend for the coordinated resources sharing, problem solving, and services orchestration in dynamic, multi-institutional, virtual organizations (Foster, Kesselman, Nick, & Tuecke, 2002). With the convergence of business and technology trends, grid computing is rapidly moving from its original home to High Performance Computing (HPC) and steps into the business-computing mainstream (Minerva, 2003).

The Shanghai city grid called ShanghaiGrid was put forward at the end of 2003 to enhance the digitalization of the city and faced challenges and captured the opportunities of grid by the science and technology commission of Shanghai municipality. The Participants are Shanghai Jiao Tong University, Tongji University, Fudan University, Shanghai University, Shanghai Supercomputer Center, Shanghai Transportation Information Center, East China Institute of Computer Technology, IBM, Intel, etc. Several other grand fundamental research projects such as NHPCE

Figure 2. ShanghaiGrid has connected several major gird nodes to form a 0.6 Tflops aggregate computing power and 4TB aggregate storage power sophisticated information environment, named ShanghaiGrid Testbed

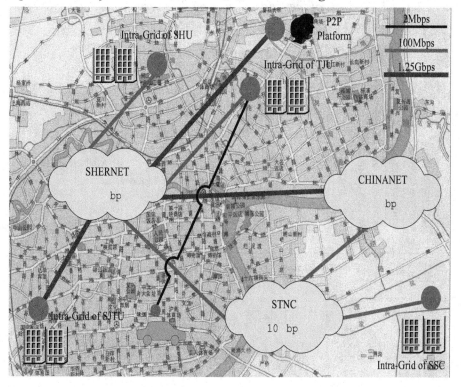

Copyright © 2007, Idea Group Inc. Copying or distributing in print or electronic forms without written permission of Idea Group Inc. is prohibited.

(1999-2001), CNGrid (2002-2006), ChinaGrid (2002-2005), eScience Grid (2002-2005), Spatial Information Grid (2001-2005), etc are also carried out in China (Li, 2003). Different from other grid projects in China that are designed mainly for scientific usage, the ShanghaiGrid focuses on information collections and services. Figure 2 shows the current main nodes of ShanghaiGrid.

The primary goal of ShanghaiGrid is to develop a set of system software for the information grid and establish an infrastructure for the grid-based applications. By means of flexible, secure, open standards sharing, and coordinating of computational resources, data information, and dedicated services among virtual organizations, this project will build an information grid tailored for the characteristics of Shanghai (Li, 2003).

The ShanghaiGrid project has several sub-projects, such as Consensus Forecast Grid, Remote Medical Service Grid, BioInfo Grid, and E-Government Grid. The potential services that ShanghaiGrid could provide are shown in Figure 3.

Figure 3. The different perspectives of ShanghaiGrid. For users, it is a set of grid services; for developers, it is GCE to facilitate the development of the grid services. Most of the grid services or Web services are designed for providing information and services to the public.

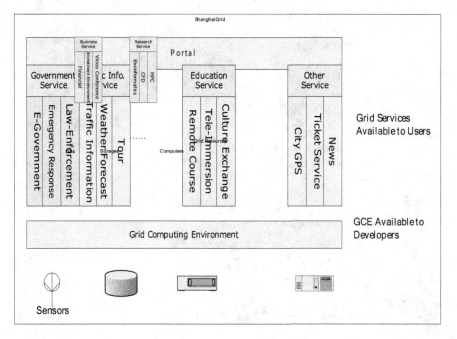

Copyright © 2007, Idea Group Inc. Copying or distributing in print or electronic forms without written permission of Idea Group Inc. is prohibited.

E-GOVERNMENT ON THE GRID

Why Use Grid Technique

With the rapid development of IT, we believe grid technology would enable the municipal government to integrate its information resources dispersed in different organizations and strengthen collaboration and information sharing. This will be invaluable for improving the efficiency of government and its emergency response speed. Currently, we build our ShanghaiGrid Operating System (SHOS) version 1.0 based on Globus Toolkit 3 (GT3) (Foster & Kesselman, 1997) which is the de facto standard in grid society as the basic infrastructure of the e-government. The main reasons that using the grid technique and GT3 are:

- Grid is an ideal way to resolve the problem of "isolated island of information." The real and specific problem that underlies the grid concept is coordinated resource sharing and problem solving in dynamic, multi-institutional virtual organizations (VO) (Foster et al., 2002). If we regard each government agency as an individual VO, then we can apply sophisticated method used in grid to coordinate each agency's resources which include databases, computational resources, storage resources, etc. Enabling integration of distributed resources is one of the important aspects in e-government.
- General-purposed, open-standard protocols are widely used in grid environment. For large distributed applications, it is one of the key issues.
- GT3 is open-source software to construct grid. Open-source is very important for the Government because government can really know what happens beneath the application, and it can be modified to meet the requirement of the e-government in which we have already designed a set of middleware to support the e-government applications. Moreover, GT3 provides good technical solutions for key problems such as authentication and authorization implemented as GSI (Foster et al., 1997), resource discovery and monitoring service implemented as MDS (Foster et al., 1997), access and integration of data from separate data sources implemented as OGSA-DAI (Antonioletti, 2005), and so on. These services and libraries lower the complexity and technical threshold in development e-government.
- Grid can provide super computational power. In most cases, e-government does not need such computational power, but in some emergency conditions such as terrorism attacks, nature disasters, and basic facility misfortune, on the one hand, we need real time data integration, on the other hand, we need super computational power to response these disasters quickly.

Copyright © 2007, Idea Group Inc. Copying or distributing in print or electronic forms without written permission of Idea Group Inc. is prohibited.

Figure 4. The conceptual framework of e-government on the grid

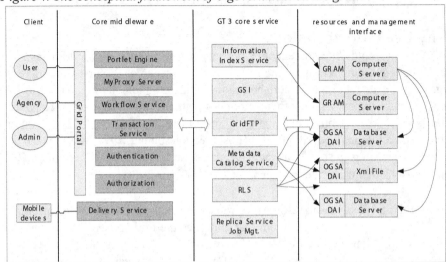

E-Government Conceptual Framework

The e-government project was launched in 2003 as a part of the ShanghaiGrid project. Currently we put focus on the design of the core middleware to support the e-government infrastructure. SHOS provides high-level services, middlewares, as well as developing tools, which we will discuss in the next section. The conceptual framework is shown in Figure 4.

IMPLEMENTATION OF CORE MIDDLEWARE

Workflow Service

First of all, we believe that workflow is very important for e-government. Workflow is defined as "The automation of a business process, in whole or in part, during which information or tasks are passed from one participant to another for action, according to a set of procedural rules" (Hollingsworth, 1995). Workflow has grown to be a primary method in managing process. A well pre-defined workflow can provide efficient and easy-to-use service for end users. Users do not need to know the process, only fill in information, and wait for results. All the processes are transparent for users.

Traditional workflow applications are widely used in government agencies. But they lack the ability of interoperation and rarely across agency. In grid environment, we can compose Web services or grid services distributed in various govern-

Copyright © 2007, Idea Group Inc. Copying or distributing in print or electronic forms without written permission of Idea Group Inc. is prohibited.

Figure 5. The framework of workflow middleware

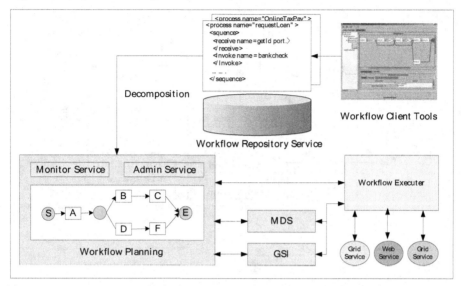

ment agencies into one workflow. Figure 5 shows the framework of the workflow management system. More detailed work could be found in Li et al. (2004). So far, workflows are composed by administrators using the existing grid services and Web services with Business Process Execution Language for Web Services (BPEL4WS) (Andrews, 2003). A set of client tools were developed to support that mission.

Transaction Support

In building reliable distributed applications, transaction is a fundamental concept. A transaction is a mechanism to insure all the participants in an application achieve a mutually agreed outcome (Gray, 1981). Traditionally, transactions have held ACID properties-Atomicity (executes entirely or not at all), Consistency (maintains the integrity of the data), Isolation (individual transactions run as if no other transactions are present), and Durability (the results are persistent) (Gray, 1981).

In grid environment, we also face the transaction problem. The coordination behavior provided by a traditional transaction mechanism can only suit for the short-lived transaction that performing stable state changes to the system, but fails to suite for structuring "long-lived" application functions, and has less capability to handle the coordination of multiple services. In order to solve that problem, we divide transactions into (1) Atomic transactions (AT). AT is used to coordinate activities having short-lived application and executed within limited trust domains. (2) Compensation transaction (CT). CT is used to coordinate activities having long-lived application. In order to improve the concurrency, a compensation model must be applied in CT.

Copyright © 2007, Idea Group Inc. Copying or distributing in print or electronic forms without written permission of Idea Group Inc. is prohibited.

Figure 6. Grid transaction framework

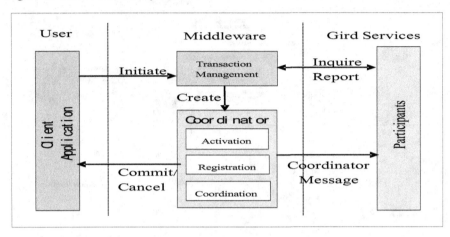

The transaction framework is shown in Figure 6 and the detail implementation of the transaction model can be found in (Tang, Li, Cao, & Deng, 2003).

Data Integration

In e-government, data are usually distributed in several government agencies, and they have different database engines, different front-ends systems, different operational systems, and are distributed in different physical locations. In order

Figure 7. The Data Proxy Server in e-government

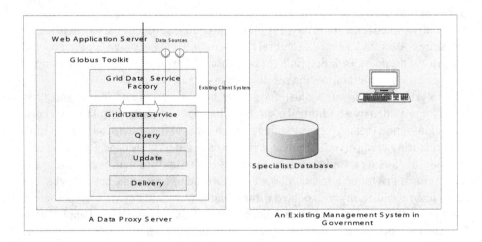

Copyright © 2007, Idea Group Inc. Copying or distributing in print or electronic forms without written permission of Idea Group Inc. is prohibited.

to integrate data and minimize the work of these systems, the Data Proxy Servers (DPSs) are placed in these systems to provide Grid Data Services using OGSA-DAI. Figure 7 shows the details.

DPS is used to provide the Data Service (DS) to query data from already existing systems using OGSA-DAI. The Grid Data Service Factory (GDSF) is a persistent grid service, while the Grid Data Service (GDS) is a transient grid Service, which means the client must indicate its lifetime. The GDSF is registered in the grid Information Service.

For every specialist database existing in the e-government, there are one or more corresponding data proxy servers providing a Grid Data Service (GDS) to other grid applications. The Grid Data Service Factory (GDSF) is a grid service used to create a new GDS for pre-defined data resources. The GDSF is a persistent grid service, which means GDSF service is automatically created when the container starts up. In that manner, data can be integrated using GDS.

Portal Tools

In the ShanghaiGrid e-government project, the grid environment provides information (news, forms, weather reports, traffic status, financial information, and so on) to the end users rather than providing computational power, storage resources, etc., which are the key activities in computational grid. Based on this, the aim and functionality of the e-government grid portal and computational grid portal is not quite the same. For example, the computational grid portal helps alleviate the complexity of task management through customizable and personalized graphical interfaces for the users (mainly scientists) and emphasizes the need for end users to have more domain knowledge than the specific details of grid-resource management, such as how to create a job, schedule and monitor its running in distributed resources, get the results, and so on. In contrast, the e-government grid portal helps the end us-

Figure 8. Portal Service

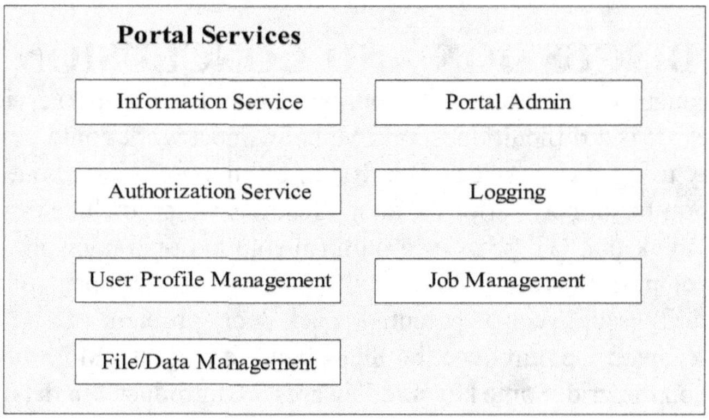

Copyright © 2007, Idea Group Inc. Copying or distributing in print or electronic forms without written permission of Idea Group Inc. is prohibited.

ers (mainly the people without much knowledge about computer science) get the information they want, such as long-term weather forecasts, financial analysis, and reports based on long-running, complex financial models, and some simple services like ticket selling and restaurant booking. The portal must shield the complexity of using such services and give the user the same experience when they access a grid portal as when they use a traditional WWW Portal. Figure 8 shows the main services in a portal.

Authentication and Authorization

Grid provides a common security infrastructure, but there still exists the problem of authentication: how we can justify ID with a real person?

The Real-Name Citizen Mailbox (RNCM) is now carried out by the Shanghai Government as well as the Real-Name Company Mailbox. Citizens in Shanghai can freely register a desired mailbox account, but he or she must go to a certain place set up by a government agency to fill in some forms. A government officer there will manually check the ID card to activate the mail account. Through this approach, government can use the mailbox account to identify a real person. The citizen can use his or her mailbox to receive bills, endowment insurance, Medicare, and other information. In the first ten days when this method was released, about 60,000 citizens registered and activated the mail account (Real-name, 2005). This is valuable information in e-government. In the future, if every person who registered the mailbox could get CA certification, many more applications could be applied in e-government. Currently, the user's mailbox account and password would be the basic authentication method for citizen. Although using a real-name mailbox is a good way to solve the problem of the citizens' identification, privacy issues must be taken into account. Investigation shows 100% of citizen's show interesting in the mailbox and about 50% of people consider the privacy issue (Real-name, 2005).

MyProxy (Novotny, Tuecke, & Welch, 2001) is used in grid environment as the repository storing grid credentials. The user who uses the portal user name and password could get certain grid credential through MyProxy.

DISCUSSION AND CONCLUSION

The frequently asked question about our model is why grid services and not Web services? It is a difficult question. We know most work could be done in the same way by using Web services. But first of all, the project is about developing a grid platform to support various grid applications which include e-government. Second, we think that GT gives us a uniform solution or framework to meet the needs of developing such applications and we can use a set of open-source projects to avoid security issues such as potential "back door" problem.

In this chapter, we introduce the ShanghaiGrid project and its sub-project e-government on the grid. Some key middlewares are introduced in detail. Although

Copyright © 2007, Idea Group Inc. Copying or distributing in print or electronic forms without written permission of Idea Group Inc. is prohibited.

grid technique and the de facto standard Globus toolkit are developing quickly, we hold the confidence that grid technique is an ideal way to build large distributed applications. A real-name citizen mailbox is introduced to solve the problem of how to identify real person with his/her electric id. The e-government project is ongoing project which we put much work on the common middleware currently that could be applied in ShanghaiGrid environment as well as e-government project.

ACKNOWLEDGMENT

This work is partly supported by 973 project (No.2002CB312002) of China, grand project (No.03dz15027), and key project (No.025115033) of the Science and Technology Commission of Shanghai Municipality. This is the developer view, not the official document of the ShanghaiGrid and e-government on the grid.

REFERENCES

Andrews, T., et al. (2003). *Business process execution language for Web services* (Version 1.1). Retrieved October 11, 2005, from http://www-128.ibm.com/developerworks/library/specification/ws-bpel/

Antonioletti, M., et al. (2005). The design and implementation of grid database services in OGSA-DAI. *Computation: Practice and Experience, 17*(2-4), 357-376.

E-Government Strategy. (2003). Retrieved October 11, 2005, fromhttp://www.whitehouse.gov/omb/egov/documents/e-gov_strategy.pdf

Foster, I., & Kesselman, C. (1997). Globus: Ametacomputing infrastructure toolkit. *International Journal of Supercomputer Applications, 11*(2), 115-128.

Foster, I., Kesselman, C., Nick, J., & Tuecke, S. (2002). Grid services for distributed system integration. *Computer, 35*(6), 37-46.

Gray, J. N. (1981). The transaction concept: Virtues and limitations. In *Proceedings of the 7th VLDB Conference* (pp. 144-154).

Hollingsworth, D. (1995). *Workflow management coalition the workflow reference model.* Retrieved October 11, 2005, from http://www.aiim.org/wfmc/standards/docs/tc003v11.pdf

Li, M. L. et al. (2003). ShanghaiGrid in action: The first stage projects toward digital city and city grid. In *Proceedings of Grid and Cooperative Computing: 2nd International Workshop (GCC 2003)* (LNCS 3032, pp. 616-623).

Li, Y., Li, M. L., Yu, J. D., & Cao, L. (2004). A workflow services middleware model on ShanghaiGrid. In *Proceedings of 2004 IEEE International Conference on Services Computing (SCC 2004)* (pp. 366-371).

Minerva, Y. (2003). Intel and grid computing. In *Proceedings of International Forum on Digital City and City Grid* (pp. 43-50).

Copyright © 2007, Idea Group Inc. Copying or distributing in print or electronic forms without written permission of Idea Group Inc. is prohibited.

Novotny, J., Tuecke, S., & Welch, V. (2001). An online credential repository for the grid: My Proxy. In *Proceedings of the 10th IEEE Symposium High-Performance Distributed Computing (HPDC-10)* (pp. 104-114).

Real-Name Citizen Mailbox Web Page. (n.d.). Retrieved October 11, 2005, from http://www.smmail.cn

Shanghai municipal informatization commission. (2005). *Briefing on the informatization progress in Shanghai.* Retrieved October 11, 2005, from http://www.shanghai.gov.cn/shanghai/node8059/

Tang, F. L., Li, M. L., Cao, J., & Deng, Q. N. (2003). Coordinating business transaction for grid service. In *Proceedings of Grid and Cooperative Computing: 2nd International Workshop (GCC 2003)* (LNCS 3032, pp. 108-114).

Copyright © 2007, Idea Group Inc. Copying or distributing in print or electronic forms without written permission of Idea Group Inc. is prohibited.

Chapter XVII

Service-Oriented Architecture for Seamless and Interoperable Service Delivery

Elena Mugellini, University of Applied Sciences
of Western Switzerland, Switzerland

Omar Abou Khaled, University of Applied Sciences
of Western Switzerland, Switzerland

Maria Chiara Pettenati, University of Florence, Italy

ABSTRACT

The delivery of seamless services is an essential feature of e-government applications. Offering seamless services presents several operational implications; a flexible and interoperable architecture is needed in order to provide some facilities to refer to, invoke, and combine e-government services in a standard way, within the context of cross-organizational workflows. This chapter presents an e-government architecture (E-GovSM) that eases the cooperation among applications of different government agencies in order to supply new added value services. Moreover, it promotes reuse of existing systems by integrating governmental legacy applications. The E-GovSM (e-government service marketplace) is a service-oriented architecture based on Web services and XML technology.

Copyright © 2007, Idea Group Inc. Copying or distributing in print or electronic forms without written permission of Idea Group Inc. is prohibited.

INTRODUCTION

One of the main e-government challenges is to facilitate citizen-public administration interaction enabling seamless services delivery to citizens through the Internet (European Commission, 2003). Regulations and administrative provisions fragment all aspects of the life of a citizen according to multiple sectors (i.e., taxation, health, etc.) (Contenti, Termini, Mecella, & Baldoni, 2003). This fragmentation often causes difficulties in delivering services to citizen; services result composed by several activities involving different agencies and frequently need to link and use data from multiple and diverse information resources. Therefore, in order to deliver seamless services to citizens, a strong collaboration and cooperation between administrations is required. Consequently, "interoperability" is the keyword to address e-government challenges. Interoperability is not only a technical issue dealing with distributed computing, but it deals also with information sharing among different administrations and the redesign of administrative processes to support more effective delivery of e-government services. Three level of interoperability are relevant to e-government issues: technical, semantic, and organizational (European Commission, 2003). The first one refers to the technical issue of connecting computer systems, defining common communication protocols, and data formats. The second one concerns the exchange of information in an understandable way even between applications that were not initially developed for this purpose. The third one refers to enabling processes cooperation. While interoperability requirements seem so obvious, today's reality is that information systems are not yet interoperable, different administrations are not able to share and reuse data or cooperate for fulfilling e-government challenges. An interoperability infrastructure is therefore at the heart of e-government applications (Office of the e-Envoy, 2003). This infrastructure has to enable cooperation among agencies and integration of legacy systems; it has to enable service reuse and composition in order to deliver ones that are more complex. To this extent, service-oriented architecture (SOA) is a new paradigm, which had been envisioned for a notion of environment where everybody provides some services for some others. Therefore, a service-oriented infrastructure is fundamental for reaching high levels of interoperability. Service-oriented architecture, by the means of Web services, can provide a standard and efficient communication means among different governmental agencies involved in providing integrated services as well as dynamic context-driven information to the citizen (i.e., services personalized according to the user, for instance, customers or employees, the device, laptops, PDAs, or smart phones, and different situations, for instance home, hotel, or office) (Sharma and Gupta, 2004). Driven by the convergence of key technologies and the universal adoption of Web services, the service-oriented e-government architecture promises to significantly improve agency flexibility and interoperability, reduce IT costs, improve operational efficiency, and facilitate inter-agency cooperation.

Copyright © 2007, Idea Group Inc. Copying or distributing in print or electronic forms without written permission of Idea Group Inc. is prohibited.

Figure 1. Trends converging to support seamless e-government service delivery

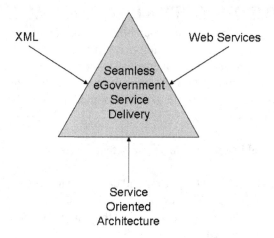

The E-Government Service Marketplace (E-GovSM) is based on a service-oriented architecture, which aims at exploiting benefits of this new paradigm in order to allow cooperation and integration among application of different agencies. The E-Government Service Marketplace facilitates the interaction between citizens and public administration by providing seamless services to citizens at transaction level (i.e., allowing the complete online handling of the service delivery process). The main design requirements upon which the E-GovSM architecture are based are the following:

- **Provide citizen-oriented services:** Provide services to citizens every time they need them, wherever they are, and in a personalized way
- **Ease public administration interoperability:** Allow integration of legacy systems and use a loosely coupled interaction among agencies by assembling on-demand Web services to automate e-government seamless service delivery
- **Respect the autonomy of the single administration:** For example, it doesn't oblige each single administration to deploy an instance of the proposed architecture by proposing an incremental integration approach
- Provide a single access point to government services via the Web, built around the citizens life events metaphor (Dipartimento per l'Innovazione e le Tecnologie, 2002) to hide the complexity of administrative process
- Perform the necessary operations for collecting the information to deliver government services instead of the citizen.

Copyright © 2007, Idea Group Inc. Copying or distributing in print or electronic forms without written permission of Idea Group Inc. is prohibited.

SERVICE-ORIENTED
ARCHITECTURE BACKGROUND

As previously stated, an interoperability infrastructure is at the heart of e-government. The main issue of an interoperability framework is the integration of a wide variety of legacy and heterogeneous systems. Service-oriented architecture enables process level integration allowing automatic communication among heterogeneous systems. A service-oriented development has the following advantages (Newcomer & Lomow, 2004):

- **Reuse:** The ability to create services that are reusable in multiple applications.
- **Efficiency:** The ability to quickly and easily create new services and new applications using a combination of new and old services, along with the ability to focus on the data to be shared rather than the implementation underneath.
- **Loose technology coupling:** The ability to model services independently of their execution environment and create messages that can be sent to any service.
- **Division of responsibility:** The ability to more easily allow business people to concentrate on business issues, technical people to concentrate on technology issues, and for both groups to collaborate using the service contract.

A SOA is a way to define and provide an IT infrastructure to allow different applications to exchange data and participate in business processes, regardless of the operating systems or programming languages underlying those applications. A SOA can be thought of as an approach to building IT systems in which services (i.e., the services that an organization provides to citizens, partners, employees, and other organizations) are the key organizing principle used to align IT heterogeneous systems thus allowing interoperability among different agencies and legacy systems.

SOA model isolates aspects of an application so that, as technology changes, services can be independently updated, limiting the impact of changes. A shift toward service-oriented architecture not only standardizes interactions, but also allows for more flexibility in the process (for instance the complete e-government service is divided into small functional units, provided by different and diverse administrations which are easily combined and composed in order to seamless deliver the final service). Moreover, a service-oriented architecture provides a standard way of describing distributed services belonging to multiple agencies thus supporting their dynamic, automated discovery, composition, and use.

A service-oriented approach allows existing governmental processes abstracting services from the various departments and orchestrating them together without requiring knowledge of department structural and functional organization (for instance one department will not worry about how another organizes their internal

Copyright © 2007, Idea Group Inc. Copying or distributing in print or electronic forms without written permission of Idea Group Inc. is prohibited.

operations). Hence, this approach is particularly suited to the development and delivery of seamless interoperable e-government services at national as well as European levels.

Service-oriented architectures have been in use for many years (CORBA as an example). However, SOA on the foundation of Web services constitutes a new era of developing business solutions (Newcomer & Lomow, 2004). So even if the idea of separating a service interface from its implementation has already been well proven (CORBA, COM, etc.), the ability to more cleanly and completely separate a service description from its execution environment is a new challenge. This ability is part of what Web concepts and technologies bring to Web services. Such a loose coupling has negative implication on system performance (in terms of service response time, execution time, etc.). However, in many cases, such as in the e-business domain, performance issues are less important than the ability to more easily achieve interoperability or easily develop more complex services by composing already existing services (Newcomer & Lomow, 2004). This is exactly the case of e-government (Castellano, Pastore, Arcieri, Summo, & Bellone de Grecis, 2005; McGibbon, 2005) were usually the delivery of service requires to link and use data from multiple and diverse information resources (agencies) as well as use common government services (such as citizen address lookup, zip code validation, etc.), with no strict requirements in term of performance.

SOA implementation key technologies are WS (Web services) and XML (eXtensible Markup Language). The major advantages of implementing an SOA using Web services are that Web services are pervasive, simple, and platform-neutral. The core Web services architecture consists of specifications (SOAP, WSDL, and UDDI) that support the interaction of a Web service requester with a Web service provider and the potential discovery of the Web service description (Kreger, 2001). Besides the core Web services specifications, a wide array of extended Web services specifications for security, reliability, transactions, metadata management, and orchestration are well on their way toward standardization exist. This provides SOA-based solutions with the necessary inter-organization-level qualities of service to support a wide variety of complex and composite multi-agency cooperations.

XML is another key technology that ensures data flow interoperability between heterogeneous systems and agencies. XML is considered the best way to exchange information; its global consensus is due to the fact that unlike other formats, humans can read it, all computer systems can be modified to understand it, and it can contain not only raw data, but information about what the data means through embedded data-description tags (Daum & Merten, 2002). Using XML representations of the data as the basis for e-government communications is therefore becoming a standard approach. We would go further and suggest that XML representations of processes, services, and documents become the cornerstone of e-government integration strategy because it is:

Copyright © 2007, Idea Group Inc. Copying or distributing in print or electronic forms without written permission of Idea Group Inc. is prohibited.

- **Open:** It is not owned by any organization
- **Transparent:** It can be read by any computer or person
- **Responsive:** New tags can be added as necessary to describe new types of data

XML is therefore the ideal way to model not only the data, but also the communication between the multitude of systems and agencies that participate in e-government. Based on the previous analysis, it clearly appears that features and advantages offered by service-oriented architecture (on the foundation of Web services and XML technology) fit with the requirements and needs of the e-government domain, thus representing a suitable solution for implementing a system for seamless service delivery. According to the design requirements previously introduced (see Introduction paragraph), service-oriented architectures ease public administration interoperability by integrating legacy systems, respecting agencies autonomy by not requiring them to implement an instance of the architecture, allowing them to provide a single access point to services via the Web, as well as performing the operations necessary for the delivery of the final service to the citizen.

THE E-GOVERNMENT SERVICE MARKETPLACE CONCEPT

The E-GovSM's (Mugellini, Abou Khaled, Pettenati, & Kuonen, 2005) main purpose is to provide quality citizen-oriented services facilitating citizen to public administration interaction. As it happens, in a traditional marketplace where a citizen can buy the products he or she needs without caring about production and delivery process, the e-government marketplace aims at providing e-government services to citizens without requiring the citizen to be aware of administrative process complexity. For instance, for the delivery of a document, citizens will not be concerned with administration responsibility or geographical location of information. The E-GovSM purpose is not only to use technologies to increase the efficiency of administrative process. It also aims to make it easier for citizens to interact with public administrations rebalancing relations between citizens and administrations, and presenting e-government services according to citizen needs. For this reason the E-Government Service Marketplace aggregates services according to "life event metaphor" (Dipartimento per l'Innovazione e le Tecnologie, 2002; Life Event Portal), for example, services are organized around events that make sense for the citizen and the citizen doesn't need to be aware of various public administrations involved in the delivery of such services. The life of citizens is described by providing a list of events that when occurring in citizen life, result in a series of transactions between a citizen and different public sector organizations. Examples of life events are "looking for a job," "moving home," "learning to drive," "pensions and retirement," "having a baby," and so on.

Copyright © 2007, Idea Group Inc. Copying or distributing in print or electronic forms without written permission of Idea Group Inc. is prohibited.

The marketplace concept of service refers to the communication, either transmission or reception, of a document, either an official document (well-structured information) or "raw" information (not structured information). When a citizen requests a service, the marketplace translates the requested service (expressed according to the life-event metaphor) into the corresponding administrative (or business) process and executes this process to deliver the document to the citizen. In order to allow the marketplace to interact with a public administration, it is necessary that this administration subscribes to the E-GovSM. Each administration wanting to join the marketplace has to subscribe to it, declaring its availability to provide services and share data with the marketplace. In order to respect public administrations autonomy the marketplace offers four different subscription profiles (see subsection "Service Manager").

Figures 2 shows the entities involved in the marketplace and possible interactions between them. From the one hand, citizens access the marketplace via a portal, from the other hand, public administrations subscribe to the marketplace in order to share data and provide services. The figure highlights three different types of public administrations (PAs). PAs of "type A" represent administrations subscribed to the E-GovSM that automatically provide data to the marketplace without requiring the citizen to interact with them. PAs of "type B" represent administrations subscribed to the E-GovSM that, even if can automatically provide data to the marketplace, require a direct interaction with citizens (for example a hospital in case of a medical examination). Finally, PAs of "type C" represent administrations that are not subscribed to the E-GovSM and hence require a direct interaction with citizens to provide data.

Figure 2. E-government service marketplace-involved entities and interactions among them

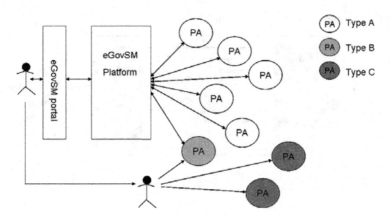

Copyright © 2007, Idea Group Inc. Copying or distributing in print or electronic forms without written permission of Idea Group Inc. is prohibited.

The E-GovSM is formalized using a set of XML Schema models (World Wide Web Consortium, 2004). This allows us to create an interoperable and open system. Public administration sector is a continuously changing world: public administration organization, responsibility, and services are always in evolution. For this reason, the design and development of an e-government system based on a set of formal models makes the system architecture more flexible and easier to extend in order to fulfill new public administration needs and requirements.

THE E-GOVSM ARCHITECTURE

General Overview

The overall E-GovSM architecture is shown in Figure 3. The platform is based on four core components: the UNIversal CITizen IDentifier Manager (UNICITIDM), the Life Event Manager (LEM), the Document Manager (DM), and the Service Manager (SM). The UNICITIDM component creates and manages citizens' identifiers. The LEM component manages marketplace services creation and presentation to citizens and all the interactions with citizens. The DM component coordinates the execution of the administrative process. The SM component manages all the marketplace interactions with public administrations in order to retrieve the required data to deliver a specific service.

UNIversal CITizen IDentifier Manager

The UNIversal CITizen IDentifier Manager (UNICITIDM) is the module responsible for managing citizen identifier (UNICITID). The UNICITID is an identifier containing citizen personal information; it is unique and not variable. Its purpose is to allow E-GovSM to find out the administrations responsible for citizen personal

Figure 3. Overview of E-GovSM Architecture

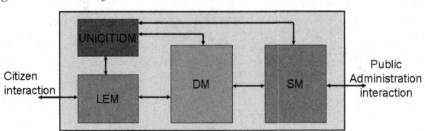

Copyright © 2007, Idea Group Inc. Copying or distributing in print or electronic forms without written permission of Idea Group Inc. is prohibited.

data. It is worth noting that the UNICITID is not for security and privacy issues, it is used by the system only to retrieve information. In order to provide a secure access to the E-GovSM, the citizen will use an electronic card, as in the home banking procedure, that will provide the citizen with a random identifier valid only for that particular session. Once the citizen is securely connected to the E-GovSM system, in order to ask for a service he or she will have to provide his or her UNICITID. While the validity of random identifier is one session (it expires when the session ends), the UNICITID has no limited validity over time. The UNICITID has a URN-like (Uniform Resource Name) structure similar to the one defined in the NIR Project (NIR Web site; Biagioli, Francesconi, Spinosa, & Taddei, 2003; Marchetti, Megale, Seta, & Vitali, 2002) that allows identifying citizens of any country by providing a uniform, but adaptable, schema for defining country-specific identifier structure. The UNICITID is created the first time a citizen access the E-GovSM platform and it is used only by the marketplace, remaining transparent to the citizen. The E-GovSM provides only the basic structure of this identifier allowing administrations of different countries to extend and to adapt it according to their specific needs. As a consequence, each E-GovSM is able to interpret only identifiers coming from its country, but, thanks to the country identifier contained in every UNICITID, it can identify the E-GovSM platform capable of managing a foreign identifier. The one that follows is an example of UNICITID:

- it:it:rossi.luca:1960-04-08:it.toscana.firenze:codicefiscale

The first field indicates the country responsible for the identifier (in this case "it"= Italy) and it is common for all the identifiers while the last one ("codicefiscale") represents a country-specific information. The E-GovSM in order to retrieve, for instance, citizen address uses the birthplace information "it.toscana.firenze" and starts contacting administrations of "firenze," then of "toscana" and so on, until it finds the searched information.

Life Event Manager

The Life Event Manager (LEM) is the manager of all the interactions of a citizen with the marketplace (Figure 4). It is the E-GovSM component that presents available services to citizen and manages citizen service requests.

The LEM is responsible for creating, publishing, and updating life events list in order to provide citizens with up-to-date and a personalized list of available services in the marketplace. LEM is also responsible for citizen subscription and authentication as well as citizen service request management. When the E-GovSM receives the citizen request, the LEM retrieves the Process Descriptor associated to the requested service. The Process Descriptor (PD) specifies the administrative process corresponding to the requested service; it describes the constraints to satisfy and the operations to do in order to deliver the service. As the E-GovSM provides

Copyright © 2007, Idea Group Inc. Copying or distributing in print or electronic forms without written permission of Idea Group Inc. is prohibited.

any kind of government services (from applying for a driving licence to filing a tax return) and each service has its own prerequisites and routing cycle, the marketplace has to be told which are the actions to perform to deliver a specific service. For this reason, a Process Descriptor is associated with each service provided by the marketplace, and depending on the citizen who is requesting it (where he lives, which are the administrations responsible to deliver the document), the number, and the type of operations to do, for the service delivery, could vary. When the requested service concerns the delivery of an official document (that is a document with a well-defined structure like a certificate), associated to the Process Descriptor there will be also a Document Descriptor. The Document Descriptor (DD) specifies the structure of this official document (i.e., the data it contains constrains associated to that data and the way the data have to be aggregated in order to generate the document).

Finally, the LEM tracks the process executed by the Document Manager in order to inform the citizen about the necessary time required to complete the service. For example, let consider that the citizen selects the service "getting your driving license." The LEM has to retrieve the Process Descriptor and Document Descriptor associated to this service. The Process Descriptor contains all the steps to be followed and the order in which they have to be executed to deliver the driving license document. For example it establishes that before collecting the data and delivering the document to the citizen, the system has to check if the citizen has or has had problems with law, or if he or she has already passed the medical examina-

Figure 4. Interaction between UNICITIDM and LEM modules

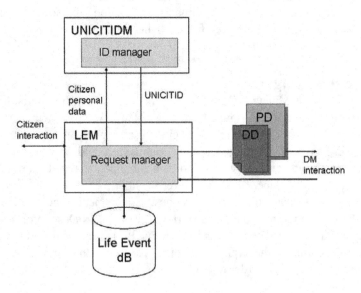

Copyright © 2007, Idea Group Inc. Copying or distributing in print or electronic forms without written permission of Idea Group Inc. is prohibited.

tion to obtain the driving license. The Document Descriptor defines the structure of the driving license document. It describes which information it is necessary to retrieve, how it has to be aggregated in order to create the document and which are the constraints associated to this information (e.g., check the validity period of the document against the citizen age).

The use of XML technologies makes the LEM module more flexible and easy to maintain (for instance adding a new life events or services requires no changes to the system but the insertion of the new element). Moreover, it can easily adapt to different citizen profiles. For instance, user interface design principles are specified in an XSL style sheet file that can automatically generate personalized user interface from the application's data model represented as XML Schemas. Thus, custom views of information for different users, devices, or contexts can be created with different style sheets without requiring modifying the system logic.

Document Manager

The Document Manager (DM) is the component responsible for administrative process execution (Figure 5).

The DM main purpose is the management and coordination of all the operations necessary to collect the required data and to deliver the document the citizen has requested. In order to do this, it uses the Process Descriptor and Document Descriptor retrieved by the LEM. The DM work is subdivided into two phases: in the first one it has to verify the fulfilment of prerequisites associated to the service while, in the second one, it has to coordinate all the operations to retrieve the necessary data. Finally, DM uses a repository to register information regarding the process execution status. In case of a process interruption, due to logical or technical reasons, the system will be able to continue and finish the process later on.

Service Manager

The Service Manager (SM) is the coordinator and manager of all the marketplace interactions with public administrations (Figure 6), providing DM with a uniform access to the heterogeneous public administration information systems.

SM also has to manage public administrations subscription to the E-GovSM. In order to allow public administrations to subscribe according to their capabilities it provides four subscription profiles. The basic profile ("Level0") refers to administrations that are not able to provide electronic data. The "Level1" profile refers to administrations that can provide elementary electronic functionalities (they are able to respond to yes/no questions). The "Level2" profile refers to administrations that are able to provide a richer set of functionalities (they can provide the marketplace with information or documents). The "Level3" profile refers to administrations that implement an instance of the E-GovSM system. In the last case, the administration

Copyright © 2007, Idea Group Inc. Copying or distributing in print or electronic forms without written permission of Idea Group Inc. is prohibited.

Figure 5. DM module. Modeling DM module with XML Schema technology allows expressing relations between different data thus allowing checking for data coherency and correctness.

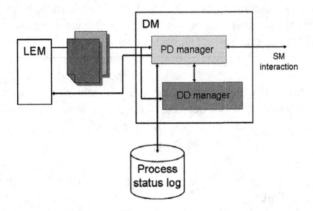

Figure 6. SM module

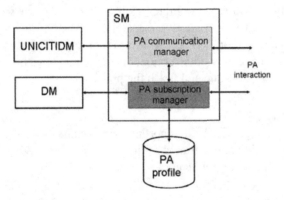

information system is fully E-GovSM-compliant and it is able to provide the same functionalities of the E-GovSM system. This will enable future collaborations among E-GovSM platforms of different countries or among administrations that will decide (without being obliged) to deploy their own E-GovSM instance.

Copyright © 2007, Idea Group Inc. Copying or distributing in print or electronic forms without written permission of Idea Group Inc. is prohibited.

EGovSM PROTOTYPE DEVELOPMENT

The validation of the whole concept of E-Government Service Marketplace has been done with the deployment of a prototype. The E-GovSM Prototype aims at testing and validating the concept of the E-Government Service Marketplace as a common virtual place where services are provided to citizens so as to hide structural and functional fragmentation of public administrations, enabling seamless service delivery at transaction level. The functioning of the prototype is further illustrated with a case study.

Implementation Choices

The prototype development is based on a .NET platform (Sharp and Jagger, 2003). The choice of such kind of platform (.NET or J2EE) is dictated by the many offered facilities, for instance the rapidity of development process thanks to the set of provided APIs and high configurability possibilities (system issues, database access, security constraints, etc). Moreover, these platforms are based on the use of XML technologies, which offers a high degree of interoperability. Finally, both the platforms fully support Web services technology, which represents the future of distributed developing approach. Our choice of using .NET platform was motivated by the following additional features:

- Support of the Office suite largely used in administrations, which facilitates administrations interaction with E-GovSM system
- Support of multi-language. NET platform supports up to 20 different languages allowing the integration of already developed applications by different public administrations
- Inclusion of a full API for the treatment of XML Schemas which eases the integration of our XML Schema models
- Easy support of the deployment of applications compliant with .NET specifications and support for implementation on Linux, "Mono" project (Mono Web site), as well as Windows operating system

E-GovSM Citizen Interface

A snapshot of the E-Government Service Marketplace Portal is illustrated in Figure 7. As shown, the interface is divided into three main parts:

- The first one on top of the page (Figure 7, reference 1) provides the service research by keywords and access policy management functionalities
- the second part (Figure 7, reference 2) provides the complete marketplace life events list, its main purpose is to help citizen navigation in the marketplace
- The third part (Figure 7, reference 3) is the principal one and it is used by

Copyright © 2007, Idea Group Inc. Copying or distributing in print or electronic forms without written permission of Idea Group Inc. is prohibited.

the citizen to search a service, obtain detailed service information, ask for a service and obtain information on ongoing service requests

It is worth noting that even if the current version of E-GovSM Portal is in French, thanks to the system modeling with XML technologies, multilingualism can be easily supported. Moreover, the system is highly flexible and easy extensible. Inserting additional life events or services, for example adding the "wedding" life event, doesn't require redeveloping the application, but it requires adding the information concerning the new life event in the database respecting the XML Schema specification and the new life event will be automatically included in the E-Government Service Marketplace and displayed on the portal.

In order to obtain a service, a citizen needs to subscribe to the E-GovSM (i.e., he or she has to provide some personal data by filling in the proper subscription form) (Figure 8). The system creates the UNICITID using these data and delivers the identifier to the citizen.

The citizen, using this identifier, can connect to the E-GovSM and ask for a service.

If a citizen doesn't subscribe to the E-GovSM, he or she can only navigate into the marketplace and access to service information but he or she cannot ask for a service (the "obtenir le service" command is disabled, see Figure 12, reference 3).

In order to facilitate citizen navigation in the E-GovSM, just below the search-by-keyword functionality the navigation path is displayed, making it easier for a citizen to "orientate" him/herself in the marketplace (see Figure 12, reference 1).

Figure 7. Access interface of E-GovSM portal

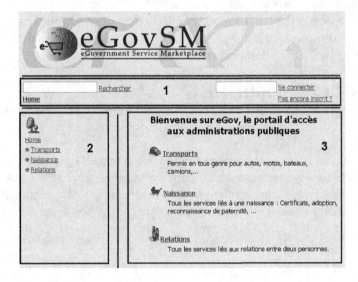

Copyright © 2007, Idea Group Inc. Copying or distributing in print or electronic forms without written permission of Idea Group Inc. is prohibited.

Figure 8. Example of citizen subscription application form

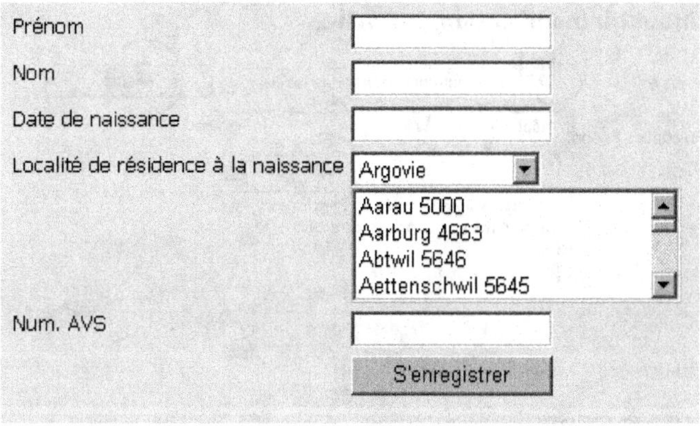

Process and Document Descriptor Creation

Figure 9 shows the Process Description creation interface. For each task or simple service ("Tâche," reference 1 in Figure 9) the following information is provided:

- The administration responsible for providing such simple service (number 3).
- The information required and constraints associated to the simple service (number 5 and 6).
- A textual description of the simple service (number 4).

Figure 10 shows the Document Descriptor creation interface. This interface allows editing the structure of a document, by inserting which information it has to include with the respective associated constraints (number 2 and 3 in Figure).

The Case of Provisional Driving Licence Delivery

To further illustrate the application of the developed framework, we used it to apply the concept of E-Government Service Marketplace for the delivery of a Provisional Driving License ("permis provisoire de voitures" in Figure 12). The case study is summarized to illustrate the main features of the framework and should not be considered as the complete and exhaustive presentation of E-Government Service Marketplace functional model. For any kind of government service, there are a plethora of official forms that citizens are requested to fill in; moreover, each form has its own prerequisites and routing cycle, each with its own fees. As a result, a simple service such as the delivery of Provisional Driving License becomes

Copyright © 2007, Idea Group Inc. Copying or distributing in print or electronic forms without written permission of Idea Group Inc. is prohibited.

Figure 9. Creation of process descriptor

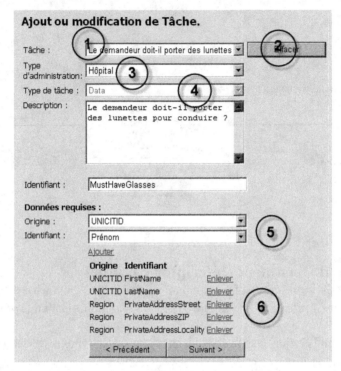

quite a complicated and time-expensive task requiring citizens to move to several governmental agencies, providing the same information multiple times.

The Provisional Driving License (named "Foglio Rosa" in Italian) is a document issued by the Department of Motor Vehicles (responsible for delivering all services pertaining to driving licenses and vehicles) that allows you to take driving lessons on the road for a six month-period. After you have been issued the Provisional Driving License, you have to pass the Final Driving Theory and Practical Driving Test to obtain the Full Driving License. The delivery of the Provisional Driving License has some conditions attached to it:

- The citizen must be 18 years old and over
- The citizen must exhibit an identity card or a passport
- The citizen must hold "moral requirements" (e.g., not to be a criminal etc.)
- The citizen must provide a medical report (including an eyesight report)
- The citizen must pay the appropriate fees
- The citizen must provide two passport-type photographs

Copyright © 2007, Idea Group Inc. Copying or distributing in print or electronic forms without written permission of Idea Group Inc. is prohibited.

Figure 10. Creation of Document Descriptor

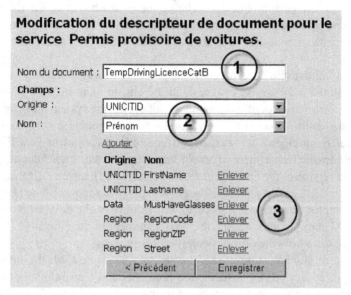

Modification du descripteur de document pour le service Permis provisoire de voitures.

Nom du document : TempDrivingLicenceCatB **1**

Champs :

Origine : UNICITID

Nom : Prénom **2**

Ajouter

Origine	Nom	
UNICITID	FirstName	Enlever
UNICITID	Lastname	Enlever
Data	MustHaveGlasses	Enlever
Region	RegionCode	Enlever
Region	RegionZIP	Enlever
Region	Street	Enlever

3

< Précédent   Enregistrer

The traditional procedure for the delivery of such service requires the citizen to go to the postal office to pay the fees, to the hospital for medical check-up, to get photos taken, and eventually go to the department of motor vehicles with all the previously collected documents and information to obtain a document ("Foglio Bianco") that allows the candidate to drive while waiting for the delivery of the Provisional Driving License. Once moral requirements are checked and confirmed, the Provisional Driving License is issued and delivered to the citizen (who has to go to the Department of Motor Vehicles again). The E-GovSM allows easing the whole procedure by reducing interaction between citizen and agencies and providing this service as a unique transaction to the citizen. Case handling, decision, and delivery of the requested service are completely treated by E-GovSM via the Web by integrating participating agencies (hospital, postal office, department of motor vehicles, and so on). The citizen wishing to apply for a Provisional Driving License accesses the E-GovSM via the portal and applies for the service ("Obtenir le service" in Figure 12). Figure 11 shows how the request is handled by the E-GovSM. The E-GovSM, as first step, retrieves the document

("Process Descriptor") describing the entire process of Provisional Driving License from a dedicated registry. This document describes in a machine-readable way, tasks and requirements that have to be executed and satisfied in order to deliver the service (for instance verifying whether the applying citizen is 18 years old or over or if he or she holds moral requirements).

Copyright © 2007, Idea Group Inc. Copying or distributing in print or electronic forms without written permission of Idea Group Inc. is prohibited.

By following the instructions contained in the Process Descriptor, E-GovSM checks whether the citizen is of age, whether he or she has done the medical examination, and paid the fees. If this is not the case, E-GovSM stops the process and informs the citizen about the requirements that have not been satisfied or missing information.

Public administrations involved in the process of service delivery are located by processing the information contained in the citizen identifier (for instance the "birthplace" information contained in the identifier tells the system the origin region of the citizen and allows focusing information search on specific governmental agencies). Once all requirements are satisfied and required tasks performed, the E-GovSM system provides the Department of Motor Vehicles with the "logic" document (i.e., an electronic version of the final document to be delivered); meanwhile the citizen is informed by the E-GovSM about the progress of his or her request. The Department of Motor Vehicles now only has to check the validity of the document, to inform the E-GovSM about it, and to issue the final document to the citizen.

Now let's see how the citizen perceives this process.

Once he or she has submitted hi or her service request, all the information concerning such service (for instance requirements and constraints associated to the delivery of such service) is provided to the citizen (Figure 12, reference 2). Once the service has been requested, the citizen is informed about service delivery progress (Figure 13).

The "checked" icon (Figure 13, reference 1) informs the citizen that the specific task has been successfully completed, while the "hourglass" icon (Figure 13, reference 2) informs him or her that the system has not completed the task yet. Two other possibilities are envisaged: a "cross" icon meaning that the task has not been successfully completed (for instance a constraints that has not been satisfied, such as the citizen is a criminal) and a "question mark" indicating that the system was not able to find the information among the subscribed administrations.

Once the service has been successfully delivered, the marketplace sends a message to the citizen informing him or her that the final administration will send a paper version of the requested document (e.g., by ordinary or express mail). At present, the prototype simulates also the generation of Provisional Driving License document (Figure 14).

In case the E-Government Service Marketplace cannot deliver the complete service because it cannot find the searched information or the searched agency is not able to provide information to the E-GovSM (the agency has subscribed with a "profile 0"), the system informs the citizen about agencies to contact ("liste des administrations," Figure 15), and for each agency provides the contact information (Figure 16).

Copyright © 2007, Idea Group Inc. Copying or distributing in print or electronic forms without written permission of Idea Group Inc. is prohibited.

Figure 11. Provisional Driving License delivery: Sequence diagram

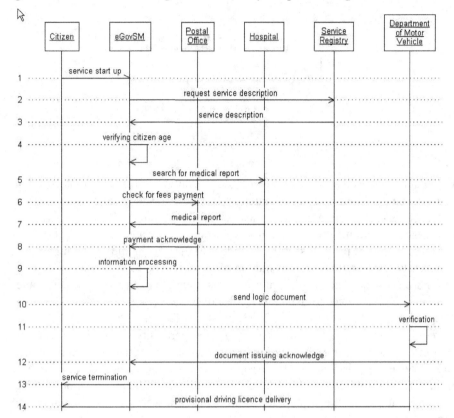

CONCLUSION

This chapter proposes a new approach to deliver services to citizens based on the concept of E-Government Service Marketplace (E-GovSM). The marketplace main objective is to provide quality citizen-oriented services (i.e., providing services according to citizen needs). In order to do this, the marketplace publishes services according to the life event metaphor, hiding from citizens the complexity of administrative process associated to each service. The E-GovSM is formalized using a set of XML Schema models and it is based on a service-oriented architecture. Service-oriented architecture is a new paradigm for the development of flexible and interoperable architecture. In a heterogeneous domain such as the e-government domain, interoperability represents a critical issues and a major challenge to address in order to provide seamless services to citizens. For this reason, service-oriented

Copyright © 2007, Idea Group Inc. Copying or distributing in print or electronic forms without written permission of Idea Group Inc. is prohibited.

Figure 12. Service detailed description

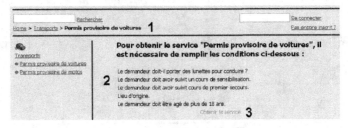

architecture represents the most advantageous solution for the development of an e-government system. Service-oriented architecture meets several E-GovSM design requirements facilitating, for instance, public administration interoperability and legacy system integration. Finally, it allows reusing and composing different services in order to provide seamless services to the citizen, hiding the underlying complexity and functional fragmentation of the public administration.

Further work is needed in order to investigate the use and the possible integration of Grid services to dynamically discover public administrations and their data resources (Dimitrakos et al., 2003, 2004). In fact, the Grid services concept represents a further step toward providing interoperability among heterogeneous distributed systems. Grid service is nothing more than "enriched" Web service (i.e., Grid service extends Web service basic concept adding additional features such as statefulness, service data, handle, etc.), which allow a better and more flexible management and more complex interactions between services in a distributed and heterogeneous environment.

At present, we are envisaging the possibility of integrating Grid service into the E-Government Service Marketplace architecture. Our intention is to improve

Figure 13. Service request execution

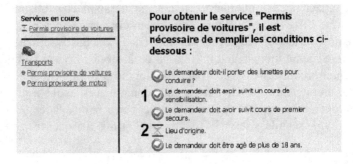

Copyright © 2007, Idea Group Inc. Copying or distributing in print or electronic forms without written permission of Idea Group Inc. is prohibited.

Figure 14. Example of "Provisional Driving License" document creation

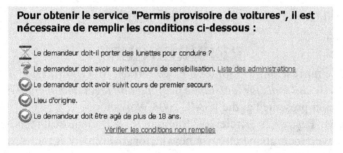

Figure 15. Display of "not-found" information

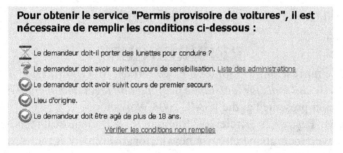

the e-government service provision so as to be able to take full advantage of the flexibility offered by Web services as a standardized mean of integrating components of heterogeneous systems both within local as well as wide area network, and of the additional functionality and reliability offered by Grid services for supporting dynamic resource discovery, life-time management of dynamic service instances, resource integration, and efficient distributed computation. This would eventually allow E-GovSM platform to dynamically discover and locate relevant public administration resources; for instance, in case of replication of several E-GovSM platforms across different countries, we can envisage the use of a Grid discovery service to locate foreign E-GovSM platforms, or to search available services on an ensemble of distributed service registries.

Copyright © 2007, Idea Group Inc. Copying or distributing in print or electronic forms without written permission of Idea Group Inc. is prohibited.

Figure 16. Administration contact information

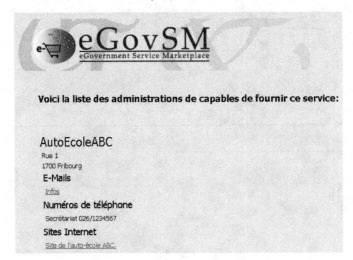

REFERENCES

Biagioli, C., Francesconi, E., Spinosa, P., & Taddei, M. (2003). The NIR project: *Standards and tools for legislative drafting and legal document Web publication*. Paper presented at the ICAIL 2003 Workshop.

Castellano, M., Pastore, N., Arcieri, F., Summo, V., & Bellone de Grecis, G. (2005). An e-government cooperative framework for government agencies. In *Proceedings of the 38th Hawaii International Conference on System Sciences*.

Contenti, M., Termini, A., Mecella, M., & Baldoni, R. (2003). An e-service-based framework for inter-administration cooperation. In *Proceedings of the 4th IFIP International Working Conference on Knowledge Management in Electronic Government*.

Daum, B., & Merten, U. (2002). *System architecture with XML*. San Francisco: Morgan Kaufmann.

Dimitrakos, T., Mc Randal, D., Wesner, S., Serhan, B., Ritrovato, P., & Gaeta, A. (2004). Overview of an architecture enabling grid based application service provision. *European Across Grids Conference*.

Dimitrakos, T., Mc Randal, D., Yuan, F., Gaeta, M., Laria, G., Ritrovato, P. et al. (2003). An emerging architecture enabling grid based application service provision. In *Proceedings of the 7th International Enterprise Distributed Object Computing Conference*.

Dipartimento per l'Innovazione e le Tecnologie. (2002). *Front-office e servizi di e-government per cittadini ed imprese*. Technical report. Retrieved July 12,

Copyright © 2007, Idea Group Inc. Copying or distributing in print or electronic forms without written permission of Idea Group Inc. is prohibited.

2003, from http://www.innovazione.gov.it/ita/intervento/normativa/allegati/avviso_allegato1.pdf

E-GovSM Web site. (n.d.). Retrieved June 17, 2005, from http://www.eif.ch/projets/egovsm/

European Commission. (2003). *Linking up Europe: The importance of interoperability for e-government services.* Technical report. Retrieved September 4, 2004, from http://europa.eu.int/idabc/en/document/2036/5583

Haya, G., Scholze, F., & Vigen, J. (2003). *Developing a grid-based search and categorization tool.* Technical report. Retrieved May 22, 2005, from http://library.cern.ch/HEPLW/8/papers/1/

Kavadias, G., & Tambouris, E. (2003). GovML: A markup language for describing public services and life events. In *Proceedings of the 4th Working Conference on Knowledge Management in Electronic Government.*

Kreger, H. (2001). *Web Services Conceptual Architecture (WSCA 1.0).* Technical Report. Retrieved January 11, 2003, from http://www-306.ibm.com/software/solutions/Webservices/pdf/WSCA.pdf

Life Event Portal. (n.d.). Retrieved May 2, 2004, from http://www.oasis.gov.ie/siteindex/by_life_event.html

Marchetti, A., Megale, F., Seta, E., & Vitali, F. (2002). *Using XML as a mean to access legislative documents: Italian and foreign experiences.* Paper presented at the 1st European workshop on XML and knowledge management.

McGibbon, S. (2005). *The case for service-oriented architecture in realising trusted, interoperable, pan-European e-government services.* Paper presented at the eGOV INTEROP'05 Conference.

Mono Web site. (n.d.). Retrieved November 28, 2004, from http://www.mono-project.com/about/index.html

Mugellini, E., Abou Khaled, O., Pettenati, M. C., & Kuonen, P. (2005). E-GovSM metadata model: Towards a flexible, interoperable and scalable e-government service marketplace. In *Proceedings of IEEE Conference on eTechnology, eCommerce and eService.*

Newcomer, E., & Lomow, G. (2004). *Understanding SOA with Web services.* Boston: Addison Wesley Professional.

NIR Web site. (n.d.). Retrieved April 17, 2004 from, http://www.normeinrete.it/

Office of the e-Envoy. (2003). *E-government Interoperability Framework (EGIF), Part1: Framework, Version 5.0.* Technical report. Retrieved October 5, 2004, from, http://www.govtalk.gov.uk/schemasstandards/egif.asp

Sharma, S. K., & Gupta, J. N. D. (2004). Web services architecture for m-government: Issues and challenges. *Electronic Government Journal, 1*(4), 462-474.

Sharp, J., & Jagger, J. (2003). *Microsoft Visual C# .NET step by step.* Redmond, WA: Microsoft Press.

Copyright © 2007, Idea Group Inc. Copying or distributing in print or electronic forms without written permission of Idea Group Inc. is prohibited.

World Wide Web Consortium. (2004). *XML schema part 0: Primer.* Technical report. Retrieved March 14, 2005, from http://www.w3.org/TR/xmlschema-0/

Zimmermann, O., Tomlinson, M., & Peuser, S. (2003). *Perspectives on Web services: Applying Soap, Wsdl, and Uddi to real-world projects.* Berlin, Germany: Springer-Verlag.

Copyright © 2007, Idea Group Inc. Copying or distributing in print or electronic forms without written permission of Idea Group Inc. is prohibited.

About the Authors

Andreas Mitrakas is legal adviser at the European Network and Information Security Agency (ENISA). He has previously been senior counsel at Ubizen (a Cybertrust company) and general counsel at GlobalSign, (Vodafone Group). He has been consulted in several security implementations in eGovernment. He is a qualified attorney (Athens Bar) and has been a visiting lecturer at the University of Westminster and the Athens University for Economics and Business. He has co-authored more than 85 publications including *Open EDI and law in Europe: A regulatory framework*. He holds a PhD in electronic commerce and the law from Erasmus University of Rotterdam, a master's in computers and law from Queen's University of Belfast, a diploma in project management from ParisTech (Grandes Ecoles d'Ingenieurs de Paris), and a law degree from the University of Athens.

Willem (Pim) Hengeveld has obtained a Diploma in physics/mathematics/philosophy from the Free University Amsterdam and a PhD in mathematics/science. After working in the labs of the Dutch PTT, he became a consultant and partner for Bakkenist Management Consultants. During 1996-2000 he was a part-time professor in ICT and management/governance at the Technical University Delft. Since 1999, he has been with Deloitte and involved in assignments that relate to architecture of complex information and telecommunication environments and in charge of innovative IT-projects for governments on all levels. For T-Systems, Deutsche Telekom Group, he now leads studies and projects in the homeland security area and related to e-government. He is also the author of numerous articles on IT and system development and a regular speaker at international seminars and conferences.

Copyright © 2007, Idea Group Inc. Copying or distributing in print or electronic forms without written permission of Idea Group Inc. is prohibited.

Despina Polemi has obtained a Degree in applied mathematics from Portland State University (USA) in 1984 and a PhD in applied mathematics (Coding Theory) from City University of New York (Graduate Center) in 1991. She held teaching positions (1984-1995) in Queens College and Baruch College of City University of New York. From 1991 to 1996, she was assistant professor (tenure track) at the State University of New York at Farmingdale in the department of mathematics. During 1996-2002, she was an associate researcher in ICCS. From 2000 to 2003, she acted as president of the BoD in a security consulting company (Expertnet—www.expertnet.net.gr) and was a technical manager of the company from 2000-2004. She now a professor at the University of Piraeus R&D department. Her current research interests are in the fields of cryptology, security, and e-business. She has more than ninety publications in the previous areas. She has received many research grants from various organizations such as the Danish Research Foundation, MSI Army Research Office/Cornell University, IEEE, State University of New York (SUNY), and The Graduate School of City University of New York (CUNY). She has been project manager (PM)/technical manger (TM) in security projects of various programmes such as National Security Agency (NSA), Dr. Nuala McGann Drescher Foundation, Greek Ministry of Defense, INFOSEC TELEMATICS for Administrations (COSACC), the Fifth Framework IST Programme (HARP, BEE, SEED, WebSig, TSEC, CORAS, RESHEN, SEED, La Mer, SECRETS), and the 6FP (e-Mayor, Intelcities, BIOSEC, SELIS). She participated in the EC security projects of the programs COST, ACTS, and NATOs' security projects. She is a member of IEEE. She serves as an evaluator, reviewer, and expert in the European Commission and consultant for the FP6.

Johann Gamper received a MSc in computer science from the Technical University of Vienna (1989) and a PhD in computer science from the RWTH Aachen (1996). From 1996-2000, he was senior researcher at the European Academy Bolzano-Bozen. From November 2000 to September 2003, Johann Gamper was project leader for the establishment of a new Faculty of Computer Science at the Free University of Bozen-Bolzano, where he has been assistant professor since October 2003. His main research interests are in temporal database and information systems and in eGovernment. He is author of more than 50 publications in national and international journals and conference proceedings.

*   *   *

Omar Abou Khaled is professor in the information and communication department of the University of Applied Sciences of Western Switzerland, Fribourg (EIA-FR). He holds a PhD in computer science that he received from the Perception and Automatic Control Group of HEUDIASYC Laboratory of University of Technology of Compiegne, and a Masters in computer science from the University

Copyright © 2007, Idea Group Inc. Copying or distributing in print or electronic forms without written permission of Idea Group Inc. is prohibited.

of Technology of Compiegne. Since 1996, he has been working as research assistant in the MEDIA group of the Theoretical Computer Science Laboratory (LITH) of EPFL in the field of Educational Technologies and Web Based Training research field on MEDIT and CR2000 projects. His current interests are in the domains of document engineering, mobile infrastructure, ubiquitous computing, and multimodal interfaces.

Claudio Agostino Ardagna received the Laurea degrees in computer science from the University of Milan, Italy in 2003. From January 2005, he has been a PhD student of the University of Milan. His research interests are in the area of information security, distributed computing and privacy, access control, mobile networks, open source, and e-government. He investigates the following issues: privacy protection and identity management, Web service infrastructure protection, access control policies and languages, XML security, remote management of mobile networks, mobile networks security, mobile phone geolocation, application of open source to e-government and evaluation of open source applications in critical environments.

Nick Argyreas holds a degree in mathematics from the University of Patras (1998) and an MSc degree in informatics from the University of Athens (2002). He has worked as system administrator for UNIX-based servers and supercomputers for a number of years. From 2004 to date, he has been with the Insitute of Informatics & Telecommunications at the National Center for Scientific Research "Demokritos" as a research associate and a member of the research staff. His research interests include biometric security, location-based services, artificial intelligence, chaos theory, and non linear mathematics.

Ruth Breu is full professor of computer science and head of the research group Quality Engineering at the University of Innsbruck since 2002. The group focuses on novel usage scenarios of models, ranging from model-based security, model-based IT Governance to workflow management, and quality assessment of models. Quality engineering cooperates with a number of companies in the areas of e-government, e-health, and e-business.

Danilo Bruschi is a professor of computer sciences at Università degli Studi di Milano, where he received his PhD in Computer Sciences at Università degli Studi di Milano in 1989. he is also director of the master program in ICT security and director of the Laboratory for Security (LASER), and teaches computer and network security and operating systems. He is concerned with computer and networks security, reliability, survivability, computer forensics, social implications, and privacy. He has published more than 60 refereed articles on his research, and he serves as referee of most major infosec-related journals and conferences. He

Copyright © 2007, Idea Group Inc. Copying or distributing in print or electronic forms without written permission of Idea Group Inc. is prohibited.

has been very active in promoting the computer security field both at national and at European level.

Mike Burmester is a professor at Florida State University since 2000. Earlier, he was at Royal Holloway, London University. He got his BSc from Athens University and PhD from Rome University. His research interests include privacy, anonymity, network security, and watermarking and he has numerous publications in these areas. He is a member of the International Association for Cryptological Research and a Fellow of the Institute of Mathematics and Applications.

Yue Chen is an assistant professor at Computer Science and Technology School at Soochow University (Suzhou, China) since 2001. He has a BA in communication and information system (South East University, Najin, China); Graduate Diploma of computer science (Suzhou University, Suzhou, China); and current a PhD candidate in dept. of computer and information technology, Fudan University of China. His main interests are grid computing and bioinformatics.

Marco Cremonini is an assistant professor at the department of information technology of the University of Milan, Italy. He has been a research assistant at the Institute for Security Technology Studies (ISTS) of Dartmouth College, USA. Among his interests, there are Web-based secure systems and applications, secure protocols, economics aspects of information technologies, and network security.

Ernesto Damiani is a professor at the department of information technology of the University of Milan. He has held visiting positions at George Mason University, VA (USA), La Trobe University, Melbourne, Australia, and the University of Technology, Sydney, Australia. His research interests include knowledge extraction and processing, secure mobile architecures, software process engineering, and soft computing. On these topics he has filed international patents and published more than 80 refereed papers in international journals and conferences. He is the Vice-Chair of the IFIP WG on Web semantics (WG 2.12) and a co-author of the book *"Human-Centered e-Business."*

Sabrina De Capitani di Vimercati is an associate professor at the department of information technology of the University of Milan. She received her Laurea and PhD degrees both in computer science from the University of Milan in 1996 and 2001, respectively. Her research interests are in the area of information security, databases, and information systems. She has been an international fellow in the Computer Science Laboratory at SRI, CA (USA). She is co-recipient of the ACM-PODS'99 Best Newcomer Paper Award.

Copyright © 2007, Idea Group Inc. Copying or distributing in print or electronic forms without written permission of Idea Group Inc. is prohibited.

Tassos Dimitriou received his BSc degree from the computer science and engineering department of the University of Patras, Greece in 1991, and his MSc and PhD degrees from the computer science dept. of the University of California, San Diego in 1993 and 1996, respectively. In 1997, he joined the Computer Technology Institute (CTI), where he conducted research on probabilistic and approximation algorithms. In parallel, he was a visiting professor at the computer science department of the University of Athens. Since 2001, he is an assistant professor in Athens Information Technology (AIT) and adjunct professor in Carnegie Mellon University, leading the algorithms and security group where emphasis is given in two distinct areas; the study of secure and energy-efficient protocols for sensor networks and the development of secure applications for networking and electronic commerce. He is a member of IEEE and ACM and a Fulbright fellow.

Christos Douligeris held positions with the department of electrical and computer engineering at the University of Miami, where he reached the rank of associate professor. He is currently an associate professor in the department of informatics at the University of Piraeus, Greece, and an associate member of the Hellenic Authority for Information and Communication Assurance and Privacy. He was the guest editor of a special issue of the IEEE Communications Magazine on "Security for Telecommunication Networks" and he is preparing a book on "Network Security" to be published by IEEE Press/John Wiley. He is an editor of the IEEE Communications Letters, a technical editor of IEEE Network, Computer Networks (Elsevier), International Journal of Wireless and Mobile Computing (IJWMC), and the Euro Mediterranean Journal of Business (EMJB).

Dimitris Foteinakis received his BSc degree in electrical and computer engineering from the National Technical University of Athens, Greece in 2002; and the MSc degree in information networking from the Carnegie Mellon Univesrity, Pittsburgh, Pennsylvania in 2004. Since 2004, he has been working for Intracom S.A. as an embedded security engineer for the content delivery systems department. Since 2005, he has been pursuing his PhD in security for constrained devices. His research interests include embedded system computing, electronic voting protocols, and wireless sensor network secure communication protocols. He is a member of the Technical Chamber of Greece since 2002.

Igor Nai Fovino received his MS degree in computer science with full marks in 2002 and he plans to receive the PhD in computer science in March 2006. He worked as research collaborator at University of Milano in the field of privacy preserving datamining. In 2004, he was visiting researcher at CERIAS Research Centre (West-Lafayette, Indiana, USA) working on secure and survivable routing protocols. Actually he is researcher at the Joint Research Centre of the European

Copyright © 2007, Idea Group Inc. Copying or distributing in print or electronic forms without written permission of Idea Group Inc. is prohibited.

Commission. He serves as reviewer for some international journals. His main research activities are related to the computer security and, more specifically, three are the main interests: System Survivability, Secure Protocols, and Privacy Preserving Data Mining. In these contexts, in the last two years he published in international journals, conference proceedings, and more than 10 scientific papers.

Fulvio Frati received the University degree in computer science from the University of Milan, Italy, in 2004. From February 2005, he has been a research collaborator at the Information Technology Department, University of Milan, Italy. His research interests are in the area of software engineering, Java programming, information security, distributed computing, access control, open source in e-government scenario, and virtualization. He investigates the following issues: introduction of Single Sign-On in existing systems, application of open source to e-government and evaluation of open source applications in critical environments, ontology management, requirement engineering, and virtualization in simulation environments.

Jeffrey Gortmaker is a research assistant at Delft University of Technology and a former project manager for Siemens Business Services at the Flemish government in Brussels, Belgium. Currently he is working on his PhD thesis involving designing a reference architecture for governmental cross-agency service-delivery processes.

Michael Hafner studied international business administration at the University of Innsbruck (Austria) and the EDHEC Lille (France) where he received his diploma in 1997. After graduation, he worked as a technical consultant for systems integration in the telecoms industry for several years. Currently, he is working as a researcher to the group of Professor Ruth Breu at the University of Innsbruck, where he is managing the project Sectino, a joint research cooperation between the University of Innsbruck and ARC Seibersdorf Research GMbH (Vienna, AUT). The research focuses on the model driven development of secure inter-organizational workflows, Web services security, and e-government.

Marijn Janssen is an assistant professor at Delft University of Technology, faculty of technology, policy and management, and a former information and communication technology consultant and architect at the Ministry of Justice. Nowadays his research is focused on designing and developing adaptive information architectures supporting business processes and collaboration in public networks (eGovernment). His research is published in a large number of conference proceedings, books, and journals.

Copyright © 2007, Idea Group Inc. Copying or distributing in print or electronic forms without written permission of Idea Group Inc. is prohibited.

Alexandros Kaliontzoglou holds a degree in electrical and computer engineering from the National Technical University of Athens (NTUA), Greece. Since 2001, he is a PhD candidate in the area of network and information systems security at the Telecommunications laboratory in the School of Electrical and Computer Engineering of NTUA. Since April 2000, he has been working for Expertnet S.A. as a security engineer specializing in Web technologies and network applications, and he has been active both in European research projects in the 5th and 6th Framework Programme (eMayor, Intelcities, SELIS, Reshen, La Mer, TSEC, WebSig) and projects of the Greek private sector. His research interests focus on the areas of IT security, service-oriented architectures, Web services, eGovernment, eCommerce, and PKIs.

Athanasios Karantjias holds a degree in electrical and computer engineering from the University of Patras (UP), and a PhD in the area of wireless network and information systems security of the telecommunication laboratory from the School of Electrical and Computer Engineering of the National Technical University of Athens (NTUA), Greece in 2005. Since June of 2000, he has been working in various companies (G.N.T S.A., Instrasoft S.A., Intracom S.A., and Expertnet S.A.) as a security engineer specializing in wireless and wired Web technologies and network applications. He has been active in both European research projects in the 5th and 6th Framework Programme (TSEC, LaMer, eMayor, Intelcities) and projects of the Greek private sector (i-Select, Web Self Care, Account Transfer, etc.). His research interests are in the area of IT security, service-oriented architecture, wireless Web services, e/m-government, e/m-commerce, e/m-business, and second generation of PKIs.

Andrea Lanzi is a PhD student with the Security Group at University of Milan, he received his MS degree with honors in computer science in October 2004, with a thesis titled "Analysis and Design of Trusted Platform Emulator." His current research interests include most aspects of computer security with an emphasis on host-based intrusion detection system, trusted computing platforms, static analysis, reverse engineering, and exploitation techniques.

Minglu Li is a full professor of computer software in the deptartment of computer science and engineering of Shanghai Jiao Tong University (SJTU). Li is subeditor of International Journal of Grid and Utility Computing and on the edit board of the International Journal of Web Services Research. He is in executive committee member of Technical Community for Services Computing of IEEE. His major research interests include grid computing, Web services, and service computing.

Copyright © 2007, Idea Group Inc. Copying or distributing in print or electronic forms without written permission of Idea Group Inc. is prohibited.

Ying Li is an assistant professor at Soochow University since 2002, and current a PhD candidate in the deptartment of computer science and engineering of Shanghai Jiao Tong University (SJTU). She takes part in the research work of several grid projects such as ShanghaiGrid and ChinaGrid. Her main interests are grid computing and wireless ad hoc networks.

Basilis Meneklis holds a degree in computer science from the University of Piraeus, Greece since 2001, and since 2002 he is a PhD candidate in the area of computer networks at the informatics department of University of Piraeus. Since 2001, he has been teaching computer science courses in post-highschool educational institutes in Athens and since 2004 he has been working as an informatics consultant for Expertnet S.A. in the areas of Web technologies, network applications, and distributed systems design. He focuses his research interests in the areas of Web services, distributed systems design methodologies, mobile networks, and e-government.

Aikaterini Mitrokotsa received her bachelor of science in informatics from the University of Piraeus in 2001. She is currently a doctoral student at the department of informatics of the University of Piraeus. Her research interests lie in the areas of network security, denial of service attacks and performance evaluation of computer networks, intrusion detection, neurocomputing, and machine learning in network security. She has also been active both in European and National research projects.

Elena Mugellini is currently assistant professor at the department of information and communication technologies, University of Applied Sciences of Western Switzerland, Fribourg (EIA-FR). She holds a PhD in telematics and information society from the University of Florence. In 2002, she received a telecommunication engineering degree from the University of Florence. Her main research interests concern network architecture for e-government seamless service delivery, information system modeling, and grid service for distributed and collaborative resource sharing.

Andrea Nowak studied mathematics and informatics at the Technical University of Vienna where she received her diploma in 1986. After her study, she was busy at Siemens Company until 1992 and then chanced to the Austrian research centers (ARCS). On the technical side, her experience is in the field of system design, database design, process modelling, and development of graphical user interfaces for big information systems for the Austrian Government. In the scientific field, she works in cooperation with the University of Innsbruck on the topic "New Methods for Modelling and Realization Security-Critical Inter-Organizational Business Processes" with several publications.

Copyright © 2007, Idea Group Inc. Copying or distributing in print or electronic forms without written permission of Idea Group Inc. is prohibited.

Nikolaos Oikonomidis studied technical computer science at the University of Siegen, Germany. He has been technical coordinator of USB-Crypt project. Currently, he is the technical coordinator of eMayor project (IST). His work and research fields are copy protection, ID-based public key cryptography, and security policy enforcement.

Maria Chiara Pettenati is currently assistant professor of the telematics laboratory of the electronics and telecommunications department of the University of Florence since late 2004. Until 2004, she held a post-doctoral research position in the same laboratory. In 2000, she received the PhD degree in telematics and information society granted from the University of Florence. From 1997 to 1999, she has been working at the computer science department (DI - LITH Laboratory) of the (Swiss Federal Institute of Technology) EPFL. Her main research interests concern network architectures for trust-enabling and personalized services delivery, e-learning and e-knowledge applications.

Christoph Ruland studied mathematics, physics, and computer science at the University of Bonn. He received a diploma in mathematics as well as a doctor degree. He worked on the development of network protocols in the industry for more than six years. He became a professor for Data Communications Systems with the University for Applied Sciences in Aachen in 1982, and a full professor with the University of Siegen in 1992. He is the director of the Institute for Data Communications Systems of the University of Siegen. His main research area is the integration of security into communication systems on all layers. He has written books and many publications about information security in networks and has been an active member in the ISO "Security Techniques" committee for 15 years. Professor Ruland founded the "Company for Cryptographic Communication Security and Communication Technology" (KryptoKom) in 1988.

Andrea Servida's main duty as deputy head of the Unit "ICT for Trust and Security" of the Information Society Technologies Programme and is planning, implementing, and managing the part of the programme on security, dependability, and privacy technologies and applications. He also contributes to the Commission policy-making and standardisation activities in the filed of network and information security. In the years 1998-2002, he held the responsibility to coordinate, at the IST Programme level, the European Dependability Initiative in Information Society. Before joining the Commission, he has worked in the industry for nearly eight years as a project manager of a number of international R&D projects on decision support systems for environmental, civil and industrial emergency, and risk management. He graduated cum laude in nuclear engineering at Politecnico in Milan (Italy) and carried out postgraduate studies in artificial intelligence at QMW College, University of London (UK) and at the Joint Research Centre in Petten (NL).

Copyright © 2007, Idea Group Inc. Copying or distributing in print or electronic forms without written permission of Idea Group Inc. is prohibited.

Pierangela Samarati is a professor at the department of information technology of the University of Milan. Her main research interests are in security and privacy, in particular with respect to access control and data protection. She has participated in several projects and has published more than 100 refereed technical papers in international journals and conferences. She has been computer scientist in the Computer Science Laboratory at SRI, CA (USA). She has been a visiting researcher at Stanford University, CA (USA), and at George Mason University, VA (USA). She is co-recipient of the ACM-PODS'99 Best Newcomer Paper Award.

Sergiu Tcaciuc obtained his diploma in computer science from the Technical University of Moldova, and a PhD degree from the University of Siegen, Germany. His work and research fields are mobile communications, Web services, and security policy enforcement for them.

Stelios C. A. Thomopoulos (StM'80 – M '83 – SM'89). He received his 5 year Diploma from the National Technical University of Athens (NTUA) and his M.S. and PhD from the University of Buffalo, both in electrical and computer engineering in 1980 and 1983 respectively. He was a faculty with the electrical engineering departments of Southern Illinois University (1983-1989) and The Pennsylvania State University (1989-1995), and a lecturer with the University of Buffalo (1980-1983). In 1994, he founded Intelnet Inc., a SBIR company specializing in the design, manufacturing, and sales of biometrics ID verification systems. In 1998, he was elected director of the insitute of informatics and telecommunications at the National Center for Scientific Research "Demokritos" were he is currently. He has published more than 160 articles in peer reviewed journals, conference transactions, and has contributed with chapters to several books. His current research interests include biometrics, wireless networks, pervasive computing, and location-based services.

René W. Wagenaar is full time professor and head of the ICT department at the School for Technology, Policy, and Management (TPM) of Delft University of Technology. He holds a PhD in physics from the University of Amsterdam and a BSc in economics from the Free University Amsterdam. He has more than 20 years of experience in ICT, both from various positions in the academic community as from working in the ICT industry. He has published six books and over 100 articles and papers in scientific and professional journals on the topics of EDI and business process networking, electronic commerce, ICT infrastructure and service design, and eGovernment. His current research interests focus on the design and management of shared ICT service systems in the public sector and the role of privacy control therein.

Copyright © 2007, Idea Group Inc. Copying or distributing in print or electronic forms without written permission of Idea Group Inc. is prohibited.

Barbara Weber is a research assistant at the University of Innsbruck where she also received her PhD degree (Integration of Workflow Management and Case-Based Reasoning). Her prime research interest is in methods, tools, and architectures for an agile management of business processes. This spans several technology areas including workflow systems, case-based reasoning, process-oriented knowledge management, enterprise systems, process mining, and agile software development. In order to allow for the exchange of ideas with practice, she is engaged in third-party funded projects with several partners (e.g., healthcare domain, logistics industry). She has been invited as PC member to several international conferences and contributed in the organization of workshops and conferences organized by her department.

Copyright © 2007, Idea Group Inc. Copying or distributing in print or electronic forms without written permission of Idea Group Inc. is prohibited.

Index

Copyright © 2007, Idea Group Inc. Copying or distributing in print or electronic forms without written permission of
Idea Group Inc. is prohibited.

Copyright © 2007, Idea Group Inc. Copying or distributing in print or electronic forms without written permission
of Idea Group Inc. is prohibited.

Copyright © 2007, Idea Group Inc. Copying or distributing in print or electronic forms without written permission of
Idea Group Inc. is prohibited.

Copyright © 2007, Idea Group Inc. Copying or distributing in print or electronic forms without written permission of Idea Group Inc. is prohibited.

Copyright © 2007, Idea Group Inc. Copying or distributing in print or electronic forms without written permission of Idea Group Inc. is prohibited.

Copyright © 2007, Idea Group Inc. Copying or distributing in print or electronic forms without written permission
of Idea Group Inc. is prohibited.

Looking for a way to make information science and technology research easy?
Idea Group Inc. Electronic Resources are designed to keep your institution
up-to-date on the latest information science technology trends and research.

Information Technology Research at the Click of a Mouse!

InfoSci-Online
⇨ Instant access to thousands of information technology
   book chapters, journal articles, teaching cases, and conference proceedings

⇨ Multiple search functions

⇨ Full-text entries and complete citation information

⇨ Upgrade to **InfoSci-Online Premium** and add thousands of
   authoritative entries from Idea Group Reference's handbooks of research and encyclopedias!

IGI Full-Text Online Journal Collection

⇨ Instant access to thousands of scholarly journal articles

⇨ Full-text entries and complete citation information

IGI Teaching Case Collection

⇨ Instant access to hundreds of comprehensive teaching cases

⇨ Password-protected access to case instructor files

IGI E-Access

⇨ Online, full-text access to IGI individual journals,
   encyclopedias, or handbooks of research

Additional E-Resources

⇨ E-Books

⇨ Individual Electronic Journal Articles

⇨ Individual Electronic Teaching Cases

IGI Electronic Resources have flexible pricing to help meet the needs of any institution.

www.igi-online.com

Sign Up for a Free Trial of IGI Databases!